From Newport
To
The Somme

A Collection of Letters.

Compiled
by
Alan Stroud
and
Richard Brimson

Acknowledgements

We would like to thank the following for their kind help:

Colin Fairweather for the use of photographs from his personal collection, Robin Freeman, Managing Director of the County Press, who kindly allowed the use of County Press copyright material,
Andy Walker and Elspeth Jackson of the Council Library Service for solving some literary conundrums for us, and
James Warren of auctioneers Warren & Wignall Ltd. of Lancashire, for kindly providing the photograph on page 266.
Thanks also go to our partners, Mary Brimson and Sue Stroud for proof reading the first draft of the book and we both thank Tom Stroud, son of Alan, for his usual incisive and thoughtful contributions.

Finally, special thanks go to Linda Smith who discovered the letters and encouraged their publication, and to her late Father, Ralph Brimson, who unknown to us, ensured their continued preservation for some 30 years after Mabel's death.

Design and Layout by Alan Stroud.
Published by Now and Then Books : nowandthenbooksiw@googlemail.com

From Newport To The Somme

A Collection of Letters.

"What I should like to do would be to have a week right away from any railway somewhere, where there was a wood – and a body could sit in the shade of a steamy hot evening and smell wood smoke, and sweet briar, and damp earth and ferns, and see little bits of blue sky through green leaves, and know that when I had to light my pipe I could wander off to the village pub and call for a pint.

Gott straff the Kaiser – Amen.

So long, Bob, old man. Take care of yourself and make haste home and let us foregather and talk. Oh, let it be soon."

Archie Snow to Bob, May 1917.

In the summer of 2013 a remarkable discovery was made in a Victorian house for sale in Newport. It had been home to members of the Brimson family for nearly 100 years and during the disposal of the property a collection of nearly 400 letters written during the First World was discovered. The letters had been written by Bob Brimson, a soldier serving in the Royal Engineers in the trenches on the Western Front and his family on the Isle of Wight, and in particular to his fiancée, Mabel Attrill.

The letters provide a fascinating glimpse into how an ordinary Island family coped with one of their own taking part in "the most disastrous war in history."

Royal Engineers in a communications trench, France, 1916.

When war broke out in the summer of 1914, Ernest Gordon Brimson, known as Bob to family and friends, was working as a painter and decorator at Whitecroft Asylum. Within a few weeks of the official announcement he and a close friend and work colleague, Charlie Dyer, had joined the Army, enlisting in the Royal Engineers. They went to the recruitment office together, receiving consecutive service numbers, and within weeks joined thousands of other new recruits for training at St Mary's Barracks, in Gillingham, Kent. It was from there that Bob wrote his first letter home and it was the beginning of a correspondence with friends and family that would continue until his discharge from the Army in February 1919. Much of the correspondence is between Bob and his fiancée, Mabel Attrill, known in the family as Mabs. The remainder is to and from other members of the family. It forms a truly extraordinary snapshot of family life over one hundred years ago.

Not only have Bob's letters survived, but also hundreds of the replies he received in return – letters from his mother, sister and friends, and in particular, those from Mabs. Clearly, Bob held the correspondence in some regard for during his four years in the Front he managed to keep them from harm and carefully preserve them. Periodically, he would send them home where someone in the family then kept them safe. It seems that from the outset, the letters were never intended for disposal.

The letters contain no accounts of heroism in no-man's land, nor are there tales of men single-handedly overcoming enemy machine-gun posts. And this is their strength. Military historians of the period are already well served; literally thousands of accounts of life in the trenches exist. This collection of letters, however, offers a rare window into the other side of war, the everyday concerns and hardships experienced not just by someone at the Front but also the family back home. They are first-hand social history – a pure, unvarnished, contemporary account of the effects of war on an ordinary family.

The letters provide an intimate insight into the everyday practicalities of having a member of the family serve at the Front, and often in the smallest and most revealing detail – the type of detail that usually goes unrecorded elsewhere. How heavy can a food parcel from home weigh? Can fresh vegetables be sent to the Somme? Can clothing be sent to the trenches? The letters provide the sometimes surprising answers to all these questions and they also contain a miscellaneous wealth of minutiae regarding life during the war, both at home and away.

What they do not contain to any great degree are displays of overt emotion. That is not to say they are soulless – far from it – the concern family members have for one another is all too clear on many occasions, but the concern is always understated. Only occasionally are the mechanics of making war referred to by any members of the family. In November 1915, for instance, Bob, almost casually, writes to his mother, "The air being so frosty they (the Germans) can hear us working so they don't forget to send a few across. I had one through the loose part of my top boots the other night." Bob's mother begins her reply to that letter not by immediately referring to what was by any standards an alarming incident but instead, first reflects on the weather and then goes on to ask how long Bob is allowed to spend in bed. Only after these niceties does she address the near death of her son. "That bullet through your boot top was a very narrow touch for you," she writes, before swiftly moving on to more comfortable territory, "I hope you will have got my parcel by the time you get this letter."

On occasions Bob does refer to life at the Front. In August 1916, during the Battle of the Somme, he writes, " I suppose there will be a time when this affair will come to an end. We get fed up at times, especially with the sights we've seen lately," but Bob, like his mother, then moves on, "Well, I hope you are all keeping quite well at home."

Perhaps Bob had remembered Mabs' admonition in October 1914, when he had just begun his training. In an effort to protect Bob's mother, Mabs had cautioned, "I wish you hadn't told your mother you were training for the Front." Equally perhaps, it may have been the thought that his letters home were subject to the gaze and scrutiny of the censor that kept Bob from going into his activities in any great detail. On occasion he is plainly conscious of the fact that his letters home are being read by a third party. In March 1918, writing from Italy, he tells his sister Kath, "We are not very far from the sea and not far from the place where you drive about the streets in boats."

The correspondence continued faithfully and regularly even after the war came to an end in November 1918 – by which time Bob was in Italy. Three months later, in February 1919, he was finally discharged from the Army after four and a half years service.

He returned to Newport where he and Mabs were married in 1920, Bob aged 34 and Mabs aged 26. They set up home in a terraced house in Trafalgar Road, Newport and lived there for the rest of their lives, Bob dying in 1970 aged 85 and Mabs dying in 1982, aged 88. At some point during those years someone decided to put the collection of letters in the loft. Fortunately, when Mabs died the house was still in family hands and so, unknown to anyone at the time, the collection of letters remained hidden.

They were rediscovered in the autumn of 2013 when the house was finally sold. During the house clearance the box of letters was discovered and they were passed on for safekeeping to Richard Brimson, a grandson of Bob and Mabs, and co-author of this book.

It was obvious from the outset that the letters deserved a wider audience. They contained little, if any, personal or confidential information regarding the writers and it was felt that Bob and Mabs and the other writers would approve of their publication after this distance of time. It is a body of work for them to be proud of and they would be pleased that their letters, only ever intended to have a life of days, have survived a hundred years to become a lasting testimony to life – and death – all those years ago.

The Brimson and Attrill Family Tree
showing the relationship of the letter writers.

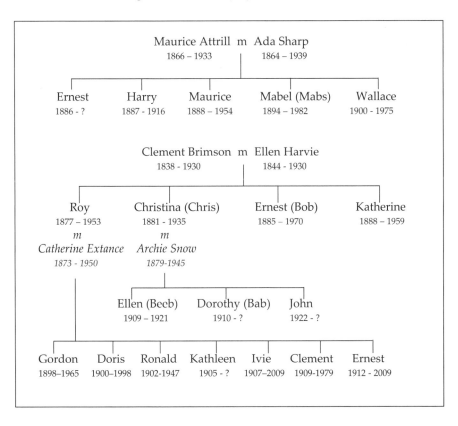

Who's Who

Ernest Gordon (Bob) Brimson : Bob was born in Ventnor in 1885, the son of Clement and Ellen Brimson. The family moved to Chesterfield in Derbyshire just before the turn of the century where Clement began a business as a painter, decorator and paperhanger with his son Roy. While there, Bob had his first experience of Army life. In 1902, aged 17, he enlisted in the Sherwood Foresters Yeomanry, a Territorial unit. Unfortunately, no records of his service have survived but he probably served for the customary six years. The family are known to have still been living in Chesterfield in 1910 but by the time war was declared they had moved back to the Island to 49, Carisbrooke Road, Newport. Bob was then working for Alderslades, the Newport glaziers. At some point he left them to join his father as a painter and decorator at Whitecroft Hospital, possibly with Westmores, a Newport builder, and he was still working there when war broke out.

Detailed service records were kept of the six million soldiers who served in WW1 but in a twist of fate, two thirds of these records were destroyed by enemy action in World War 2 and unfortunately Bob's records were amongst those that were lost. Fortunately, we know from the correspondence that on September 4th, 1914, Bob went to the recruitment centre at Newport Drill Hall with his friend Charlie Dyer, where the two of them joined the Royal Engineers. They received consecutive service numbers, Charlie becoming 46869, Sapper Dyer and Bob becoming 48970, Sapper Brimson.

Events moved fast and within days Bob was in an Army training camp, St Mary's Barracks in Gillingham, Kent. Britain was ill-equipped for a war and the influx of new men soon exhausted the available equipment. Arriving at training camps, Bob and his fellow volunteers (there would be no conscription until 1916) frequently found there were no uniforms for them, no instructors, no cooks and no kitchens. The men paraded in their own clothes and weapons drill was carried out with broom handles. It was from St Marys Barracks that Bob wrote his first letter to Mabs.

At the end of training, in May 1915, Bob's company, the 87th, moved to France but Bob did not leave with them. After suffering a bad reaction to an inoculation he was hospitalised for three months and as a result didn't join the BEF (British Expeditionary Force) in France until August 1915.

At the outbreak of war Bob has an older brother by seven years, Roy, and an older sister by four years, Chris, who is married to Archie Snow, one of Bob's childhood friends from Ventnor. Bob has another sister, Kath, three years younger than him.

Bob writes well. His letters are business-like and uncomplicated but full of interesting everyday minutiae. They can be affecting on occasions : "The wounded Bluejackets were out on the balconies. We all cheered them as we marched by and they waved back to us – those who had arms to wave with."

Mabel (Mabs) Attrill : Mabel Isabel Attrill, known to her family as Mabs, was born in 1894. Her parents, Maurice and Ada Attrill, were tenant landlords of the Bedford, or Bedford Inn, a pub on the Mall, on Carisbrooke Road, Newport. Mabs lived and worked there for the first two years of the war. The pub was evidently a successful one, so much so that when the Bedford and its six-day operating licence was auctioned in 1911, there was what the *County Press* described as "spirited bidding for the property, in which the representatives of several important brewery firms took place." The winning bid came from W.B. Mew & Langton, then the biggest brewers on the Island, who paid £1870, a huge sum for those times, an indication of the pub's success.

Just three years later, war was declared, by which time Mabs had met Bob, who lived just along the road from the Bedford, at 49 Carisbrooke Road and it is clear from their subsequent letters that by the time war was declared they had already decided to marry.

By the summer of 1916 Mabs was working at Saunders of East Cowes, who had come to the Island in 1907 to set up business as boat builders and aircraft manufacturers. It becomes apparent in the letters that Mabs found other employment as the war went on but the exact nature of the work is not known. The Bedford remained in family hands until its closure in the late 1960s, the last landlady being Alice Attrill, Mabs' sister-in-law (her name can be seen just above the door in the photograph on page 17). The premises then became a printing and copying centre for many years before being demolished in 2006. Today, residential housing stands on the site of the Bedford and its gardens. In a nod to the past the original postbox used by Mabs all those years ago has been incorporated into the wall of the new development and is still in use today.

Aged 20 at the outset of war, Mabs writes well. She is obviously well educated and well-informed, and has a witty, spirited sense of humour. She can be waspish, even feisty, on occasions : "It's your fault I send short letters. I rack my brains to put into four pages what I usually put in eight and that's all I get for it. I thought you hadn't time to read the longer letters as you never half answered them."

Mabs has three older brothers, Ernest, Harry and Maurice, and a younger brother, Wallace.

Ernest Attrill, (Ern) : Aged 28 at the outset of war, Ern is a professional soldier in the Hampshire Regiment; he was at Gallipoli and France and wounded several times. His letters tend to be strait-laced but on occasions are infused with a dry humour : "I am writing these few lines to let you know we are quite happy listening to the shells bursting," and on another occasion, "There goes another shell. No wonder the writing is shaky."

Harry Attrill : Aged 27 at the outset of war, Harry is a leading signaller (later promoted to Yeoman Signaller) in the Navy, which he joined as a boy. He serves on battleships HMS Tiger and HMS Queen Mary.

Maurice Attrill (Morrie or Morry) : Another of Mabs' older brothers. Aged 26 at the outset of war, he was also in the Navy, having joined before the outbreak of hostilities. Morrie served on HMS Owl, HMS Royal Sovereign and HMS Furious. He writes chirpy, conversational letters, : "I'm a full-blown Ship's Cook now, four shillings and threepence halfpenny a day for nothing, only to chance having a sky trip from a German submarine. I suppose Bob is looking forward to a medal as big as a frying pan."

Wallace Attrill : Mabs' younger brother. He takes up an apprenticeship with BTH of Rugby (British Thomson-Houston) suppliers of lighting, radio and signalling gear to the Royal Navy, joining them shortly after war broke out, aged just 14 years old.

Ellen Brimson : Bob's mother. Aged 68 when war broke out, Mother's letters were the most problematical to transcribe. She wrote as she thought, with little or no punctuation, and her thoughts tend to move rapidly from one subject to another. Her cheery and conversational letters are a little whimsical at times, "I have put a bit of wadding in. I should put a piece in your ears to keep out the earwigs." It is clear that she is concerned for her son's welfare but with the reserve that permeated the age, she never directly addresses the subject.

Clement Brimson : Bob's father; aged 76 when war broke out. Although he is referred to on many occasions, he appears as a writer only once. He, like Bob, was a painter and decorator at what was then called Whitecroft Asylum.

Katherine (Kath) Brimson : Kath, 26 at the outbreak of war, is Bob's younger sister by three years. Confined to a wheelchair due to a childhood accident, she lives at home with her parents. She is close to Bob and great friends with Mabs. Kath makes a small income as a portrait artist and by making and selling soft toys.

Christina (Chris) Snow : Bob's older sister, aged 33 at the outbreak of war. She is married to Archie Snow, a solicitor's clerk, and they live in Clapham, London. They have two daughters Ellen (Bee, Bebe or Beeb) 5, and Dorothy (Babs), 4.

Archie Snow : Five years older than Bob, Archie is his brother-in-law, having married Bob's sister Chris, (see above) in 1908. Archie and Bob grew up in Ventnor and despite the age gap of five years became close friends. Archie has two brothers mentioned in the letters, George and Jim, living in London.
His letters are a delight to read. He is a skilled, even gifted writer who clearly enjoys putting pen to paper. He writes fluently and is obviously well-educated and well-informed, with a fine wit. Archie is a man who clearly wrote to be read. He would be delighted to know that his letters have survived and are being appreciated over 100 years after he wrote them.

Fred (Roy) Brimson : Bob's older brother, aged 37 at the outbreak of war. He is married to Kath or 'Kit' and lived in Melbourne Street, Newport. He works as a painter for various employers during the war years, and almost joins up. They have seven children : Gordon, 16; Doris,14; Ronald, 12; Kathleen, 9; Ivie, 7; Clement, 5, and Ernest, aged 2.

Gordon Brimson : Roy's eldest son. He works in Newport employed as a clerk for the Freshwater, Yarmouth and Newport Railway Company. In May 1917, aged 18, Gordon enlisted in the 3rd Hampshire Regiment and served in France.

Doris Brimson : Roy's eldest daughter, aged 14 at the outbreak of war. When her brother Roy joins the Army, she takes on his clerical position with the Freshwater, Yarmouth and Newport Railway Company in their offices at the bottom of Hunny Hill. It is from there that she usually writes her letters. Even at the age of 14, Doris possesses a well developed sense of humour and like Archie, she writes letters that are a joy to read. She is a confident and witty writer for someone of her age. Her letters can be quirky on occasion, but they are, without exception, always amusing.

Charles (Charlie) Dyer : Bob's best pal. He and Charlie worked together at the 'Asylum' and enlisted together just days after war had been declared, receiving consecutive service numbers – Bob, 46870 and Charlie, 46869. They joined the Royal Engineers together but ended up attached to different regiments. Their paths occasionally crossed at the Front.

The Outbreak of War

On Sunday, June 28, 1914, Archduke Franz Ferdinand of Austria was assassinated by a Serbian terrorist while riding in a motorcade to City Hall in Sarajevo. Within days the Austrian government declared war on Serbia, a move that precipitated a chain of defence alliances between the major European countries. Events moved rapidly and just five weeks later Europe was at war. With prophetic and eerie accuracy the *Isle of Wight County Press* had already prepared its readers for just such an outcome. The August 1st edition had warned readers, "Events have developed with alarming rapidity. Yesterday reports came to hand that Russia, Germany and Holland were mobilising and the most pessimistic telegrams stated that well-nigh the last hope of averting the most disastrous war in history had gone." The gloomy note of pessimism was not misplaced. Three days later, German troops marched on France, making their way through neutral Belgium as they did so. The British government, who had pledged allegiance to Belgium, were honour-bound to assist, and as a result, on Tuesday August 4th, Britain declared war on Germany.

The outbreak of war had two immediate consequences for the Island. Cowes Week, which was due to begin on the following Monday was immediately abandoned and a dramatic mass exodus began of the several hundred Germans present on the Island, mostly workers in the hotel trade. There was also a sizeable number of German tourists on the Island and ironically, the most prominent amongst them was none other than the Kaiser's youngest son, Prince Joachim, who happened to be holidaying in Shanklin. Immediately recalled to his regiment, he hurriedly left the Royal Spa Hotel where he had been staying and quickly made his way to Ryde Pier where he discreetly caught a late boat to Portsmouth on the Monday evening.

There was nothing remarkable in the fact that there were so many Germans on the Island, for at that time there were over 50,000 Germans living in Britain – it was a time when Britain considered it had much in common with Germany. The royal family, after all, was of German descent and the Kaiser, Queen Victoria's grandson, was an Admiral of the Fleet and a Field Marshal in the British Army. Overnight, these cordial relationships came to an end. The 'Aliens Registration Act' was hastily passed and many of the Germans in Britain were instructed to leave the country immediately while the remainder were to register with the police. On Wednesday August 5th, it was the turn of the Island's German inhabitants to leave. Several entire German families left Ventnor and there was a wholesale clearance of German waiters from local hotels, the *Daily Mail* declaring, "Ventnor, in the summer practically a German watering-place, is no longer polluted by Germans."

Simultaneously, a national recruitment campaign began. On the Island, the *County Press* front page for August 22nd carried a recruitment advertisement for the Isle of Wight Rifles (see page 21). "Men of the Wight! If you treasure the honour of the Empire and you venerate the memory of British heroism, come forward and help to protect your Island and your homes. For years you have been warned and threatened with this German menace. Trouble has now come. Proceed to the Drill Hall to enlist." Inside, an editorial referring to the 'stirring appeal' left readers in no doubt as to what was expected of the Island's young men: "While we have nothing but praise for the young citizens who have joined the local Territorial battalion, we think a great reproach rests upon those civilians who, while possessing the requisite physical qualifications for service, are remaining outside." Throughout the paper other exhortations to join up appeared, couched in similar, powerfully persuasive terms.

The following week's edition of August 29th carried another front page address to the young men of the Isle of Wight (see page 20), this time from Lord Kitchener. It was direct if nothing else. "The National Emergency," it informed potential recruits, "demands the patriotic self sacrifice of the able-bodied young men of England." Despite the menacing tone the campaign was effective and there was a tremendous response to the call on the Island. Under the headline, "Enthusiastic Recruiting Campaign - Huge Gathering at Newport," the *County Press* of September 12th reported, "There was a gigantic gathering in the Newport Market on Saturday night last, when the recruiting meeting for the capital took place. The Market was hung with flags and crammed with dense crowds.... After rousing speeches which were well received, a trumpeter sounded the 'Fall in,' a number of recruits then came forward and received rosettes from the Mayor. They were afterwards examined and attested at the old *County Press* premises."

There were similar scenes all across the Island and at the end of the week over 700 recruits had signed up, the *County Press* reporting, "Stirring and enthusiastic scenes have been witnessed at Newport Railway Station this week in connection with the departure to various depots of the recruits for Kitchener's Army, particularly on Monday, when the Mayor and a large number were present to wish *bon voyage* and good luck to the brave fellows."

The campaign was also a success nationally, so much so that on a single day in early September, 33,000 young men signed up – more than the entire annual enlistment the previous year – and within a fortnight, 80,000 keen young men and boys were on their way to the battlefields of France.

The Letters

Most of the letters survive complete with their original envelopes, some of which are a source of information in themselves, being overprinted with a variety of official postmarks and censors' stamps. A selection are shown on the inside covers.

They are the work of over a dozen writers who comprise a mixture of friends and family. Not all the letters have survived, possibly due to having been passed around various members of the family at the time, meaning that on occasion there are no answers to questions posed in some letters because the letter containing the reply has not survived.

Because of the sheer length of the letters some editing was inevitable, however, nothing of any consequence has been removed. Where editing has occurred it has been confined to inconsequential family or domestic matters.

What remains is a strictly faithful transcription of the contents of each letter. Nothing has been added or altered. On a handful of occasions a word has been inserted where it is clear that the writer has mistakenly omitted it, leaving a sentence making little or no sense.

Being faithful to the letters has led to various anomalies and if on occasion a passage seems disjointed or curiously constructed, it is not an error in transcription or a typographical mistake – it is the way it was in the original text. Similarly, the lack of punctuation in many of the letters has left some sentences open to more than one interpretation depending on where the commas or full stops might have been placed. Hopefully, the correct version has been chosen for this text.

The Sketches

In May 1917, Bob asked for a sketchbook to be sent to him and received one from Kath which he used to document scenes on the Front. He later used another book to sketch scenes in the Italian countryside. Both books have survived and were found with the letters. The colour sketches in this book are all taken from these sketchbooks.

The Royal Engineers

The Royal Engineers motto, '*Everywhere*' is an apt one – during World War One they were indeed, everywhere, as they serviced the British Army's every need. They provided and maintained roads, water supplies, bridges and transport. They serviced and installed telephones, wireless and signalling equipment, designed and built front-line fortifications, maintained guns and other weapons and built camps and stables across the battlefields as and when required, carrying out much of this work under enemy fire. When Bob joined the Royal Engineers in August 1914, the force consisted of just under 25,000 men. Such were the demands of war that by 1917 it had grown to nearly 300,000.

Calendar of Events of 1914
(Bob's activities shown in italics)

August 16 - Original landing of British Expeditionary Force in France.
August 23 - Battle of Mons.
September 4 - Bob enlists with Royal Engineers.
September 5 - End of retreat from Mons.
Early September - Arrival at St Mary's Barracks, Gillingham, Kent.
September 9 - German retreat from Marne.
September - Bob begins his training and drill.
October 12 - Battle of Messines.
October - Bob moves to Royal Engineer's training camp, Seaford.
November 1 - Messines taken by Germany.
November - Training, trenching and wiring.
December 21 - First aeroplane air-raid on Britain at Dover.

─────────────◆─────────────

The first letter in the collection is from Bob, who has just been posted to Gillingham camp for training.

From Bob
4th Billeting Co, R.E., Cricket Pavilion, Park Rd, Gillingham.*
                                        Saturday, September 12, 1914
Dear, Mother, Dad and Kath.
I hope you are all getting on all right at home. We had to rough it the first night we arrived here. That was about 8.30 or nine. We were dished out with one blanket apiece and we had to sleep on the bare boards of the tent – twenty of us in one tent. There were those worse off who had to sleep out in the open all night. This was at St Mary's Barracks. All the barrack rooms were overcrowded. There must be over 3000 recruits here and still they are coming in by hundreds every day. Every country is represented here including Ireland, Scotland and Wales; young men of all kinds and descriptions.
On the second day we were marched out and billeted in different houses round the town, mostly houses of people who have got relations at the Front or in the Navy, and we are very comfortable too. We shan't be here long though, I'm afraid. They will be moving us in a week or two's time to different units; either Aldershot, Hounslow or Ireland.
They parade us every day on what they call the Lines. It is a great big common and there are troops drilling as far as the eye can see each way. Yesterday it rained, so five hundred of us were marched to a Picture Palace close by and had a few films and songs from our own chaps. Today it is raining again so we've got half a day off. I should like my razor sent and two collars to 26 Upper Milton Road, Gillingham, Kent.
                        With love to all, from Bob.

* See photograph page 56

Bob and Mabs, just before the war. Bob was photographed at Whitecroft where he was employed as one of the maintenance workers.

The Mall, looking towards the top of Newport High Street. Bob's house, 49, The Mall, is hidden behind the large tree on the right hand side.

The Bedford photographed in the 1960s. Above the door can be seen the licencee's name – 'Alice Attrill,' Mabs' sister-in-law.

From Mabs
The Bedford, The Mall, Newport.   Monday, September 14th, 1914
My Dear Boy,
We went out to see Uncle George at Atherfield. They are some more people who can't do enough for one and I like uncle George better than ever. Poor old chap has got a cancer but he puts up with it much better than Uncle Isaac with his asthma.
It was a grand day but when I got to the top of the hill before Atherfield and saw the Freshwater cliffs and then the Niton cliffs on the other side, it was getting too much. It made me think of holidays we had had. There now – it's too bad to talk about those things but it isn't me, it's the pen. Anyway, we will say it is, because it is your pen, or one you gave me. Elsie's sister-in-law was here with her little boy so we all went down with Uncle George on the shore to have our tea. We paddled too. Uncle took his telescope and we were able to see two troopships go out by Ventnor, absolutely packed with men. Ern's draft was supposed to go out in one of those but they sent to say they were full up.
I went over with Kath last night but it wasn't like with you – especially when 10 o'clock came. Never mind. We shall be able to make up for it one day.
I had a grand dream Saturday night. You came and looked in my window, the same as you always do. The only fault was that you were in dress uniform instead of khaki but you made a splendid soldier, and then I woke up just when I could have gone on dreaming for hours. Dreams are beastly things sometimes. Have you seen anything of this chorus?* It is to be sung in some of the Halls. I don't know the verses yet but it looks nice.

> Oh, we don't want to lose you,
> But we think you ought to go,
> For your King and Country,
> Both need you so.
> We shall want you and miss you,
> But with all our might and main
> We will thank you, cheer you, kiss you,
> When you come back again.

Well, goodbye my Sweetheart, with best love from Mabs.

From Kath
49, Carisbrooke Road, Newport.   Tuesday, September 15, 1914
Dear Bob,
You're a fine one and no mistake. Say you've been waiting for a letter from us? We have been waiting against the door all the week for one from you. 'Stead of that, nothing comes but a measly postcard. We wanted to know how you liked the place and what you have been doing with yourself and who you found there. Did you find anybody you knew?
It seems queer here without you, especially Sunday seems awfully quiet, not

---

* "Your King and Country Want You" was published at the start of the war. It was written as a 'Woman's Recruiting Song' to be sung to persuade men to volunteer.

that you made much noise. I saw Min Jones out of the window yesterday. She asked me if we had heard from Bob and if he was getting on all right. I said "Yes, he seems to be getting on fine so far." She said, "Oh, I'm so glad." Mabel has just been in, (In yah! I get all the kisses now, there's too bad it is, poor old Boy.) Poor old Dad got nearly home tonight and found the keys in his pocket and had to go right back with them. John H. got talking to him about you so Dad went off and forgot all about taking them up. Dad gets along all right out there. He says it's a lot better than going to Cowes. He says they all want to know how you are getting on.

Charlie hasn't left Hurst Castle yet. He wishes he could. He is getting sick of it there. Just fancy old Jim joining. I can't imagine him a soldier, can you? We are half expecting to see him walk in. Mabel says there are a hundred a day coming from London and Winchester.

I'm just going to have my supper now so goodnight Bob. Mother and Dad send their best love.

Heaps and heaps of love from Kath.

From Morry
HMS Owl, c/o GPO   Tuesday, September 15, 1914
Dear Bob,

In answer to your postcard, I'm glad to hear you are still in the pink. We have been having a time of it here. Shan't know the way to walk when we get ashore again. I had a letter from Harry. He is A1. We haven't been far away from each other but it might just as well be 1000 miles – we can't see each other. He said they were all right there but he didn't care about the small ships job. Talk about looping the loop. It ain't in it! I had a postcard from Mabel to say she said the Scout was doing his bit. He had better arm himself with my revolver. There is one thing – they will have a decent job to poison our water.* That's a dirty move of theirs, poisoning the water, but it won't save them. They've got to go through it. I only hope to get through all merry and bright so as to get back and wet it up. If I don't there will be all the more for someone else. Don't drink it all on chance. I got a mascot carrying around with me, a stuffed owl I got in Scotland. I expect a 155 shell will ruffle his feathers if it comes too close. Thank Kath for the postcard I received today. Tell her I shall be glad to come round and call for you again one of these Sundays. This is all now, hoping this finds you quite well as it leaves me the same,

Morry.

From Bob
26 Upper Milton Road, Gillingham. Kent.   Saturday, September 19, 1914
Dear Mother, Dad and Kath,

I received the vest all right today and also the postcard. I was pleased to get it as I don't know when I shall get the kit dished out to me. There are so many of us that they cannot cope with the great demand so they have issued orders that

---

* False rumours had circulated that the water supply of Brussels had been poisoned by German agents

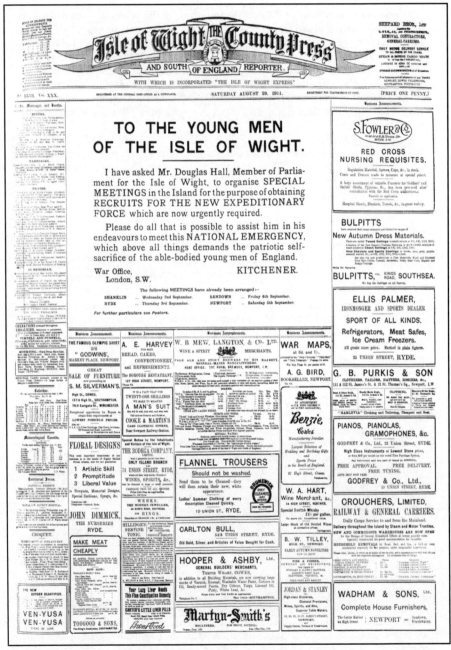

The County Press front page for August 29th, 1914, three weeks after the declaration of war.

THE ISLE OF WIGHT COUNTY PRESS—SATURDAY SEPTEMBER 5. 1914.

☞ TO THE MEN OF THE WIGHT!! ☜
YOUR KING AND COUNTRY NEED YOU.
ANOTHER 100,000 MEN WANTED.

Lord Kitchener is much gratified with the response already made to the Appeal for additional men for His Majesty's Regular Army. In the grave National emergency that now confronts the Empire, he asks with renewed confidence that another 100,000 men will at once come forward.

TERMS OF SERVICE: (Extension of Age Limit).

Age on enlistment 19 to 35, Ex-Soldiers up to 45, and certain selected Ex-Non-Commissioned Officers up to 50. Height, 5ft.3in. and upwards. Chest, 34 inches at least. Must be medically fit. General Service for the War. Men enlisting for the duration of the War will be able to claim their discharge with all convenient speed at the conclusion of the War.

PAY AT ARMY RATES,

and Married Men and Widowers with Children will be accepted, and will draw Separation Allowance under Army conditions.

HOW TO JOIN.

Men wishing to join should apply in person at any Military Barrack or at any Recruiting Office; the address of the latter can be obtained from Post Offices or Labour Exchanges.

The following **MEETINGS** in connection with the Recruiting Campaign in the Isle of Wight, organised by Mr. Douglas B Hall, M.P., at the request of Lord Kitchener, have already been arranged, and others will be announced later, and the Speakers named are assisting in the Campaign:—

PLACE	DATE.	SPEAKERS.
NEWPORT	Saturday Sept. 5th	Douglas B. Hall, Esq., M.P.
FRESHWATER & TOTLAND (Joint Meeting)	Monday „ 7th	Sir Godfrey Baring, Bart., M.P.
		Major-Gen. R.S. R. Fetherstonhaugh,
YARMOUTH	ditto	Lieut. Viscount Wolmer, M.P. [C.B.
VENTNOR	ditto	C. Seanmanga-Ralli, Esq., J.P.
		Col. H. P. Benson, R.A.
BEMBRIDGE, BINSTEAD, & ST. HELENS (EAST)	Tuesday „ 8th	Col. J. E. Rhodes
		Col. C. du P. Powney
EAST COWES	Wednesday „ 9th	Lieut.-Col. C. W. Clark, R.A.
NORTHWOOD	ditto	Major C. Sweetman
		The Hon. A. R. D. Elliot, M.A., J.P.
WHIPPINGHAM	Thursday „ 10th	Rev. S. Herbert
SEAVIEW	ditto	Sir Edgar Chatfeild-Clarke. J.P.
		Major C. Gordon Brodie
BRADING	Friday „ 11th	Rev. C. H. Thompson, M.A.
		The Hon. & Rev. W. E. Bowen, M.A.
ST. HELENS (WEST)	ditto	Major Arthy, R.A.
COWES	Saturday „ 12th	W. A. Glynn, Esq., D.L., J.P.
CARISBROOKE	ditto	Victor Middleton, Esq.

"GOD SAVE THE KING."

A recruitment advertisement, which appeared in the County Press of September 5th, 1914, the day after Bob enlisted.

if we have one good suit of clothes, pair of boots and topcoat to go on with until we get our khaki uniform, we shall be compensated with half a sovereign so I should be pleased if you could send me that brown showerproof coat of mine. It will be quite good enough for knocking about down here with and I will send you a postal order during the week but please send the topcoat carriage forward, as the government is paying all carriage and it will cost you nothing. I have had a fine flannel shirt and a thick pair of socks supplied me up till now. We start parade at 7.30 each morning up till 12.45 with plenty of rests in between and from 2.30 to 4.45, mostly foot drill and Swedish drill. I feel as well and fit as I ever did in my life and I've no trouble with my feet to speak of. Sundays we don't start till 9.30 a.m. and finish earlier. Gillingham is a fine healthy place. When you get to the top of our street you can look right down in the valley and across to the Kentish hills in the distance and on the right lays Chatham within easy walking distance. It is beginning to get very cold here in the mornings and night. We haven't any idea when we shall be moved from here yet but I'm comfortable enough. I'm glad Dad is getting on with his work all right. Does he find the walking too much for him?* Remember me to all the boys and girls at Whitecroft, also those in the workshops. What lot has Jim joined? He ought to have come with us as a clerk. I was pleased to get Kath's letter. Tell me everything that is going on in old Newport. I should like a paper now and then. I found out that we have got a hero at Brading – the boy who stuck to his guns when all his comrades were killed. Do you remember seeing the picture in the paper? Well, dear Mother, it is getting too dark to write any more just now so I will finish,

from your affectionate son Bob

From Mabs
The Bedford, The Mall, Newport.   Sunday, September 20, 1914
My Dear Bob,
I will have no more of writing once a week. In future I shall write twice or even seven times if I feel inclined.
This week has seemed like a dozen weeks rather than one. How have you managed this time? You have made a good start. I hope you are still keeping a good heart. I am glad if you can manage that all right because it makes everything go better then. I started this letter Sunday evening. I had to stop because Mother and Dad went out so I went over with Kath. Dolly and Doris were there too.
I had a postcard from Harry on Friday. He said he was glad to hear you are making a name for yourself. He hopes you are settling down all right. Morry is going on all right. He managed to get ashore one day. He said they had a six mile walk to get a pint (Perhaps).
Kath had a letter from Archy. He said he was going down to see you to keep your spirits up and then Kath told me I was evil-minded because I wondered whether it would be Irish or Scotch. I shall have to take some lessons from Arch in the art of letter writing. I can't get along with this at all.
It was a good thing I hadn't finished this letter because yours has just come in.

---

* At the age of 77, Bob's father walks two miles each way to work at Whitecroft six times a week.

I'm glad my letter was satisfactory. I had my doubts about it. As far as we know Ern is safe. He sent a card to let us know that he had arrived somewhere safely. It might have been Jericho for all we know. We didn't even know which country.

Kath was saying last night that you would hardly know what to do with yourself on Sunday, especially Sunday evening. As for me I don't like Sunday evenings any more, in fact if it wasn't for Kath I should wish them further. Upward and his pals still come round in the evening. We get all soldiers up to 7.30, some of the swanks too. There were five sergeants and two sergeant majors in Saturday night. Three of them were so tall and big built that when I went in it felt like this: IIIi. Of course the little one is myself. I suppose they fancied themselves.

Flo is home again now. I suppose that means a tramp down to Whiterails every week now. It will break the monotony a bit. Mr. Wray very kindly mended that pendant free of charge. Goodbye my love for a little while,

with heaps of love and good wishes from Mabs.

From Mother
49 Carisbrooke Road, Newport.   Wednesday, September 23, 1914
My dear Bob,

I sent your coat yesterday. They wouldn't take it in the Post Office unless I paid 6d. I expect they will refund it to you when you receive the parcel. Let me know if there is anything else I can send you. Do you march out like the soldiers do here? There was such a lot out yesterday. There never was so many passed by before. A lot had white canvas clothes – great big fellows. They say the Hampshires are going to Portsmouth. They keep sending more here. Do you see anything of Dyer? They keep on asking Dad how he is getting on. Dad is getting on very well but the ladders – he finds them very heavy which, of course, they are for one man. Finds it a bit trying on the ladder all day. Mabel has taken Kath out this afternoon and she is over there to tea. I got a letter from Harry Harvie. I will send it to you after Charlotte has seen it.

Isn't it sad – the three ships sunk? So many lives lost.* Have they given you another shirt and socks? I hope you will get the coat too, all right.

Love from us all,

your loving Mother E. Brimson.

From Mabs
The Bedford, The Mall, Newport.   Wednesday, September 23, 1914
My Dear Boy,

I had to rush that last letter because I nearly heard the postman's footsteps. Things are still going on about the same here except that we are to have a real live General in residence in the town. He has taken that house on the Watergate Road where Doctor Coombes lived. Flo hasn't come in today after all so there is

---

* On September 22nd, three cruisers, Aboukir and her sisters Cressy and Hogue, were sunk by just one German submarine while on patrol. 1,450 sailors were killed and there was a public outcry in Britain at the losses. The ships, contrary to practice, had failed to zigzag.

County Press advertisements, 1914

no walk back to night. Loud cheers because I have been out with Kath this afternoon. We went out Monday afternoon as well. We mean to make the most of the fine weather.

I was just going to tell you that Cecil Hall was in the Bar Parlour all alone up till now but two more have just come now. They are saying now that the Hampshires have all got to go to Portsmouth and the Warwicks stop here. I hope not. I expect we shall see more of the Warwicks now. There was one in tonight who always went to the Saracen's Head when he was working in Rugby and he says there are some more know it up there so I suppose he will be bringing them along. The Bar Parlour isn't the same without you.

I often forget now and look at that door expecting to see you come in but the curious part about it is that is always your Father or Roy comes in then.

If you were to hear all the good things they have to say about you I'm afraid you would never stop blushing. Roy has just come in and they are going it as hard as they can about Rheims Cathedral.*

Rotten luck for those cruisers. It's a great pity they couldn't rescue the men although we can't afford to lose the ships. I hope they won't be after our first class ones with all those men on board. Upward and Co. can't get enough beer before nine o'clock** so they take it away with them now and drink it under the hedge.

I shall have to rush again now with a big goodnight kiss for you but it would be so much better if you were here to take it my sweetheart.

With Best Love,
from Mabs.

From Ernest Attrill. Envelope endorsed, "Passed by Censor. 107 A.R.Gill."
No address given.   Saturday, September 26, 1915
Dear Mother and Father,

I am writing these few lines to let you know we are quite happy, listening to the shells bursting. Jack Pope got wounded but I'm glad to say Jerry and Bert and myself at time of writing are A1.

We are well looked after. Plenty of food, fags and tobacco so we can't grumble as it is brought up regular, which is good as it is a very bad country to get about in as the roads and villages are all damaged in this part of the country.

I suppose you have heard from Harry and Morry. I hope they are quite well as we don't get much news of the Fleet.

I will say au revoir from your affectionate son,
Ernest. XXXXXX
There goes another shell. No wonder the writing is shaky. So long.

---

*Rheims Cathedral was all but destroyed by German shellfire on 20th September 1914, leading to accusations of German "barbarism". By the end of the war only the Cathedral walls were still standing.

**At the end of August the Government introduced the 'Intoxicating Liquor Act,' curtailing the current drinking hours which allowed public houses to open at 5.00 am to midnight. Under the new Act opening times were restricted to noon to 3pm and 6.30pm to 9.30pm.

From Bob
26 Upper Milton Road, Gillingham, Kent.   Sunday, September 27, 1914
My dearest Mabs,
You don't know how grand it is to get your letters. As I've told Kath, it's all
we've got to look forward to in a way. I had a postcard from Arch to say they
are coming down today and the weather is lovely so we shall be able to have a
look round. I only wish you were coming as well – I should be happy then.
I've got a dear old landlady. She will do anything for me. I've had a beastly cold
so she made me onion gruel for three nights and the old chap put brandy in my
tea. I believe I should have been laid up if it hadn't been for them. I don't go
much on this Yankee that is here with me. He's too much brag like all the rest
of them (the old chap's just brought me in a glass of beer – hooray!) although
he's not so bad in other ways. I went up to the barracks for my final trade
approval yesterday. We got up there at 9.30 a.m. and laid about on the grass till
12.30 before it was our turn to go before the Major and we done practically
nothing in the afternoon so we get it easy sometimes. We have formed
Regimental football teams now and also concerts and boxing matches. We've
got some jolly fine teams amongst our lot I can tell you. The officers are getting
these things up. They are not very old themselves; one or two not more than 18,
but good sports. You and Kath must make the best of each other while I'm
away. I only hope it won't be long before we shall be able to get married when
I do come back, £40 or not. I don't draw my full pay until I've learnt all drills.
We are learning semaphore and knot tying, two things the R.E. has to know. I
get 10 shillings a week now so I'm better off than the line. Well, my sweet, I
must finish till next time with lots of kisses,
                              ever your true love, Bob.

From Bob
26 Upper Milton Road, Gillingham, Kent.   Sunday, September 27, 1914
Dear Kath,
I received overcoat and papers all right and also Mother's letter. I might
mention that letters are practically all we've got to look forward to, so write
plenty. We had two route marches as yet and we passed the Naval Hospital.
The wounded bluejackets were out on the balconies. We all cheered them as we
marched by and started singing 'The Boys of the Bulldog Breed' and they waved
back to us – those who had arms to wave with. They do look some wrecks, some
of them. Chatham and district has suffered heavy in the loss of those three
ships. Nearly every street there is someone who has lost a husband or son. One
of the chief PO's is a friend of our people here. He was on the HMS Aboukir and
came up to see us a few days before they sailed and brought his little curly-
headed boy with him. We all had quite a nice evening together but his wife has
had no news of him one way or the other. They've brought 300 of the survivors
back to Chatham. It's quite a common sight now to see the Red Cross motor full
of wounded on their way to the hospital. Although we finish at 10.30 Sundays
for the day, I believe we have to get a pass to leave the town but I might have a
chance later on. We are having lovely weather here, that's one good thing. I've

got all my new underclothing now; thick lambswool pants that make you shiver to look at them and a fine brown Cardigan jacket. Now I shall have to finish. Write soon.

With Love to all, yours ever,
Bob.

From Mabs
The Bedford, The Mall, Newport.   Sunday, September 27, 1914
My Dear Bobbie,
As soon as I had posted your letter Wednesday night, in walked Minnie and Sally. They might just as well have come before so that I could tell you! Of course they wanted to know how Mr. Brimson was. Sally said you were a brick and they were both quite sure you would be all right.
Minnie told me that Read is at the Front. I was surprised because I didn't know that he had been in the Army before, did you?
I went over with Kath after nine o'clock last night and I have been over again tonight. Well, it's past eleven and I'm supposed to be in bed but I feel like writing for ever now. I hope Archy went down to see you after all. He'll be severely spanked if he didn't, or at least if he doesn't go this week.
We had a letter from Morry this week. He said he thought you would have to follow the crowd. He also said that the Germans have said that the cowardly English disguised their fleet as a fishing fleet. He says picture the Iron Duke or Queen Mary floating round as fishing smacks. I must give you another extract from his letter, "I have been made a P.O. dating from July 1. More money for the wagonette party when we go to Berlin, 'Fall in and Follow me.' Tell Ern we will meet him there and he must save a drop in his water bottle." I think he must be in Scotland now. He says he is 'up' somewhere where it is getting very cold. By the way it is Saturday afternoon. You will be able to come round now but when will they let you come? Have you got to wait till Christmas?
Jim Curling is a full-blown Corporal now (Hants) and young Jock is a Lance Corporal. Did you know Cecil Barrett, a brother of that Barrett who sings? He was killed at the Battle of Mons and I am afraid Shiner Haines' brother was too. We're not quite sure of that. Anyway, I hope it wasn't him.
Is there anything you want that I can make for you? Please let me know if there is. Would it be any use knitting that white sweater? I suppose I may as well do it for when you come home if you don't want it now. I think it is nearly time I stopped. You'll have to get a week off to read this lot.
What has happened to Dyer? Is he with you now?
Another beastly Sunday evening coming. I suppose I shall have to go down with Flo. Your father says he thinks you must have been glad to get away from the Asylum. He says it gets on his nerves. Ben Sykes, Frenchy Flood and Mr. Chaplin were in last night. They were wedged up in a corner while a crowd of soldiers took possession of the rest of the room. There was a racket when they all tried to sing at once. It was Waterloo night last night for the Hants. Is that what you call pay-day? I must stop now my dearest, XXX

With love from your own Mabs.

Kath (Katherine) Brimson.
"I was pleased to get your letter last night and also that lovely photo of yourself"
Bob to Kath, 5th Dec 1915

From Kath
48 Carisbrooke Road, Newport, IW   Tuesday, September 29, 1914
Dear Bob,
I received your letter of today. I thought it was about time I did have one for my share. Mother was very glad to have the money, Bob. Very much obliged, too. We were very glad to hear that Chris and Arch came to see you. I expect you had a good time. It must be dreadful to see those poor sailors, Bob. It made you feel queer inside at first, didn't it, to see them?
Mother is glad to think you are being mothered. You won't be feeling homesick. Yes, you do sometimes. I know very well you do. We miss you more now than we did at first.
Mabel was over this morning. She made an excuse to come over but I believe she really came to talk over your letters. She likes to (only for goodness sake don't tell her I said so). That's why I said write different parts of the week, so we needn't be telling each other the same news. She was in last night too.
Dad, Roy, Doris and I went up on St George's Down Saturday afternoon to pick blackberries; that Roy brought a rope with him. When we got to the long lane to the right of Pan Down, he tied the rope on my carriage one end and the other on to a gravel cart that was going up, the varmint, but we got to the top in double quick time. Came back over Pan. Gordon has been promoted to every other Sunday, at the Carisbrooke Station. He'll be up an inch higher now. I'll be saying goodnight now, Bob. I will write again soon. Just beginning to get fond of it.
Heaps of love,
from your loving sister Kath.

From Mabs
The Bedford, The Mall, Newport.   Wednesday, September 30, 1914
My Dearest Boy,
If it is such a treat for you to get a letter, you can guess what it is like when I see yours come. I don't know what would happen if the postman didn't come in at 11.10 a.m., Monday with a letter. I can wait patiently till then but I don't believe I could wait another minute after that.
Monday afternoon I went off with Mrs. Reynolds to get some blackberries and mushrooms. Yesterday afternoon Kath and I went for a ramble round one of the old haunts. We went through Dark Lane into Gatcombe and back by the Asylum. It was six o'clock when we arrived home. I don't think I shall go up that hill from Gatcombe any more. It is easy enough to go down but it was jolly hard work getting up.
I expect when you think it over sometimes you feel glad that you joined up. All that exercise is bound to make you more fit. You won't know yourself when you come home. I believe there was a photo of Harry doubling round the deck with some more chaps in the Daily Mirror of the 26th. I noticed the likeness in the 'Mail' photo, but I didn't take any more notice of it as it was a bad print. Of course the other may not be him, but it is uncommonly like him.
I hope your cold is better now. You really must not lie about on the grass at this

time of the year unless you are obliged to. You want looking after still. I shall have to come round there to take care of you.

I shall disappear about nine o'clock to play Ludo. I wish you could come too, my dearest. However, it seemed as if you were here on Monday. I had such a grand dream about you. I couldn't shake it off all day. Our bell has vanished out of the bar parlour again. It went on Saturday. We must tie the next one on.

It is nearly time I stopped or you will have to read it in instalments, at odd minutes. Goodbye my love for the present,

With best Love From Mabs.

From Morry
HMS Owl   Friday, October 2, 1914
Dear Mabel,
Just a few lines to thank you for your letter and beer etc. I should like to have tasted it on the lawn but we have got that to come perhaps. I saw Shiner. He told me he had some pears and to thank you for them. The last lot I had were a proper mess. The parcel had broken open and they put them in the mailbag at London, but still, what there was, was very acceptable. We are going out again tonight. Of course, the same as usual – don't know where or how long for. We had some terrible weather last week, nearly as bad as a China typhoon. I have got pretty well all my clothes spoiled and the Owl I have got for a mascot has fell off his perch a couple of times and spoiled his feathers. I had a big photo of the ship to fetch home but it got soaked with water. I shall have to send it somewhen. That was a bit rough about them cruisers but I suppose it's what anyone would have done under the circumstances. I don't think a thing like that will happen again. Forewarned is forearmed. Have you heard from Bob lately? I suppose he will soon be off in the thick of it. Must close now, mail just going.

Your Affectionate Brother, Morry.
Goodbye.

From Mabs
The Bedford, The Mall, Newport   Sunday, October 4, 1914
Dear Bobbie,
I hope you received the last letter all right. I had only just put it in the letterbox when your card came.

Kath and I went up to the Barracks this morning.* We were just in time for the last Hymn and Prayers. We saw them march off and then we stopped to listen to the band. They played a few selections.

Flo came up this afternoon so we went for a walk after tea out to Shide and saw Mount Joy. It was grand on Mount Joy. The sun had just set, the sky was a beautiful red one side and on the other, the moon was just rising. There were just enough clouds to make it perfect. We went in to see Kath before we went to Whiterails.

There was a postcard from Ern yesterday. I expect he has been in it by now. He sent it on the 28th and they could hear the guns then, so they were not far away. There is another draft of about 200 Hants leaving tomorrow (Monday).

---

* See photograph page 76.

Ernie White managed to get through all right but his friend was wounded. His foot was shattered. Did you hear about Bert Westmore's narrow escape? The heel of his boot was shot off without injuring him.

It is terrible to think that they (our people) have had to lay mines around. I suppose the danger will be greater than ever now. I wish they could pop off all the enemy's leaders and end the wretched war.

You needn't laugh at those violets. I always said that no-one but you should have my buttonholes so I have sent them – with a kiss on each one for you. Kath and your Mother were having a game at your expense the other evening. Your Mother said she wouldn't call you Bob any more; it would be Ernest for the future, and Kath has christened you Don, so by the time you get a few more names you won't know who you are.

There was great excitement over the postcard. Of course, Sykes had to tease because I was looking at it with a magnifying glass. Well, I really must stop now or there won't be anything done this morning, my dear.

With best love, To my own Love.

From Chris
28 Barnard Road, Clapham Junction.   Wednesday, October 7, 1914
Dear Bob,

I expect you are thinking we are still on our way home. We might have been. That was a journey. We didn't get home until after 10, tired out. We will come a better way next time. Poor Jim is still under canvas and getting poor food. He wishes he could be transferred into your regiment. We managed to get down to see him last Sunday. He was very glad to see us. Bee's birthday made her very happy. First, she had a Bear that we had bought her, then came Mabel's parcel with two lovely books and chocolates for both of them. They have been reading ABC's ever since. Kath sent a work basket and dolls and sweets so they were well set up. Take care of yourself. I wrote to Mabel last night. The children often talk about you. Let us know when you make a move.

Love from Chris.

From Mother
49 Carisbrooke Road, Newport.   Wednesday, October 7, 1914
My Dear Bob,

Mabel gave me your address so I posted off the County Press to you. I hope you are comfortable. If you have a cold and it seems too thick to you, try and get rid of it. What do you think of St Mary's Barracks? And I wonder where you will be sent to next. Have you got enough clothes to wear and how do you get it washed? Mabel and I both think you don't answer the questions.

Charley is gone to the Front, and a lot more from this place. George Urry tells Minnie his chum was shot down at his side and killed. A close shave for George wasn't it? Do you think it will last much longer? What do they say up your part? I am afraid you don't find it very easy to write as you did when you were in lodgings. You will see those people when you can, won't you, for their kindness to you? Did you find anyone you knew in the Roll of Honour last week? I must thank you for the Postal Order. I was glad of it but I have not been able to pay the L bill yet, Mr. Brakie sent. I suppose you got the trenchcoat all right or I should have heard. Kathie is over at Mabel's today. We are having beautiful weather. Your father has not gone to work Saturday morning. He finds he needs the rest after the five days. It seems to pick him up again for Monday. I can't get used to your empty room yet, Bob. Do you think you will be able to come at Christmas? I can't think of anything more that will interest you, for I expect Mabel tells you plenty so I will close with love from all.

I am ever your appreciative mother,

E. Brimson.

From Mabs

The Bedford, Newport.   Sunday, October 11, 1914

My Dear Boy,

It was a relief to get your last letter. I was afraid that your cold had got worse and that you were in Hospital. I was very glad to find there was nothing wrong after all. I hope you will be able to get home sometimes. The soldiers here have a dreadful bother to get a pass to go away. I hope you won't be served the same. Things go on still about the same except that they are waiting for stray bombs from Zeppelins now. I had a letter from Morry this morning. He has been having a rough time. He said that it was worse than a Chinese typhoon. All his clothes are spoiled, the water must have gone everywhere. Two aeroplanes went over today. Great excitement. Shouts all round as to whether they were German or not. We haven't heard any more of Ern lately. Wasn't it terrible? You will have seen how badly the Hampshires caught it.* Well, one of the Captains up here told them this morning that it was our own men did it. They had not been told that the Hants were there and when they came up, it was dusk. The other English, thinking it was some more German treachery, fired on them. That's how it was there were so many.

I wish you hadn't told your Mother you were training for the Front, although I suppose she would have to know if you did go. Everybody wishes to be remembered to you. Well, I suppose I must stop now, it is post time my dearest.

With heaps of love from Mabs.

Seaford Camp, situated on the coast between Brighton and Eastbourne, was one of many tented training camps that sprung up across Britain between 1914 and 1915 to accommodate the tens of thousands of volunteers who responded to Kitchener's recruitment campaign. Bob left his digs in Gillingham and arrived at Seaford in early October.

From Bob

87 Field Company. R E Camp. Seaford. Sussex. **   Sunday, October 11, 1914

Dear Mother,

We moved into our final destination yesterday. Hardly any food all day until we went into the town at night and bought some. We had a jolly good feed then.

---

* During the Battle of the Aisne, gun crews of the Hampshire regiment were mistaken for German forces and fired on by their own side. There were no casualties.

** See photograph page 56

We are once more under canvas, sleeping twelve in a tent. The 88th company are coming Monday to join us. We are attached to a Division here composed of the Welch Regiment, the South Wales Borderers, 3 battalion of Liverpool Regiment, the Cheshire Regiment, the Staffordshire Regiment and N and O Shropshires and the Manchesters – the worst of all – the scum of the city, but we are away from that lot, thank goodness. Our Major Lloyd Owen told us this morning on parade that here we undergo our final training and in four months time he hopes to get us ready for the Front. We have got a lot to learn yet and some long hours to put in. I got the topcoat all right. I washed all the small things myself but the shirts and pants we send out. We have got a working uniform issued out to us so I have made a parcel of my other clothes. I have kept the trousers and waistcoat back and sent the coat, one pair of pants, one shirt, six collars, tie and one or two other things. Be careful of the coat because there are some letters in it. The parcel will be sent from St Mary's Barracks by the officials on OHMS so there will be nothing to pay. Please see that everything arrives safe. Am I too late for any of our tomatoes? They will be very acceptable. I think I would rather be in Chatham than here. We have just got comfortable in Barracks. Dad ought to take it easy this winter as he has nothing to worry about. I shall try to come home for a weekend later on when we get a bit more settled. As for Christmas leave, I shall try and get that off. The County Press is very welcome. I saw my name in the last one you sent but I wish you had seen that it was spelt properly.* Has Roy got any work yet? Tell him to drop a line now and then. George Urry's luck was in that time. Remember me to his mother and father. Now I must close with love to you, Dad and Kath and all the rest,
from your affectionate son, Bob.

From Kath
49 Carisbrooke Road. Newport   Wednesday, October 14, 1914
Dear Bob,
I'll have one more try. If you don't get this one, nary another one will I write. After thinking I'd surpassed myself by writing two letters in one night, one to you and one to Jim, I didn't get an answer to either of them. Neither of you got them, I don't believe. I don't reckon much to your fat-headed Barrack postmen. Did you get your tomatoes? If you didn't, it's his fault – take my word for it. Give him a thick ear for me. There, I won't be growling any more, only it might as well have been somebody else's letter you didn't get – Mabel for instance. She can scribble off yards in two minutes, whereas it takes me hours.
Dad told me to tell you that he is working over at the farm, papering two rooms. Mr. Salter has left; another young fellow is put in there. Mabel and I went out Sunday afternoon and on the way we met Min. Of course, she wanted to know all about you and wished to be remembered to you. 'Spect she would have sent her love if Mabel hadn't been there. Anyway, she seemed a bit downhearted about her boy. Said she had a letter from him; he was only 100 yards from the firing line while he was writing.

---

* In the County Press for Saturday, October 3, 1914, the Island Roll of Honour lists County Asylum staff who have joined 'Kitchener's Army' as C. Dyer, O. Salter and R. Brimsdon.

You told us you wouldn't be likely to be sent to the Front, young Bob. You know very well you did. Suppose you thought you sneaked off very well with that fib. I wish you'd come back. I'm about fed up with hearing Mother and Mabel's conversations all about you. I'm sure they will be coming to a fight before long. It's something like this: Mother says, "I wish I had a nice long letter from Bob," then Mabel will say, "Oh dear! Anybody would think he was your young man instead of mine." Then Ma flares up, "So he is, indeed – until you're married, then I'll give him to you – but he'll be mine all the same." And I've got to sit and listen to all that! Perhaps it will be safer for you to stay away or they'll be tearing you to pieces between them. Never known such women.

Just had a letter from Arch. He is just about worried about your boots. Every letter lately, he has done nothing but rave about yours and Jim's boots! Whatever is the matter with them? I should like to see them. Have you got your clothes yet? Don't come home till you have.

I forgot to give you Ivy's message. She was saying the other day to me, "Won't Grandma be pleased when Bob comes home, and you will, won't you?" I said, "I should think we will, and won't you be glad to see him? You'll let him pump down your neck as much as he likes, won't you?" She said, "Course I will, if he wants to." She said it quite seriously as if she meant it. She is a funny little kid. If there is room to say goodnight, I'll be saying it now.

Heaps and heaps of love,
from your loving sister, Kath.

From Kath
49, Carisbrooke Rd, Newport.   Friday, October 16, 1914
Dear Bob,
Your parcel came yesterday with no shirt but the coat, pants, collars, tie, letters and braces managed to get here. The parcel came in a very untidy condition and Ma wants to know if you want a pillow? Tell us when you write if you do. Did you get the tomatoes? I suppose you have been washed nearly out of your tent, haven't you? These poor chaps have up the barracks; they have been pretty well soaked. Goodbye,
heaps of love from Kath.

From Bob. On YMCA paper
87 Field Company. R.E Camp. Seaford. Sussex.   Saturday, October 17, 1914
Dear Kath,
I was pleased to get your letter, although it was a short one, and I'm glad to know everything is going on all right at home, also that Roy has got work. There is plenty of work for carpenters down this way. They are working all over the place, putting up these wooden huts, working Saturday afternoons and Sundays. I shall be glad when they are finished so that we can move in. It has been nothing but rain these last few days and the parade grounds are up around your ankles in mud. The other night I woke up with the rain coming through the tent on my face and blankets. I had a letter from Chris and Arch this

morning. They want me to come up for a weekend. I shall see later on. Mrs Attrill's bread pudding was very nice. We don't do so bad in our tent now for feeds. Each chap sends home for cakes or something, so nearly every day a parcel arrives which is shared all round. We have quite a variety at times. It all helps to make it better for us. You never said whether you received that postal order I sent the other day. I'm glad my coat arrived all right. I was beginning to think that had got pinched too. We get marched down to paddle (don't laugh). We have got to bathe our feet in the sea whether we like it or not. There are some of the chaps who go for a swim but it's rather too cold for me. It's cold enough putting your feet in with the north-east wind blowing. There are heaps of limpets and winkles, also starfish. It is a very rocky shore in some parts and no sand anywhere along. I wish I'd been there for the duck the other Sunday dinnertime but I'll have my share at Christmas, all being well. Is Dad working inside still? I hope he is. Tell him to remember me to all of them at Whitecroft. Love to Mother and Dad and yourself, not forgetting Roy, Kit and the kiddies, and tell Nip to get busy,
From Your loving brother, Bob.

From Mabs
The Bedford, Newport .   Sunday, October 18, 1914
My Dearest,
What a dreadful time you must be having lately. It was too bad to take you down to that one-eye spot at this time of year, especially as you were just comfortable in Barracks. I hope they will soon get those huts up. They are putting some up here now. You may guess what a pickle the Warwicks were in last week, in their field. I bet there's a fight to get a drink over your way, something different to the Bar Parlour here. It won't hurt to have a glass less a day. Everybody wishing to be remembered to you. I should fill two or three sheets if I tried to name them all. Woodford and Ashley, and Mr. and Mrs Leal are some of them. The Leals and Ashleys have been to tea today. Jock and Flo were here too. Kath and I went up to the Barracks to fetch Jock to dinner. The band played, 'The Girl in the Taxi'* while we were waiting. That is coming to Portsmouth this week. Don't you wish you were off to see it again with Johnnie and I? Barclay Gammon was there a week or two ago. It will be a treat to see you here again. I do hope you can manage it sometimes.
There was a dreadful accident here last night, Saturday.** It was caused by an explosion from one of those electric lamps. The explosion was underground near the standard outside the old County Press offices. The force was so great that it blew up a big paving stone and made a big hole there. A Territorial named Belcher was standing near and he was killed. The stone hit him on the head as it fell but they say that he was electrocuted before the stone hit him.

---

* The title music from the 1912 London production of the musical farce, 'The Girl in the Taxi.'
** An explosion in a manhole at the junction of Pyle Street and St. James's Street blew the cover thirty feet into the air. The descending cover struck Bandsman Edward Belcher of the Isle of Wight Rifles on the head, killing him instantly. Ironically, he was on the point of leaving the Rifles, having been certified medically unfit for further service.

The Attrill family photographed in the garden of The Bedford. Seated, Mabs' parents, Ada and Maurice, with Wallace in between and standing, left to right, Harry, Ernest, Mabs and Morry.

An Edwardian picture postcard of Whitecroft Asylum .

However, I expect you will see all about it in the paper next week. You must please excuse my writing in pencil as I forgot to fetch the ink in here (I am supposed to be in bed).

It was hard luck losing the Hawke* and all those men but the enemy were well paid for it when their four destroyers went to Glory. Who says our chaps are asleep!

Please remember, if you make me wait till Friday for a letter again I'll make you wait a week (See). You didn't tell me whether you have that other letter. If you don't answer questions when I ask them, you wait – see what you will get my lad. I shall write so much but I suppose that would be a relief instead of a punishment. Your Mother quite expected you home this week. She thought you would smell that duck they had for dinner. I asked you in one letter if you wanted anything but you never took the trouble to say anything about it.

I am glad you are a good boy but you might know I could trust you as well over there as I can here. I am sure I should love you as much if you were not the dear old boy that you are. Other girls won't worry me my sweetheart, so you can rest in peace. With Love to the best Boy,

from Mabs.

From Morry
HMS Owl   Sunday, 18 October, 1914
Dear Mabel,

I received a parcel today but could not sort out the grapes, tomatoes and tarts – they were all squashed up. The cake and apples were all right. We have had a little excitement the last couple of days. It's getting a bit warm here now they managed to catch the Hawke. It's a bit hard lines having to fight what you can't see. There's no mistake we are up against it. Things are not very bright yet. We collected £130 for fags and tobacco and had them made up in packets and marked with the 4th Flotilla's compliments and had them sent to the Front. I don't know whether Ern will get any or not. I'm a full-blown Ship's Cook now, 4s.3½d a day for nothing, only to chance having a sky trip from a German submarine. I suppose Bob is looking forward to a medal as big as a frying pan. Hoping you are quite well.

Your Affectionate Brother, Morry.

From Mother
49 Carisbrooke Road, Newport.   Monday, October 19, 1914
My dear Bob,

We were so glad to hear from you this morning and to know you were quite well. I'm always wondering what you are doing. Eh, Bob, I did want you to dinner yesterday. Mrs Attrill sold me a nice duck for 2/6. I felt upset when I sat down and you was away, knowing how you would enjoy it. Now can't you possibly come before Xmas or will it mean you will be able to get more time if you don't have any weekends? You ought to find out. I will be glad to send you a cake and I will before the week is out. The bother is I am always so short of

---

* On October 15th, HMS Hawke was sunk off Aberdeen with the loss of over 500 men.

money, the post and stuff together, but I will do my best. I have posted three papers for you tonight. I will send the handkerchiefs with this letter. What do you lay on?

Don't the rain make everything wet? I have put a bit of wadding in. I should put a piece in your ears to keep out the earwigs. I am sorry the tomatoes was spoiled – I was afraid they would be. I think a lot of the Card, Bob. Everyone can easily pick you out. Dad took it out to the Asylum and only brought it back tonight.

It's getting dark in the mornings now at six o'clock. Do you get up at that time? I hope you get your shirt aired, and socks. Who made them? Tuesday. Your father says he don't quite know why Salter left. He is up at Parkhurst now and his wife lives in New Street but they offered her quite her husband's wages, but she was not satisfied. I hope you got the papers this morning. If you are glad with the Lloyds*, tell me. I won't send it else.

Goodbye Bob. Keep your heart. The General who lives here says the war will be over by Christmas.

Every your loving mother,
E.B.

From Mabs
The Bedford, Newport.   Sunday, October 25, 1914
My Dear Bob,

Just think of it – only eight weeks now to Christmas, but I wish it wasn't so long. I do hope they will give you a decent holiday after waiting so patiently. I have just come from your house. Mr. and Mrs Reynolds have been to tea today and Mother's cousin came to dinner and tea. His name is Albert Everton. He is a lance corporal in the 1st Royal Warwicks. He went to the Front and was wounded at Mons so that is how he comes to be with this Regiment. He expects to go out again soon. He is another young lad about my age but he is as big as you. I have to smile when I compare him and Jock – there is such a difference in their size. I must tell you about him when you come home.

You shall have something to eat my dear. I did not send this week because your Mother sent the cake but you shall have something soon. It was as well to go on strike concerning that inoculation. Some of them here have refused to be done at any time. Of course, they won't be allowed to go away. I don't think they will mind that. Some of them will do anything to get back from the Front.** I have been helping the Club money up, Kath's and yours, but I had only been paying sixpence a week on yours. If you want any alteration, you must let me know. How do you like the life? Is it all right or do you make the best of it?

Another letter from Morry this week. He is in fine style again now. They

---

* A weekly newspaper so popular that the music hall artiste, Mathilda Wood, changed her name to Marie Lloyd "because everyone's heard of Lloyds".

** Vaccination against smallpox was compulsory for all troops, but anti-typhoid inoculation was voluntary and became an individual liberty issue. Kitchener, a supporter of anti-typhoid immunization declared that men who did not accept inoculation would not be sent abroad. Soldiers refusing inoculation were accused of unpatriotic behaviour by the medical profession, who declared, "Microbes kill more men than bullets." By the end of 1915, 90 per cent of troops were submitting to inoculation.

captured an oil ship so they felt very pleased with themselves. We have had no news of Harry for some time now. I suppose we shall get about half a dozen letters in a bunch soon. I had a card from Ern. He is all alive, and the old woman, and Jerry too. They have been fighting but he thought that battle would soon be over. The Hants are leaving the Island this week. I see Kitchener is applying for another half million men, so he is not satisfied yet. Mr. Curling is Sergeant and George Attrill is to be Sergeant Major as soon as they move, so he is going on all right. There is a rush and scramble from 6.30 till nine o'clock every evening now. I don't know how it will be when the Hants leave, though. If it wasn't for the soldiers we should have scarcely any trade at all.

I must close this 'tommy rot' letter now. My brains won't think because they keep flying away to you. I keep on wishing you were safe here and then it is goodbye to the news. Never mind my love, I will write again soon.

From Your Loving Mabs.

From Mabs
The Bedford, Newport.   Tuesday, October 27, 1914
My Dear Boy,
Mother heard you wanted bread pudding so you will get it with a vengeance if the postman doesn't eat it on the way.

The box is going by the same post as this and biscuits are in the pudding. I will send you biscuits alone another time. I hope you are all right and it won't be too long before you write to me this week. We were worried to death with Regimental Police last night. They have had a lot of trouble with the Warwicks this week so they must be out of the pubs by five minutes to eight now unless they have a pass. If any are caught without passes, the house is to be put out of bounds. It applies to all soldiers here (no bottles to be served to them either). I saw Mrs Spink this afternoon. She sends her love (tut, tut).

We had a letter from Ern, Monday. He says they are well looked after there, both in food and clothes. The Frenchmen tell them that they will be home for their Christmas dinner. We are still waiting for news of Harry. Wallace suggested taking the chocolate out of the parcel in case you did not get it. Everyone wishes to be remembered to you as usual.

Did I tell you in the other letter how disappointed Albert Everton was because he was wounded and did not see a German? Some more troops have come from India. There were a few Newport chaps amongst them. This is all now, my sweetheart.

With Best Love From Mabs.

From Kath
49, Carisbrooke Road, Newport.   Tuesday, October 27, 1914
Dear Bob,
We had your card yesterday but you needn't think we are going to be satisfied with measly cards. That was a good long letter you sent last week to me – we'll have a few more like that. Mother was very glad you liked her cake, and the

other boys too, but she can't seem to make out how you shared out 12 pieces and still had a big piece left. Oh, before I go any further, you said you had sent your coat or were sending it. Well, we haven't got it. I don't know when you sent it. Anyway, we haven't got it.

Mabel has just been in and gone again. She is in a hurry to pack something off to you from Mrs Attrill before the post goes. I hope you will like it. She has been in two or three times today. She doesn't leave us long to be lonely and young Nip's popping in and out at all times. He doesn't seem to know what to get up to. There doesn't seem enough of him to go to work. He told me today that he thought, but wasn't quite sure, that he was going to the Grammar School next week. Mabel hasn't said anything about it to me so I expect it's one of his make-ups. I was to be sure and tell you from Roy that he packed the cake. He was very fussy about it – said if he let Mother do it, it wouldn't have got there, or rather you wouldn't have got it. He says, tell Bob I'll write to him as soon as I've got time. He is working for Mr. King again.

I have begun my cards again. Chris and Arch are coming this Christmas as far as we know at present. I hope so. It seems such a long time since they were here, and you too Bob, try and get a nice long time off, can't you? Haven't got anything more to say now. There's heaps of love and kisses,
from your loving Kath and Mother and Dad.

From Chris

28 Barnard Road, Clapham Junction.   Thursday, October 29, 1914
Dear Bob,

Your letter has just come in – at the right time too. I was trying to make up my mind to write. Archy has gone out on business somewhere but I expect he will drop you a line. He is fearfully busy. We had made up our minds to come down and look at you one day but it doesn't seem as if we shall get a chance now with such a rush of work. Anyhow, you come up as soon as you can. Jim has had two weekends off already. He has got some blue clothes. You don't say whether you have got a uniform. He is as swanky as ever, stands in front of a glass to put on his cap and must have the folds in his coat just right. Let me know when to expect you. The children still call the spare room 'Uncle Bob's room,' and I don't suppose it will ever get called anything else. They keep on writing letters to you and Jim but I'm afraid they don't reach their destination. You wouldn't know London at night now. It is a hole. We have only one lamp light in our road, no lights outside any of the shops and only so many inside. It is miserable to go out at night. Up in town, it is worse. Buses and trains with lights shaded or blinds down, and the great searchlights look very weird. I hope you will be able to get off at Christmas, us too. We are looking forward to it. It will cheer them up so, and poor old Kath, she must be very dumpy lately, although I suppose Mabel is good to her. Have you told Kath about the club money? I think you ought to now, if you haven't, in case she can come up. You see, she will be getting her things together. I'm glad you have got some mattresses. I don't think Jim has – he didn't mention it. Have you got a decent set of men in your tent? I suppose you get newspapers and books to read. If there is anything we can send you down, you must let us know. The children have been very quiet this last week again. I tell them they won't be able to go to Granma if they don't get better quickly. That upsets them. I will write again soon. I daresay Archy will add to this. We don't like picture postcards. You can't get enough writing on them unless they are photos; then we don't mind. Goodnight now, Bob. Be a good boy, mind,

love from us all, your loving sister, Chris.

From Harry
No. 4-0 Mess, HMS Tiger. 1st Battle Cruiser Squadron   Possibly October
Dear Bob,
Sorry to keep you waiting so long. I have had a shift round as Tiger was rather short of signalmen. Everything is all gay. I expect you are longing to get to the Front. I had a letter from Ernest. He's quite well but doing plenty of time in the trenches. Haven't anything exciting to report this time except to say the Germans wouldn't bite,

yours sincerely, Harry.

From Mabs
The Bedford, Newport.   Sunday, November 1, 1914
My Own Dearest Sweetheart,
'You're My Baby' – No, I forgot – I meant to say, I'm surprised at you. You should want something a little more loving (you will get it too). I am very sorry for you if you will have to be under canvas till Christmas. It must be rotten. I hope you're taking care of yourself, Dear. I have been over to see Kath since I began this. Flo and Albert Everton went with me and we played Ludo. You see, Doris was there, so Flo looked on while we played. Albert won. By the way, I shall refer to him as 'Toffee' in future.*
He says that is his common name. You would like to know him, I am sure. Now then, there is no need to be jealous. You know there is no one but you for me. He is only another brother. Enough of him. Let's get to something else. I am very pleased (now don't be offended at what is to follow) to say that I haven't any time to miss you up to 9 o'clock. We have to keep moving now and no mistake. I'm glad that the bread pudding was all right. The only fault was that Mother forgot to put the fat into it.
I do wish it was summer instead of winter. It would be nice in Camp then and then I should be able to come to see you sometimes. I wish it had been you instead of Toffee playing Ludo tonight but we will have a good time to make up for it won't we, Lad? There was a nice fire in the front room in your house tonight, but no Bob to sit by it.
I wonder whether we shall hear from Harry tomorrow. We have had nothing more yet. Morry is going on in fine style. He says he's 'Ship's Cook', with full pay for doing nothing except wait for a sky trip from a German submarine, so I suppose they are beginning to get a bit scared of them now. He also said he supposed you were on the lookout for a medal as big as a frying pan. That

---

* Albert Edward John Everton, born in Lutterworth, 1895, enlisted 1910 and served in India and then with the Royal Warwickshire Regiment.

would be a very good thing to go to war with, perhaps you wouldn't get hit so easily. My head aches now. I think it must be straining my eyes reading when I ought to be asleep. The 'Owl' has not been in this week but they have been expecting the 'Prince of Wales' in for three weeks.

You ought to have been here Saturday night (Harry, Morry and Ern too). That Upward and his pals got old George Cooper on the string with his songs and their choruses, much to the delight of some NCOs who were in there. Of course, Roy was there to help. He is going to write to you sometime. I have got about ten letters to write at the rate they are mounting up. I shall have to start writing as soon as I get up and keep on till I go to bed.

By the way, do you know I never get your letter until Friday? There is no delivery here Thursday night. I really must stop now. I can hardly see the writing at all. Well, goodnight my love, and be a good boy. I suppose there is no need to tell you that. I don't suppose you get any more time than I do to miss anyone, except Sunday. I am looking forward to the time when this confounded war is over and we can have our old happy times again, with lots of love and kisses.

To My Dearest Boy, from Mabs.

From Mother
49 Carisbrooke Road, Newport.   Monday, November 2, 1914
My dear Bob,
I must thank you for the postal order. I received one from you, Bob, while you was at Gillingham and I remember thanking you for it; it was for two shillings. You will be glad to know we are all keeping well. I am glad Mrs A sent you the puddings and you can get extra feeds, all you boys. I will try and send you something this week. I wish I could have the little hamper again. It was capital to send you anything in but perhaps you find it handy. I will manage somehow. I will put on the outside when I post it, then you let me know when you get it. I shall know then how long it is on the way for if I send you anything in the way of meat things, such as sausage rolls or pies.

The Hants up at Parkhurst is very bad and they are busy putting up wooden huts – as if they couldn't have done it months ago. A lot of them are ill up there and I suppose it is the same at your place. Herbie Cornish is on the Grantham now. He's only been moved from the Ship Hawke, which was all right for him. Mabel and her husband and four children are on their way home from India with the regiment. I hope they will get home safe with so much trouble about. They only have 48 hours allowed them before they are off again to the Front. They have come home from Egypt three weeks ago, and a fortnight ago came home from India.

Poor Jack Cornish's time was out in August. What a shame it is now. Perhaps he will get killed at the Front – Mrs Reynolds three sons as well. George Urry is having a very rough time out there. He keeps asking for things to wear and all sorts of things. Don't you want any extra things? Do you get supplied with enough? Let us know if you do. Now I can't think of anything more to tell you.

Ever your loving Mother, E. Brimson.

From Bob (YMCA postcard)
Royal Engineers Camp, Seaford, Sussex.   Monday, November 2, 1914
Dear Mabs,
Received box all right. Thanks very much for it and please thank you or Mother for the bread pudding. We all enjoyed it. It will be a treat for Morry if he can get home for a weekend. I wish I could, but Christmas isn't far off now.
                                        Yours, Bob.

From Mabs
The Bedford, The Mall, Newport.   Wednesday, November 4, 1914
My Dearest Bobbie,
Your Mother sent you a box today. Kath was afraid to put a letter in because she thought it was against the rules. You ought to be all right between your Mother and Chris. I wrote to Chris, Monday. Now please take warning – if you dare to go to London without coming here you'll be mincemeat when I have finished with you.
Punch Drake managed to get into the Army after all. They put him on a Staff job. We had news of Harry yesterday after all this time. He didn't have much to say. He is quite well but very busy and they are, all the while, dodging submarines. Well my dearest, how do you find knitted socks? Mother has given me orders to knit some for you and the other boys. And what of gloves? I expect you could do with some, couldn't you dear, or won't they allow you to wear them out?
Kath says if you send that ship you had better fill it with socks to darn. I tell her to let you learn how to do it – see how nice it would be when we get married, but it is only fun. I hate darning myself so I wouldn't be so cruel as to give it to you to do. I must close now, my Love, as it is bedtime again.
With heaps of Love and kisses,
                                I remain Your Loving Mabs.*

From Bob
87 Field Company R.E Seaford, Sussex.   Thursday, November 5, 1914
Dear Mabs,
We have struck something great here. Last Sunday we went for a walk and met a lady who is the essence of kindness. She is doing a lot for us. This postcard is not big enough to explain it all on so I will tell you all about it in a letter. I was delighted to get your lovely cake this morning and also the books. It was very thoughtful of you. I am writing this card in a big seaside residence. Of course, you will be surprised to hear this but more about it later.
                                        Yours, Bob.

---

* The word 'From' had been overwritten to read 'I remain' and each letter of 'Mabs' had been spelt out in tiny kisses.

Bob, third from right in back row, with fellow maintenance workers at Whitecroft Asylum. Seated on the ground are five patients; in all likelihood, some are mentioned by name in the letters.

From Kath
49, Carisbrooke Road, Newport.   Thursday, November 5, 1914
Dear Bob,
It's very glad I am, to get your letters. You write very decent ones, plenty of news, but it doesn't matter how much I write to you (or any of us) you still want more. You're as bad as that Dickens boy. I shall soon be an expert letter writer, what with you and Chris.
Mother hopes you got your pastry all right. She says it wasn't quite so good as she expected it to be – she'll try and do better next time. We found it shook about after it was packed up, so we think it must have been smashed up a bit by the time it got there but you will manage to eat it all right, I expect. Oh! I mustn't forget to tell you – Nip's strict instructions were that I was to inform you that he made the biscuits purposely for you. He was here when Mother made the pastry, so of course he must have his finger in the pie, so Ma let him make the biscuits for you. He also made some for Clem and Ivy. They came to tea yesterday.
What's this curious card about that Mabel has just brought over to show us? Who is this mysterious Lady, for gracious sake. I should think she has bewitched you. It's the queerest I've read from you. Write and tell us about it properly, do.
I expect that cake came from Chris if only you knew it. She told us she was going to send you one. You remind me of a boy away at School, having hampers sent you. I've a good mind to send you some toffee and candy. Speaking of toffee reminds me of that sort of cousin of Mabel's. He's ever such a nice boy. You needn't be a bit afraid of him. Mabel is always ramming you down him. I believe she's always talking to him about you. He makes out he is looking forward to seeing you at Christmas but I believe he'll be sick to death of you before then, poor chap, only for goodness sake don't tell Mabel I said so. She is a dear, though. I don't know what Mother and I would do without her.
There! Mother came in last night, in a fever, saying they wouldn't allow the soldiers to cross the water. They won't let Charlie come or Eldridge, so of course Mother is afraid they'll be stopping you. What do you think about it?
I'm just going to have my supper. I wish you were here to have some too. This is just about enough of this jabber. There's nothing in it after all, but it shows I'm thinking of you. Goodnight Bob,
                                        ever your loving Kath.

From Mabs
The Bedford, Newport.   Tuesday, November 10, 1914
My Dearest Bobbie,
Upward and his pals are still here. I don't suppose they will ever join, although Upward says he thinks sometimes he will finish up at the Docks and join.
Roy keeps on talking about writing to you but he says he wrote so much the first time he can't find any more to write about. I will make you one of those helmets. I would have made one long ago when you spoke about your nocturnal visitors (beetles) had I known you wanted one. We had one here but I sent it out to Ern

last week. You know that nice old lady who lives in the flat over Chris? She sent Harry a parcel of socks, cigarettes, etc. It seems to me that everyone we know wants to do something for Harry and Morry. I had a letter from Harry at the same time as your letter came. He is still in the best. He managed to exchange messages with Morry the other day. They passed within signalling distance but of course, they didn't meet.

Another draft of 210 Royal Warwicks (with great emphasis on the Royal) left on Sunday. I expect some of the Hants will go now. We had a card from Ern. He said they had just come out from some of the heaviest firing they would get through the war. One of the Officers up here told his men that only 400 men of the first Battalion were left. We went up to the Barracks on Sunday to hear of the Royal Warwickshires and, thank Heaven, it's a bit better than the Hants.

I went down to have a tooth out on Saturday. It began to ache so I thought I would be rid of it before it got worse. It is all right now.

By the way, you can go to London if you like, dear. I didn't know it was so easy to get there. I must stop now. I have got lots of things to do. If I have forgotten anything I shall be writing again in a day or two, so it won't matter.

So now 'Au Revoir.'

From your Loving Little Sweetheart, Mabs.

From Mabs
The Bedford, Newport.   Friday, November 13, 1914
My Dearest Boy,

You are very slow at writing. Your Mother has been waiting all the week for news of you but nothing comes.

I haven't sent you anything more that is eatable because you seem to be doing so well for the present. I know you like chocolate so I am sending you a little to go on with. Before I forget, Billy Reynolds' brother is a prisoner in Germany so you may rejoice that you don't live next door to the old lady now.

Frank Coleman is also a prisoner and Toffee's cousin too.

The Royal Warwicks must have lost very heavily for they sent out 1000 men in ten days from Parkhurst. 600 left on Wednesday with about 200 Hampshires.

They had no idea the night before that they were going so soon. They were away by eight o'clock in the morning. One poor chap fainted and died on the road. He was too excited. The Warwick's band is up in the Workhouse – a nice place for them. Still, it's better than being under canvas.

You can go to London if you like, dearest. I didn't know it was so easy to get there. It would be a nice change for you. Only six weeks now and you will be here again but I do wish the weeks wouldn't be so long.

Villain! I have been waiting for the postman and he didn't call here. You don't deserve a smell of this choc. I was going to put some cigars in but thought the flavour would be too strong. Goodbye my sweetheart,

with Fondest Love from Mabs.

From Mabs

The Bedford, Newport.   Monday, November 16, 1914

My Dear Sweetheart,

Thanks for letter received on Saturday. What a lively time you have had, although I believe it is been worse since then. I hope you have not been quite blown away. Poor Jock is down for the Front, probably this week. He says the sooner the better. There is one thing – I expect he's too small to hit so he will be safe. I expect you will be sorry you could not get to Atherfield when I tell you that poor old Uncle George is very ill with that beastly cancer. Not expected to recover.

The fires have been started in the rooms now and it does seem strange to have the vacant chair by the fireside. Flo and I went over to your house to tea yesterday. We had some more Halma and I actually beat Kath. Flo went home alone. There is some wretched fiend in the next room trying to play 'Echoes of Killarney'. I'm sure I shall go and kick him in a minute. I should think he's got 'ragtime' on his brain by the way he jerks it out.

Nearly all the Hants have left for Gosport today. There is only the draft and a few employed men left up here now.

Tuesday: I had to give up last night. That idiot made such a row. It is a beautiful day so I am off to Atherfield presently. I will let you know then how Uncle is going on. Mother went to a sale yesterday afternoon and she thought she had bought two or three lots of those Staffordshire figures (one, twelve inches high) for me, but the fat-headed clerk had put them down to some other woman at less than Mother's bid.

We have heard nothing of the boys this week. I suppose they are busy again. I must close now, my Love, because there's a lot to do.

With heaps of kisses (When you come home),

I Remain Ever Your Loving Mabs.

From Mabs

The Bedford, Newport.   Thursday, November 19, 1914

My Dear Boy,

It's no use, I can't wait any longer before writing. I said today I wouldn't write to you till I heard from you but I changed my mind. How do you get on through this horrible weather? I hope you don't find it too much.

I hope you will have some Halma at Christmas. I have beaten Kath three times now and I want to beat you, then I shall rejoice. I might get a look in with draughts then.

We had a very interesting letter from Ern today. He is quite well and as happy as a cricket. I am going to get the County Press to publish his letter next week so you will be able to read it. (See page 48.)

What of the beer? Threepence a pint. You'd have to be a TT now and drink shandy. Roy looked in the shop tonight to ask the price of beer. He didn't stop, he took a bottle off with him.

Only three weeks now. I do hope we shan't be disappointed after all.

I went out to Atherfield and the Doctor says that Uncle George won't be here at

Christmas, so he is very bad now. He doesn't seem to trouble about it.
Goodnight now my love,
from your own little sweetheart, Mabs.

County Press Saturday, November 28, 1914
"HERE THEY COME! – THEN THE BAND PLAYS."
NEWPORTONIAN'S SPIRITED ACCOUNT OF GERMAN ATTACK.
Private Ernest Attrill, Hants Regiment, son of Mr. Maurice Attrill, of The
Bedford, Newport, writing home from the Front on November 12, says: "Just a
few lines to let you know I got both parcels and papers all together this morning,
with a letter. We could not get them before, as we were having a game with the
Germans in the trenches and it was rather too hot for them to be sent in. …. We
were at it last night, in fact we have been at it the last 12 days and nights in the
trenches. We had one night's shelling. We had a beautiful thunderstorm last night,
with 'bags' of rain, and I can tell you that just for a few seconds it makes you think
of the empty bed at home when you are soaking wet through with no roof over
you. But you soon get reminded of where you are when you hear the joyful words
whispered from man to man, 'Here they come.' We let the Germans get close, and
then the band plays and the cinematograph commences, but you don't pay at the
door for these picture shows. They are at it again on the left. I have had a couple
of squeaks, one by a shell burst, which injured my mate and snipers had a go
when I was making for the trench. …. There are thousands of German helmets
out here in front of our trenches, but I shall wait till later before taking one, as
one has quite enough to carry about. You ought to see the game we have with the
Germans. We fire at them with their own rifles and bullets, of which we get
plenty. We had a 'beauty' the other morning in a big fog. The Germans thought
they had us, but they forgot that the British bulldog sleeps with one eye open, and
they soon found out. We let them get quite close, and as we brought them down
we shouted, 'Take this to Berlin' or 'How do you like this one, Sausages?' &c.
In another letter, written from hospital at the Front on November 23rd, Private
Attrill says: "Just to let you know I am being treated quite well. I have got
rheumatism in the legs. We were standing in trenches half-full of water, and of
course, the frost and snow helped it on. It is hard luck after being in the semi-
final, but I hope to get in the final, which will be about a fortnight or three weeks,
and then we will sweep them off the map."

From Bob, on YMCA headed notepaper
87 Field Company, R.E., Seaford, Sussex.   Friday, November 20, 1914
My dearest Mabs,
I received your last letter alright, also the box on Sunday. It came just right.
They were ever so nice and I enjoyed them no end. I shall have a lot to make up
for when I come home. Fancy Jock going out. He doesn't look more than a kid,
but don't tell him I said so. I have put in for a pass to London this week, from
Saturday midday until Sunday midnight. That is all the leave they will allow us
and then there are only so many passes issued. It will be a treat to get out of the

camp for a few hours.

I have had a soft time all the week, back on the old job, painting and signwriting. I was lucky enough to be picked out for it. All the rest of them have been trenching but I shall get my turn of that next week. It is not sappers' work really but we have to learn it practically, because later on we have charge of the infantry who dig them while we direct.

I'm afraid I shall have to cut this letter short because there is a Welshman behind my chair waiting to write a letter. You would be surprised to see how this place is patronised. You have to wait a deuce of a time to get a pen and a chair. Every night is the same.

They have some decent concerts here two or three times a week, mostly young ladies too. What do your father think of Lloyd George now? And what he has done? I bet he doesn't half rave about him. I fancy I can hear him arguing the point in the bar now.

Well, I must finish this now and I will tell you more news after I have been to see Chris, only it will seem funny without you there this time. I send you my deepest Love and fondest kisses,

                    from your Loving Sweetheart, Bob.

Love to all at home.

From Bob, on YMCA headed notepaper

87 Field Company, R.E., Seaford, Sussex.   Friday, November 20, 1914

Dear Mother,

I have been keeping fine lately and we are having some fearfully cold weather but I don't seem to suffer from it like some of the fellows do.

 I have not received the County Press this week. I always look forward to it. I have put in for a weekend pass to go up to London this week for the sake of getting a bath more than anything, as it is impossible to get one in Seaford.

I have been working at painting and signwriting all this week, the field letterbox and noticeboard and NCO's mess room, so I have been excused all parades. I was on guard last night. It was pouring with rain and about six inches of water underfoot. I spent a good bit of the night in the sentry box with the rifle stuck up in the corner. There were no officers about, as it happened.

Tell Kath she can knit me a muffler if she likes or is she too busy with Christmas cards? Does Roy find plenty of work at Kings? I have not heard from him for a long time. It is only five weeks to Christmas now, although we have not heard whether there will be any leave yet. It will be a treat to have a roast dinner again.

Is George Urry still alive? I expect he is having a tough time out there, trench digging and fixing barbed wire. We are getting a lot of that here now.

 We go to that house on most nights. They have a nice fire in the room. It is quite cosy. There are five of us go there so we can easily make enough for a game of cards and we usually get back to camp at 9.30 and turn in. We have physical drill every morning before breakfast, from 7 till 7.30. We don't feel sleepy for long. Well, dear Mother, I must finish now, with love to you and Dad and Kath,

                    from your Loving Son, Bob.

From Mother and Nieces, all in one envelope)
49 Carisbrooke Road, Newport.   Monday, November 23, 1914
My dear Bob,
  I'm glad you don't feel the cold so much. Are you still in the tents? If so, you
will be glad of the helmet cap Mabel sent you yesterday. Mrs A. Stratton made
it. It was very kind of her, wasn't it? Don't forget to send her thanks by Mabel.
By the way, don't you keep her waiting for letters. She feels neglected, I think.
She is a proper good girl, Bob. She is with us every night, and so good to Kath.
Most afternoons they walk together.
What dreadful cold weather we are having. It isn't like November – more like
January. Dad feels it very much.
You will see a letter in the County Press from G. Urry. (*See opposite*) His mother
heard from him last week. She always enquires for you and tells him. Mrs
Reynolds oldest son, Jim, who is in the King's Royal Rifles, is missing and he is
out of his time some months back.
I suppose you like going about writing instead of drilling. I have been trying to
write this letter under great difficulties – Wallie and Kath chipping in, then
Doris, then Roy, so please excuse mistakes.
I hope you managed a good laugh and had a good roast dinner. You would be
glad, I know, also to get in a nice bed. Now, about those Old Ladies. Will you
tell me their address? I should like to thank them for their kindness. Those sort
of people expects it.
How glad you must be to be able to sit by a nice fire, and do they still give you
a supper every night, the dear souls? I do hope you will be able to come home
at Christmas. We will try and have a good time. I think you won't mind sleeping
up in the attic, will you? I will make it as comfortable as I can for you. At any
rate, it will be better than the tent, won't it?
Have you had a cake lately from anyone? I am sorry you did not think much of
the pastry I sent. I will try and send you something this week. We will try and
let you have a muffler soon.
Roy is all right. He done a very good job this last week. He is painting Mr.
Attrill's house round by the Church. Mr. Spink has joined the Flying Corps –
went a week ago. Kathie is busy painting cards and will write to you soon.
                    Now goodbye my Son,
                ever your Loving Mother, E Brimson.

*From Ivie**
Dear uncle, I don't want you to be in the hospitle if you come home at Chrismas
I hope you will be able to give us a present each and I will give you a present at
Christmas   perhaps you and Kathy may come up and let there be rejocing I no
that grandma does-not want you to go, but I want you to because you save our
country   it is very kind of all the soadures to keep our country for us.
                    Love from Ivie Brimson.

---

* Ivie is seven years old.

1914

From Ivie
Dear uncle bob,
I hope you will be well at chrismas and come home and have rejocing with us and not be misrible then. at this time there will be rejocing and a lot of carls held at that time. I hope you will be well at the time. I no grandma will be sorry if you are in the hostpitle. We will all sit round the table in chairs and each one will have given a pece of cake and or a pece of plum pudding. I don't no if to send you a lot of flowers it does look pretty across the pretty green fields. the Indien children are always dressed in bright coulours when anyone dies they dont dress in black clothes but in white clothes. baby has not been well the last to or three days it is very cold out of doors now we are making cuffs, coats thick better for you do you think it is very nice of us to do such a thing for you bob are you nearly in the hostpitle I have not had pumps down my neck since you have been away and I do miss you a lot while your away now is it very nice out there while you are garding the germans are you at seaford we are just going to have tea now and I wish you was hear
Egiptoin children Egyt has very narow roads and their is camales and donkey in Egyt if you go to egyt you will have two pickup your diner with your fingers
your loving freind Ivy.
Nobody told her what to say, Kath.

County Press Saturday, November 14, 1914
A SAPPER'S LETTER TO THE "COUNTY PRESS."
Sapper G. Urry, R.E., of 12 Field Company Royal Engineers, South Division, Expeditionary Force, writes: "I see by your paper, the *County Press*, that some of the Newport men who are in the firing line have written letters home which have been published. They mentioned about the food; the food we are getting here is very good – indeed, you could not wish for better under the circumstances. The Engineers have been kept very busy digging reserve trenches in the daytime, and at night we are in the firing line putting up overhead cover to the trenches and also putting barbed wire in front of them. This is a very dangerous job, as everything has to be done without any noise and when it is dark. We get everything ready before setting out, and then we crawl up to the trenches, and the infantry send out a covering party for us. We have to be very careful, as the Germans have a lot of snipers (crack shots), who take up positions in empty houses or ricks. When we are attacked we lie down flat or crawl back to the trenches. We have to clear out of the trenches before dawn, as we should only be in the way if we remained. Some of the Engineers here are building bridges, others are road making, and some are destroying buildings so as to give a clear field of fire. Our infantry are meant to be proud of – they are, indeed, bricks. They seem quite happy in the trenches, and most of them form a sort of cave in their trenches, in which they place straw, and these places they use for sleeping in and also for cover from shell bursts. I will write again when I get time if this is of any use to you."

From Arch

Undated.

Dear Bob,
Your welcome letter duly to hand. I'm working late as anything. If we haven't written, it's not for want of thinking of you. We'll make a cake and let you have it, but it would be fine if you could run up for a weekend. I wonder what Mabel would say if you had to tell her you had a weekend off and had spent it in London. We have blokes route marching past our office every day singing, "Here we are, Here we are, Here we are again!" I suppose you do too. The London Solicitors tried to get up a corps but although 1200 of us said we would join, the War Office wouldn't give us permission.* We may be able to manage it yet. Do you get any firing exercise? Jim don't yet. He is waiting to be transferred to Windsor for that. Wonder what they think of the war down at the Eight Bells. I expect there's some profound wisdom going round, what with Woolley and Roy and various old seafaring blokes. We close pubs at 10 here now. (*See below.*) No use living in London. It's just the same as the Country. I got to stop now Bob, Ma's waiting to go to bed. Best love and all that.
Ever your loving brother, Arch.**

County Press, November 21, 1914
"CLOSING TIME OVERDONE."
In an article with the above title, the Daily Mail, dealing with the order closing licensed houses in London at 10 PM and forbidding the sale of alcohol in clubs after that hour, says it has considerably restricted the harmless pleasures of the public. There are many, indeed, who ask with what object and for what reason this order has been issued. If it represents an attempt to force temperance upon the country, even the strongest teetotaller will agree that the method is somewhat unfair which applies such a regulation during a great war on the excuse that it is demanded by patriotism and the safety of the nation. If it is required for military reasons let us be told so plainly. At the same time we do not believe that the British soldier or seaman of today is a man who is in any danger of drinking to excess. Thousands of the best of our youth are serving in the King's forces and they are perfectly capable of exercising self-control. But if the contrary were the case, then it would scarcely be needful to close at this early hour licence houses and restaurants in which a soldier is never seen.

From Mabs
The Bedford, The Mall, Newport.   Wednesday, 25 November, 1914
My Dearest Bob,
I am very sorry I called you names over that last letter. Well, you didn't know that I did, but I was wild because I thought you had gone to London without letting me know. It wasn't your fault after all. I hope you had a good time there. I should think it would be a treat to get away from the Camp for a time. Only

*Only the Inns of Court were permitted to form a regiment but despite this, thousands of London solicitors, articled clerks and barristers joined various infantry battalions.
**Although Arch invariably signs his letters to Bob as "your loving brother," he is actually his brother-in-law.

another month and you will be able to come down here. I shall have to chain you on when you do get here. I am sure I shan't want to let you go again. It gets worse every week instead of getting used to it.

I hope the helmet suited. Mrs Stratton made it. I was going to do it but she wanted something to do so Mother let her do that.

How do you like trenching? They are doing it all roundabout here to defend Newport. It was nice to get back on the old job. Don't you wish you could stick to it? Things are looking much better all round now I believe. Perhaps you won't have to go out after all. We had a postcard from Ern today and he is in hospital through standing so long in the water. He seems disappointed but I should think it nice to get a rest. Bert Branton, who went in the car, is lying seriously wounded in France. Morry says he thinks he was married to Mrs Simmonds' sister at the Freemason's. Kath is over here very busy knitting. I think I must finish now. With best Love, to My Dearest Boy.

From Mabs.

From Roy
31, Melbourne Street, Newport.   Wednesday, November 25, 1914
Dear Bob,
Sorry to have kept you waiting so long but wrote so much last time I got spent out. Well, I saw Punch Drake, Monday. He is at guard in Aldershot. He is chairman in the canteen. The other agent on his firm is pianist, that chap Taylor. Used to come in the Bedford sometimes. Played like blazes. Punch persuaded all he could to come up there. He said he owed Morry Attrill 12 shillings but he should have it somewhere.

Poor old Starkes is nearly bankrupt. He has been walking about almost crying because he don't get any work. We done a little job together, earned 8/6 each. I heard today he was down the Quay shifting timber, 5d per hour. He only married last Easter. As you know, Walt Jacobs has gone coal heaving down Cowes. He's making good money down there but haven't they made a mess of the pubs down here, this extra penny on a pint. They started taxing last Thursday here. There wasn't a soul in the Bedford that night, hardly. I've got to go short now. I finished for King a fortnight ago, Saturday. I am painting Morey's house round against St John's Church. Ern and Rob sold some pictures for me in London and I've got to do two more. Ron got 3/- a week in that Laundry shop on the top of the town and with Sonnie's money we scrape along somehow. He gets 10/- one week, 12/6 the next week. Every other week he takes Stationmaster's place at Carisbrooke Station.

I think it's a pity Dad, Mother and Kath didn't get a claim from the government. It would have made no difference to you and it would have been a good seat for them. There is only Arch Meech, George, Sis, that chap down County Press, Sid Lipton, and Percy the fisherman that walks about in civilians clothes. George Harvie is master tailor again in Ireland. Charlie is in Selsey Bill.

Are you in huts yet? Punch says they have just got in up there. I've seen enough

of the poor Devils up Barracks here sleeping in water. Nearly all got cold in the chest. Walter Warne is home, him that was up Camp Hill with us. He was on the Cressy. He ain't half sick of it; most uncomfortable ship that was ever built. Can't sit up and lay down anywhere. I must finish. I want a wash now, 8 o'clock p.m., else I shan't get a pint down Morry's,
                        from your affectionate brother, Roy.

From Mabs
The Bedford. Newport.   Friday, November 27, 1914
My Dearest Boy,
I have just been reading about you in Kath's letter from Arch. It's a treat to know that you are going on all right, but I wish you had let me know you were going to London. Just think of it! I might have landed there too. I can't understand your post at all. It takes a letter as long to come from there as it does to come from France, and that box you had on Sunday was posted Friday morning. Now, before I forget again I must tell you about Ern. I expect you thought I was a bit gone when I wrote that last letter. I am sorry I left that blank space. I wanted to tell you that Ern had rheumatism in his legs but not being sure of the way to spell it, I left the space so that I could fill it in later and promptly forgot about it in a hurry to get it posted. I had a card from Ern this morning and he expects to be about again very soon. He is another who is dying for a cake.
What a terrible affair that Bulwark disaster was. I'm sorry to say that poor Teddy Bond was aboard her, unless by any lucky chance he was transferred lately. If not, I am very sorry for his people as he was a proper favourite all round. Aunt Clara thought as much of him as she would her own children so I don't know what she will do.
Jack Cornish was here yesterday and today. He says he may be in England till after Christmas so perhaps you will have a chance of seeing him. He had to leave his wife in India. Georgie Reynolds is home too. I suppose there will be some more Irish wailings when he has to go away again. By the way, before I forget, your Mother said I was to thank you for the present you sent her. She is sorry she did not mention it in her letter but there was a crowd and they drove it out of her head. Don't forget to send Ivy a little letter when you write home again – she would be so pleased. Don't you think she managed that other one all right all by herself?
You ought to be here to hear about Lloyd George. The first night or so, it was dreadful but we don't hear much now.
Mrs Newnham must be a dear old soul to look after all you boys like she has done. Our boys seem to have no end of Fairy Godmothers to send them things. Did I tell you that Morry had been in his bunk for two days with the touch of ague? It was Mrs Newnham's parcel put him right then. He got into the socks and things as soon as he saw them and said he was as fresh as a daisy next day. It is past bedtime again so now goodnight beloved.
                        From your ever loving Mabs.

From Mother

49 Carisbrooke Road, Newport.   Friday, December 1, 1914

My dear Bob,

Have received your letter this afternoon and was so glad to know you was all right. You are having a dreadful rough piece of it, I am sure. Do tell us if there are chances of your going into Huts on the Barracks. If the wind is so rough your way last night as it was here, I am sure the tents must have been blown away and you poor soldiers with them. I must thank you for the postal order very much, and am sorry I forgot to last week. Dad has not been over to the Asylum today for it has blown a hurricane all night and all the day, with rain pouring down. Did you get the paper this morning and what do you think of Ern's letter. It was sad about the Bulwark, wasn't it?* The Germans says in today's paper they have the credit of doing that. Mabel says they have put Harry on the Tiger. I hope it won't prove unlucky.

We have had a letter from Arch telling of your visit. It was nice for you and I would try and go again. You must have felt the pleasure of the bath, I am sure, also the roast. I wish I could cook a Sunday dinner for you every week. Mrs Attrill and I will send you something this week.

I think I will conclude now, with much love from Dad and Kath, myself, also many thanks for the enclosed postal order,

ever your loving mother, Ellen Brimson.

From Morry

HMS Owl c/o GPO   Wednesday, December 2, 1914

Dear Bob,

Sorry to keep you waiting so long for a reply. Glad to hear you are getting on all right. What do it feel like to be a soldier? What time do you have your shaving water? I suppose you are pretty well ready to go and give an account of yourself now.

I saw in the paper that Bert had been wounded and was at some hospital in France, dangerously ill. He married that girl before he went out. Cole was amongst the missing too. I wonder what he did with the car we left him, or rather what remained of it after we had finished. I don't think there will be anything more doing in the joyride line. I expect Jimmy is out there too. Do you ever feel any effects of the bump on your head now?

We have been getting it pretty rough here but we are getting used to that now. Sorry I can't let you know what we have been up to. This is all now, hoping this will find you quite well.

Yours Truly, Morry.

---

* On November 26 1914, HMS Bulwark was blown apart at her moorings on the River Medway by an internal magazine explosion. Out of 750 men onboard, only 14 survived. The explosion, which shook buildings six miles away, was blamed on the overheating of cordite charges stored alongside a boiler room.

St Mary's Barracks, Gillingham, Kent.
Bob arrived at St Mary's for his initial training in early September 1914, just days after enlisting. *"We were dished out with one blanket apiece and we had to sleep on the bare boards of the tent – twenty of us in one tent."* Bob to Mother, September 12, 1914.

Seaford Camp.
Located on the south coast, between Eastbourne and Brighton, Seaford was Bob's second training camp. *"We moved into our final destination yesterday. Hardly any food all day until we went into the town at night and bought some."* Bob to Mother, October, 11, 1914.

From Mabs
The Bedford. Newport.   Friday, December 4, 1914
My Dearest Boy,
Your mother has been at it again, as you will see by your parcel when it arrives. Your mother has sent a cake, and my mother has sent some tarts, while the violets were mine. I hope there will be enough jam in the tarts. I hear you are very particular, respecting jam in tarts. I should have sent plain tarts if I hadn't heard of that, because I thought you had plenty of jam.
Wallace is going to Rugby to the BTH works. I told Kath this morning that he wasn't, so I don't know what will happen when she knows he is.
Only three weeks now, my dearest. It seems to me if you are going to make up for all those kisses you have lost, you will be doing nothing else all the time. Why, if you only allow for one day it will be something like 100. Kath is the only one who gets any now except one or two stray ones that go to Flo.
Harry has been moved to the Tiger, No. 40 Mess Hall, and Tiger is his address now.
May came down from London today. Hard lines – it has been so peaceful here lately. I am sorry for the neighbours; they hoped she would go altogether. We have had a new order now. Nine o'clock every night we have to close now, and although the soldiers are allowed out till nine, we mustn't serve one after eight o'clock.
I had a nonsensical letter from Arch on Monday. He composed a little verse in your honour. It runs like this, Robert is a soldier man, a Royal Engineer. The two things that he misses most are Mabel and his beer.
Well, if I don't soon stop this nonsense I shan't get it posted tonight; I shall have to go down to the town with it, as it is. I hope you have had that photograph taken, or haven't you got your full uniform yet? Goodnight my Love,
                                    from your everloving Mabs.

In the next letter Bob makes the first of several references to what he calls his 'allotment.' He is referring to the Separation Allowance (See photo page 133). This was, and remains, a payment to ensure that a soldier's dependents are not left destitute because of losing what could be a sizable part of their household income due to a family member serving in the Forces. Usually referring to wives, the allowance was also awarded to mothers who had been dependent on the soldier's income.
The allowance in 1914 was made up of a compulsory 'allotment' of money from the soldier's own wages, usually 6d a day, (half the basic shilling a day earned by privates) which was then matched by the government.

From Bob
Seaford.   Tuesday, December 8, 1914
Dear Mother,
I am sorry to have kept you so long without a letter but we have been so upset again lately owing to the rough weather. It has been awful lately and it has not

altered yet. It started a week last Saturday about dinnertime. It rained in torrents and came right through the tents wetting everything and some of the chaps had to go in town and sleep. It stopped a little on Sunday but started again Monday morning and rained all day without a break and the wind howling something chronic. We called round to the lady's house in the evening and when we got back to camp about 9.30 we found the tent half blown down and all the rest of the fellows gone and we heard they had been billeted in the town. We managed to find a tent or two that had withstood the storms and crowded in and slept the night in the wet.

Next day, ten of us were told to stop in camp and guard the stores and we had to do our own cooking. We didn't mind – it was fine sport. We stopped there till Friday when we were marched to the police station and billeted out. Seven of us were taken to the house where we are now.

It is a big lodging house with fine rooms and we have been having jolly good food but it is too good to last. Mrs Yeomans has had a letter from the wife of a Major who is at the Front who, it appears, had previously booked the rooms a month ago and she insists on having them so we have all got to turn out again this week.

The policeman is downstairs now so we shall get settled some time. I will let you know our address as soon as we arrive there. I received the paper today but have not read it yet. Is Dad still getting along all right? I hear there are one or two more enlisted from the Asylum.

As soon as they are settled at the office I will arrange about that allotment if they will allow me. It will be a little help. Is Kath getting on all right with her Xmas cards? Well I must finish now,

from your loving son, Bob.

From Mabs

The Bedford, Newport.   Wednesday, December 9, 1914
My Dearest Bobbie,
I think you are growing very hard-hearted, unless it is hard-worked. Fancy keeping me till today – ten days and not a line from you.

I am very sorry to hear that you have had such bad times and sincerely hope, my dearest, that your troubles will be ended now. I hope your new quarters will be as good as the first.

That was a great secret about the holidays. We shall be so pleased to see you that Christmas won't worry us. I only hope it won't be very long after, if you are not lucky enough to get that week. It will be ever so much better if you can get it because of Chris and Arch being here. If you can't I suppose we must make the best of it.

I am housekeeper again for a few days. Mother went up to Rugby with Wallace on Sunday. He started yesterday in the office, beginning with 10/- per week, so if he likes to keep his head and stick at it, he will be all right.

I went to a Concert last night; the first time since I was in London. It was given by the Newport Choral Society in aid of the Belgian Relief fund. It was splendid. They had two professionals there who were very good. Their orchestra was a

very good one too. I happened to know the gentleman at the door so he planted me right in the front, nearly next door to our MP. I was doing it in style then.
We heard from Ern on Sunday. Ern is at Rouens now. I don't think Harry likes the 'Tiger' so much as the 'Queen Mary.'
Did you know that young man Dunford? He has been to the Front. He used to play the piano once but he won't be able to any more – he has lost two fingers of his right hand. I was surprised to find he was a soldier. Although I have known him such a long time I hadn't any idea that he was in the Army. He was in the Hants.
Did anyone tell you that 'Frenchie' Flood had joined the Household Cavalry? I don't know which branch. I saw young Gifford in uniform, too, this morning.
I have some secrets for you now. One is that Morry is coming home shortly – at least we think he must be. We had a card today telling us to send him a white shirt and collar and not to send anything for the 16th (which is his birthday), and to keep the Mall open, so I think that means business.
The next secret is that Ern is in England but we don't know which hospital he is in yet. The last and most important is concerning the 'Tiger'*. Of course, you will see nothing of it in the papers, so you will have to keep it dark. The fact is, she is crippled up off Sweden. I expect Harry would be surprised if he guessed we knew. The crew are all quite safe.
It appears that all the machinery was made at the BTH works** and somehow a piece of faulty iron got into it with the result that it can't move. The men to repair it went from the BTH while Mother was there so that is how we know of it. A rotten start for one of our latest men of war. I think it's about time I finished, my sweetheart.
With fondest Love and Heaps of kisses,
From Mabs.

From Harry
40 Mess. HMS Tiger. *Envelope stamped, "Passed Censor."*   December, 1914
Dear Mabel,
You must excuse me keeping you waiting so long for a letter. I haven't been up to the mark just lately but am feeling better now. I received your letter safely, also papers. Thank you very much for the trouble you have taken sending papers etc. Should very much liked to have been down there with Morry but I am afraid there is no luck now, especially as I have shifted ships.
We are getting settled down onboard the Tiger now. Have also had a couple of all nights in, the first since the war began. I am doing Yeoman duties on board here as they were short of Yeomen but do not yet get the pay, worse luck. Patience will be rewarded in good time, I hope.
It's great sport trying to find our way around the ship now as, of course, we

---

*Tiger was built by the John Brown shipyard in Clydebank and commissioned into the Royal Navy on 3 October 1914, at the cost of £2,600,000, It was still under construction when war broke out. Tiger was commissioned into the 1st Battlecruiser Squadron.
** During the First World War BTH, a major employer of Rugby, produced electrical equipment for the Navy.

have no lights showing on board whatever now so you can guess what it is like when you have to go on watch in the middle of the night finding your way round, but one gets quite used to seeing in the dark.

The only thing that annoys us is not being able to see through fog as the Germans, who bombarded Scarborough* and those places would have known with a vengeance if it was possible. It was awful, wasn't it? I expect you wondered when the Isle of Wight's turn would come.

What did you think of our Squadron off the Falkland Islands? Great, wasn't it? They soon made short work of the crack gunnery ship. That's only a lull before the storm to what will happen to their High Sea Fleet when we get there. I don't think the time is very far distant now as they have had a little bit of rope. Was quite surprised to hear Wallace had started at the BTH Works.** I hope he will like it and make a name for himself. I expect you miss him at home.

I had a parcel from Rugby the day before yesterday, also a letter from Wallace. He appears to be enjoying himself but didn't say what work he was doing. I suppose he will have to give up Scouting now and start studying.

I didn't tell you about the Tiger. She is about 1000 tons heavier than the Queen Mary and quite a smart looking ship. She is probably the largest Man of War afloat and there is no doubt she will prove herself when the time comes.

The Signal Boatswain was a Leading Signalman with me in the Signal School so the war helped him along all right as they appointed all the people who had passed to all these new ships commissioning. He is a very nice fellow. It is rather a big responsibility for him coming to a ship like this directly he was passed.

Wishing you all a Merry Xmas and a Happy New Year.

Love to all from your Loving Brother, Harry.

PS. Cannot get you a present for Xmas so have enclosed money order for 10/- to get something yourself. Should your choice be more expensive you can let me know as there is plenty more where that came from.

---

*On December 16, 1914, two German battlecruisers bombarded Scarborough, killing 18 people including a 14 month old baby. Churchill, then First Lord of the Admiralty, described the Germans as "the baby killers of Scarborough". The attack resulted in public outrage towards the German navy and also the Royal Navy for its failure to prevent the raid.

** Ironically, Wallace, then aged 14, began work at BTH at the same time as the Tiger was out of action – seemingly due to faulty BTH machinery.

Calendar of Events of 1915.

(Bob's activities shown in italics.)

January 19 - First Airship raid on England.

January - Bob and RE's training in trenching and pontooning, Seaford.

February 18 - German submarine blockade of Britain begins.

February - RE's transferred (march) to Aldershot.

March 10-13 - Battle of Neuve Chapelle begins.

April - Manoeuvres near Aldershot.

April 22 - Second battle of Ypres and first German use of gas.

May 7 - Lusitania sunk by German submarine U20

May 8 – 12 Bob has Four days leave prior to leaving for France – Attached to 87th RE Field Company.

May 27 - Bob hospitalised due to bad reaction to inoculation.

May 31 - First airship raid on London area.

July - Bob leaves hospital joins Depot Co. Newark on Trent.

July 15 - National Registration Act becomes law.

August 4 - Bob arrives in France.

August 6 - Landings at Suvla Bay (Dardanelles).

August 15 - Bob attached to 80th Field Co. (Location unknown).

August 22 - Attached to 3rd Entrenching Co. (Locations unknown).

September 25 - Allied 'Autumn Offensive' begins, Battle of Loos .

October 6 - Joins 95th RE Field Company, Assar near Bethune – wiring and trench repairs.

October 8 - Battle of Loos ends.

October 15 - Gorre. 95th take over La Barre Canal to Givanche section of line.

December 8 - 95th Field Co. move to Tirancourt, Amiens – pontooning, constructing stables etc.

December 20 - Evacuation of Suvla and Anzac (Dardanelles) completed.

From Bob

C/o Mrs Turner, Downlands, Salisbury Rd, Seaford. Saturday, January 2, 1915

Dear Mother,

I expect you have been waiting for a letter from me since I got back but we are working harder than ever now and going through examinations so that our pay in the future will depend on what we have learnt, so it will pay me to know as much as possible.

We are leaving Seaford again in about a fortnight's time and going to Brightlingsea, somewhere near Colchester for 'Pontooning'; that is making pontoon bridges across rivers. We shall be there perhaps three or four weeks and then we are supposed to come back here again. Dyer will be coming home next Tuesday. He is going to call in and see you sometime.

Three of our chaps in our billet have gone home on leave so there is only three of us left. I got back in good time last Saturday. They were all having supper as I came in. The old gent that is lodging here bought us all a pipe each and a big box of Woodbines for us and we had other parcels of cigarettes sent us from different people so we haven't done at all bad and the other chaps had a very decent Xmas too while I was away.

We seem to have started the New Year badly with a naval disaster* and the railway smash** but a bad start is a good finish as a rule. Well I shall have to finish now as I have not much else to say and I shall be glad to hear how things are next week.

Ever your loving son Bob.

From Mother
49 Carisbrooke Road, Newport.   Tuesday, January 5, 1915
My dear Bob,
I was glad enough to get your letter. I had been wondering all sorts of things and poor Mabel's eyes glistened with water last night when I told her I had heard from you. I hope she will have one today. Oh dear, I wish the rain would stop. We did miss you after you went. Shall you like the change to Brightlingsea? Wasn't it kind of the gentleman to treat you all so well. You wanted a pipe, too. I shall be pleased to see Mr. Dyer. There has been a lot on leave. They keep going back with their kit bags. That tells.
Dad says the new doctor is making new rules out there. One of the lady patients tells him that he is altering things and she believes it will be much better for them. Dad didn't go to work yesterday. T'was bad weather. Today has been fine – for a wonder he came home dry. Now goodbye, my dear Bob. Take care of yourself. Love from all,

your loving Mother, E Brimson.

From Morry
January, 1915
Dear Mabel,
Hope you received money order I sent you for Christmas. I am enclosing orders for £3, "more winners next Goodwood." Tell Dad to give George Cooper the best in the house, also himself and Mother and any other old friends whom he thinks that come in and deduct expenses for same from enclosed. I expect Ernest was too ill to give the lads a treat this year. Give my best and hope he is getting better again now. Glad to hear you were busy. Did Bob keep getting in the way? "Sorry." Hope he enjoyed himself and that you both had a good time. Thank you for your card, also for papers I received today. Pleased to see the casualty list wasn't too great in the Island last week. It was a bit tame this Christmas. We will try and make up for it next with a bit of luck.
Sorry we didn't sink a few Germans for a Christmas present but they wouldn't come out. It was sad about Formidable. The old ships seem to be having all the bad luck. Perhaps our turn is to come. I said "perhaps". Well, there is nothing

---

* On New Year's Day 1915, the battleship HMS Formidable was torpedoed by the German submarine U-24 in the English Channel. 547 men were lost.

** On New Year's Day 1915 an express passenger train passed a signal at danger and collided with another passenger train that was stopped at Ilford railway station. The collision killed ten people and injured 500.

more of interest to tell so will close. Hoping you are all in the best of health. Am
A1 myself.
Love to all from your affectionate Brother,
Morry.
Thank you for parcel just received. I received Mr. C's cigarettes.

From Mabs
The Bedford. Newport I.W   Wednesday, January 6, 1915
My Dearest Sweetheart,
I should think I did anxiously wait for a line from you. I began to think you had
forgotten me – writing about not hearing from home. It wasn't likely you would
hear until they knew where you were. I have had that ring altered and it fits a
treat now and the eyes of the whole world are upon it (Praps). As to the bill,
prepare yourself for a shock. The grand total is 0. Mr. Wray kindly did it free of
charge. I hope you don't have to overwork yourself, my dear, because while you
have been working I have been playing. At least, I went to another concert last
night. It was splendid – account in the paper so I needn't worry you with one
now. Madame Anna Shergold has a beautiful voice, so has Mrs. Taylor but Mr.
Harwood ought to be squashed and Mr. Norton nearly killed us with his comic
songs. We have been very lively here until the last two nights. Sally and Minnie
were in tonight. Albert Hawkins arrived in England today so I suppose Flo will
be feeling very pleased with herself. I am glad.
Do you know Phoebe's sister, Flo (Harris)? Mickey has discovered her so he has
been taking her out lately. He had a narrow escape from being sent to the Front
again last Monday. He was put off at the last minute again. Well, my Love, I
really must stop – it's time all good children were in bed. Morry sent a postcard
to say that he arrived safe and Harry sent me a long letter. They spent Christmas
day prepared for action but he said they made up for it after.
From your Own Sweetheart,
Mabs.

From Mabs
The Bedford. Newport, I.W.   Tuesday, January 12, 1915
My Dearest Bobbie,
You are a good boy to write so soon. I hope you will keep it up. You were right.
It was a sweet one of those sloppy message sweets with, "You are the girl of my
heart," or some such tommy-rot on it. Ern went back this morning. I believe he
is going to Romsey before he goes to Winchester because the 2nd Hants are
there.
Albert Hawkins arrived on Saturday and leaves today. He doesn't look so thin
as he did last time although he is not better yet. He wished to be remembered
to you and he seemed very pleased to hear that you were one of the boys (R.E.).
I think it would have been better to have a plain ring this time. I had to take the
other to be seen to this morning. One of the pearls came out last night. I didn't
lose the pearl.
You remember that Aunt I went to see while you dived into the pub opposite?

Well, you won't have a chance to see her now – she died last Thursday; it was very sudden too. Arthur Bull is a Leading Stoker now. It is to be hoped he will keep it. He is coming home tomorrow. I saw in the paper last night that they had picked up three of the bodies from the Bulwark and one was identified as Edward Bond, so I suppose that will be a relief for them.

Your mother thought you would be able to come home for your birthday but as you can't do that, just see if you can manage for mine. Kath, Kitty and I are going to Mrs Bull's to tea today (Tut Tut), there was no escape. If we don't go today it will have to be another, so we may as well get it over quick.

From your Little Sweetheart,
Mabs.

From Bob
c/o Downlands, Salisbury Rd, Seaford.   Wednesday, January 13, 1915
Dear Mother,
I received your letter and also papers all right and I should have replied before only I had a letter from Archy about the allotment, so I waited until I got the reply to the letter I sent him. The papers have already been sent up to the War Office so we shall know the result shortly. I tried to arrange it so that you would get as much as 15 shillings per week but it depends on what view they take of it. If they think it is a deserving case you will secure as much as 15 shillings down to about eight shillings. Of course a few shillings will be stopped out of my money but it will be worth it if you get that much every week.

We have been out trenching every day this week. We take our lunch and have a hot dinner when we come home. I am sending my insurance card. You must hand it to the collector when he comes and I rather fancy he has to send me a new one in return. Be sure to tell him an 'Army Card'. This card has been filled up from the time I left work so I have not lost a week. We leave here the end of this week. We shall have to march from Victoria to Liverpool Street station. It will take us about half an hour. I must close now with fondest love to you all.

From your loving son Bob.

From Mabs
The Bedford, Newport, I.W.   Friday, January 15, 1915
My Dearest Boy,
I didn't even see the tail end of Dyer's coat while he was home so I don't know what sort of a soldier he made. You have got a nice little walk through London, I hear, when you get there. I wish I was in London. I expect you will go through some of our old walks on the way.

Arthur Bull is home this time. He arrived yesterday till Monday so you can guess what May is like now. I hope you will be able to get home after you have been to Brightlingsea. I wish, though, you hadn't to go away again. Confound the war and the Kaiser and all such things. It looks worse again now. Kathie is here now waiting for me to finish this so I mustn't keep her too long.

Your mother had a visitor today. I went over this morning and who should I

find there but that Kate from Scotland. I was surprised – in fact they all were – and Kath says she will believe anything after that. Wallace is going on fine but he has had to be apprenticed after all, for five years. Kitty has started school at Carisbrooke House Convent School. She is delighted with it. Don't forget to let me know as soon as possible where you are or – well, I won't say any more my Dearest. And now I must finish with fondest Love and heaps of kisses,
From Mabs.
You needn't worry about Toffee any more. He doesn't come near and as for Mick, well, he doesn't either.

From Mother
49 Carisbrooke Road, Newport.   Wednesday, January 20, 1915
My dear Bob,
you will spend your birthday all right on Saturday, I think, for they are sending you a nice parcel from over the way and Kathie is sending you something we have ordered for you. If we can't get it by in time for your day, you will have it next week.
I am sorry, Bob, I can't do anything for you yet, for I am troubled with your father. He has not been well for some time. I have been doing short time for some weeks now but this week he has been in bed with bronchitis. I'm afraid he won't be able to go out yet for a bit. He being over 70, he can't have a doctor. I only hope we shan't want one. I am sorry to tell you but I think it is best to let you know. We will hope things will be all right again soon. I am glad you have seen to the affair of the allowance. I mean, it will be a grand help if I can get it. If they are liberal with the payment and your father is all right at work then I shan't have your money. I shall hope to do without it. Mabel Cornish with her four children is home with John. Her husband is taken from the trenches, frostbitten in the legs and is at Manchester in hospital where he is better. He tells Mabel he is to go back to the Front and George Reynolds is wounded in hospital. How well Mr. Dyer looked. We were pleased to see him. He says he will be back again in a few weeks. Shall you be able to come? We will keep your birthday then so I hope you will have a happy day and many more, please God. Write soon, won't you?
Ever your loving Mother, E Brimson.

From Bob
c/o Mrs. Minter, National Villa, Station Road, Brightlingsea.
Thursday, January 21, 1915
My Dear Mother,
I am very sorry to hear that Dad is in bed with bronchitis. He must stop there until he is quite well again and I will try and send you what I can in the way of money. As soon as I hear about the allotment I will let you know and then he need not bother about work so much. We are getting on well with pontooning here. The Colonel says we are making great progress. When we get back to

Seaford we stop there a week or so and then we pack up and move on to Shorecliff so that we shall be attached to the 12th Division.

Dyer and me are going to try and get a few days off together so that we can come home before we leave Seaford. I have had my photo taken. I shall get the proofs at the end of this week. If they turn out all right I will send them on to you as soon as possible. We have been having lovely weather until last night. I done 24 hours guard and it has been raining ever since. Pontooning is fine fun especially when you have to go in the sea up to your knees but we only do half a day at a time which gives us a chance to dry our things. We were not very far away from the Zeppelin and this time they seem to mean business. I'm glad you are not living on the east coast. I am sending you a 10 shilling postal order or note. I hope you will get it safe and I will send you some more in a few days. Don't be afraid to let me know if you are in trouble.

I will do what I can. I hope Dad will soon be better and you and Kath must cheer up and keep smiling.

Love to you all and kisses from your loving son. Bob.

I will write to Mabs very soon.

From Mabs

The Bedford, Newport, I.W.   Friday, January 22, 1915

My Dearest Bobbie,

It is too bad having to write to wish you 'Many Happy Returns' but I hope we shall have better luck next time and that you will be here safe and sound. I posted your parcel this morning so I expect it will be there when you get this.

Mother is responsible for the cake and the pies but I made the ice (I mean the coconut ice). I was expecting a letter from you today but it appears I must go on expecting. I hear that your mother has had one instead and you told her that you were coming home as soon as possible. Well, let it be soon then, lad, although I should like you to be here for the 14th.

Ern is up at Parkhurst again but all the 3rd Hants are off to Gosport on Monday so he won't be here long. I had a letter from Morry on Monday and he sent me his box that Princess Mary sent him for Christmas.*

Kitty has finished with that Convent School so she goes next door now. She wanted me to send three packets of 'Wild' ones for you but I couldn't very well put them in the box. Perhaps they will fit in the letter. Kathie had to mend my ring at last, because the pearl came out again the first day I put it on after I had it done at Wray's. It seems to be all right now. I shall have to stop now. With best wishes from us all. I hope the watch will suit. It won't be much to lose if it does get 'pinched.' I hope it won't frighten you.

With fondest Love and kisses,

From your Loving Mabs.

---

* Everyone in uniform serving overseas on Christmas Day 1914 received the gift of a pressed brass box engraved with a picture of Princess Mary, paid for by public subscription. It contained a pipe, one ounce of tobacco, twenty cigarettes and a lighter. Non-smokers' boxes contained a 'bullet-pencil' and a packet of sweets instead.

From Bob

Friday, January 22, 1915

My Dearest Mabs,

I have got an hour or two to spare so I will try and let you know how I am getting on. We are having some lovely times here with the pontoon bridging. We woke up this morning and found about three or four inches of snow on the ground. Now it is about a foot thick and still snowing. We have been down to the waterside all the morning. We got the river bridged across and by the time we had finished I was swamping wet through – you could have wrung a bucket full of water out of my white canvas suit. The major dismissed us about 11.15 and I had to change every stitch of clothing. The housekeeper here is very good to us.

Dyer and me are billeted together. A dance and social was held in the Forrester's Hall here last night for us and it wasn't at all bad. Yesterday morning we had the news read out to us. The Colonel had orders from the War Office that we will be attached to the 12th Division, and that as soon as we get back to Seaford we pack up and leave for Shorecliffe. So we now belong to the first new Army Corps and it is only a matter of weeks now before we go out to the Front. You needn't tell them at home. I shall try and manage to get home for a few days. Well my dearest, I shall have to finish as they are waiting to lay the dinner. Hoping to hear from you soon,

ever your sweetheart, Bob.

From Mother

49 Carisbrooke Road, Newport.   Saturday, January 23, 1915

My dear Bob,

I am sorry we let Kathie's letter go without thanking you for your kind letter and enclosed postal order. It was so kind of you and I am thankful to you for it. I hope you got Mabel's parcel all right. We are posting Kathie's tonight. Hope you will like it. Am glad you are trying to get a few days off.

I have got a paper to sign but I don't know quite what to say for I shouldn't like to answer a question different to what you have stated so Roy copied it off. Will you look it down and anything you think I ought to say, I will put on the paper. The paper speaks only of me but I'll state about your father's age and Kathie. Don't you think it well to do so? Now goodbye. Many happy returns of the day,

ever your Loving Mother, E. Brimson.

For the County Press the war was one of their finest hours. Thirty years old by this time, trusted and authoritative, it was to become the most important source of war news for Islanders and throughout the war the County Press printed many hundreds of letters home from soldiers at the Front.

Living next door to the Brimsons, at 50, Carisbrooke Road, was the Urry family, and George Urry, serving at the Front, had written home to his mother. She passed the letter on to the County Press for publication.

County Press, January 23, 1915

A THREE WEEKS' TRUCE IN THE TRENCHES

NEWPORT ENGINEER'S INTERESTING NARRATIVE.

Sapper George Urry, R.E., writing from the Front to his mother at 50 Carisbrooke Road, Newport, on January 11, says: "Just a line to let you know that I am quite well. We have been very busy here this last week or so. The heavy rains have caused a lot of work for us, as it is very flat country here and the trenches are flooded. We have been employed putting up some new ones above the ground. It was a new experiment, and has proved very successful. Being placed behind the old firing line, it is much drier, as the old trench used to drain the land and had to be constantly pumped out. It has been very quiet in this part of the line, where we have the Saxons in front of us. They are suffering the same as we are, as we can see them throwing water out over the trench. This is the part of the line where the truce has been made, and at the time of writing is still being kept up. They seem to be doing the same as we are, as we can see them working in front of their trenches. Our infantry are getting wood from a farmhouse that has been partly destroyed between the two firing lines, and the Saxons are doing the same, not only at night, but in day time. Not a shot has been fired since Christmas Day. It is wonderful to note the coolness of the people here. Some of them are living quite close to the firing line. I saw yesterday a farmer ploughing in a field close to our reserve trenches. Owing to the flatness of the country it is very dangerous because when an attack is in progress, thousands of bullets flying about and anywhere from a mile to a mile and a half is very dangerous. In some of the houses which are facing the lines, the doors and the brickwork are studded with bullets, and yet people are still living in them. Another most noticeable thing in this country is the use that dogs are put to. Every farmhouse uses dogs to churn the butter and cut up mangels etc. This is done by means of a big wheel which is placed outside each farm. Another thing which is very common is the use which dogs are put to for drawing small carts. I saw two dogs yesterday drawing some milk cans and a man sitting up in the cart. Everything is being done for the troops here, and they are relieved as often as possible."

From Bob
c/o Mrs. Minter, National Villa, Station Road, Brightlingsea.

Tuesday, January 26, 1915

Dear Mother,

I received Kath's nice present and the letters all right. It's a splendid picture of Mabs and it is a handy thing to carry about. I have been interrupted in this letter by the officials coming round with the order that the windows must be darkened or else all the lights must be turned out. The village is all in darkness, no street lamp alight and all the shops with the double thickness of blinds; it's quite a job to get about after dark. This order has only come out today and it affects the whole of the east coast. Of course, they are taking precautions against the Zeppelins. We had our first night shift last night. We started work at 7 pm, building a pontoon bridge in midstream. We had to work silently. We hadn't to speak to one another or make the least noise with the planks. We worked up to

9.30 pm and we were praised by the Colonel for the way in which we carried it out. When you send the form in, let the officials know as much as you can how you are situated and it will be all the better for you. They are stopping three shillings a week out of my money so you should get 15 shillings a week and also the back money from when I first applied – that is about 10 days ago. Try and get as much as you can out of them but try and keep to the answers I put to the questions, as they are the same as I signed on the form. I will try and write to Mabs a bit later on. I believe we are on day and night work as well tomorrow but I will write as soon as possible. I will close now with love to Dad and Kath and yourself.

Ever your Loving son, Bob.

From Mabs
The Bedford. Newport, I.W.   Thursday, January 28, 1915
My Dearest Bobbie,
I am sorry to hear that you're having such a rotten life in Brightlingsea. I hope you will soon get used to it if you have to keep on with it long. We had a postcard from Harry last night, just to say that they had got through the battle safely and he thinks Morry was in it. He also said that the Tiger sank the Blücher.*
I am sorry to have to tell you that Uncle George of Atherfield died yesterday morning. I am glad Mr. Brimson is going on all right now; he quite worried me last week. He looked so ill, but he looks more like himself this week.
It's nice for you to have Dyer with you. It will be a little like Newport. The Hants are having a 'jolly' night tonight because they are leaving for Gosport tomorrow.
With best love to my own love,
From Mabs.

From Mother
49, Carisbrooke Rd, Newport, IW.   Wednesday, February 3, 1915
My Dear Bob,
I have not heard anything from the War Office yet. I filled in the paper alright, I think, and sent it. Have been looking hard every day for an answer. I hope it will come soon. Your father has not been able to go to the Asylum yet. Three weeks now I have only had the ten shillings that you sent me. He had a few shillings so we paid the rent with that, the first week. Now I couldn't pay this week. Roy went to Cowes last week, so he had three days pay. They lent me three shillings. I am sorry to ask but I should be pleased with a little help as soon as you can send it. I would have written before but kept putting it off, waiting for the post. Mabel says she has written twice. I hope you will be able to come. We wrote and told them in London but they haven't sent anything. Kath and myself are pretty well. Dad and Kath send love to you and will be glad to see you soon. Now goodbye my son,
ever your loving Mother, E. Brimson.

*The Blücher was sunk in the Battle of Dogger Bank on 24 January, 1915. Between 750 and 1000 men were lost.

From Bob

87th Field Company, R.E, Shorecliffe, Kent   Thursday, February 4, 1915

Dear Mother,

I should have written before, only we have been so busy on day and night work almost up to the time we left Brightlingsea. We left on the Monday morning for Shorecliffe. We are in barracks and we are occupying the married quarters, six men in each. We are a tremendous height above the sea and we have to go down a steep hill, something like Tulse Hill, Ventnor, to get down on the seafront. I am sending you a letter from our landlady in Brightlingsea where we were billeted. I was waving my hat out of the train when we were leaving and the signal post knocked it out of my hand and I had to wear my stocking cap so I sent her a postcard to try and get it for me, and she was lucky enough to claim it as my number was inside.

I am sending you a couple of 10 shilling notes. It is all I have except for a few shillings. Try and make it till next weekend and I will try and manage to send you a bit more. The War Office is very slow but still, you will secure all back payments from when I first applied.

We are doing our firing at Hythe ranges next week so I might be able to get a weekend leave after. There's plenty to see here. We see the boats leave Folkestone for Boulougne. They are accompanied by submarines. We can just see the conning towers sticking out of the water. We see plenty of aeroplanes. One came down today not far from us. I was very pleased to receive the nice presents. Kath made a splendid job of that watercolour of Mabs. Well I shall have to close now, with Love to all, hoping things will soon be all right again.

From your loving son,

Bob.

From Mother

49, Carisbrooke Rd, Newport, IW.   Sunday, February 7, 1915

My dear Bob,

Did you get the card to tell you that I received your letter with the two postal orders, of which I sincerely thank you for? I really did not know what to do. I got a letter from the office in Pyle Street, Newport, asking me to come down. I went and he asked me if the 15 shillings you allowed me was for board and lodgings. Of course, I said yes, then he asked how much did I think it took for your keep out of that, and I said eight shillings, so he said I should be allowed seven shillings from the War Office. So I wish you had said you paid me £1 a week. I asked Arch to tell you to say that, but never mind. It will be a help and will pay the rent and soon, if the weather breaks up and your Father gets alright, things will be better. He is a bit better but this continual rain is dreadful. He would be getting wet through and that would throw him up again.

Bob, do try and get a few days off soon for it worries me, you being sent to Thorncliff. It's so near the boats for France, you might be shipped off. You seem to have been very jolly at your lodgings. What a nice letter your landlady wrote; she must be a nice person. It's a good thing you got your hat again. You would have had to buy another, I expect.

I never sent you the paper last week for I did not know where to send them. I

am sending two now. You will see Harry Attrill's letter (*see below*) – they haven't heard from Morry yet.
Now I will leave off, hoping to see you soon, love from all,
ever your loving Mother, E. Brimson.

County Press February 6, 1915
NEWPORTONIAN'S THRILLING ACCOUNT OF THE SINKING
OF THE BLUCHER

Leading-Signalman Harry Attrill, of HMS Tiger, writing to his parents, Mr and Mrs M. Attrill, of The Bedford, Newport, on the latest North Sea battle, says: "Sorry to keep you waiting so long, but we have had rather busy times, exciting too. We have had what I call a glorious Sunday. We had orders for 'full speed' on Saturday night and went off like a ton of hot bricks in the direction of Heligoland. Everyone on board was full of excitement, as we had an idea there was something doing, and we were not far wrong. The ship had not been in action up till that time, so you can guess we were all itching for a scrap. We had orders to keep a sharp look-out for enemy destroyers on Saturday night and have the ship cleared for action and stations manned by 7 o'clock on Sunday morning. I had the middle watch, a nice four hours staring into darkness, but nothing took place until Sunday morning, when we received information that the light cruisers and the destroyers were in touch with the enemy. That was the time! Up went the signal '22 knots' and the battlecruisers were straining like some huge greyhounds to go off at full speed, when we suddenly sighted the enemy. Off went the alarm, and everyone was at action stations before you could look round, except the captain, engineer-captain, commander, and signalman. The enemy were evidently about to make one of their raids on the East Coast, for soon as they sighted us they turned tail and started off at full speed in an easterly direction, so it was going to be a race. Our squadron gradually worked up until they were going at full speed. The enemy were then seen to alter their course to starboard, making towards Heligoland as hard as they could. The chase went on for some time and we were gradually overhauling them. We were now up with our destroyers, who reported seven large ships in line ahead and an enemy's destroyer flotilla. Then the flagship, Lion, made the signal to our destroyers to give chase. You should have seen them nip hot on the enemy's trail; they were off like a shot from a gun. Morry's (the writer's brother) boat was amongst them. We were at fever pitch with excitement, as we were gaining on them every minute now. It was about ten minutes to nine when the enemy fired the first shot at our destroyers, as they were worrying the German ships. About 9 o'clock the Lion opened fire on the enemy, when they were about 12 miles off, to get their range. Then our commander asked the captain if he should try a shot, and was told to try his luck. The action then began in earnest, the captain and engineer-captain (who was killed) going down to their station in the conning tower and the signalmen to their war stations below decks, except myself and two other signalmen who remained on the bridge looking out for submarines, &c., until such time as it got too warm for us. We had begun to get their range lovely, several of our broadsides getting home on them. We were having a splendid view from the bridge when it began to get a bit warm, enemy shells falling just short and just ahead of us, so we had orders to come down to the conning tower. Everything was going splendidly when we got down there. The captain was giving orders as cool as a cucumber, as if we were merely carrying out some every day evolution. We were right in the thick of the battle then and the noise was terrific with our broadsides and the enemy's shells exploding around us. But try as they might they could not seem to hit us. We had already set fire to two of the enemy's ships and had taken the lead of our line, when the captain ordered the fire to be directed on the Blucher, which was soon seen to be in difficulties, dropping back from the remainder. We altered our course so as to close on her, and that was when our casualties commenced, as we had to close to within her range to finish her off properly. Shells were whistling all round us. All of a sudden there was a terrific explosion, right underneath me. It was about the nearest thing I ever had. When I picked myself up there was a heap of wounded officers and men right at my feet and Engineer-Capt. Taylor not an arm's length away, mortally wounded. I shall never forget it. His last words were 'Remember my wife and daughter.' He expired before he could finish the word 'daughter.' It was that shell which accounted for the majority of our dead and wounded. All I got was a bruised forehead. We avenged them by sinking the Blucher. The remainder of the enemy by that time were miles away and with little hopes of capturing them before they got under cover of their minefields, &c., we considered it a good day's work and sounded the 'ceasefire.' It must have been awful on board the German ships. Well, I think this is all for the present; we hope to have another 'bump' at them next week."

From Tester Bros

Monday, February 8, 1915
"Tester Brothers. Art Photographers. Dealers in photographic materials, fancy stationery, music etc etc ,. Seaford. Telephone 22."
Dear Sir,
Your note to hand. Please find enclosed two photographs. Mr Tester printed them, then had an accident and smashed the plate, so we shall have to trouble you to have another sitting on your return to Seaford.
Yours, H. Tester.

From Mabs
The Bedford, Newport, IW   Wednesday, February 10, 1915
My Dearest Boy,
Thank you very much for the photo – it is a splendid one. I believe we shall have a house full here on Sunday – Mrs Leal's crowd, your Mother, Father and Kath, perhaps Toffee – but I wish it was only you.
I expect life in Barracks is a shock after billets, but I hope you will soon settle down. Mick Richardson has joined the Royal Army Medical Corps and is going to Aldershot on Monday.
We have heard from Morry at last and he has been in hospital in Pembroke but he hopes to be better soon. He didn't say what was the matter with him. Ern is

in hospital again too, with his feet.
I hope you didn't put anything very terrible on that postcard. I left it especially for you to fill in. Wilfred Woodford is always making enquiries for you; he hasn't joined up yet, neither has Upward.
    Goodbye now my love, with heaps of kisses, from your loving sweetheart
                                    Mabs.

From Bob
                                    Sunday, February 14, 1915
My Dear Mother,
Glad to know you got the notes. I am sending another five shillings this week. It is all I can manage – they stop 3/6 every week out of my money for your allotment. Are you receiving it yet? You said you would only get 7/6 but I think that would be separate from the 3/6 that I pay, which with the two combined, would make it up to 10/6 or 11 shillings. Let me know as soon as you receive it. I am only supposed to pay one third and the government pays two thirds.*
I couldn't come home if I had a pass as I have no money to pay my railway fare. I think we shall be leaving here shortly and going to Aldershot, so I shall be a bit nearer home. I believe the whole of this division is going.
    I am glad you are going to Mabel's to tea today. It will be a nice change for you all. I couldn't buy her a present as they put me on twenty four hours guard the very night I was going into Folkstone. I couldn't get a very nice one either because I'd only about half a crown. I shall have to buy her one when I can manage to get home. You had better not show her this letter.
Glad to hear Roy is still in work. There should be plenty about now. I will close now,
                    with Love and kisses from your loving son, Bob.

From Mabs
The Bedford, Newport, IW   Monday, February 15, 1915
My Dearest Boy,
What in the world happened? Are you acting on Mother's advice of saving stamps by writing only once a fortnight? Just think of it. A fortnight tomorrow and no letter. Of course, I have had the postcards, but I have been waiting for a letter. Harry sent us a splendid account of their last battle. It will be in this week's paper so you can read it there. We are getting a little bit anxious about Morry. We have heard nothing from him and Harry says he was there.
Ernest is soon off to the Front again. He was silly enough to volunteer so he was transferred to the 2nd Battalion at Stratford on Avon. He might have waited a

---

* In 2009, *Sapper Martin's War Diary* was published, an account of Jack Martin's war as a sapper with the Royal Engineers. In February 1918, serving as an RE in Italy, he wrote, "Yesterday we received slips of paper to stick in our pay books showing the new rates of pay. Through getting Separation Allowance for my Mother I am 6d. a day better off as the government now pay the 6d. a day allotment that I made. Also I get 1d. a day war pay, having done over twelve month's active service. When I have completed the second year I shall have another rise of a penny. At present my daily rate is 2s 3d and I feel quite wealthy." *Sapper Martin's War Diary, Bloomsbury. 2009.*

bit before going again. He said they go on the 15th.

They had a tremendous fire in Portsmouth Dockyard last Sunday night.* It began before 10 o'clock and it was 3 o'clock before they could get it under control. They won't allow anything to be published about it because they think it might have been a spy. It was in the offices; Dad saw it from here when he went to bed so you can guess what a blaze it was.

Kath and I went to the 'Rink' on Wednesday night, the first time since I was in London. It was a decent show too. When is that photograph coming that you were talking about? It's a long time – are you afraid we shall see it?

With love and heaps of kisses from Mabs.

From Mabs

The Bedford, Newport, IW.   Tuesday, February 16, 1915

My Dearest Boy,

I expect by now you will think I have forgotten you, but I have been busy for a change lately, so I have had very little time to write.

Morry and Ern are both going on all right, up to the present. I had birthday cards from both of them. I wasn't disappointed not having a present from you. You know that wouldn't worry me. I hope your parcel arrived safely and not squashed. Don't blame me for the jelly. That was one of Mother's tricks; she would put it in.

I don't know, but I should think I was one of the luckiest girls in the Island on Sunday. I had shock after shock. Presents seemed to roll in and they were all such splendid ones (for all you care). There are still plenty of kindhearted people left in the world yet.

Dad gave me a bracelet, set with pearls, and £5, and Mother gave me £2.10.0 so she says if you want to borrow £5 you will know where to come. I hope you will soon be able to come here again. You can go to Aldershot as soon as you like provided it doesn't mean you will have to go to the Front soon. The party went off very well.

I think you have a cheek telling me to write longer letters. It's your fault I send short ones. I rack my brains to put into four pages what I usually put in eight and that's all I get for it. I thought you hadn't time to read the longer letters as you never half answered them. I suppose you will have heard by now that George Urry was killed, but I may as well tell you in case you have not.

I was very pleased to see that Brewer (George Grossmith) has got a DCM. He has something to be proud of now. I suppose Harry's last letter was such a long one he can't manage another one yet, but I suppose we shall hear in a day or so now. Wallace is going on well with his work but he is a lazy beggar for writing. He has only written about three times since he went.

Well, its past bedtime again. I have put a list on the back; you might be interested, if not, don't look. With fondest love,

from your little sweetheart, Mabs.

P S I am longing for the time when you can come home again.

---

* On the night of 31st January 1915, a fire broke out in Portsmouth dockyard. Large quantities of stores and valuable machinery were lost and two jetties were destroyed. Saboteurs were suspected but an offer of a reward by the Admiralty produced no suspects.

Present List - Mrs Brimson, fancy box (for jewels she said). Mr. Brimson, pair of pictures, beautiful ones, Gibraltar and another. Kathy, crocheted cake d'oyleys. Flo, jam dish and spoon. May, photo frame. Alice, Ethel and Ivy Ham, scent and handkerchief. Mr. and Mrs Seal, Maud, Ashley, Alice and Arthur, pair of silver candlesticks. Aunt Kate, iced cake and silver candlestick. (I have four birthday cakes altogether) Wallace, scent spray. From all at Lutterworth, gold brooch with pearls. Nelly, table centre (Indian). Doris, sugar basin. Kitty, silver sugar tongs.

From Kath
49, Carisbrooke Rd, Newport, IW.   Wednesday, February 17, 1915
Dear Bob,
I'm glad you like the picture; and so do we like your photo; we think it's a splendid of you. You couldn't have a better one done if you try all your life. I suppose you will be more conceited than ever if I tell you you look like an Officer; that's what we said, first look. Today has been dreadful, wind and rain all day. It nearly blows my bedroom inside out so I am going to turn into your bed tonight to see if it feels any safer.
Mother was ever so glad with your letter Bob, yesterday. She is sorry it is running you up so short with money, especially if it keeps you from coming home. Beastly War Office people don't send; they are such a long time; it would just put things right.
I suppose Mabel has told you about poor old George Urry.* It was Saturday morning when Mrs. Urry came staggering round here – she could hardly stand – with a letter in her hand from his Sergeant Major to say George had been shot through the head. Died instantly, of course. She made Mother read it to her, poor woman. She was dreadfully upset. And poor Minnie too, she'd had a letter as well, and one George had written to her, ready to post. He had been so lucky all through, up till now.
And there is another one – Kit's brother, Caleb, went down in the Vicknor, that armed yacht. He was coming over to see her last summer, only the war came instead and stopped him. He had had two lucky escapes before that, too, but the next one did it, the same as George.
Oh, before I forget it, you might cut out that letter of Harry's and put it in your next letter home. I wish you had saved those others with your name in, and Ern's letter, but I suppose they are gone now.
We had a very jolly evening over Mrs Attrill's last Sunday. We wanted you there. I did wish you had been there to see Mrs. Leal waltzing with Mr. Stratton; it was a beautiful sight and no mistake. She did it so gracefully, too. That Arthur Stratton is an idiot. He and Mrs. Leal are the most comical pair I've ever come across. He bobs down all of a sudden into her face, "Hullo, little mummy." Makes her jump off her seat nearly. She yells out, "Drop it, Mike, you fool!" They nearly killed me. Mr. Leal, I like him. He's a nice old chap, isn't he? He was dead nuts on the ham at supper – he couldn't leave it alone. In between the conversation it was, "Jolly good ham, Ada," and then, "Yes, I'll have a bit more

---

* See page 77.

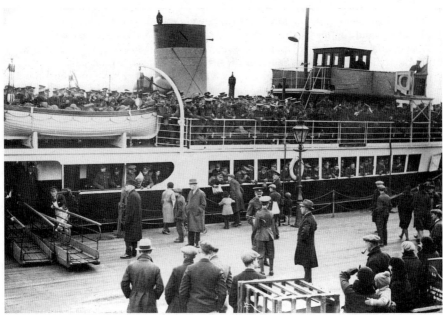

Troops embarking for the Front from Victoria Pier, Cowes Esplanade.

Entrance to Albany Barracks.
"Kath and I went up to the Barracks this morning. We were just in time for the last hymn and prayers. We saw them march off and then we stopped to listen to the band. They played a few selections." Mabs to Bob, October 4th, 1914.

please," then his Missus would say, "No, you mustn't have any more Jack. You won't sleep all night," and he'd turn round – "You go and fry your face! Jolly good 'am, Ada," and that's how it went on.
I'll finish now. Mabel is going to post it.
Heaps of love and kisses from us all,
ever your loving Kath.

County Press February 20, 1915
THE ISLAND AND THE WAR
ANOTHER NEWPORT MAN KILLED.
Yet another gallant Newport man has been killed at the Front in the person of Sapper George Henry Urry, R.E., the only son of Mr. and Mrs. H. Urry, of 50 Carisbrooke Road, who was in his 26th year. The sad news was conveyed to the parents on Saturday in a touching and sympathetically worded letter from the major commanding No. 12 Company Royal Engineers to which the deceased belonged.
It stated that Sapper Urry was engaged in work near the trenches at night on February 9th. Desultory firing was taking place, and he was struck in the head by a bullet and died almost at once. The major added that he was sure "George must have been a good son, as he was a good soldier." Sapper Urry had been in the thick of the fighting since the commencement of the war and we have had the pleasure of publishing several interesting and well-written letters from him. He had had many wonderful escapes from death during the exceedingly dangerous work, which the gallant men of the R.E. are so nobly carrying out. In a letter to his mother, written two days before he received his mortal wound, he tells of such an escape. A shell struck the building in which he and other men of his section were at tea. It penetrated an 18in. wall and burst in the room. The company bugler had his leg blown off and six other men were wounded, but Sapper Urry escaped. The bugler boy died four days latter, and in a letter to his "young lady Sapper Urry relates how this gallant bugler's last words were, "Tell mother I died like a man," and how the whole company attended his funeral on Sunday February 7th. Sergt. W. Park, who is in charge of the section to which the deceased belonged, has also written to Mr. Urry giving further details to the effect that his son was shot through the head by a sniper and killed instantaneously. The sergeant added, "I express the feelings of the whole section when I say that we have lost a cheerful, willing, and good comrade, whom we shall miss very much."
Sapper Urry's many friends at Newport greatly deplore his death, and the deepest sympathy is extended to the bereaved parents in their great sorrow. It is interesting to note that Sapper Urry, who was a plumber by trade, made six trips in that capacity to America and back on the Royal Mail liner Astoria, the hospital ship which the Germans so basely endeavoured to torpedo off Le Havre recently, Mr. and Mrs. Urry desire to return their very sincere thanks for the numerous letters and expressions of sympathy they have received.

From Bob
Kent   Sunday, February 21, 1915
I'm glad you like the photos all right. I have just received another ten which makes up the dozen. As I told you before, they smashed the plate of the other after they had only printed two so I had to act again on the Sunday afternoon we arrived back from Brightlingsea, as we were leaving Seaford the next day, and as I had lost my hat I had to have it taken without. It was a great shock for me when I heard George Urry's fate when he's been so lucky up till now. Dyer has just received his County Press and has been reading the account of it. Sorry to hear about Caleb too. I believe that's the one that has a wife and two or three kiddies.
We are leaving Shorecliffe tomorrow and marching to Aldershot – somewhere about 100 miles. It will take us about seven days to do it. The section that I am in, which is No.1, is the advance. We go on ahead with the Army Service Corps and the whole of the Division will follow in about two days after Cavalry Royal Field Artillery and the different infantry battalions. It will be a fine sight for those that watch them go by. You mustn't expect to hear from me until some time next week when we get to Aldershot. I'm glad you had a good time over at Mabel's. You seem to have enjoyed yourself all right. Mabs received quite a lot of presents. It was nice of Dad, Mother and you to give her one each.
I am sorry to be leaving Folkestone. It's such an interesting place. It's just like being across in France as everywhere you go you hear French or Belgian. Little kiddies stop you in the street and beg for your cap badge or letters. They ask in their own language but we know what they mean because they point to their caps. There seems to be more foreigners than English here.
Well dear Kath, I must close now.
                    Love to you and all at home, from Bob.

From Mabs
The Bedford, Newport, IW   Monday, February 22, 1915
My Dearest Bob,
It is a shame that you have to move again although I am glad when I know you will be able to come home. I like the new photo very much. I didn't expect to see such a perfect one as the other. Of course, having no hat makes a great difference, you never do look the same without a hat as you do with one. Sally and Minnie were in last week and they asked how you were so I showed them the photo. They were delighted with it and Sally passed remarks about the handsome moustache so I told her that was a different tale to the one she told you when you started it. They have made enquiries for you two weeks running now, so I think I shall tell them you send your love next time (tut tut).
Minnie told me that Tom Read was coming home from the Front on leave but I don't think he has been yet. Thank you very much for the postcards of Brightlingsea that you have sent me. How would you have liked being in Brightlingsea on Sunday when they made that air raid?
If the weather your way is anything like it has been here today, you have my sympathy on that march. I don't see why you have to do it. It snowed for nearly

two hours this afternoon, after pouring with rain all the morning, and now it is raining again. I am very pleased to say that Mother is nearly fit again now. I can't say the same of Morry, though. He won't tell us what is wrong with him but I think he must have been very ill because he is too weak to walk yet. He says he can have a cheap 'drunk' now – he only has to stand up and he is done for because everything begins to spin. Something has gone wrong in his ears; he says there is a noise like a German band in them all the time. He thinks he may be sent to Portsmouth from the hospital. You may have a chance to see him then.

Ernest is back in Gosport again now. I suppose he isn't fit to go out again, although the doctor up here asked him what he wanted to come home for when he examined him. Ern ought to have told him he came for fun.

I have been over with Kathie this afternoon while your mother went out to tea. When Mr. Sykes saw your photo he advised me to get married to you when you were in your uniform because you look so smart. I hope you will be able to read this dreadful scrawl but I am writing in bed under difficulties. I do hope the weather will be all right for the rest of your journey, and make haste and come home when you get there. I won't grumble at your letters any more. They are such splendid letters and it's such a treat to get them.

From your loving little sweetheart, Mabs.

You can have the kisses when you get here.

From Bob

Gibraltar Barracks, Aldershot   Monday, March 1, 1915

My Dear Mother,

We arrived in Aldershot today, about 1 pm, and joined the rest of our company in Barracks. We had quite a lively time on the march although we were rather fagged at the end of each day. We left Shorecliffe barracks at 7.30 am on Monday morning the 22nd – that is No 1 Section, about 36 of us all together, and marched to Hythe where we picked up the main body of the column which composed the RF Artillery, the Buffs, the Queens, the West Kent's and the East Surrey's and the mechanical transport of the Army Service Corps, about 70 or 80 big motor lorries. We reached Ashford at 1 o'clock that day where we put up in an empty house for the night and had our dinner of bully beef and bread and a drop of tea. Started away at 8.30 next morning for a place called Cranbrooke. That was our longest march – 22 miles. As we were having a day's rest day we had to put up in an old barn for that night, and the next. We couldn't get much sleep as it was so cold, the ground was covered with snow next morning.

On the Thursday morning we left Cranbrooke for Tunbridge Wells, which was another long march, and we put up in an empty house there for the night. Next morning we left early for East Grinstead. Had an empty room over a shop to sleep in. Left next day – we marched to Horsham and slept in a motor garage. Left next day, Sunday, for Godalming where we actually slept in a feather bed. The town being full of troops they had to put us two in a cottage. Me and another chap got in a house with some very nice people and they gave us a jolly good supper – the first square meal I had since I had been on the march. We left there this morning and arrived here at 1 o'clock, having marched 112 miles all through Kent, Sussex and Surrey into Hampshire – and I feel as fit as ever I did in my life. We did it with the valises on our backs, and full up too, as well as our rifles. I dare say we should be having some leave soon now that we have come here. I will write to Mabel within a day or two.

Love to all at home, ever your loving son Bob.

From Mother
49, Carisbrooke Rd, Newport, IW.   Wednesday, March 3, 1915
My dear Bob,
What a relief and pleasure your letter gave me and all of us. I expect as long as you live you will never forget the walk you had last week. I got a paper from the War Office last week telling me to call at the Post Office, Newport, on the Tuesday of this week, then I should receive 8s. 9d. weekly. I went down yesterday. They had not any book for me. I am to go down this Friday. I will write again when I get it and let you know what I get. You will be glad to know your father went to work four days last week; started Monday sharp this week. Roy is still at Cowes so things will be looking up brighter now. How do you like Aldershot? Six splendid Indian officers went up by yesterday, to the Castle. I expect there are the spotted fever up the Barracks, they say, but one don't hear much about it. Love from all,

ever your loving Mother, Ellen Brimson.

From Mabs
The Bedford, Newport, IW.   Monday, March 8, 1915
My Dearest Boy,
Thanks very much for the letter I received this morning. The idea of you saying I should get sick of reading it! I shall begin to think that is what you say to mine. It was a very interesting letter – you evidently see sights there (especially after a night on rum hot).
Now listen to my tale of woe. I quite expected you home for the weekend. I can't think what gave me the idea. However, I wasn't the only one. Your mother had the same idea and even got your dinner ready for you. Never mind, you will be home soon to make up for it. Ern was home this weekend, he went back yesterday. He expects to go to the Front again shortly but I don't expect he will because his foot is still bad. It appears there is a bone broken in it, so I don't see how he can go out yet.
Your mother thinks you won't have to go to France, of course I have to lie low and say nothing, but I do hope you won't have to go, although I don't believe you would be happy till you did. Kathie has painted such a splendid picture of you, for me, but the one with the cap.* I like the one without the cap. It is more like my old Bob than the new soldier Bob with the soldiers cap.
Morry wasn't wounded. I suppose we shall know what it was. I think he has lost his hearing powers. He says something has given way in his ears. He was ill onboard for a week before they sent him into hospital. He supposed they were afraid of losing him but he says he won't go back on the Owl if he has anything

* See page 131.

to do with it.

Harry is very pleased to get on the Queen Mary again. He wasn't very comfortable on the Tiger. He said they never are for the first year of the commission. I shall have to stop now till tomorrow; the blinking candle is just about to go out, drat it. I'm sure I shan't be up in time to finish it for the first post.

Well I didn't manage the first post. The fire alarm sounded about an hour ago. I was in bed and thought the brute would never stop. I heard the engine go tearing by here and I have heard since that the fire is at Yafford.* Old George was in the Bar Parlour trying to sing, Saturday night, but there was no one to lead the chorus. The soldiers wouldn't because they said it was a shame as he was so old, tut tut! They don't know George. It's nearly time I wound up or you will want a day off to read it. I hope you are keeping quite well and don't get that dreadful spotted fever. There are some here.

From your loving sweetheart Mabs.

From Kath

49, Carisbrooke Rd, Newport, IW.   Wednesday, March 10, 1915

Dear Bob,

I had made up my mind to write to you tonight to let you know how Mother got on about the money, only Mabel came over today and said she had two tickets for the Rink. She wanted to take me, told me to be ready by six. Now it is seven and she hasn't come yet – I could have written while I been waiting. Mabel has just come in. She has biked over to Hatherfield today, and did not get back early enough so we are going tomorrow instead. Brought back some primroses for me.

Well, Mother had to go down the Post Office three times. Anyway, Friday, the last time, she came back with three pounds and some change. She nearly went off her head with the shock of having so much all at once. She set off and paid everybody she could manage. It was a tremendous help to her but she said she would rather have you, Bob.

We had another mile long letter from Arch yesterday, all about their visit to you. You seem to take some getting at. What a lot of grand people you have been seeing lately. Getting mighty swanky now, I suppose.

Do you know, we all seemed to get it into our heads that you were coming home last Saturday – I don't know how it got there – but there was Mother, prepared your bedroom, cooked a nice dinner, a pie, put your dinner up ready, even laid your place at table. It did seem beastly when you didn't turn up after all. Don't go playing us tricks like that any more, mind; sending us wireless messages and then not keeping your word.

Dad says it is a very nice doctor they have got over the Asylum now. I suppose Mr. Holt must have said something to him about Dad not being well lately because the doctor went and examined Dad and gave him a big bottle of medicine, and Mr Holt was very nice too – told Dad he needn't come to work till next Monday.

---

* The County Press of March 13th reported, "A fire in a field close to Yafford House destroyed a large wheat rick belonging to Mr. Carver of Wolverton Manor, on the previous Thursday morning."

We are getting in plenty of jam for when you get home. You couldn't possibly live without it, now I suppose. Roy says, "Tell Bob I'm disappointed that he never writes to me – I don't know what I've done." It's 9 o'clock now, past. Mabel has just come so she can post it. Goodnight now, dear old boy.

Heaps of love and kisses,
ever your loving Kath.

From Mabs
The Bedford, Newport, IW.   Thursday, March 18, 1915
My Dearest Sweetheart,
I am sorry I didn't write sooner, but I won't do it again. I know you didn't grumble. Still, I expect you have been patiently waiting.
They let Morry out for a walk from the hospital last Saturday. He may be in Pompey after all, this week. There is still no news of Harry. It is to be hoped he isn't ill, too. The latest whisper round here is Ernie White is going to buy Ethel Snell an engagement ring, tut tut! She gave the other chap the push because she couldn't go out with him in the evening as he had to work till 9.30.
Have you been inoculated yet? I hope it won't serve you too badly when you are done. You know those creatures were very near having a row here, Saturday night. They did finish it somewhere and none of them have been in since. Jolly good thing if the 'tigers' don't. (I don't mean the Hampshire Tigers).
Sally saw Charlie Dyer Saturday night. By the way, I think the Army has improved Dyer. I should hardly have known him. Kathie didn't take any notice of what I said about the picture, as she wanted to alter the chin, so I have taken it back again. I do hope they will let you come as often as possible now. Especially if you are due out there next month.
Wallace is 15 on Sunday. He calmly informs us that we can buy a bicycle for him, between us. Wallace never wants much. There was a letter from Harry this morning. They had been out to sea and didn't get back till Thursday. Fancy it being only last Sunday you were here. It seems months since then.
I must wait patiently for the next weekend now. I hope you will have your usual good luck.

With heaps of kisses, I remain your loving sweetheart,
Mabs.

From Mabs
The Bedford, Newport, IW.   Tuesday, March 23, 1915
My Dearest Bob,
I am not trying to write a long letter this time for two reasons : 1. This is about the worst pen nib in the world and I can't get a better one now, and 2. I haven't enough time.
I really want to tell you that Morry is home. He came home last Saturday till next Monday so if you are able to come this week it will be all right, although he says he thinks he can come back again for Easter. I do hope you can manage a weekend together. He wants someone to liven him up a bit. He can't sleep at

night and he mopes about when he is indoors – not a bit like he used to be. His head worries him. Still the doctors could make nothing of him in hospital but you will understand better when you come home.

I had a letter from Chris and one from Mrs. Newnham today. Chris and Arch hope to get here for Easter and Mrs Newham's letter was full of our brave boys including, 'Mr. Bob', as she calls you.

Did you know that Nurse Bridger had a brother in the Navy? Morry told me about him. He says he is a seaman on the Owl. Our class finished today and we had afternoon tea to celebrate the event. Now if you do come this week get as long as you can but, of course, you will do that without telling. Now I must close, my love, but you shall have a nice long letter for Sunday if you don't come. With fondest love to my own love,

from Mabs.

From Bob
Stanhope Lines, Aldershot.*   Sunday, March 28, 1915
My Dear Mother,

I am trying to come this next week for a few days if I can get a pass. I should like to have seen Morrie. I hope he will be able to get home again. Is Archy and Chris and the kiddies coming down this Easter? I hear that they are running no excursions but perhaps they will manage it somehow.

 One of our men has been down with German measles and the doctor has turned us out of the barrack rooms and we are under canvas again, and have been for over a week, practically isolated. There seems plenty of it about here too, and spotted fever. The doctor asked me to enquire if I ever had the measles. I don't remember if I had or not. Will you write and let me know? We had no band for church parade this morning as they are nearly all isolated.

I met Charlie Harris' wife's brother last night, he is in the reserve signallers of the R.E.s, and I received the County Press this morning, also the socks and handkerchiefs you sent. I am sending you five shillings this week I hope you are managing to get along all right. Has Dad been to work much lately?

The weather seems to be getting better but still cold. I am still working on the same job, writing the carts. Our No.1 section had our photographs taken in a group with that lieutenant in the centre. If I can arrange to get home next week I will bring it with me.**

I wonder what's wrong with Morrie. Did you notice much difference in him? They ought to allow him a few weeks at home. I suppose he will go into Barracks at Portsmouth for a bit. Well dear Mother, I must close now as it is getting near dinnertime. Love to you, Dad and Kath,

from your loving son, Bob.

Have just had orders that all men who hasn't had measles to parade at 2 o'clock today and leave here for Thistledown camp, wherever that is, so I have got to pack my kit once more. Will let you know more later, Bob.

---

* Stanhope Lines and Bob's previous address, Gibraltar Barracks, were both part of the 8000 acre Aldershot army camp.
** See page 84.

Aldershot, 1915.
The original photo is titled *"No.1 Section 87th Field Company, Royal Engineers, Aldershot, 1915."* Bob is seated second from left in first row and Charlie Dyer is first from left, top row.

From Mabs
The Bedford, Newport, IW.   Wednesday, March 31, 1915
My Dearest Bob,
I expect you will be thinking nasty things of me for not writing to cheer you up. Poor old boy, I believe you had the blues properly when you wrote my letter. I have tried two or three times to write but I don't seem to have a minute to spare now. It will be all over tonight, though – Elsie from Atherfield has been staying here since Sunday, but she is going home today.
May White was here from Thursday until Sunday to keep Morry company. Beastly little flirts, the pair of them. Elsie and I went to Ryde yesterday on the bicycles. It was a beautiful day. Ryde is a spanking place for shopping but I would rather have been in Ventnor with you.
Your mother thinks it will be a rotten Easter this time. Arch and Chrissie won't be here now and if you don't come I shall send to the Commander-in-Chief and tell him what I think of him (Perhaps). Your mother says you have had the measles.
I am still thinking you might come. We will make up for it later if you don't. Morry will be in Portsmouth for a month or two now. Shiner Haines is home now and Harry Matthews. Mother is just yelling about me writing this now, so I must stop. With love to my dearest,
from Mabs.

From Mabs
The Bedford, Newport, IW.   Friday, April 9, 1915
My Dearest Boy,
I hope you have managed to settle down again after your holiday. Holidays are all very well but I never like the return part of them, though I suppose we ought to be content. I do want you to come again soon, but I don't like the idea of that four days. I hope that won't be for some time yet. Your mother has guessed what that means. I told her that you wouldn't be going away for a long time yet (chance whether it is true), because you had nothing to go with.
To make matters worse, your father said last night that Dyer was coming for three days, which would be the last, so your mother is beginning to think she won't see you again.
By the way, a dreadful thing has happened. I have lost my badge. I lost it, I believe, on the Asylum Road on Tuesday. I suppose it serves me right for saying that I wouldn't give it away. Did you manage to see Morry after all? We haven't heard anything of him.
I sent Harry some violets yesterday. I expect he will smile when he sees them. He is lazy when it comes to letter writing and Wallace is just as bad. Kath and Gordon are both going to fix him when he comes here again.
We are having real April weather here today. High wind and terrific showers mixed up with bright sunshine. There are several thousands of Kitchener's Army passing through Rugby. They think it will take them a week to pass through.
With love and kisses to my sweetheart,
Mabs.

From Mabs
The Bedford, Newport, IW.   Friday, April 16, 1915
My Dearest Bobbie,
I expect you have been patiently waiting for a line from me. I am a wicked
sinner and I'll try to mend my ways by writing at the proper time. Well, my dear
boy, you can just imagine how the news was received that you will be safe for
a bit longer. I hate the thought of your going away knowing that each time takes
you one nearer the last. Now I am at it again – but I can't help it sometimes.
Poor Morry was upset because he didn't see you. I wish I hadn't been so selfish
in keeping you at Ryde. He was waiting at the gate, from 4.30 till 6 o'clock, and
then being fed up with waiting, he went inside. It was a pity he couldn't get out;
you would have seen him all right. He sent a postcard this morning to know
whether you would be home, as he will be out Sunday. I suppose he thought
you would soon have your four days, because he said he would be out on
Thursday in case you were home next week.
I had a letter from Chris on Tuesday. They had just had a letter from you. Do
you remember Dave the sailor, who came over from Whale Island* for the
weekend with Morry? He has been made Warrant Officer, so I suppose May can
swank now when she goes out with him.
Kathie, Kitty and me went off to Gatcombe Wilderness yesterday to get
primroses to send to London. I am sending a Pictorial this week. You will have
to be content with this for now; I haven't time to write more. Dad is cutting the
grass for the first time this year.
We haven't heard from Harry yet. Mr. Devereux was enquiring for you the
other night. He was disappointed because he hadn't seen you. With fondest love
and kisses.

                                    From Mabs.

From Bob
Stanhope Lines, Aldershot.   Friday, April 16, 1915
My Dear Mother,
We have been very busy on the ranges this last fortnight but I think we finish
tomorrow and then we start on manoeuvres for a few days, about 10 miles out
of Aldershot. We left Aldershot this morning and we are now in Berkshire
under canvas at a place called Finchampstead. We marched all the way in full
kit with the Division and the tool carts and the pontoons – practically all the
whole of the 87th company in full marching order.
Our camp is on the Finchampstead Ridges, very high up, overlooking about 50
miles of lovely country. The weather is beautiful too and there is heather all
around us and just across the road is a forest of Scotch firs. There are a lot of
other regiments here besides us. Please tell Mabs I received her letter and
Pictorial all right. I will try and write to her later. Well I must say goodbye.
                 With love and kisses from your loving son, Bob.

---

* Whale Island is a small area of reclaimed land in Portsmouth Harbour. It has been home to a Royal
Navy base since the 1870s.

From Mabs
The Bedford, Newport, IW.   Wednesday, April 21, 1915
My Dearest Sweetheart,
I hear that you are so hard at work that you haven't much spare time this week. Perhaps you will find time to read this.
At last we have had news of Harry. He is quite well and it appears he only writes when he is in harbour, and only then if there is anything of importance to write about. As it happened, he wrote from sea this time with nothing more than a submarine attack to report. They were all too quick for the submarine. Ern was over for the weekend. He said he was granted special leave before leaving for the Front. He was supposed to go Tuesday. I don't know whether he did. He may be gone, but I don't think they would pass him yet. He can't walk any distance now. He was sorry you didn't come home but I told him if you didn't meet before, you would see him in Berlin. They all think they will meet there.
Albert Hawkins was here for Sunday and Monday; he is still getting fatter. He was quite disappointed at not finding you here so he wished to be remembered to you. He thinks he will have to go to France soon.
Toffee is a blighter; he gets on my nerves. We are not even on 'Good morning' terms now. He will be sorry for it yet.
                    With fondest love from your loving sweetheart, Mabs.

From Bob
Stanhope Lines, Aldershot.   Sunday, May 2, 1915
My Dear Mother,
I'm sorry to have kept you waiting so long for a letter, but I believe we have finished manoeuvres at last and I should have more time now. I sent a postcard from Clapham last Sunday to say I was up there for the weekend. I had a very nice time with them. Chris and Babs are all right but Archy and Bee have very bad colds. Jim was home on sick leave again. I don't know how he manages it – I can't do it.
On Friday we done 32 miles in full marching order. I was about finished when I got back to Barracks that night as we had nothing to eat since 4.30 that morning except oranges we bought on the road. That was the longest march we ever had done as yet. There were two divisions of troops out. It was also one of the hottest days we've had this year. I had to change all my clothes as they were wet through with perspiration. I was jolly stiff the next day but I am all right now.
There is talk of us moving to Winchester or somewhere near Southampton. We can't place much reliance on what we hear but still, I hope we do. Well, Mother, I must finish now with fondest love to all,
                              ever your loving son, Bob.

From Mother
49, Carisbrooke Rd, Newport, IW.   Wednesday, May 5, 1915
My dear Bob,
I was so pleased to get your letter. I hope it won't be long before you get a few days off. C. says you will be having it together. He told us all about that long march last Friday. I am sure you must have been dead beat, and such a hot day. C. Harvie is off to the Front today. Aunt C. says George is at Aldershot but is not sure. Father keeps on all right out at the Asylum. Kath has painted a nice head of Mrs. Green and daughter and has to do one of the little girl. The girl that she painted is in a Post Office in London, very pretty girl; she did do it beautifully. Now goodbye my dear boy,
                          ever your loving Mother E. Brimson.

From Mabs
The Bedford, Newport, IW.   Friday, May 7, 1915
My Dearest Boy,
I have managed at last to write. I didn't write last week because I heard that you were in Winchester. Morry will be over Saturday afternoon with a chap named 'Ginger'. Mrs White was quite all right this time. She didn't have a word to say against you and she didn't think you looked as old as you are. Fancy that now. Morry sleeps there every other night now, so he gets all the jaw. It seems months since I sent you a line. I hardly know where to begin now, there is so much to tell. I think it will be best to wait till you come home.
Billy Millgate had his four days last week. He came from Edinburgh. He saw Harry up there, but he had to go on board to him. He says Harry is looking better than he has seen him for a long time. Morry is going on fine now. It is a good job he won't have to go back to the ship again.
Fancy sending Ern out again so soon. About 700 Warwicks left Sunday morning; they all met at Southampton. George Almer (the groom) was there too. Ern said he saw him. We had a postcard from Ern this morning and he has arrived at the Base.
I am sorry to say that I shall not be glad to see you soon, unless it is only a weekend. I don't like that four days because from rumours I have heard it means you may have to go this month. I hope not, although I suppose I have no business to.
                    With heaps of kisses, from your loving sweetheart,
                                    Mabs.

From Mabs
The Bedford, Newport, IW.   Friday, May 14, 1915
My Own Dear Boy,
I couldn't rest till I did write to you. It eases my mind a bit when I can write. I am glad you were able to see Morry on Monday. He came over to take May back on Wednesday. Well, holidays are all very well but it is very hard to see you go away again.
Were you in the carriage with a man in a naval uniform? I was down by the

Quay when the Ryde train went out. I thought I saw you and Dyer, and put up my hand to catch your eye. The other chap thought I was waving to him and he waved too, silly duffer. Your train was very late. Mother and May didn't get back till 6 pm on Monday.

Kath, Mrs Spink, Norah, and Alma and I all went to Gurnard on Tuesday. We went through the forest. It was grand in there. We had such a beautiful day so we are going again another day.

I have specially scented this for the benefit of certain young men to get a sniff. I hope they won't be jealous. If you don't want any more of this notepaper, let me know and you shan't be teased again.

They had a sort of a recruiting night here last night. I don't know how many they had. They showed that 'Wake Up' picture at the Rink and the Royal Warwicks played there. I haven't lost the new badge yet, I must get a chain to put it on in case I do. Well I must finish now my love or there will be a row. They are just getting busy. It's Waterloo day today, if you know what that means.

With love and kisses from Mabs.

From Bob
Stanhope Lines, Aldershot.   Sunday, May 16, 1915
My Dear Mother,
Just a few lines to let you know we are settled down once more for a little while. I met Morry when I got over to Portsmouth and we had an hour or two together. I got back to Barracks in good time. We have got our regimental band down here from Chatham. It numbers about 52 but there are a lot more. They play on the parade ground every dinnertime, and the officers' mess at night. It's a splendid band too. It's nice to see them in their red and gold uniforms after so much khaki. Have you heard from Chris and Archy yet? I wrote to them but they never answered. I had the first dose of inoculation yesterday. It hasn't half given me beans but I expect it will be better again by tomorrow. We were supposed to have been reviewed by Sir Archibald Hunter last Wednesday but it rained all day. We turned out with our wagons and everything, but Hunter didn't, so we had to go back after getting really wet through. I expect we shall be leaving here soon and moving a bit nearer home. I'm just about fed up with Aldershot so I shan't be sorry. What did Mrs Green say to Kath's picture? She couldn't have done it better – it's exactly like her. She should put a decent price on it too. Well, dear Mother, I must close now as it is getting near dinnertime and will write again shortly. Love to Kath, Dad and yourself,
Ever your loving son, Bob.

From Mabs
The Bedford, Newport, IW.   Monday, May 17, 1915
My Dearest Bobbie,
I don't know what to say to that letter this morning. Of course I was very pleased to get one but I am very sorry to hear of your moving so soon. I suppose there is no chance of you coming over again now. I hope that you will be

somewhere near Southampton, then if you can't come here I might be able to see you there – and yet sometimes I think it would be better as it is, because it is so hard to be left behind.

You must have been having a rotten time with that inoculation. Is that only the first time or is it the second?

By the way, how many more times am I to talk to you about Everton? Mother had to tell Morry that yarn because he couldn't understand why he never came here now. Of course, she didn't want to tell him the truth because you know what Morry is if anyone upsets him, so now just be quiet and don't get jealous anymore.

I like the boy, and it worried me because he has been so silly in not coming near, but you ought to know now that you are always first and if he was a perfect angel it wouldn't worry me. Another thing, you know it isn't his nature to worry over one girl. There are more girls than me in the world and if you don't think there are better ones, lots of other young men do. Now don't worry any more or I shall deliver a lecture, fierce and strong.

There is a young man all alone in the next room nearly breaking his heart. I've a good mind to ask him if he has had a row with his girl. He has been to a funeral (4th Warwick's) so perhaps he feels downhearted. I can't help it if he does – if he sniffs much more I shall bite him.

Well goodbye my love till next time.

Yours ever, Mabs.

From Kath

49, Carisbrooke Rd, Newport, IW.   Tuesday, May 18, 1915

Dear Bob

I am writing this letter in between my supper. We were ever so glad to get your letter yesterday morning. Mabel told me that you said we might as well write once a week. Well, we always seem to wait for your letter first when you go back. Of course, we know you haven't got much time for letter writing but we are always looking out for them. That was a nasty trick of Sir Archibald's, bringing you out for nothing but to be soaked.

We did go for our picnic after all. That fat-headed May, of course, didn't come but we enjoyed ourselves without her. We went through the forest. It was lovely. The others all did their share of pushing so they said it came very hard.*

We thought about you and talked about you too, Bob. I like little Alma, she is a nice little girl. We had a letter from Chris and Arch; they quite expect Mother up there, and now she has got a scare about London. Do you think they mean business this time?

Mabel was over this afternoon, and she will be over again in a minute, so I am trying to finish this before she comes; it is just a quarter past nine now.

I do hope your arm will be better soon. No – Worse! So that you will be sent home on sick leave. Mabel has come so I will be saying goodnight now,

From your loving Kath.

---

* Kath is being pushed in her wheelchair.

From Mother
49, Carisbrooke Rd, Newport, IW.   Tuesday, May 18, 1915
My dear Bob,
I want this letter to go tonight so I am just sitting down anywhere to write it
with lead pencil. I was glad to hear from you. I was hoping you was going to
say you would be home this Sat. I think you ought if your arm is bad. Charlie
came home. Have you had the other one done yet? I expect it is bad for you.
Have C. Dyer had his done yet? Can't be expected to do much work, so they
ought to let you off. Kathy is writing. I don't know what. Perhaps we shall be
doing the same thing – I mean, telling you the same.
They keep on wanting me to come up to London but do you think it sensible
when they mean to raid the place? Everyone says they mean to set it afire. I
hope you will be moved nearer us.
There was a lot of your fellows went by today, all in private clothes in the rain.
The pictures went home today. The Greens were very pleased; the little girl
looked beautiful. Kathie charged 5/- each. I am sure they were worth it. Dad is
on papering out there now. Hoping to see you soon. Believe me,
ever your loving Mother, E. Brimson.

From Bob
28, Bernard Rd. Clapham Junction. London S.W.   Sunday, May 23, 1915
My Darling Mabs,
You'll be surprised to know that I've got a few more hours off, but not enough
time to slip down and see you all, as I have to be in tonight at 10 pm. We did
not leave Aldershot on Wednesday after all, but we go for certain this week as
we have handed all our kit in and we only possess just about what we stand up
in, except for a change of underclothing.
Two divisions have left this last week for the Front. It has cleared Aldershot of
a great number of troops. We were out Thursday and Friday nights,
bivouacking and trenching, so we have not had much sleep, therefore I had a
job to wake up this morning. Gordon is up here as well. They did not know I
was coming, it was a surprise. In fact I did not know I was coming myself or I
should have let you know so that you might have tried to come up as well. We
went to the 'Grand' again last night. 'Phil Ray' was there and also a decent
review called '1915'.
Thanks very much for all the explanation regarding Everton. It has lifted a great
weight off my mind. I know quite well that you will be true to me in spite of my
wicked ways. I could not have chosen a better girl if I had searched the whole
world through, and the dangers and hardships I shall have to go through these
next few weeks will be eased a lot by the thought of you waiting for me at home
– if it is my luck to get through all right. I must say goodbye now Mabs, for the
present with heaps of love and kisses,
ever your loving sweetheart,
Bob.

From Mabs
The Bedford, Newport, IW.   Tuesday, May 25, 1915
My Dearest Bob,
It was a relief to get your letter this morning. I began to wonder if they had taken you straight to the Front on Wednesday. I didn't write before because, of course, I didn't know what to do. It didn't worry me much (I mean the holiday). It wasn't like a holiday without my Bob. Morry came over in the afternoon – he was over on Saturday too. I knew that letter came from London as soon as I saw it but I thought it was from Chris until I saw the writing then I guessed where you had been to. I should have liked to be there but I expect they were full up with Gordon and you. I expect Gordon enjoyed it. We had two postcards from Ernest today. One to say that he was going on all right in his second turn, but one four days later that says he is wounded again, and being taken down to the base. That was all on that one. I will let you know as soon as possible how Ernest is going on.
Elsie is coming in from Atherfield today. She is to be married next week. I suppose our turn will come in time.
I am glad your mind is set at rest concerning Toffee. He only recognises any of us at a distance, the same as when we saw him last. If we get too near he turns his head so that he doesn't see us. He is 21 next month. I hope he gets some older brains by that time instead of being such a baby. I expect his second stripe has raised him so high in the world that he can't look down.
I was supposed to take one young man to Church and another one for a walk after, on Sunday night, but I took Kath over St George's Down (our old walk). She enjoyed that. It is dinnertime now so I must finish or there will be a row. Don't forget to let us know as soon as you move.
                        From your Loving Sweetheart,
                                Mabs.

In his last letter Bob had told Mabs that he was finally off to the Front, "We go for certain this week," he had confidently written. Instead, within days of writing that letter he was hospitalised at Aldershot and would not see the Front for another three months.

From Bob
87th Field Coy, 12th Div, Stanhope Lines, Aldershot.   Thursday, May 27, 1915
My Dear Kath,
Just a few lines to let you know I am still alive and have not left Aldershot yet. I have been in hospital with something the matter with my chest and arm, probably through inoculation. I am getting on all right though and shall be out in a few days. I don't like hospitals at all and that's the worst of the Army. They always send you there if there's anything the matter with you at all. It saves the regimental doctor the trouble of looking after you. I have not had a letter from either of you this week. Perhaps you thought I had gone from Aldershot. They keep putting it off. They don't seem to know their own minds two days

together. We should have left last Tuesday but it dropped through. You had better address letters to the Barracks as usual because I might be going out any day and then I might not get them at all. We had a nice time in London. Archy, Gordon and I went sightseeing on the buses and got back in time for dinner and went up on the Common with Chris and their kiddies in the afternoon and they all came down to Waterloo in the evening to see me off. Well Kath, I must close now with love and kisses.

From your loving brother, Bob.

I forgot to tell you that I got Charlie Dyer to ask his mother to have two photos taken off of the one he has; I mean the group.* She is having them done down at Kymes and they will be only a few shillings so if Mother would pay for them and let me know how much they are, I will refund the money. Mrs Dyer is bringing them up home when they are finished.

From Mabs

The Bedford, Newport, IW.   Friday, May 28, 1915

My Dearest Boy,

I'm sorry to hear that you've been ill again. I do hope you will soon be all right again. Was it anything very serious? Not blood poison, I hope.

It is a relief to know you are still safe in Aldershot. I have been hating the sight of the postman lately for fear he should bring the news that you had left.

I can see I shall have to keep my eye on Kath, to see that she keeps up her correspondence.

Did Kath tell you about our picnic that we had yesterday? We had a beautiful day and I am quite sure we were as bad as the little ones; we enjoyed it quite as well as they did. We saw a fox and whole families of baby rabbits. Some of them were black, like the one you brought home. I mean to take Kath to Ventnor soon now, before it gets too hot.

The 12th Battalion Warwicks left today for a place in Dorset. It didn't make much difference here though, we were just as crowded again tonight. If they go on as they are now we shall have to get five or six barmaids to look after them. Archie Street was here on Monday. I couldn't go near him. I told Mother I would when he wore khaki, not before. She said he thinks of joining up now. He might when he has to. It will make a few of them hop if they really mean compulsion. Thank heaven my boy had pluck enough to go without being driven. Well goodnight my love, because it is bedtime now.

With fondest love and kisses, I remain,

yours ever, Mabs.

From Kath

49, Carisbrooke Rd, Newport, IW.   Saturday, May 29, 1915

Dear Bob,

Your letter came this morning. We were glad to get it but very sorry to hear you're in the hospital. So you don't like hospitals? Don't you know they ain't very nice places? Is that your second turn at inoculation? It has been a long time

---

* This appears to be a reference to the photograph on page 84.

Bob in tropical kit which was probably issued in Italy. *"Quite a gay time. Thousands of British troops in topees."* Bob to Mother, September 5th, 1918, writing from Tezze D'Arzignano in Italy.

getting well if that was the first.

Dad asked Mr Holt if he could have a week off and he said he could have it when he liked, so Mother thinks she will try and go up tomorrow (Saturday) week. She is writing to tell Arch now. Now – about the pictures.* Jack (out the Asylum) told Dad they would be 9/6 the two, framed. Mother thinks you must have been pretty bad to be in hospital. Do you know where you are going after Aldershot?

Arch in his letter says you will be leaving shortly for the Front. We somehow thought that was it when you were here, and Mabel told me about it. I wish you could manage to get up to London again while Mother is there. Do you think you will? I wish you could come home too. People about here have been saying the war will be ended in June. Some old gypsy woman told someone in the train as sure as they had 15 shillings in their pocket. It happened to be true about the 15 bob but it remains to be proved about the war. I guess it is a bit too good to be true, don't you?

Mabel has just drifted in so I must finish now. She is just saying they have been having a dreadful rush tonight – more than Saturday night.

Goodnight now, Bob. Love and kisses from us all.

Ever your own loving, Kath.

From Chas
Lance Corp. Dyer, 46869, 87 Field Co. R.E. Battalion.   Thursday, June 3, 1915
Dear Jack,
Just a line hoping you are quite well. I received your letter safe. Glad to say we are getting on all right. I dare say you know Bob is not come with us. He is in hospital. Ask Mother to send the paper on to me. I shall get it if you put the address on above. I must now close,

From Chas.

From Mabs
The Bedford, Newport, IW.   Thursday, June 10, 1915
My Dearest Boy,
Why on earth didn't you let us have your address before? I expect my last letter has gone travelling off to France now, after the 87th Field Company, and I shall have to tell you all the same old news. We heard that Dyer had gone out last week. I suppose you think it hard lines being left behind but I can't say I do. I know you are safe for a little longer, but what is the matter with you to keep you there all this time?

In my last letter I told you that Ern was back in England again. He has a bullet in him this time – somewhere in his shoulder. He can't move that joint yet although he can manage to write himself now. I believe he has been under the x-rays since he wrote, to find the bullet. A sniper did it. I suppose you will have heard that Mr Salter from the Asylum was killed out there. Ern said in his letter that he helped to carry him out of the trench. He said that day was terrible. The Germans were shelling them all the time.

---

* One of these photographs appears on page 44.

I wish you were a bit closer. I would very soon be there to see you then. Poor old boy. Fancy having to stay there all this time and no one to take care of you. Mother said the other day that I ought to have gone in for the Red Cross work because so many of our poor fellows are wandering about for days before they can be attended to. She says that they want all the nurses they can get. I told her I would think about it. What do you think of it?

Elsie Attrill was married on the 2nd and she has sent you some wedding cake. She said I must send it on to you because she didn't know your address. I went out to the wedding but I must be developing into a crabbed 'old maid' because I don't like weddings now, till we have ours. T'isn't fair seeing other people getting married. Aunt Kate came last Saturday and goes back tomorrow. She has been to Atherfield today with Mother to see the new brides.

Wallace is just as much of a monkey as he always was. Aunt Kate says it doesn't matter what he does that he shouldn't do, he always wriggles out of it somehow. He doesn't grow, but he gets fatter. Wilf Woodford hasn't joined up yet. I don't suppose he will till they make him.

Our Ma seems to be having a good time in London. Don't you wish we were having our holiday again now? But I suppose it is no use wishing anything now. You must excuse the scrap of paper that I'm finishing on. I haven't any more here now. Everybody is very sorry for you and most concerned because you are there so long.

Perhaps you will be able to come and see us again now. Harry has hopes of a leave in the near future. All our old boys of the Warwicks have gone to the Front. It does seem hard for them. Nearly all the last ones were going second or third time and you may be sure they didn't like it. I don't like having to say goodbye to them either after getting so used to them, but I suppose it must be. If I don't stop now I shall be filling another ten sheets. Goodbye for the present my dearest. With fondest love,

from Mabs.

From Kath
49, Carisbrooke Rd, Newport, IW.   Thursday, June 10, 1915
Dear Bob,

We had your very pathetic letter this morning. It made me want to begin answering it at once, so here am I down in the summerhouse doing it. WHAT'S the matter with you?

You don't tell us what is the matter with you. There must have been something wrong to keep you in hospital all this time, poor old boy. Mabel has written too. Now I must tell you our mother has gone up to London. She went last Saturday. She actually made up her mind at last and she seems to be having fine old games too – going out to tea every day, visiting old friends. I'm sending you her letters and I shall send yours up to her. She is looking for it. Dad and I are blowing along somehow without her. Mabel and Mrs Woodbine and Mrs Wry are looking after us, keeping their eyes on us. In fact Mabel comes over every morning and set things a bit straight for us, and again in the afternoon and evening. If her Aunt hadn't turned up from Rugby I think she would have lived with us and done with it.

We only wish you were here too, to look after – it would be just right. Oh, you ought to have seen Dad cooking dinner on Sunday. He got fairly fed up with it at last, what with burning his fingers and one thing and another. He said things, he did, poor old Dad, but it turned out pretty well except the gravy and that wasn't exactly as Mother makes it – more like melted lard – but all things considered, we get on fairly well.

Fancy poor old Dyer gone. It seems a pity you are parted although it is a jolly good job you are not gone, don't you think? Mrs Dyer hasn't brought the pictures yet. We are expecting her every day. Someone told Dad she was bringing them last Saturday but they didn't turn up. I think I did tell you, didn't I, that they came to 9/6, sixpence taken off for having two done. Dad and I are just going to have our dinner now. I've got 11 silkworms (not the dinner I don't mean, only I nearly forgot to tell you).

Goodbye now Bob, heaps of love and kisses,
                    from your loving Kath and Dad.

From Mother
28 Barnard Road, Clapham Junction S.W.   Friday, June 11, 1915
Dear Bob,

Just got your letter from Kathie. I have felt anxious, have wondered really if they had sent you away. Why didn't you write and let us know that you were still in the hospital? I am afraid you have been worse than you have said, and here I am enjoying myself and was intending to go back to Newport tomorrow, but can't do it. They are so determined to keep me until Monday. I must go back then. Archie will pay my fare, he tells me. They are so kind to me in every way. I could stay here a long time and be very happy, but for leaving them at home. Kath seems to be getting on all right and Mabel is so kind to them and does all she can but I expect Kath has sung her praises. As I have been writing this, Jim Snow has come in. He is looking all right. He is waiting for orders to return to Windsor and is going to write to you. We are all going over to the Shaw's tomorrow. A. has got the day off. I went to see Frank Gaiger, your cousin. He has got a splendid house and a very nice person, his wife, four boys well grown and nice looking. The elder has joined. Try and see them if you come to London again. Arch thinks you will get a few days now as you have been ill. Everybody sends kind love to you.
                    Your loving Mother, Ellen Brimson.

From Jim
28, Barnard Road, Clapham Junction. SW.   Friday, June 11, 1915
Letter from Jim enclosed with Mother's
My Dear Old Bob,

As you see by the above address I have just looked in to see Chris and your Mother, and as your Ma was writing to you I am scribbling a line also.

How do you like hospital old man? If it's anything like Millbank, I pity you. When I was at the Second London General I enjoyed myself no end, but Millbank – Oh Lor! On London, I think tho' that they will go a bit more careful now that we've smashed one of them up. That fellow Warneford is a plucky beggar and deserved his VC.*

Have you heard any news about the Dardanelles? I heard on pretty good authority that there had been a very big victory and that Constantinople had fallen – whether it's true or not. I suppose, Bob, that if your Company has gone off you will in all probability go with the next lot.

I don't know what they are going to do with me. About a month ago I went before a medical board meeting and am now waiting their decision. I am not fit to go out to the Front, old man. I'd sooner get my check and start work again. It's no cop staying at home doing Guard's – What? Well, Bob old man, I hope you will soon be fit again.

From your old chum, Jim.

From Mabs

The Bedford, Newport, IW.   Monday, June 14, 1915

My Dearest Boy,

I am glad you liked the flowers. You shall have some more if you have to stay where you are much longer. The garden is just grand now and the roses come out as fast as they possibly can. I am sorry I forgot to tell you where Ern is. He is at the Leaf Square Hospital, Pendleton, Nr Manchester. We haven't heard any more from him yet. Your mother arrived this evening. Great excitement at 49, you may be sure. She has evidently enjoyed it, so that's a good thing. Archie said he only sent her home because it was Father's birthday. Your photographs of the Company arrived tonight. They are fairly good but not so good as the original. Now do hurry up and get out so that when Harry comes you can slip over and see him. He is expecting to come any time now. It is nearly time too; fancy being penned up on that ship all this time. It's just about enough to drive them mad.

I am glad you are well looked after. I believe it's those nurses keeping you there, not the arm. When Morry came home from hospital he said he didn't want to stay any longer because all the nurses were men, so I shall begin to think you are as bad.

Bee didn't come after all. Archie will come down with her in a week or two. I expect he wants a trip. Perhaps we are going to Ventnor this week. Don't you wish you could go? I do. Mr Sykes called last Friday. He told me that Mr Talbot has had a rough time since he went away. He went to the Front but he was invalided out because he had something wrong with his heart. When he came home he went back to the Asylum again, but the new Doctor wouldn't have him. He said his health wasn't good enough. He has got something to do at last, as a chauffeur to some Doctor here. We heard from Ern since I started this. He says he is to go to through an operation now. The bullet is somewhere in his

---

* On June 7, 1915, Flight Sub-Lieutenant Warneford, single-handedly attacked and destroyed a Zeppelin in mid-air after chasing it from the coast of Flanders to Ghent, where he succeeded in dropping his bombs on to it from a height of only one or two hundred feet. He later died in an air accident over Paris.

back. He says that is the worst of being thick skinned – it might have gone right through otherwise.

I have been to Newbridge today to see Dad's Aunt, who lives in that quaint little cottage Mother told us about. I shouldn't like to live in that one; it isn't a bit like ours. In one bedroom you can climb over on to the stairs. In fact, you would have to if you wanted to turn round. The best part is the stairs. They finish or start (it doesn't matter which) in the kitchen fireplace. Goodnight my sweetheart, it's bedtime again now. Hoping to see you soon, with fondest love and kisses,

I remain yours ever, Mabs.

From Mother
49, Carisbrooke Rd, Newport, IW.   Wednesday, June 16, 1915
My Dear Bob,
I left London Monday afternoon. I got home about 6.30 Monday evening and found them all right. Dad was at the station. Mabel was with Kathie. They seem to have managed very well. I did have a good time. Archie done all he could to make it a good holiday. Poor Charlie is at the Front in the firing line. They say he has written to you but has not got an answer. Perhaps you haven't received the letter. They tell me C. Harvie has deserted and joined the Navy – had the cheek to come over in his sailor clothes. Oh, we have the photos but we don't like them – they are not anything so good as Charlie's and you don't look a bit nice taken and they are not so large either. Now good love from us all,

ever your loving Mother Ellen Brimson.

From Mabs
The Bedford, Newport, IW   Sunday, June 20, 1915
My Own Dear Bobbie,
Morry was home on Thursday again yesterday. I suppose you will think it's nice to be him to pop over here when he likes.

Harry hasn't arrived yet, but I suppose he will in time. Now what do you think? I had four different engagements today, besides going out to tea. I was to row down the river to Cowes with one chap, ride down on the tail of another's motorbike and go for walks with two more. I'm getting on.

The wedding went off all right, but I won't send you a piece of cake because I don't want you to die yet.

The Boy Scouts are having Litchfield House on Thursday, so Gordon said this evening. They are going out near Shide Station. They will have to build their own hut so I suppose that will just please them. We didn't go to Ventnor after all. We are going next Monday unless you happen to come home next weekend; then, of course, it will be postponed.

I remain, yours ever Mabs.

Enclosing stamps because I know you can't get them. That letter hasn't come back yet.

From Mother
49, Carisbrooke Rd, Newport, IW.   Sunday, June 20, 1915
My Dear Bob,
I was glad to get your letter to know you was getting better. Did you see in the County Press about Sissies poor boy? It is very sad. She feels it bitterly, poor thing. I met Charlie's mother Sat. evening. She said they had heard from him that morning. He tells them they have not heard from you. He is at the base and is sent out to do different jobs in trenches and so on.
I have paid them the 10 shillings. I wouldn't think of touching your B.B. Roy has gone on for Watt's at Cowes; hope he will stay there. Dad is papering at the Asylum – finds it rather hard work. Mabel was here to tea Sunday. She made me a very nice present of a table centre. She made it herself. Have put in some stamps so you can write more. Write soon.
                              Ever your loving mother.

From Bob
C2 Ward, Connaught Hospital, Aldershot.   Saturday, June 26, 1915
My Dear Mother,
I received the cake all right. It was a beauty too. I enjoyed it a treat only it would have been much better if I had been there to eat it. I got the County Press all right last week. I saw about Sissie's boy. It's a very sad affair. I should like to hear from Charlie Dyer. I can't write to him until I know just about where he is laying. I'm sorry you have had to pay for those photos. I will try and refund the money later on. Dad must find paperhanging rather tiring work this weather, especially if it is those high rooms. I used to find them awkward enough. I'm glad Roy has got plenty of work. There's plenty about for everybody now by all accounts. Well Mother, I must close now,
                              ever your loving son Bob.
Thanks very much for the stamps.

From Mabs
The Bedford, Newport, IW.   Sunday, June 27, 1915
My Dearest Bobbie,
I am sorry you have had to wait a long time for this letter. We have heard from Ern at last. He has been through the operation, but they can't get at the bullet, so he says it will have to stay there to help make weight. It is to be hoped that it won't always affect his shoulder. He couldn't move it at first. He didn't mention whether he has been able to since.
Harry hasn't been home yet and we have had no news of him since.
I expect you will be sorry to hear that the little Welshman (Jones) was killed in France, I mean the one who used to come with Fred Hayles and those others. It hardly seems possible that he can be killed. I was sorry to hear it although he was such a tartar.
As long as your illness isn't very serious, I certainly won't wish you were out of

the hospital. You are far safer there than expecting every minute to be either blown up or poisoned. So now you just be quiet and don't growl any more, or you will be severely spanked. How are the nurses getting on? Don't, please, elope with any of them when you do come out.

Kath and I have been for a walk tonight – that old walk along Clatterford Road, down the hill into the farmyard where the hound lived, and through the little lane. Hang the place. I don't believe there's a square inch of it that you and I haven't been through. I can't go anywhere without thinking of the splendid times we used to have. I wonder if they will be just the same again, but I suppose we shall be older and staid, then.

We are going to Ventnor tomorrow. If it wasn't that I had promised Kath for such a long time, I wouldn't go near the place till you came home again. Well goodnight my love, or I shall never get to sleep tonight,

I remain, yours as ever, Mabs.

From Mother
49, Carisbrooke Rd, Newport, IW.   Monday, June 28, 1915
My Dear Bob,
Glad to get your letter but you did not say if you was any better. Mabel, Kitty, Kath and myself have been to Ventnor today – the long talked of visit has been done at last. We have enjoyed ourselves; the place is looking beautiful. We went to see Mrs Sims. She was glad to see us. She made Mabel promise to bring Kath out and spend the day with them. She says W. Murphy helped to save the Hill 60.* Gassed twice and now he is wounded. She doesn't know where Dick is.

I have sent this letter so you should have Dyer's address. He is so anxious to hear from you. You don't seem to say anything about coming home. Bob, it's a pleasure I'm afraid we shan't have now.
Believe me, ever your loving mother,
Ellen Brimson.

From Kath
49, Carisbrooke Rd, Newport, IW.   Wednesday, June 30, 1915
Dear Bob,
In your last letter you didn't tell us any different, so we concluded you were still in bed. Best place for you – you bide quiet. You have heard of our trip to Ventnor? It was grand. First we went up to St Boniface Road to have a look at 'Cromwell' – it did look nice.** Mother marched off to see 'Auntie Mall' and while she was in there, we (Mabel and Kitty and I) thought we would go on down to the pond. We ought not to have gone because then we lost Ma. I stayed by the pond while the others looked for her, and she was looking for us half over Ventnor. We found her at last, found her down the High Street and she wanted a cup of tea badly.

We went into a teashop and Ma asked for a pot of tea from the girl in the shop

---

* The Battle of Hill 60, near Ypres, 17 April to 7 May, 1915. The hill was captured quickly with only seven casualties. German attacks on the hill included the use of gas.

** 'Cromwell' was the family home of the Brimsons prior to leaving to go to Chesterfield.

and this girl kept looking at me. Presently she came up to me and said, "Before I go any further I must ask you, are you Kathie Brimson?" 'Course I said, "Yes," and she said, "Don't you remember me – Mabel White?" She was a little girl used to go to Clifton school the same time as I did. She used to come up to Cromwell sometimes and she remembers you making faces at us over the area steps. Said she knew me directly we came in the shop. Wasn't it queer? happening to go in that very shop. Well, after that we went to see Mrs Sims. She was so nice. We didn't go in and May Sims was exactly the same as ever she was, only bigger. She isn't a bit stuck up and she has got the dearest little baby. Mabel likes her ever so much and they want Mabel and me to go out there and spend all day with them soon.

Then we went down on the Esplanade. The Cascade was lovely, great improvement, but the sea was best of all. It was too rough to go onto the shore. We went to the far end of the Prom. The wind was high and the waves beating on the rocks. I would like best to have stayed there all day but, of course, the others got cold (just like 'em) and it was time to be off, so we spent the rest of the time up in the Park. Just the same old Park. The peacocks were not there that you and Mabel told me about, but there was a great big Hippodado there; and that was the end of our day.

Ivy says you haven't answered her letter yet and Gordon is Stationmaster at Calbourne again while the other is away on his holidays. He likes that job.

I must say goodbye now Bob. With best love and kisses,
Ever your own loving sister Kath.

From Roy
31 Melbourne Street. Newport, IoW   Friday, July 2, 1915
Dear Bob,
The above is my address, as you know, but I am now on the boat crossing to Southampton to paint the bottom of the yacht Liberty.* She is a hospital ship now. We are going through the transport ships now. There are about 30 moored off here. Start about 3 pm today, Friday, finish tomorrow Saturday. We get 30 shillings each for the job, get home about 5 pm, Newport.
Poor old Llewellyn has been killed at the Front, you remember Kitchener Dick, the Polo boys, so Dad told me last night. I am working for Messrs. Watts, Cowes. He has got part of the work in the docks on the torpedo boats. I am on deck work when we are there. Eightpence per hour. Will write again soon.
Yours Affectionately,
Roy.

From Bob
C2 Ward, Connaught Hospital, Aldershot.   Sunday, July 4, 1915
My Dear Mother,
I am pleased you sent Dyer's address; now I can write to him. As regards myself, I feel grand now only I've got to pick up again – I've lost a little weight. It will not be long now before I shall be out of it. I had a letter from Roy

---

* Liberty was a steam yacht built for Joseph Pulitzer and one of the largest private yachts of its day. She served as a Royal Navy hospital ship during World War I and was returned to the owner, Lord Tredegar, in January 1919.

yesterday. He said he was on his way to Southampton onboard the Liberty – a nice little trip for him.

You had a nice time at Ventnor by all accounts. Mabs and Kath tried to give you the slip, the wretches. I should like to come home. I'll try anyway but don't expect me until you see me.

Our lieutenant has been wounded. He is on the group in the centre. It was in the 'Daily Chronicle' but I saw no other casualties of the men. I received the County Press this morning. It comes just right for Sunday morning.

Well Mother, I must finish now as it is near dinnertime and I'm hungry,

Ever your loving son,

Bob.

From Mabs

The Bedford, Newport, IW.   Monday, July 5, 1915

My Dearest Sweetheart,

I didn't take a gloomy view of things because that pearl dropped out. I only meant that they were unlucky because they will keep on falling out. I have such a lot to write about this time that I expect it will take a week to write it.

Morry did go on the Thetis but he was able to get over on Tuesday, and was to come again on Saturday but they began ten days isolation on Thursday, so he wasn't able to come at all. They all had to leave the Barracks owing to an outbreak of spotted fever.

I intended to tell you all about my invitation in the last letter but I hadn't time to write a lot. Mr Holt asked your father who he would like to go out there for the Sports, so of course he said there was Kathie, Mrs Brimson and a friend. Mr Holt wasn't satisfied with being told that the friend was a young lady, he wanted to know if it was Bob's girl. Then he said Bob's girl must have a special invitation from him. It was very kind of him.

He came over to us in the grounds. He asked me if I was Miss Attrill, wanted to know all about you and said that as you were away he had sent the invitation just as if you had been there. These were nearly all fresh faces amongst the men. Mr Samuels, Mr Morris, Leadbeater and Mr Gayler were the only old ones I saw. Sykes and Devereux both stayed in. They had the Sanders band. They have only two left in their own band. We saw Peter still in his Dutch costume, Your father sent him some tobacco. Wasn't he pleased when I gave it to him? I couldn't help laughing when he said, "Thank you very much for it when you see him, won't you?" George Younger was still a Chinaman. I gave him some tobacco and he immediately fell in love with Mrs Reynolds and presented her with a Rosebud, which he had given him. He is still as mad as ever. He told us his old mother hadn't been to see him for a month, and she was over 80, but they sent her an invitation.

So villain, I hear you called us wretches in your mother's letter. You daren't say it in mine. Dick has joined up in Portsmouth. It must have been his name in the Roll of Honour

We all went for a grand joyride yesterday afternoon. Uncle, Mother, Dad, Kitty and myself. We went through Shorwell, Brighstone, Mottistone and Brook to Freshwater. Then to Totland, Yarmouth and home through Shalfleet. I wish you

County Press advertisements, 1915.

had been there. We shouldn't have ill-used you, my love. We are still waiting for Harry and we have heard nothing of him yet. Ern has been moved to Facit, near Rochdale.* He expects to come home soon.

Your Lieutenant must have been hit nearly as soon as he got there; it was rather hard luck. I wonder how the others are going on out there. Dyer writes but I never hear what he writes about.

Do you remember Gerry who used to come with Jock, Ern and the 'old woman,' we called him 'Monkey'? He was here last Saturday; he was wounded in April. He came over from Gosport to fetch a prisoner. The 'old woman' was all right when he came home in April but Jock is suffering with shattered nerves. Monkey has been recommended for the DCM and said he had earned it two or three times when he was home at Christmas, so I suppose he has got it now. It is Russian Flag Day here, today.** The band will play in the town at about 6 o'clock then they are to go to the Recreation Ground to play till 8.30.

You remember the little girl who was at the Asylum from Sandown? She died a little while ago. Her people took her home when they knew she wouldn't live. She had gone quite blind.

Well, it's nearly time I wound up. Goodnight my love, with fondest love and kisses. I remain, your loving sweetheart,

Mabs.

From Chas
46869, 87 Field Co. R.E. Battalion 12th Division, BEF.   Wednesday, July 7, 1915
Dear Bob,

I was very pleased to hear from you today. I thought you must have been shifted for I have written two letters to you. I suppose you have not received them. I am glad to say we are getting on all right out here. We are in Belgium now. When we landed in France on 2 June, we found we were at Le Havre. We stopped there all day for the horses and tool carts then we went to a rest camp at a place called Sanvie. We were there till 11 pm the next night, then we marched down to the train and left at 5 am next morning. We were 20 hours in the train; must not say where we are. You know that some of the sections work night and the others day. No.1 are sapping and mining, also some of No. 2, 3 and 4 are repairing trenches. It was on 24th June when the first casualty was. Poor Billy Lloyd was killed by a shell and Blanch was wounded in the shoulder. He is in England, about a mile from his home, and Fred Chappell was hit in the head but he has joined us again, and Cecil Brims was hit in the elbow. He is well again. They were carrying timber along the trenches at the time it happened; that was in France. We have shifted since that on Monday. Sal Guyford in No. 2 was shot through the leg last night. No. 3 were out and Corporal Bailey was shot through the chest. They think it has gone through the lung, so you will see the 87th has been near it. I have not been down to the trenches yet. I am Sanitary Inspector, looking after the camps. We are in separate camps, No's 3 and 4. No's

---

* Mount Pleasant Auxiliary Hospital, Facit, Rochdale. At the outbreak of the First World War the British Red Cross set up temporary hospitals as wounded men began to arrive from abroad. The patients were usually less seriously wounded than at other hospitals.

** British towns held 'Russian Days,' where Russian themed Flag Day badges would be sold to generate funds for the Russian war effort and in return, selected Russian cities would hold British Flag Days to raise funds for Britain.

1 and 2 are together and headquarters. Our chaps are working right up in the firing line, only about 80 yards from the Germans in some places. What about the lads that said we should never get to the Front? We are sleeping in a barn. It is quite comfortable. We have no blanket now. It was very sad news about G. Salter. Fancy Ern Attrill being in the same trench. He seems unlucky – wounded again. I had a programme sent to me of the Whitecroft sports on Saturday, and am sending it to you. I should have liked to have been there but no luck. I will drop a line to your mother and let her know how things are out here. All the boys have been asking after you – somebody every day. I must now close, Hoping to see you soon,

from your old pal, Charlie.

From Mother
49, Carisbrooke Rd, Newport, IW.   Friday, July 9, 1915
My Dear Bob,
I was glad that you are feeling so much better. I suppose you will be out soon. Your father was talking to Mr Holt the other day about you. Dad told him you was still in the hospital. He says, tell him he is in a damn sight better place than at the Front. What do you say?
 I have been to the sports. Went with Mab and Kath and Mrs Reynolds. It was a long and hot walk but I enjoyed it very much. We had a good tea which put us right. I thought of Dad and the long walk for him after his day's work. Dick Murphy has joined up. They don't know where he is. He has five children. You never say if you want anything. Let me know if you do, won't you? The garden is looking so pretty in the front and the back is splendid. We have had some rough winds; it has blown the pears down a lot now. Goodbye, Bob. You shall have the paper Sunday,

ever your loving Mother, Ellen Brimson.

From Bob
C2 Ward, Connaught Hospital, Aldershot.   Saturday, July 10, 1915
My Dear Mother,
I am practically all right again now and I expect I shall leave here sometime next week. It is all very well for Mr Holt to talk but I can't stop here simply because I am better off – we hear it quite enough from the wounded that are here in hospital. I've got one of them in the next bed to me. He's been out almost from the start. We hear plenty of tales but we are used to them. I'm rather doubtful whether I shall be sent to my old company. I might be in another one altogether, which won't be very nice as they will all be strangers.
I am glad you had a good time out at the Asylum. It is a long walk as I found out many a time. I should like you to send me some tobacco, St Bruno and B.D.V. mixed. We can get plenty of cigarettes but it is a hard job to get tobacco. Well Mother, I must close now. With love to you Dad and Kath,

ever your loving son, Bob.

From Mabs
The Bedford, Newport,   Sunday, July 11, 1915
My Own Dear Boy,
At last I have managed your letter. I hope the last one didn't make you faint. I am at my usual game; writing instead of going to bed. I did hope to see you this weekend. I quite expected you till about 8 o'clock Saturday evening and then I suddenly thought you were not coming. Harry wrote this week. He is still living in hopes of getting leave shortly. He is sorry for you being ill all this time.
I am a thick-headed idiot. I keep on forgetting to ask you if there is anything you would like sent to you. If there is, be sure you let me know, although I hope you would not have been afraid to ask if there was anything you wanted. I am sending you some cigarettes. I expect those will be all right. Ern wrote in the week. He still says he can't use his arm – he thinks it will take a long time – otherwise he is quite all right. Our Territorials are supposed to leave for the Dardanelles this week. Hoping you are still getting better.
                              Your loving sweetheart, Mabs.

From Charlie
87 Field Co. R.E. Battalion 12th Division, BEF.   Wednesday, July 14, 1915
Dear Mrs. Brimson
Just a line hoping you are all quite well as it leaves me at present. I had a letter from Bob the other day. Very glad to hear he is getting on all right. He has had a rough time of it. We shall be looking for him out here very shortly. All the boys are asking when he is coming. We are billeted in a barn somewhere in Belgium – nice and comfortable. We have got used to the noise of the guns now. They are firing all day, and every day and night we are very busy. Plenty to do out here in the trenches. I must now close.
                              From Charlie.

From Mother
49, Carisbrooke Rd, Newport, IW.   Thursday, July 15, 1915
My Dear Bob,
I was pleased with poor C. Dyer's letter. Dad and Kath and the Attrills have read it and Dad has taken it out to the Asylum. They liked to read it and now his brother has taken it to Charlie's Mother. When they seem to be very busy at shooting out there it seems a sorry thing that if you do go that you should not be in the same Company. All the same, you will be glad to get out of the hospital for it must be very depressing at times. What tales you must have heard and bad sights. Try and write to Archy and Chris. I hope C. Dyer will write to me. I shall be pleased to answer it. We are having a lot of wet and it is bad for the children. Lea Pashey, Mabel and Kathie has just gone down to the Rink and is wanting me to come to see Dick Turpin*. I think I shall go, so goodbye my dear. Have put a stamp in. Write soon. Love from us all,
                              ever your loving Mother.

---

* A Newport cinema on the Lugley Street/Hearn Street corner. That week's County Press reported, "At the Rink, the film depicting Dick Turpin's ride to York proved very popular." The Rink opened in 1911 and closed in 1935.

A pontoon bridge constructed by Royal Engineers over the Marne at La Ferte sous Jouarre, France, September 1915. *"We parade about 7.30 in the morning for exercise and then after breakfast we do a bit of trenching or pontooning on the river."* Bob to family, December 16th, 1915.

Chateau Tirancourt

"We are in the park of a large French château. I believe it has been deserted by the owners as the dresses and clothes are still hanging up inside and the kids' toys are laying about. The Germans came through this part when our army was retreating from Mons." Bob to family, December 16th, 1915.

From Bob
Connaught Hospital, Aldershot.   Thursday, July 15, 1915
My Dear Mother,
Just a line to let you know I am going out of hospital tomorrow. They are sending me to Newark, close to Chesterfield. Our reserve section are there so there will be some fellows I know. It's better than going to a strange company. It does not look as if I shall get any leave but it can't be helped. I might be lucky and get one later on. Some of the Sherwood Rangers Yeomanry that I belonged to came from there. I will write and let you know particulars later on. Received the baccy all right; just what I wanted. Love to all at home,
                                         ever your loving son Bob.

From Mabs
The Bedford, Newport, IW   Thursday, July 22, 1915
My Dearest Boy,
I expect you think me a hopeless case by this time but never mind. I expect you will feel better when you see this. We (Ethel and Nellie) left here about 6.45 am, Tuesday, and went out to Shorwell with the mail cart. From there we walked to Blackgang, through Chale. We went to see the Chine. It is a grand place but not so nice as Shanklin. It is a totally different Chine to that at Shanklin, much larger, and very wild and bleak. We roamed around in there for some time then found our way over the Downs to Niton. From there we walked on into Ventnor. It was a glorious day. We all enjoyed it and were none the worse for it. Of course, we came home by train from Ventnor.
It was all right for you to be able to see Chris when you went up. When I do write again I shall just about talk in plain English to them, lazy beggars. You shall share my secret now, my dear boy – If they are going to keep you there for a long time and not let you come home, I think that I will be up north when I get my holiday, instead of going to Bristol. How would that suit? I haven't said anything about it to anyone except Mother and you. Albert Hawkins has sent Flo her ring. It has red and white stones – very pretty, but not like mine. I have had our initials engraved on it like this EB O MA – the circle represents the centre of the ring. I suppose it ought to have been EGB but never mind, it won't hurt on that. With fondest love and all the kisses,
                                         yours as ever, Mabs.

From Bob
No.5 Depot Co, Hawton Road Camp, Newark-on-Trent, Saturday, July 24, 1915
My Dear Mother,
I received the County Press all right (*see over*) but have received no letters. As you see by the above address, I have been moved again. We have left the huts and gone under canvas. The company I belong to now supply the draft for the Front, or rather we go to the base and are then sent to any company that are short of men. They give us two days notice when we are going. There were 160 left last Sunday night for France. I am practically all right again now. I am having seven days light duty; have not been parading with the rest yet. I managed to get out at Clapham Junction and see Chris and afterwards Archy

came as far as King's Cross with me. There are plenty of fellows from the 87th company down here which makes it a bit better. Hoping to hear from you soon,
Ever your loving son Bob.

County Press, July 24, 1915
Private Ernest Attrill, eldest son of Mr. M. Attrill, of the Bedford, The Mall, serving in the Hants Regiment on the Western front, has again been wounded, this time by a bullet in the shoulder, and is in hospital at Manchester.

From Mother
49, Carisbrooke Rd, Newport, IW.   Sunday, July 25, 1915
My Dear Bob,
I was glad to get your letter this morning. I had been wondering how you was after so long an illness. About going to the Front – I suppose it is what you and all the others are looking forward for, or at least expecting, but I hope you will have got your strength up well before you go for it is very rough do's out there I think. Oh, I do hope you will be all right and be near Charlie. I had a letter from him last week, not a very big one, but now I have heard from you I will answer it. Morry and Harry have just come in. Harry came home yesterday and will go again tomorrow. Morry seems to come home whenever he likes. Harry is looking well and jolly as ever. Mabel has just come in for us all to go over to tea; Doris and Kath will go. Dad goes out to the Asylum all right. Let me know of anything else you may want. I hope you will soon be strong as ever.
Ever your loving Mother, E Brimson.

From Bob
No.5 Depot Co, Hawton Road Camp, Newark-on-Trent, Thursday, July 29, 1915
My Dear Mother,
I got your letter on Tuesday morning. I was lucky to get it too, as the postman was just going to take it back and then it would have gone to the Front somewhere; you have to be on the spot when he is calling them out. I did not get the County Press or John Arum's letter. I don't suppose I shall now.
I am practically all right again now and have done a couple of marches with the Company. There was another draft picked out yesterday morning but I don't know yet whether I shall be one or not; I was vaccinated anyhow. It isn't much cop waiting about here. They hardly know what to do with you to pass the time away. We had a VC visit the town last night. He is one of the Sherwood Foresters. They had a band to lead the way and then a lot of R.E.s. Then came the VC in a motor with the Mayor and then heaps of other motors with recruiting posters on them and of course, followed up with the Boy Scouts. The town was decorated with flags and you couldn't move for people. He gave a speech in the big market square. I daresay you will see something about it in the papers. They didn't give Harry a very long leave. I suppose he is still on the Queen Mary or is he in Barracks? Morry is having the best time. Am sending a packet of letters home. You needn't open them; you can put them in my box upstairs. Hoping you are all keeping quite well.
From your affectionate son Bob.

From Charlie
87 Field Co. R.E. Battalion 12th Division, BEF.   Sunday, August 1, 1915
Dear Mrs. Brimson,
I had a letter from Bob yesterday. So glad to know he is quite well again. He said he might be put on Drafts at any time. I do hope he will come somewhere near us so I shall be able to go and see him, for I have not met anyone I know out here yet, outside of our own chaps. You want to know a little about Belgium. Well it might be all right in peace time but it is not up to much now. The part we are in, the villages are smashed to pieces. Last week a church on our right, about 300 yards away, was set on fire by a shell. It is the same all round here – nothing but shells flying about all day and night. We have got used to the noise now.
We are camped in a farm. It is very comfortable but not like home, for we have no blankets here. They were taken away soon after we arrived in France but we can do without them now for the weather is grand today, something like summer, but it has been very cold and wet. I have not been up in the trenches very much for I am on duty in the camp – quite a bit of luck for me. We are not allowed to say very much about things out here. I expect you know that, but I hope I shall be able to tell you some day. I don't think there's any more now.
From Charlie.

A year after enlisting at Newport, Bob finally arrived in France.

From Bob
80th Field Coy., R.E, 18th Div. B.E F   Sunday, August 15, 1915
My Dear Mother and Father,
We left Rouen last Sunday, about 22 of us, and we are now a few miles behind the firing line, 'Somewhere in France'. We can see the Germans shelling our first line of trenches in the distance. There was great sport yesterday. A German aeroplane was scouting overhead and we were shelling it. We could see the shells bursting all round it against the clear blue sky. Some of our planes chased it but whether it was brought down, we don't know. He had some pluck and no mistake, as some of the shells exploded quite close to him. We can't get any papers here so I should like you to send me a weekly paper – any one will do. We have heard rumours that the Allies have forced the Dardanelles. I hope it is true.
We are living in an old barn in an orchard. The one thing we are troubled with is flies. I've never seen so many in all my life as there is in these French villages. The peasants are dirty people. The women seem to do most of the work about here ploughing and working in the fields.
Will you please send me some writing paper and envelopes as it is impossible to buy anything here, even if we had any money. Be careful how you address the letters. Please let Archy and Chris know my address so that they can write. Best love to you all at home, hoping to hear from you soon,
your affectionate son, Bob.

1915

From Kath

49, Carisbrooke Rd, Newport, IW.   Wednesday, August 18, 1915

Dear Bob,

Here have I written two long letters to you, and you say you haven't got either. Just fancy my doing all that for nothing. Mother will write in a day or two and says you must let her know if you get this letter safely, for she wants to send you a parcel. Chris and Arch are coming on Saturday. Oh, if only you could come too, wouldn't it be fine? But that is to come. We don't know how long they will stay. We have had Doris down here all day helping us get a bit ready for them. It will be nice to have them, a nice change. Mother has just been laughing at me for being so long writing this but it's no use, I can't write in a hurry, especially when everybody is talking. Doris has finished hers and now Mabel has begun; perhaps I shall finish this by the time she does. You didn't say a word about Charlie. Have you heard from him lately – and I suppose haven't seen him? Now you are in an orchard I suppose you get plenty of fruit. Mother is going to send you some pears, they are nice now. Doris is tucking them in like mad. I really can't think of anything more to say now. Heaps and heaps of love and kisses from us all,

ever your loving, Kath.

Roy has got a job up Parkhurst; sends his love.

From Doris

31, Melbourne St. Newport.   Wednesday, August 18, 1915

Dear Nunk Bob,

I am writing this letter at 49, Carisbrooke Road. I have been here all day helping Grandma to get ready for Chrissie and Uncle Archie, Marjorie and Dorothy who are coming on Saturday. Your letter arrived at dinner time. Grandma was upstairs at the time. She saw the postman coming across the road and didn't I race down the stairs to get the letter? Grandma read it out to us. You seem to have put so much on such a small piece of paper. Kathie did not quite know if you had her letter or not, for you asked for the very things she had thought to send you. Grandma is getting some envelopes etc. ready now to send to you. I hope it will reach you all right, because if it doesn't this 'ere letter won't, for I think it's going in the same envelope.

The weather here has been rotten. It is ever so changeable. Clouds keep on rolling up, and between the clouds and rain you get a glimpse of blue sky. Mabel and Kathie and Kathleen and me (and some friends of Mabel's) arranged for to go for a picnic on a lovely day last week. It was lovely for two days before but on the day we went it was cloudy but we did go up to "Bukkum up" in that pit up there and the weather was fine after. We are having our summer holiday now but three weeks have gone already. Daddy is working at Parkhurst now. A little while ago he was working at Week's the confectioner, and did he bring some sweets home? Bought them cheap. We had to sign the National Registration papers on Sunday and we wanted four in our house, Daddy, Ma, Gordon and me. In one column you had to state whether single, married, or widowed and daddy put Married as big as you like. One of our school teachers brought the papers round. I saw in the Lloyds on Sunday that lots of labourers left Lancashire and roundabout for Ireland, so as to miss the registration, and farmers were left with no one. There was another train smash at Weedon between Northampton and Rugby and about 12 killed. We had more air raids in England. Have no more room now and must close.

From your loving niece, Doris.

A week after his arrival in France, Bob joined the 3rd Entrenching Battalion, one of the many temporary units formed during the early days of the war. The Battalions were used as pools of men, from which drafts of replacements could be drawn by the infantry battalions.

From Bob
R.E., (Attached) 3rd Entrenching Battalion, B.E.F c/o GPO
Sunday, August 22, 1915

My dear Mother and Father,
You will see by the above address that it is altered again. The 80th are going away today and for the present we are attached to the infantry. It might be altered again any day but this will find me all right. I got the packet of writing paper and envelopes and letter enclosed all right. Thanks very much. Kath says she has sent two letters but I have not had them, and only one of Mabel's which she sent on the ninth. It took 11 days to find me. I should like you to send me out a pipe if you could manage it, one with a bone mouthpiece or something similar. Be careful to pack it tight.

I am glad Archy and Chris have managed to come down. I should like to be there myself. I meant to have asked you if you got my kitbag all right and if you are receiving the extra money yet. We are allowed five francs per week out here but of course there are no shops, just one or two inns where they sell red and white wine which tastes like vinegar – we don't trouble it much. There was a terrible bombardment last night but as a rule it is pretty quiet during the day. It is a common sight now to see them potting at the aeroplanes but they never seem to hit them – at least we have never seen one struck. I think I would rather take my chance on the old earth all the same.

Remember me to the folks at Whitecroft, Dad. I have written to Charlie Dyer but I have had no answer as yet so I don't know how he is going on or where he is. It was a very nice letter that Doris wrote; she can write some more. Well I must close now.

Ever your loving son, Bob.

I was too late to get this posted today but since writing it we have witnessed a fight in the air. A German plane flew right over our heads and very soon was chased by the British. Our guns were shelling it all the time and then our plane opened fire on her with a machine gun. Soon after, a French monoplane joined in the chase. The French was the faster one and appeared to overtake the German. They then disappeared from sight so I cannot say what the result was but I don't think it was possible for the German to escape.

From Bob
(Attached) 3rd Entrenching Battalion, BEF   Thursday, August 26, 1915
My dear Mother and Father,
Just a few lines to let you know I am going on all right. Just got the County Press now, and also a postcard from Mrs A. I hope there is nothing wrong with you all at home. I wrote to Kathy last. Did she get it? I like to hear from you once a week at least. I have had one letter from Mabel and I have not had any of the postcards she promised to send. Are you getting your money again all right now? If not, you had better write to the Paymaster at Chatham again and wake them up.
I think Dad might drop me a line now and again. Remember me to all of them at Whitecroft. I have had two letters from C. Dyer. He is getting on all right and wants to come and see me but I hardly think he can manage that as he is in Belgium and I am in France. He must have forgotten he is at the Front. Roy promised to send me an Anglo-French dictionary but I haven't got it yet. I keep looking forward to all these things but they are a long time turning up.
We are having nice weather here and we get plenty to eat. We are a lot better off than the Island Terriers at the Dardanelles; they seem to be having it pretty hot out there. The cake you sent out was a real treat. Don't be long before you send another if you can manage it. Best love to you all at home,
                              your affectionate son, Bob.

From Bob
(Attached) 3rd Entrenching Battalion, B.E.F. c/o GPO Tuesday, August 31, 1915
My dear Mother and Father,
I have just received another of your letters written last Wednesday, and also the County Press. It is a very interesting account of the Island Terriers in action, they are making a name for themselves (*see opposite*). Referring to the bag I sent, it contained a suit and a pair of boots, a towel and my brass cleaning gear and one or two other little things. Someone must have been helping themselves.
We had an exciting time last night when half the village was burnt down. The houses here are mostly built of mud plaster and wooden beams – very ancient places. The fire started in one of the outhouses and it quickly spread right and left to the adjoining houses. The outhouse belonged to a farm and there were stables and cow houses all round the yard. Of course, all the soldiers were called out and they had no fire brigade of any kind in the village. All we could do was to pull down parts of the stables to prevent the fire from reaching the house. I worked jolly hard for an hour and a half saving cattle and carrying pigs out under my arms and saving the furniture or what we could. The heat was so terrific I had a job to stick it.
The French people seemed to lose their heads altogether. They never attempted to help, at least not where we were. There was a lot of straw laying about and also hay ricks which of course helped the fire. I think we managed to save most of the furniture for the people but there were plenty of pigs refused to be caught and so got roasted. The fire stopped just a short way from the old barn where we are billeted. There happened to be a brick gable-end on that house which prevented it going further. It was a good job for us that it stopped where it did.

I wrote to Mabs on Saturday. I hope she got it all right. I shall be glad of a parcel any time, especially one of your cakes – a thing we can't get here – and also a stick of shaving soap. Tell Roy he can send me that French dictionary. It is just what I do want. I will drop him a line later on. I hope Chris and Arch and kiddies are having a good time. I should like to have been with you on Bowcombe Down. It will be lovely up there now. Well I've not much more to tell you this time. Love to you all at home,

from your affectionate son, Bob.

County Press July 17, 1915

VENTNOR ARTILLERYMAN'S TRIBUTE TO ISLAND TERRITORIALS.

Sergt. Percy Channlng, R.O.A., who is serving in the Persian Gulf, in a letter to his father at Ventnor, says : "I am proud to say our No. 1 gun was the first to fire in the action: Sergt. Arthur Honeybourne (another Ventnor man and an old schoolfellow of the writer's) was second. It was a fine sight. All our guns were laid on the enemy's position, and the first gun was the signal for the others to open fire. The gunboats and all were in it. Our infantry went up in boats. We only had 12 casualties. Cannot say how many of the enemy 'went west,' but hundreds were captured and a terrible lot killed. Even when we brought the prisoners in they still had their hands over their ears, so awful had been the bombardment. Just tell some of those fools at home who want an extra penny an hour it is ammunition that wins a fight. If we had not had the ammunition in this fight our infantry must have been wiped out. We are driving the Turks up the river. We hear they have already retired 60 miles in two days. We also sank a gunboat of theirs above here, and nine guns have been captured. I was with A. Honeybourne and Francis Hess last night. The Terriers made a name for themselves in this fight. Their shooting was a credit to any Regular battery. Everybody is talking about it, and you can tell them at Ventnor that the work of the battery has made a great impression here. The heat is terrible. 140 degrees in the shade. Honeybourne, Hess, E. Wright, and. W. R. Langdon were among those who volunteered from the 4th Hants (Ventnor) Battery for active service in the Persian Gulf.

From Bob
Attached 3rd Entrenching Battalion, B.E.F. c/o GPO

Thursday, September 9, 1915

My dear Kath,

Another of your letters has turned up; also one from Mabs and another from C. Dyer. They were dated July 31st and addressed to Newark. The three of them were tied up together and they have been all over the show but anyway, they have found me at last. A quarter of an hour ago I actually met a fellow that was in hospital with me at Aldershot. They have just arrived in this village and he happened to stray into our billet. It's very funny how you meet people, especially in such out of the way places.

I have not had any letters this week except the odd one that has just arrived, and a weekly paper. I expected to hear from Archy but have not heard anything yet.

I hope Mother and Dad are keeping all right and that she has heard something about the money by now. They are awfully slow with anything like that.
Tell Mother she needn't be frightened at sending parcels and they must be packed very strong. I have a craving for sweet stuff now and we look forward to letters and the parcels. I read the account of the Island 'Terriers' in the last County Press. There are three or four of the chaps I know in the casualty list. I think they have done jolly well out there. We are still going on the same here. We keep living – that is the main thing – and look forward to the time when we can get back to 'Blighty' I hope Mabs got my last letter although it was a short one. I shall be writing to her again in a day or two. Remember me to all our friends and tell them I'm in the pink.

Ever your loving brother, Bob.

From The Regimental Paymaster,Chatham,
To : - Mrs Brimson   Monday, September 13, 1915
As your son E. G Brimson has increased his Allotment of 6d per day to 1/9d per day, I enclose herewith Army Money Order for 53/9d., being arrears of 1/3d. per day from 3.8.15 to 13.9.15. Your Postal Draft book has been recalled for adjustment to weekly rate of 17/6d from 14.9.15.

A P K Sinclair, for Regimental Paymaster. Chatham.

From Clement *
31, Melbourne St, Newport IW   Sunday, September 26, 1915
Dear Uncle Bob, I am Standard 1 in the big boy's school. I went and got some blackberries in my jersey down a lane, when I got home Ma gave me a hiding 'cos I juiced my jersey.

From Clement.

From Kath
49, Carisbrooke Rd, Newport, IW.   Saturday, October 2, 1915
Dear Bob,
Your letter came this afternoon. Ma and Dad had a collision in the passage running to pick it up. It made us wild, though, that the box had been broken open and those nice little scissors lost, and looking glass, but Mother has just bought a glass up from the town, like the one you spoke about in your letter, an unbreakable one.
Mother is just off up to see Mrs Dyer; they pay each other a visit now and then and talk about their boys. Wouldn't poor old Charlie be pleased if you could get near him? I wonder if he is all right. Fancy you not getting half the candles, the very things you wanted most, but we will be making up another box. It shan't come open then – Mother will see to that. Somebody told Dad they were no use unless sewn up in canvas, so Ma's going to stitch the box up in canvas every time now, unless a better kind of box turns up. Mabel came over to tea yesterday (Sunday) and we got Dad and Ma to play Ludo with us. Well,

---

* Clement is six years old.

you see, we have got to play those idiotic games; we do nothing else but talk about 'War' and it gets on your nerves a bit sometimes. It does on Mother's, so anything is better than that. It makes us want you here, though. Arch said in his last letter they had Jim and George in last Sunday night, "If only they could have had Bob too."

Glad Chris wrote to you. She hasn't written down here since she went back; left it to Arch so far; that's just like her.

Mother says she will see about that money of yours when she goes down to the Post Office tomorrow. Those Post Office people doesn't seem to know what they are up to, seems to me.

I'm beginning my cards again. Got an order for two miniatures for Miss Walcroft and a dozen Christmas cards for somebody else. This kitten of yours is worse than a monkey. He is all legs and eyes at present; growls and bites and scratches and plays all the same time, nags his old mother to bits. Yours ain't a 'common or garden' cat. He is learning to stand on his head and bite his tail now like this (*see front inside cover*) When it gets like this, it shows I haven't got any much more to write about. Well goodnight now, dear old boy.

Ever your loving, Kath.

After six weeks with the 3rd Entrenching Battalion, Bob joined the 7th Division, 95th Field Company, Royal Engineers, where he was to remain for the rest of the war.

From Bob
Royal Engineers   Wednesday, October 6, 1915
My Dear Mother and Father
Just a line to tell you that I am on the move again. There are ten of us picked out to go to the 95th Field Company, further up the line, and a lot nearer to where Charlie Dyer is. I am quite all right and in the best of health. I hope you are all quite all right at home. I got a letter – in fact a lot – from all the kiddies at Roy's. They were quite amusing, especially Clem's and Ivy's. I will try and answer them when I have a bit of time. I had a nice parcel from Mabel. It is a treat to get them out here. I hope Kath got the last letter I wrote to her. Is Dad still going out to Whitecroft? Make use of my money whenever you want it. Don't Forget. Well Mother, I must close now.

With fondest love from your loving son, Bob.

War Diaries were handwritten or typed documents providing a daily account of the activities of Army units on active service. The Diary was written up each evening by a junior officer and usually signed off by a senior officer. In addition to the daily entries there might also be sketches, maps and Operational Orders included. The War Diary of the 95th Field Company covering the period from August 1915 to November 1917 is in the National Archives and a scan of the complete document can be found on their website,

The Raid

"Bert! It's our officer!"

"We go up in the trenches mostly at night and the Germans keep us illuminated with their starlights. They send them up right along the battle line as far as you can see each way." Bob, October 15th, 1915.

A Bruce Bairnsfather cartoon from Mab's collection of *The Bystander* magazines. See footnote page 152.

www.nationalarchives.gov.uk; reference WO 95 1645 4. The 95th Diaries for the remainder of the war also exist but at the time of writing, 2016, they have not been transcribed and are not available online.
From now until November 1917, each of Bob's letters are accompanied by that day's Diary entry. They are verbatim transcripts.

War Diary : "Beuvry, nr. Bethune - Carried on work on 2nd Line straightening C Trenches where they enter it from Front and providing wiring loopholes."

From Bob

95th Field Company, 7th Division. BEF   Friday, October 15, 1915

My Dear Mother and Father

Just a few lines to let you know that I am still going on all right. I got two letters on Tuesday and the parcel arrived yesterday, quite safe and sound, for which I thank you very much. It is nice to get parcels out here. Now we are farther up the line I expect they will take a bit longer to come. The razor and the scissors are just what I did want. They are fine. I forgot to tell Kath that chewing gum* was A1. I've seen heaps of fellows with it out here.

The sweets are very nice as we can't get any water when we are up in the trenches. We go up mostly at night and the Germans keep us illuminated with their starlights. They send them up right along the battle line as far as you can see each way. The nearest I have been is 30 yards off their frontline and they were sending 'whizz bangs' over then.** They are things I don't care for much about as they travel so quickly, but we are giving them a terrible pasting with our artillery. They are being bombarded continually, night and day. When we are up there we can't hear ourselves speak for the noise. They are getting what they asked for now.

I will write to the ladies at Seaford as soon as I get a little bit more time. We don't get quite so much as we did before. I hope Dad and Kath and you Mother are keeping all right. Whatever you do, you must not worry about me as I shall be all right. I am glad you are trying to get the rest of the money from Chatham. Live as comfortable as you can with it.

Where we are now we can get English beer and stout, and we can buy almost anything we want. The French people do our washing for us, they are a better class altogether. Well, I must close now.

Ever your loving son,

Bob.

PS I forgot to tell you we get lovely baths out here. There are hot shower baths and about 20 of us go at once. Tell Mabs I am writing to her soon.

---

* Chewing gum first appeared in America in the 1860s.

** 'Whizz bang' refers to the noise made by shells from German field guns due to the fact that the shells travelled faster than the speed of sound – the soldiers heard the "whizz" noise of a travelling shell before the "bang" issued by the gun itself. Whizz bangs were much feared since there was virtually no warning of incoming fire.

*During late 1915 a British aircraft crash-landed very near Bob and his fellow
soldiers on the frontline. Unfortunately, Bob's letter home giving an account
of the crash has not survived, only Mother's reply to him in this next letter. It
has not been possible to positively identify the plane but research suggests it
was probably a Royal Aircraft Factory B.E.2.*

*Bob managed to secure a piece of the wing canvas of the plane for himself,
a part of the RAF roundel, and sent it back to Newport. The canvas still exists,
now in the possession of Richard Brimson. See page 132.*

From Mother

49, Carisbrooke Rd, Newport, IW.   Sunday, October 17, 1915

My Dear Bob,

By your last letter to Mabel you say that you are much more comfortable. We
all feel glad for you but we are afraid you are in the war more than you have
been.

Mrs Dyer called the other day. She had just heard from Charlie. We all think
you must be near one another. I hope it is so. He sent this envelope now, to be
sent to you so that you can see how his letter went about to find you, and after
all, came back to him. By the stamps it seems they do their best for you boys to
get your letters. Send it back when you write; we will keep it safe.

How startled you must have been for the aeroplane to come right over you like
the one did. Glad you sent the piece. Now it is being taken great care of. Mabs
thinks a lot of it. She will have it put in a frame for the war it comes of.

I hope they will let you have all the letters. Archie says ask Bob if he gets the
Pictorial and letters. He don't get an answer. He would like to when you have
time. Everybody is anxious to know how you are and sends their love to you,
Bob. Ern was in today. He is got thin and seems so quiet. He was on the list last
week to be sent away, then stopped for a bit, so he don't know how soon now
that he may go.

We have had your dad home for a week with a cold. He thinks of going out
there tomorrow. He don't seem to be able to manage the ladder. It is heavy, he
says. Now I will stop. I am looking for every post and will answer very soon.
Dad sends his love, also Kathie. Hoping this letter will find all right and in good
health.

Believe me, ever your loving mother,
Ellen Brimson.

War Diary : "Gorre - Working on Parapet Fire Steps and Communications Trenches."

From Bob

95th Field Company, 7th Division. BEF   Monday, October 25, 1915

My Dear Kathie,

I thought I would write to you this time as you haven't had one for a long while.
I have heard from Chris. They sent me a parcel, a cake that Archy made, and
chocolates that the kiddies saved their money up to buy. I had a letter and some
very funny sketches that they drew. I am enclosing them. They have been

having some frights by all accounts with the Zeps. It's getting a bit too thick. I had a big surprise on Friday last. I was coming back to our billet, which is a big brewery, when who should I see standing outside but C. Dyer. I think it was the happiest day that I've had in France – we had such a lot to tell each other. He couldn't stop long that night, as it happened, so I went to see him next day. In fact all the company, what is left of them, they were all pleased to see me and want me to come back; they are quite close to us. Charlie came to see me on Sunday afternoon but I had gone up to the trenches so I did not see him again. Talking about the trenches – they are awful. Up to your knees in mud and water and we have to wade through it all. It is pleasant now so I could do with it. We have been back in the firing line a week now, we seem to be always on the move somewhere.

So poor old Ern's come out for his third round. I expect he has gone to Serbia this time. Is Dad still keeping all right, and Kathie – you are awfully slow with your letters, somehow it seems such a long time since I heard from you.

Did you settle the allotment business all right? It is time you heard something. Well I must close now, with my best love to you all.

Ever your loving son, Bob.

From Kath

49, Carisbrooke Rd, Newport, IW.   Tuesday, October 26, 1915

Dear Bob,

It's about time I wrote again, I find. Mother sent your last letter for Chris and Arch to see, and it came back this morning with one from Chris. She tells us they have sent you a nice parcel with cake and chocs and marzipan. We do hope you get it. We had Mrs Dyer in yesterday (Monday). She brought in a letter from Charlie to his brother. She says you have been able to meet at last. Fancy you two only three miles apart where you are resting. I expect you were just glad to see him and Charlie was too. He says you have cut your hand with that beastly barbed wire. He says it isn't serious but I expect it is bad enough, isn't it? Mother wonders if it will prevent your writing.

It's a shame you don't get the papers; we send you two every week regularly and Arch has been sending some too. What do you think of Jim being a Corporal now? Getting on, isn't it?

Dad has started work again. Mother told you he had been poorly. He was home a fortnight. Came in tonight a bit tired, said he had got on pretty well today.

I've just been giving Mabel a painting lesson. She is putting some pansies in an autograph book; it looks quite decent.

Dolly sends love to you and mustn't forget to tell you she is a Red Cross nurse now. Got her uniform, she is waiting to be sent anywhere in the Island (not out of it). We hope it will be Gatcombe, then we shall see more of her.

The children are still waiting for their letter when you have got time to write to them. I don't know what to say about 30 yards, it's plenty close enough.

With love and kisses,
Kath.

From Mother
49, Carisbrooke Rd, Newport, IW.   Wednesday, November 3, 1915
My Dear Bob,
I am sending you some socks. I am sure you must want them now, so tell me of anything else I can send you. I was glad Mabel sent the air pillow. Does it answer and do you find it comfortable? You mustn't blow it up too hard. I do want to know what things they serve you out, in the way of clothes, for if you can't get enough warm things I will send some. Mabel is a good girl. She is working hard to get the jersey done. We will send it to you next week. I shall make a parcel up with it, as well, for you. I'm afraid you are finding it very cold now. I am so sorry you have to be in wet up your legs. How can you get dry? Have you much chance in the brewery to do so? I was, as we all was, so glad you and Charlie was able to meet. You felt it like a touch from home, didn't you? Can't you manage to get back with them? But you know best, for perhaps you are more comfortable your way, if there is any comfort that way at all. Oh dear, I do wish it was all over and you was all marching home again. I am glad you are thinking of writing to the ladies at Seaford. I wonder if Charlie has told them where you are? He said he would. Your father is better again; he went three days last week. It was raining hard all day Monday this week so he started Tuesday and went today. He says Devereux is writing to you and will tell you all the news he can. Of course, it is no use to look for you boys this Christmas. Mab says there's seven weeks yet and we won't know what might happen by then. So we must hope for the best, Bob.
Every day we are talking about you. Father and Kathie send the kindest love to you. Now my dear boy, I will wish you goodnight,
                    ever your loving Mother, Ellen Brimson.

             Gorre, Bethune. The War Diary page for this date is missing.
From Bob
BEF, France   Monday, November 8, 1915
Dear Mother and Father,
I received your letter last evening. I wrote to Mrs. Ricketts at Seaford the other day and I got a very nice letter back. She said she was sending me a parcel. We have left the village where we were billeted in the brewery and moved into a large town for a few days. It is impossible to say how long we shall be here but it is quite a change. We can buy bread here – a fairly large loaf for fourpence halfpenny – but the butter you have to pay two francs for a half pound, so it is a luxury. We very seldom get a taste of it.
I am glad you are sending me the socks. I am drawing a pair from the stores so I shall be well off for them, and there is plenty of other clothing. We have also been served out with boots which come right above our knees, watertight for working in the trenches.
I have not seen or heard any more of C. Dyer so I don't know where he has moved to. I expect I shall drop across him again sometime. I am glad you are all going on all right at home. I wrote to Roy. Did he get the letter OK? I also wrote to Chris but have heard nothing.

I think there must be something the matter with the Huns. They have been coming across to our trenches where I've been working and giving them selves up saying they were starving. They were only too glad to exchange cigarettes for bully beef so it shows it must be right about the famine. Well I must close now. Remember me to all our friends,

ever your loving son Bob.

From Mother
49, Carisbrooke Rd, Newport, IW.   Wednesday, November 17, 1915
My Dear Bob,
We were all so glad to know that you were all right and well. It's well you have those high boots, for by the papers there has been a lot of rain in France. I hope you have got the parcels. It is kind of the ladies, you will write directly you get theirs. Don't mind telling them of anything you want for they seem anxious to do anything they can. Poor Mab couldn't get the jersey done for this week, things have been anyhow with having her Aunt ill and dying, but it won't be long now. But you being moved about makes it longer for things to get to you. I shall send some flowers of sulphur – you rub some on your body and your clothes – it keeps insects away they tell me. Chrissie is sending you another parcel so you will be well off.
There are such a lot of young fellows joining up. I see them continually going up to join, somewhere up Castle Road.* I feel so sorry for them. I can't think what you feel like Bob, it must seem so hard for you and so far away from us all. I am always wondering and hoping if you are all right. I suppose you all try to cheer one another up. We have been having such frost lately, quite like thick snow and they have in London, snow three inches deep.
I hope you will come across C. Dyer again soon. My dear boy, hoping to hear that you are all right. Write again soon. Love from us all and I do hope it won't be long before we shall have you home with us again.

Ever your loving Mother and Father, E Brimson.

From Doris
31 Melbourne Street. Newport. IOW.   Thursday, November 18, 1915
My Dear Gay Uncle,
Have you been blown away yet? Anybody would think all the pens and ink had, by the short and sweet little letters you write. Gramma wants you to write a real letter. I'll tell you next time what kind. If you don't hurry up and write now, I'll ————— .
What is that about barbed wire and loop holes in houses? Do you mean to say they are doing such things as that? If you write one big long letter not under 16 pages, you need only write one for Kathie, Gramma, Grampy and me. I don't know what to say. You must do all the "say" in your next letter. Don't forget – I have finished.

With love from Your Giddy Niece Doris.
PS. Kathie will tell you about the giddiness next time.

---

* The recruiting office was located at 'Woodleigh' 34, Castle Road.

Gorre : The War Diary page for this date is missing.
From Bob
95th Field Company, 7th Division. BEF   Saturday, November 20, 1915
My Dearest Mabel,
At last I am able to write to you. We have been back in the firing line a week now and up to our eyes in mud and work but as it happens I am not going up to the trenches till tonight. I have a bit of spare time to write.
First of all I must tell you how very sorry I was to hear of your aunt's death. You must have been having an awful time lately. All the same, it was nice that she spent her last few days in comfort at your place – far better than being in London. I am not surprised that Ern is sent out again. We get them back here almost as soon as they are out of hospital. I expect he is gone to Serbia; they are crowding a lot of troops out there now.
I received the parcel quite safe, thank you. It was a treat. You are getting quite clever at making things; I shouldn't have believed it unless you told me. I got one from the ladies at Seaford the same day, it was almost about 10 days in coming, and received one from Chris last night. I sent you and Mother letters, both in green envelopes, posted the same time. Did you get them? Archy hasn't said whether he has had his, or Roy.
I've had a big parcel of books from someone in Southampton. I haven't the least idea who they are from as there wasn't a note of any kind. I should be glad of that sweater as soon as you can send it. I am sorry to trouble you so much only it is so beastly cold here we are glad of anything like that.
I hope you are all keeping all in the pink at home. I should like to be home for Xmas but I am afraid it won't come off. Well Mabs, my pet, I must finish now. With my best love and kisses.
Ever your sweetheart,
Bob.

From Mother
49, Carisbrooke Rd, Newport, IW.   Wednesday, November 24, 1915
My Dear Bob,
I am always thinking about you and we are often talking about you. I am glad you got the parcels. You didn't say what the Ladies sent. I am sending one to you tomorrow; cake and soap, half a pound of fresh butter and some flowers of sulphur – they say if you rub it on your pants and vest inside it helps to keep insects off – also walk-easy ointment. Mab put you in some chocolate. I will get you some more socks next week and send. Perhaps the ladies will send you some.
You left a woollen scarf here. Shall I send it out to you? And do let me know of anything I can send. Can you get a bath now? I hope you can. It is a nice box I am sending. Can you send it back with anything I can wash or mend for you? I should be pleased. I am sorry if you was disappointed about the letters. I expect you got mine soon after you sent yours to me, didn't you?
You mentioned about the money. I did write to Chatham but have never got an answer. Can you speak to anyone? I said in my letter that you was leaving all your pay and that I was supposed to get 21/- but am only receiving 19/6d. I am

putting in the bank for you every week as much as I can. I have been obliged to use some when Dad never worked in the bad weather in the last weeks – you said I might, didn't you? But I will do what I can for you. Wouldn't it be lovely for you and C. Dyer to come home for a bit? I hope this will find you well,

ever your loving Mother,

Ellen Brimson.

War Diary : "Gorre – Three sections with 700 Infantry on Breastwork. Pouring rain on frozen ground hampered work considerably. Hurdling completed in the section worked by company."

From Bob

95th Field Company, 7th Division. BEF   Monday, November 29, 1915

My Dear Mother and Father,

We have been having some pretty hot times this last few days or nights; rather, when I say hot times, I don't mean the weather, which has been very hard frosts and snow. We are working on ground which is almost as level as a billiard table. There is absolutely no cover for us at all and the Germhun snipers have a clear sweep right across, and the air being so frosty they can hear us working so they don't forget to send a few across. I had one through the loose part of my top boots the other night. Last evening (Sunday), we went up there at 8.30 and did not get back until 4.30 this morning; there was an awfully cold wind blowing too. We only had two wounded this time.

I think by the time you get this we shall have left the firing line and gone back for a rest, and we can do with it too. I should be pleased if you would send that khaki scarf on and also the pair of mittens if you still have them. Mrs Ricketts' parcel was a home-made cake and a box of chocolate. I wrote back to her and thanked her but have had no reply yet. I shall be glad of your parcel when it comes. I shall have to write to Chatham myself when I get time. I am only too glad for you to have the money as I know how expensive things are at home now.

If there is any possible chance of my getting any leave, I shall be after it. Your parcel has just arrived quite safely, and also a letter from Mabs. We are leaving for the trenches tonight so it has come just in time.

Well I must close now with fondest love to you all and to all our friends.

Ever your loving son,

Bob.

From R. Holt on headed notepaper.

Whitecroft, Carisbrooke I.W.   Thursday, December 2, 1915

Dear Brimson,

This small parcel is the result of a wish expressed by the men in my department. Everyone was pleased to join in. Dyer is having a similar one. Hoping it will reach you safely and is what you require. Should there be anything you would like, any article you require, let us know. We shall be pleased to send it on.

With greetings from the whole of the men and myself, trusting you may fall in with Dyer and have a decent time.

Yours sincerely, R. Holt.

War Diary : "Gorre, Berguette, nr. Lillers - Church parade."
From Bob

Sunday, December 5, 1915

My Dear Kath,

I was pleased to get your letter last night and also that lovely photo of yourself.*
It is a real good one. I showed it to some of the boys and they want to come
home with me when I go – to be introduced to my nice looking sister. Don't you
feel flattered? It's 'tres bon.' We are back from the firing line again for a rest.
They say it is for some weeks but we never can tell. We have earned this rest as
we have worked hard lately. I've been keeping in good health myself. It never
affects me whether I am in the trenches or out, but I think it would if we had
many more weeks like last. It wasn't the people opposite exactly, it was the
terrible weather that we experienced at the same time. However, we are away
from it for a while.

I had the pleasure of meeting Dyer again. We are resting about two miles from
him, lower down the road. It was a surprise too. They had been there four or
five days before we came. I was with them Thursday and also yesterday. We
don't seem to get very far away from each other. I had a letter from Arch. It is
all very well his wanting me to come home for Christmas. Trust me, if I get the
chance. Mother, Dad and you are to buy yourselves a nice present this Xmas
from my money, whether you take it from the bank or from the other, as I shall
be unable to be there myself.

There are notices stuck up out here that all parcels are to be posted before the
15th. It is the same at home, I suppose. It is rather too expensive to send parcels
from here. Well Kath, I must close now.

Ever your loving brother, Bob.

From Mother

49, Carisbrooke Rd, Newport, IW.   Thursday, December 9, 1915

My Dear Bob,

Nice for you to see Dyer. He tells his brother that you are looking well. I would
like to know what you do while you are having a rest. Can you stop in your bed
whatever it is, as long as you like? That bullet through your boot top was a very
narrow touch for you. I hope you will have got my parcel by the time you get
this letter. There is a little pudding – hope you will be able to make it hot – and
cake, a few nuts and bull's-eyes. I would like to send you a lot more but is not
allowed for a month, then I shall. And we all shall think of you so much this
Xmas.

They are coming down or are trying to. I hope they will for we feel so lonely.
Mabel tells me the Ladies sent you some socks; I am glad of that. Kath's photo
was nice wasn't it? She was amused at your remarks; she says it is the first time
she was ever told that she was nice looking. She has been very busy at Xmas
cards and golliwogs and other things for some time now.

Your father seems well lately and is going over to the Asylum. He didn't go this
Monday for it was raining very hard and it kept on all the day.

It was all right for Mr Holt to send to you wasn't it?

Oh, I must tell you that Minnie Jones is walking out with Percy Fry; he goes out to her. She will sharpen him up a bit, won't she? It doesn't seem as if this dreadful time is near an end to see the hundreds of men joining up. They have been going by all this week. Mabel is sending off your parcel today. I have given her your scarf and mittens, also nightcap, with a tin of coffee that I couldn't send with the other parcel. You seem to get the parcels all right, don't you? I am glad your Aunt Elisa sends to you. She is very kind to me and Kathie.

Now I will finish, Bob. Hoping to hear from you again very soon. I think you have been very brave through your hardships.

From Kath with Mother's letter

We had a letter from Arch and Chris yesterday. They meant to come down for Xmas but poor little Bebe and Bab have chickenpox so they can't be sure. Arch says he wrote you a long letter and told you to try and get leave. He said if you do he'll expect a brass band instead of a trumpet because it will be his doing.

I don't know what sort of Christmas it will be. I think it will be pretty rotten for all of us, but we will have to put up with it this year. Hope it will be ever so much better next. We do hope you got the last parcel safely with the coat; you must want it dreadfully bad. It will be beautiful and warm for you.

I'm putting in a letter from Ivy. She likes to write to you. It's quite her own and Doris has half written one, she says. I've been very busy and Mother has been helping me. We have made six golliwogs, two for Bebe and Bab – they save buying, and Mrs Attrill has ordered one; it is nearly as big as Baba. It is going to Lutterworth.

Bob – Mabel told me about the place you are in. We haven't told Mother or Dad, but I hope to goodness you will be out of that trench as soon as you possibly are able. I shall keep thinking about it until we hear from you again.

Heaps of love and kisses, from Kath.

From Kath

49, Carisbrooke Rd, Newport, IW   Sunday, December 12, 1915

My Dear Bob,

We were ever so pleased to get your letter this morning. We are always looking forward for them coming and glad as anything when the postman comes. You just ought to hear Ma rave at the men when they knock like the postman – it's generally the fish man. She says to him, "I won't buy any fish now for knocking like a postman," and he chips in, "Alright mam. If you don't buy any, I'll knock like him again next time."

I'm glad you like my photo.* They all say it's good. Well indeed, there's flattered I do feel, ach, i, fi (*sic*). Fancy 'em saying nice things like that. Mind you give 'em my love next time you come across them. We can talk French now can we? I looked in the book to see what it meant. Let's see you write a letter in French, Bob – Come on. Doris has just come in. She says up at the recruiting office it is so crowded that the men have had to get in and out of the window; three rooms

---

* See page 28.

blocked up and the doorway on the road too. It's true. They have been crowding up the Mall in dozens the last two or three days and today being Thursday they have flocked like sheep, in fifties.* It seems as if they wanted to put it off to the very last minute. Doris being here, it's a hard job to write letters, so I'll be sure to write you a long one next week. With best love and kisses – lots of 'em.

Ever your loving Kath.

War Diary : "Tirancourt - Pontooning. Trench digging. Building latrines and Stables in area. Major Dobson R.E. arrived to take over command."

From Bob

95th Field Company, 7th Division. BEF   Thursday, December 16, 1915

My Dear Mother, Father and Kath,

I received the lovely parcel quite safely. Everything was quite all right. The cake is beautiful – the pudding I am going to warm up. I have not sampled it yet but I know it is nice. The nuts are the first I had since I've been in France. Mr. Holt and the men have sent me a parcel. I wrote to him to thank him for it. We are right away, back from the trenches now, in another part of France. We shall be here some weeks yet so we shall have Xmas here. We are sleeping in a large barn on straw. We parade about 7.30 in the morning for exercise and then after breakfast we do a bit of trenching or pontooning on the river.** It is rather pretty round this part. In fact, we are in the park of a large French château.*** I believe it has been deserted by the owners as the dresses and clothes are still hanging up inside and the kids' toys are laying about. The Germans came through this part when our army was retreating from Mons. I am glad you are all keeping well at home and hope you will have a decent Xmas. It will be nice if they can come down from London. I'm glad the lads are joining up before they are forced to as they will have a pretty rough time if conscription comes in. I will write and tell you what sort of Christmas we've had as there doesn't seem much chance of any leave yet, not for a month or so. You might send me half a dozen candles if you can manage it please. With my best love to you all.

Ever your loving, Bob.

From Arch

28, Barnard Road, Clapham Junction. SW   Friday, December 24, 1915

Dear Bob,

Glad you received the parcel. Your letter just arrived. Pleased to think the writing was 'tres bon'. Trust the contents of tin were 'tres bon'. Yes, what about Roy? Bow wow. I also had a try but got knocked out by the doctor. George wears an armlet. All the family are getting the military aspect. We can't go to the Island this year on account of funds being low. We sent them a hamper. We are sorry we can't wangle it but it's no go. I've got to get to work so this must stop. Well well, toodle-oo. So long, Olive oil, Bon jour, Love and luck and good wishes from us all,

your loving brother, Arch.

---

* Thursday was early closing day in Newport.

** See photograph page 108.

*** Chateau de Tirancourt. See photograph page 108.

From Charlie Dyer to Bob's mother
46869, 87 Field Co. R.E. Battalion 12th Div, BEF.   Tuesday December 28, 1915
Dear Ma,
Just a few lines in answer to your nice letter and card which I received quite safe. I think the card is lovely; I shall keep it and bring it home with me when I come. I was very pleased to see Bob the other week. He is looking well. He came and spent a day with the lads. They were all pleased to see him. We had dinner and tea together just like old times.
I hope it soon be all over so we can get back again. The weather is terrible; raining every day; mired up to our knees. Never mind – we are doing our best and we can do no more. I am the same as Bob said the other day, we are glad we came when we did. I thank you and Kathy for your good wishes. Glad to say we had a nice Xmas. Hoping you had the same and wishing you all a happy new year.
From Charlie.

From Kath
49, Carisbrooke Rd, Newport.   Wednesday, December 29, 1915
Dear Bob,
I thought it would be better if I wrote to you after Xmas was over to tell you how we went on. Well, to begin with, Chris and Arch couldn't come down and what with you being away it didn't seem very Christmassy at all, but we didn't expect it to be much better this year. We went over to Mrs Attrill's to tea on the 25th, and supper.
Chris and Arch sent the usual hamper down with the usual nice things in it. We had them all down from Melbourne Street on Boxing Day. It wasn't so bad as it sounds; there was lots of room at the table for more (two tables together) and of course, we played Tippett* later on in the evening and of course, just when it grew most exciting we had to leave off.
Mabel had to go home about eleven and Kit said it was late for the children (Doris, Wallie and I could have gone on playing all night). The kiddies were ever so good. At teatime Clem couldn't understand why Roy kept eating celery and watercress. He said, "Look at Daddie. Is that all he came down for?" It all went off all right; the kiddies enjoyed it. Mabel made me a lovely navy blue carriage rug. It looks ever so nice.
We put your present money together to get some extras for the tea party. It was ever so nice of you, thank you ever so much from all of us. Dad had from Saturday until Tuesday off. Ma bought him a lantern to light his way through the copse; he went off today with it. Doris is here telling me to finish it quick so that she can post it, and we haven't had dinner yet. Now you must tell us quick how you spent your Christmas.
Now, good morning, heaps of love from us all and good luck for the New Year.
Ever your loving, Kath.

---

* 'Tipit' is a centuries old game involving two teams who have to guess which player is hiding a coin in their hands.

Ellen (Mother) and Clement (Father) Brimson in a 1927 painting by Kath.

Bob

Painted by Kath from a photo of Bob taken in 1915. *"Kathie has painted such a splendid picture of you for me, but the one with the cap."* Mabs to Bob, March 8th, 1915. See page 80.

The original wing canvas removed by Bob from the roundel of crashed Royal Aircraft Factory B.E.2 aeroplane.

"*How startled you must have been for the aeroplane to come right over you like the one did. Glad you sent the piece. Now it is being taken great care of. Mabs thinks a lot of it. She will have it put in a frame for the war it comes of.*" Mother to Bob, October 17, 1915. See page 120.

G. R.

SOLDIERS' SEPARATION ALLOWANCES

INCREASED RATES from MARCH 1, 1915

Increased Separation Allowances for the War are now given to the wives and children of married soldiers and to the dependants of unmarried men and widowers.

WIVES AND CHILDREN OF MARRIED MEN.

The New Weekly Rates are as follows :

	Private and Corporal.	Sergeant.	Col.-Sergeant.	Quarter-Master Sergeant.	Wt. Officer (1st class).
Wife - - - - - -	12s. 6d.	15s. 0d.	16s. 6d.	22s. 0d.	23s. 0d.
Wife and child - -	17s. 6d.	20s. 0d.	21s. 6d.	27s. 0d.	28s. 0d.
Wife and 2 children	21s. 0d.	23s. 6d.	25s. 0d.	30s. 6d.	31s. 6d.

With 2s. extra for each additional child.

These rates include the usual allotment of 3s. 6d. a week for privates and corporals, and 5s. 10d. for other ranks.

Adopted children are admitted. The ordinary limit of age for children is now 16, and the allowance is continued up to 21 in certain cases (for higher education, apprenticeship on a nominal wage, or physical or mental infirmity). Soldiers marrying AFTER enlistment are now eligible.

An extra 3s. 6d. a week is paid in the case of soldiers living in the London postal area at the time of enlistment if the families continue to live there.

MOTHERLESS CHILDREN.
5s. a week clear for each child.

OTHER DEPENDANTS OF UNMARRIED SOLDIERS AND WIDOWERS.

If a soldier who is unmarried or a widower (or one whose wife is not drawing separation allowance because she was living apart from him before the war) had any person or persons (whether related or not), including children, actually dependent upon him before he enlisted, the Government will pay that dependant a weekly sum provided the soldier contributes a share (one third or less) of the amount. The intention is to allow to the dependant, within certain limits (see below), the same amount weekly that the soldier paid him or her before enlistment, less any portion that went to pay for his own keep.

As an example, if the soldier had paid 17s. 6d. a week to his mother, and 7s. 6d. of this was needed for his own keep, the allowance admissible will be the remaining 10s. Towards this the soldier will contribute 5d. a day from his pay.

The amount the Government will pay to any one dependant of a soldier will not exceed the amount of separation allowance for a wife (see table above), but that limit will be raised if more persons than one were dependent on the same soldier.

NOTE.—As it is impossible to explain all the classes of cases on a poster, intending recruits can obtain fuller information from the two pamphlets for married and unmarried men, revised to 1st March, 1915, which they can get at any Post Office.

Forms of Application for Separation Allowance can be filled in at the Recruiting Office.

PUBLISHED BY THE PARLIAMENTARY RECRUITING COMMITTEE, LONDON.   Poster No. 72.   H. W. & V. Ld. ...

Many households suffered a loss of income when husbands and sons went to war. The Separation Allowance was an attempt to redress the balance. See page 57.

Calendar of Events of 1916.
(Bob's activities shown in italics)

January 27 - Conscription of all single men aged 18 to 41 begins.
January - 95th at Naours – Preparing standings for 200 horse, preparing billets.
February 21 – Battle of Verdun begins.
February - 95th Field Coy move to Meaulte, Albert, preparing machine gun emplacements, wiring.
March 31 – German airship raid on England. Airship brought down by gunfire near mouth of the Thames.
April 1 - Morlancourt, trench working.
April 14 – Attack on Constantinople and Adrianople by Royal Navy aircraft.
April 24 – Rebellion in Ireland.
May 16 – Conscription extended to married men.
May 17 – After 9 months in France Bob has his first leave, of 14 days.
May 21 – German attack on Vimy Ridge.
May 31 – Battle of Jutland Harry Attrill on HMS Queen Mary and five other ships lost.
June 2 - Battle of Mount Sorrel (Ypres) begins.
June – 95th at Grovetown Camp, usual work in trenches.
June 13 - Battle of Mount Sorrel (Ypres) ends.
July 1 – Start of Battle of the Somme; Battle of Albert.
July 14 – Battle of Bazentine, Le Grand Wood & Caterpillar Wood (Somme).
July 23 – Battle of Pozieres Ridge (Somme).
July end – 95th at Dernancourt and Tirancourt. Drill, overhauling equipment etc.
August early – Constructing German prisoners' camp.
September 2 – Fourteen German airships raid London and parts of England.
November 18 – Battle of the Somme ends.
November 23 – Mailly Maillet. Return to trench work.
November 27 – Zeppelin raid on the East Coast of England.
December 7 – Lloyd George succeeds Asquith as Prime Minister.

From Mother
49, Carisbrooke Rd, Newport.   Friday, January 14, 1916
My Dear Bob,
We was all so glad to get your last letter to know you was all right for Xmas. I think you must have enjoyed yourselves pretty well but it is a great shame that the parcels didn't come to your Company for Xmas. As you say, there must be plenty of poor fellows who would be glad of them. I hope they will come; it will be better late than never. Surely someone would write about it else – especially to the County Press – for I know everyone done all they could, even I did. Mab went to Chris's yesterday. We do miss her. She is expected to be back Sunday. Kath is using the machine so it shakes the table.
You find it better to be further in France, don't you, for to be away from the sound of the guns? It must be bad for your head. I am glad you are in such good health, and with all the roughing it, so much as you have had to. I think it is a

great wonder. Morry was home yesterday. He is at the Barracks at Portsmouth. Are you glad Aunt E. sends you papers? I heard from her the other day; she always wants to know how you are getting on. George Reynolds is expected home next week. He has been in hospital three months, a very bad wound in his leg. Jack Cornish was here from Winchester last week; he says there isn't a bit of feeling in his feet, yet he can't get anywhere near the fire. We all hope it won't be long before you will be home again.

Ever your loving Mother E B.

From Charlie Dyer

46869, 87 Field Co. R.E. Battalion 12th Division, BEF. Sunday, January 16, 1916

Dear Bob,

Just a few lines hoping you are still keeping fit. Glad to say all the boys are quite well and wish to be remembered to you. I had a letter from Jack Farmer last week. He is at Rouen, been wounded in the leg with shrapnel but glad to say he is going on all right and hopes to be back up with the line again before long. He has been up round Dixmude, Ypres and Amentieres – rather hot that way he said. He wished to be remembered to you. Glad to say I am quite well up to the present. We are back for a rest about a mile from where I came and found you the last time. I suppose you have had your leave by this time.* I have not had any luck yet but it will come some day. Write soon.

From your old pal Charlie.

War Diary : "Naours – Preparing billets in Naours, Wargnies and Havernas for troops. Repairing barns, lettering streets and numbering billets. Quarrying chalk for horse standings, felling trees and work in sawmill and shop framing latrines."

From Bob

95th Field Company, 7th Division. BEF   Thursday, January 20, 1916

Dear Mother and Father,

I received your letter of the 14th yesterday and I have also had the County Press's all right. We are still away from the firing line and shall be for some time yet, but all the same we have plenty of work to do. I have been employed at the old job, sign writing, for the last three or four weeks. We are all employed on certain work of which I can't tell you anything by way of correspondence but I shall probably be home for about seven days about the end of February or the beginning of March. All the company is having leave and I think my turn will come about then. We are working from daylight till dark, Sunday as well, so we don't get any time off to do anything. I believe we are moving further back still next week.

I got Doris's letter all right. She writes quite a nice one. I also had a letter from Archy yesterday. He told me about Mabel's visit and also of Morry coming to see them at the same time. I hope he will be able to get off when I am home; I'm longing for the time. It seems years since I was in England; it's getting on for seven months. Dad must get a week off from work. Please thank Aunt E. for the papers she sends me; it is very kind of her to think of me. We have been having

---

* Bob did not receive any leave until May, four months later.

marvellous weather lately, hardly any rain and also very mild. There are heaps of snowdrops in the gardens of the cottages round here and some of the trees are budding out. It is almost spring weather; it's been a god-send for the troops out here. Well, I have not much more to say as nothing exciting has happened lately. I am writing to Mabs tomorrow night.

Ever your loving son, Bob.

From Mother
49, Carisbrooke Rd, Newport.   Friday, January 28, 1916
My Dear Bob,
We were so thankful to get your letter and know you was all right and quite well – especially to know that you hopes to be home soon. How thankful I shall be to see you again after all this dreadful, anxious time. I shall send you some more candles. I meant to put them in Kit's parcel with some more things. Of course, I would help to pay postage but she has been waiting for a lot of chocolate that is coming to her. She wants to send it to you.
Harry sent me a very pretty New Year's card but no letter. He tells his mother that they have had a very long dry season.
They are saying that we are to have 2000 Derby's billeted in Newport, and all those that has joined up here are to be sent away somewhere else. I hope they won't put any in our house, but I suppose I mustn't refuse. Of course, if it did happen I would do my best for the poor fellows.
How very dear everything is getting.* It's quite a business to manage now. Is it the same where you are?

Ever your loving Mother, Ellen Brimson.

War Diary : "Méaulte and Derancourt, nr. Albert."
From Bob
Royal Engineers. BEF   Tuesday, February 8, 1916
Dear Mother and Father,
Just a few lines to let you know that I am still going on all right. I have been getting the County Press all right, but as we have been on the move just lately they have been somewhat delayed. I have been expecting a letter from Kath but perhaps she has been busy. I have not had a parcel since the one Mabel sent a few days before my birthday. Archy said he was sending one and I think you said you were as well, but nothing has arrived. Still, don't bother if the things are getting too expensive.
We are not quite so well provided now as we were at first and we get paid once in about three weeks – and not very much at that – but all the same I don't want you to spend your money on me as I know that you will be finding it very hard to get along now. Our issue of tobacco and cigarettes has gone down too and I see in the papers that they are stopping the import of the weed in the raw state, so that will go up in price. I expect it will be a good job when all this lot is over for all of us.
I am glad you are all keeping well at home. The weather is a lot colder here but

---

* According to Board of Trade figures, prices increased by 61% in the first two years of the war.

we are getting used to it now. I am in the best of health anyway. I should be pleased to have that French book you told me about if you could send it. I have got on well enough to make myself understood by the people and they can also understand me. It pays anyone to understand the lingo out here.

Remember me to all of them at Whitecroft, Dad. I'll come and see them when I come home which I hope won't be long now. I hope you won't be troubled with any soldiers billeted at home as I know some of them are an awful trouble. Of course, it depends what sort you get. Well, Mother, I must close now,

ever your loving son, Bob.

From Chris
28, Barnard Road, Clapham Junction. SW   Thursday, February 17, 1916
Dear Bob,
You will be wondering what has become of us. I think we have been waiting for another letter from home from you but it hasn't come so I had better write. We must get your parcel at the end of this week. I'm so glad you are getting a few days leave. Of course, we shan't expect to see you up here. You will want all your time for Mother and Mabel; they will be so glad to see you.
The worst of it will be the going back. That will be harder now than at first. I wish to goodness it was all over; it is all so horrible you can't forget it night or day. I'm glad you have made some friends; time will go quicker for you. Have you seen Charlie Dyer again? Archy is out tonight and taken his pen so I must make do with this pencil. I sent Mabel a little present for her birthday. Haven't heard from her since. Sure you didn't forget the date?
I haven't got much news. Jim is still in the place. I believe has a weekend off pretty often and George is a Special Constable, and also wears an armlet. He thinks he might be called up but can't tell yet. Hope you get the Pictorial all right. Let us know if there is another you would like better. Look after yourself, there's a good boy

Ever your loving sister Chris.

War Diary : "Méaulte and Derancourt, nr. Albert - Revetting frontline in Guildford continued. Laying of trench boards in King's Avenue. Work interfered with by enemy bombardment. Bonte dugouts completed. Divisional bathhouse begun."

From Bob
Royal Engineers. BEF   Saturday, February 19, 1916
Dear Kath,
It seems about a fortnight since I heard from home and you don't know how I look forward to a parcel, especially when the other chaps keep getting them. I have almost forgotten the taste of Mother's cake and yours as well; you mustn't start experimenting with your pastry as it is lovely the way you make it. It doesn't do for everyone to make things alike. I wish I had some now. Tell Mother to be careful how she runs for this letter and to see there is no varnish cans in the way.
We had a rather rotten night last night. It blew a hurricane and torrents of rain

Refuelling aboard HMS Hindustan.

Harry Attrill is in the second row, left hand side, with black face and cigarette. *"Every single officer and man that can be spared, should get into the collier to dig out the coal."* Rear Admiral Sir Christopher Craddock on coaling warships, 1908.

all the time. We were all wet through, the rain running down inside my puttees into my boots however, we don't have to get up early in the morning when we are on nights, so we have plenty of time to dry our things.

I was lying in bed this morning when the Germans started shelling. As they dropped in a field on the right of our billet no harm was done. They passed over our head like an express train. I thought if one happened to drop through the roof how nice it would be to snuff it in bed, comfortable. Anyway, they were all rotten shots this morning.

There is one question I should like to ask. How it is that Jim Snow doesn't have a turn out here? I should very much like to see him when I come home. If this war keeps on for a few more years I suppose young Gordon will be called up. I should like to see it finish this year but there seems no end to the Huns, they seem to spring up like mushrooms. Harry, Fred and Ernest and Hugh Shaw as well. There's plenty of time for them to do a bit yet.

Every your loving brother, Bob.

I should like Mother to forward me five shillings if she could manage it please.

From Mother
49, Carisbrooke Rd, Newport, IW.   Friday, February 25, 1916
My Dear Bob,

So glad to get your letter this morning to know you are all right but so sorry that you have been disappointed so about the parcels. I do hope you will have got Roy's by this time – then Mrs Attrill sent you one last night. I am getting one for you and will send it early next week. I daresay you do feel disappointed when you see the others getting letters and parcels, poor boy. I want you to know that I don't wish to be neglectful to you a little bit but one and another has been saying they are sending to you so I waited. Have you got the little book? I hope it will be useful. I am hoping every day that comes you will get through it safe. It must be awful in those trenches when it rains so heavy. We are having a lot of snow and very cold weather this last three weeks. It is snowing very heavy now and everywhere is white. We shall have it deep if it goes on like this till the morning. I am very glad it's Friday for Dad won't go tomorrow. He has braved it out all this week.

Kath is busy making a picture – very nice. She has to leave off every now and then to warm her hands. You asked about Jim Snow; he was down here the end of December. He told us that he is a clerk in an office. He told Kathie he only got a shilling a day but he don't have to march or drill – he is out of all that. He don't think he will be sent out but he can't be sure. Gordon is in the Cadet Corps. He is measured for his khaki this week and will be 18 this May. He is a very nice lad; always coming in to know if we have heard from Bob. George Harvie is in hospital, the last they heard from him. I am going to the Post Office directly Dad is settled after he gets home, to get the order for you and send it off at once. I hope you will get it all right. Now goodbye,

your loving Mother, E. Brimson.

Kath's 'large' painting of Harry Attrill, painted six months after his death. *"I think I told you I had finished the miniature and large picture of Harry. They were very pleased with them."* Kath to Bob, November 19, 1916.

From Roy
31, Melbourne Street. Newport.   Sunday, February 27, 1916
Dear Bob,
We sent you a parcel weighing 7lbs but we don't think you could have had it or we should have heard from you before now. We sent it about the 15th of February. I hope you will get it – it takes such a lot of time to pack one and get one together. We don't mind that so long as you get it. When do you think you will be home? Now the place is about skinned out it is a job to find anyone to talk to in the pub. It is all khaki – Derby recruits everywhere.* Gordon joined the Cadet Corps for one year. They are now going to dress them in khaki and bring them in the Isle of Wight Terriers. I shall have to go in them, or the Hants. We go up in June. I hope it will be over by then. Old W. Jacobs got to go at last. I shall see him tonight up the Red Lion, Carisbrooke. I wish you were here to go with me. You can picture me up there every Sunday night between 7 pm and 9 pm. I am still working at Camp Hill. Only 49 men left now – all old men. I am thinking about going down the docks again. If I get a chance to join up what would you advise me to do, R.E.'s or Infantry?
            From your Affectionate Brother (good luck to you) Roy.

From Mother
49, Carisbrooke Rd, Newport.   Tuesday, February 29, 1916
Just a line my dear Bob, with this parcel. I hope you will enjoy the contents. Kath made the pastry but she is not satisfied. She says she will make the next lot better. They have told me today that all leave in France is stopped for a while. Have you heard that? I do feel disappointed. Let me know if you are wanting socks or anything and if you find the tin of cocoa useful, then I will send more.
Kath : Mother's sorry she has had to take out some things. We can't send more than seven pounds. She has taken out the tin of cocoa and milk. She thought you would rather have the food. Send the tin next week.

From Kath
49, Carisbrooke Road, Newport.   Tuesday, March 7, 1916
Dear Bob,
We had your letter Sunday morning. We were glad to know you received all the things safely. You seem to get them all right in time.
It must have been a grand surprise to meet Walter Baird. I expect you are always keeping your eye open for somebody you know. By the letter you wrote to Mabel, you seem to have more things to think about. That barbed wire work must be awful – working on a lot of snuffed Germans too. Expect it makes you feel a bit queer inside doesn't it? It's a good thing you have got a nice place to dry your things in. I suppose it's still snowing; it is here.
Mother is sending you another parcel tomorrow. She has baked the cake today. It will be a good thing if we can get to find out about the ten pound parcels you

---

* In October 1915, Lord Derby, Director-General of Recruiting, introduced a programme often called the Derby Scheme. Men could volunteer for service but remain in their jobs till called up.

spoke about; we shan't have to keep taking something or other out that we want to send because it just weighs over the seven. It's a nuisance when it happens like that.

Roy expects to be called up soon so last night he was off down to the Recruiting Office to see if there was any way of getting out of it. We haven't heard if he has managed it yet. Did they tell you that Gordon is Lance-Corporal in the cadets now? He is mighty proud of it. I was disappointed with those tarts, Bob. They didn't turn out a bit like I wanted so it didn't matter much that they were obliged to take some of them out again. Never mind; I'll have another try soon.

Ever your loving Kath.

From Mabs

The Bedford, Newport, IW.   Wednesday, March 15, 1916

My Dearest Boy,

Harry has been home at last and he left again today at 1.10 pm. He will stop the night in London because he has to catch the 10 am train for Scotland at King's Cross. I hope he will see Archy and Chris. I do wish you could have managed to get here at the same time but never mind – we will make up for it when you do come. Harry does look well and not a day older; the sea agrees with him all right. As to the war, I don't believe it would worry him if 500 German men of war came out after him. He has great hopes of the war being over this year. I think that is the general opinion though. They are very stingy with some sailors' leave. Harry had six days. He arrived here Saturday afternoon and had to go back today so it made a very short six days. We had a letter from Ern on Saturday. He says he is going on fine but he can't get much water. He couldn't say where they were but they are not with the Rifles now – I should think it must be somewhere very hot. I think I'll go there too until the summer.

We went for a spin in the motor yesterday afternoon. Morry came over so we all went off. It was all right, but a little bit cold. We went out through Shorwell, Brighstone, Brooke and Calbourne, then down to Wootton to call on Uncle George. It would have been a lot better if you had been there (and perhaps it wouldn't have been so cold). Well, I suppose I shall have to stop again, it's just getting busy time, Saturday.

With fondest love to my dear old boy from your loving sweetheart, Mabs.

From Arch

28, Barnard Road, Clapham Junction. SW   Friday, March 17, 1916

Dear Bob,

Many thanks for your letter. You can't think how important we feel when we get a letter from the Front. I had been meaning for some time to send that Hazelden book to you as I know you appreciate his Little Willie and Big Willie designs.* When you have quite finished with it you might let the Huns have a squint at it so that they can see what we think of the Kaiser and the Crown Prince. That parcel was a long time overdue and in fact we had prepared one first about the time of your birthday, or shortly after, but couldn't find anything

---

* Big Willie and Little Willie were nicknames for WW1 tanks. Hazelden was a Daily Mirror cartoonist.

at that time to send it in. We had an idea that in these days it must be tins and nothing else. However, we thought we would chance it in a box this time, and it seems to have answered all right. You shall have another one soon.

Jim still sticks at Windsor in the Orderly Room. I told him you wanted to know why he didn't come out to France. He said he would watch it. It would take two or three generals, the commander-in-chief, and the Secretary of State for War to get Jim to move out of the Orderly Room and go out where nasty, disagreeable Germans are waiting to be scrapped. Not that Jim lets on to be contented. He's as discontented as anything. There's too many creature discomforts for Jim, of course. Windsor, where he still hangs out, is crowded out with soldiers and Jim, as I may have told you before, sleeps in a scullery basement on the floor and there are five of them all together in the same room. Better than the trenches anyway. But the fact is they bring their beer in from the canteen, and I suppose the Orderly Room Sergeant is a bit of an old soldier and is up to a dodge or two so there's always plenty to make the poor dears sleep well. Jim says he wouldn't get any rest scarcely if it wasn't for the beer, on account of the bugs and lice. The lice is worst. Sometimes they wake up and have a hunt in the middle of the night. I've heard tell that out there in the trenches they get to be quite pets and will sit up and beg for bully beef. Is this so? Jim gets off a weekend every fortnight. Don't it make you wild? No wonder he don't want to go to France.

George is a Special Constable now, as well as in a Derby Group. He doesn't know whether the Borough Council got him exempted or not; there was some muddle about him. But I expect he was exempted because it would be very difficult at the moment to find anyone to take on his job. George comes over here nearly every Sunday morning just to see if the pubs open at the proper time, you know. He mostly stops to have a morsel of dinner.

Fancy your running into an old Chesterfield pal. I dare say there are a good many out there in different regiments. We often wonder if Harry Edge joined up in any of the overseas battalions. He would be just the sort. Markham that he used to work for, has been making himself a nuisance in the House of Commons lately.*

My word Bob, I wish that next Sunday we could all meet up at 49 Carisbrooke Road, and after a leisurely breakfast and walk round the castle, drop in at the Cutters**, or the Eight Bells, before finally returning to dinner and talk over things as they seem to be to the enlightened. May the time come soon.

In the meantime you may take it that if thoughts could make themselves seen, you would see some of ours every day. I don't suppose a day passes but that we speak about where you may be and what you are doing; so do the children. I reckon we know a certain young woman who thinks about you more than we do ever. We haven't heard from her lately as all her time must have been occupied in writing to you. Well so long, Sapper, love and kisses from all of us.

Ever your loving brother, Arch.

---

* Arthur Markham, MP, fought against the recruitment of under age soldiers during the war. Prior to conscription in 1916, boys as young as 14 had found their way into the Army. Markham accused the Government of turning a blind eye, declaring: "There has been fraud, deceit and lying practiced by the War Office."

** The Cutters Arms pub, on Carisbrooke High Street, between the church and Priory Road.

Bairnsfather cartoon from *The Bystander* magazine.

From Mabs
The Bedford, Newport, IW.   Monday, March 20, 1916
My Dearest Boy,
I received your letter this afternoon. I'd begun to wonder what had happened, you see it took six days for your letter to come to me. Well, I am glad you shall keep clear of German shot and shell, but it is a great shame that they should keep on smashing up the towns and villages as they do. Still I suppose those are a few of the 'fortunes of war'. The wretches have been to England again with their bombs, but one of them got captured this time. I wonder why they always choose Sunday to come here? I think the damage was rather bad this time. Morry has heard that he may be sent to the Royal Sovereign. He is just about delighted with that. He hoped he would be sent to her. Of course she is the largest man-of-war in the world and this is her first commission. Ern is still keeping well and they are not very busy now. Wallace is going on well too. We have just had a letter from him. He is 16 tomorrow, the 21st. He fancies himself now. He tells us last week he earned £1.2s.0d so I suppose he is smart at his work, for he wouldn't get so much. Thank you very much for the postcard; it is very pretty but I think Kath beats the French people for Regimental Crests. Mr Brimson is a brick and no mistake, to go off over there like he does – it's a jolly sight more than a good many young ones would do. By the way, your nephew and namesake is growing up. Why, he even smokes a pipe now, because he says cigs are too expensive. Tut-tut! Fancy our Gordon with a pipe. Ludo seems to have a great fascination lately. Halma is quite knocked out, and whist, until you come home again. I do wish you were here now, but hang it all, it's no use wishing. I shan't know how to walk if you stop away much longer. I do miss our evening walks; I rarely get a walk at all now. I hope they will soon start your leave again so that you can get home. The forget-me-not is the first one out of the garden.
                Heaps of kisses from your loving sweetheart, Mabs.

From Charlie Dyer
87 Field Co. R.E. Battalion 12th Division, BEF.   Wednesday, March 22, 1916
Dear Bob,
Just a few lines hoping that you are still keeping fit. Glad to say that I am quite well. We are in a warm place now – been here for six weeks. Very sorry to say we have had some bad luck here. Lieutenant Alderson and Lieutenant Latham and Sapper Renouf were killed and a lot wounded, two officers. Glad to say Bertie Paskey and WH Chappell and the lads in No1 are all right and wish to be remembered to you. I suppose you will soon be going on leave. Ours start again on Sunday. My turn might come soon if I get any luck in the draw. Well, I wish you the best of luck and good time when you go home, hoping that I shan't be very long after you.
                From your old chum Charlie.

This print was found by Bob in a ruined farmhouse on the Somme battlefields in 1916, by which time it was already six years old. It is a list of Saints' Days for the year 1910 and bears the title 'The Somme Weekly - 1910.' The caption at the top reads, 'The Sufferings of Joan of Arc.'

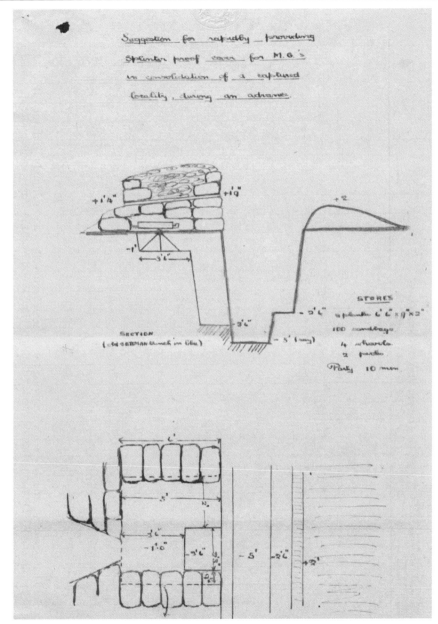

95th Company, Royal Engineers' War Diary for June 14, 1916.

The firing platforms in German trenches faced the enemy. When the trenches were captured by the British they were modified to face the other way. The War Diary set out the precise procedure, complete with measurements.

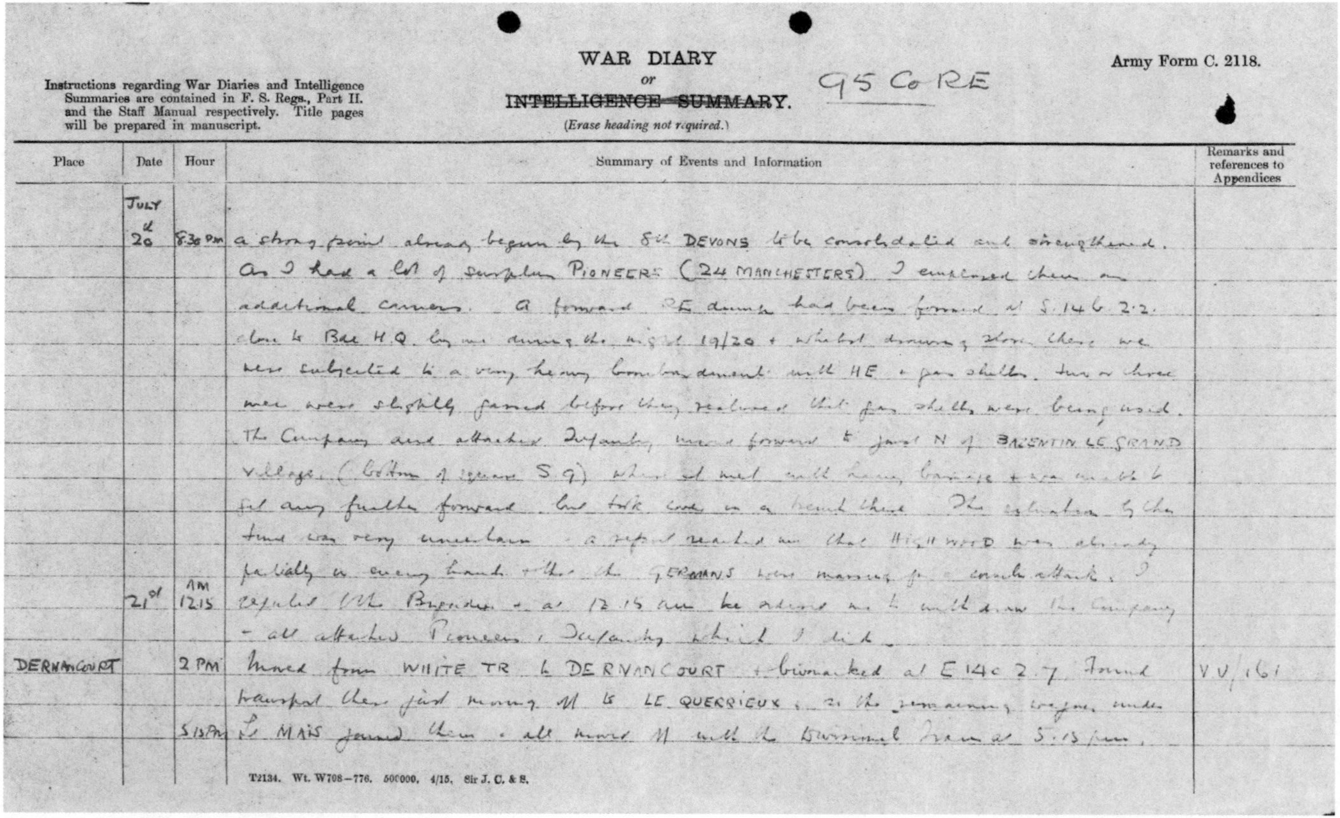

WAR DIARY
or
~~INTELLIGENCE SUMMARY~~. 95 Co RE
(Erase heading not required.)

Army Form C. 2118.

Instructions regarding War Diaries and Intelligence Summaries are contained in F. S. Regs., Part II. and the Staff Manual respectively. Title pages will be prepared in manuscript.

Place	Date	Hour	Summary of Events and Information	Remarks and references to Appendices
	July 20	8.30 PM	a strong point already begun by the 8th DEVONS to be consolidated and strengthened. As I had a lot of surplus PIONEERS (24 MANCHESTERS) I employed them as additional carriers. A forward RE dump had been formed at S.14 b 2.2. close to Bde H.Q. by me during the night 19/20 + whilst drawing stores there we were subjected to a very heavy bombardment with HE + gas shells. two or three men were slightly gassed before they realised that gas shells were being used. The Company and attached Infantry moved forward to just N of BAZENTIN LE GRAND village (bottom of square S 9) where it met with heavy barrage + was unable to get any further forward but took cover in a trench there. The situation by the time was very uncertain – a report reached me that HIGH WOOD was already partially in enemy hands + that the GERMANS were massing for a counter attack. I	
	21st	AM 12.15	reported to the Brigadier + at 12.15 am he ordered me to withdraw the Company + all attached Pioneers + Infantry which I did.	
DERNANCOURT		2 PM	Moved from WHITE TR to DERNANCOURT + bivouacked at E 14 c 2.7. Found transport there just moving off to LE QUERRIEUX + as the remaining wagons under	VV/161
		5.15 PM	Lt MAIS joined them + all moved off with the Divisional Train at 5.15 pm.	

T2134. Wt. W708—776. 500000. 4/15. Sir J. C. & S.

This War Diary page records the events involving the 95th between 8.30pm and midnight, 20th July, 1916. At 8.30pm the 5th and 7th Divisions, having captured most of High Wood by the morning, came under sustained German attack by high explosive and gas shells and just after midnight the REs were ordered to withdraw, together with the Pioneers and Infantry. High Wood was to be fought over until 15th September.

S E C R E T.   Copy No.

7th Division Operation Order No. 83.
by
Major-General H.E.Watts, C.B., C.M.G.,
Commanding, 7th Division.

Reference -
    MARTINPUICH Sheet   Divisional Headquarters.
    1/20,000.   17th July, 1916.

    1. (a) The Fourth Army will continue the attack to morrow.

        (b) The XIII Corps will be attacking GUILLEMONT and
GINCHY.
                 The objectives of the III Corps will be the Switch
line west of the Railway (S.2.a, 0.2) and POZIERES Village.

        (c) The XV Corps will capture HIGH WOOD and the German
Switch line between HIGH WOOD and the Railway (S.2.a. 0.2),
7th Division being on the right, 33rd Division on the left.

        (d) The enemy's position immediately east of HIGH WOOD
will not be attacked.

    2. (a) The 7th Division have been directed to capture
HIGH WOOD and the portion of the German Switch trench west
of the WOOD as far as the central north and south line
through squares M.33 and S.3.

        (b) The attack will be carried out by 20th Infantry
Brigade. One battalion 22nd Infantry Brigade will be
attached to 20th Infantry Brigade for the operation as
Brigade Reserve.

        (c) The infantry will assault at a zero hour which
will be notified later.

    3. The dividing line between the 7th and 33rd Divisions
will be central north and south line running through squares
M.33 - S.3.

    4. (a) Artillery.
             The attack will be preceded by a bombardment in
accordance with instructions issued by the XV Corps. The
last five minutes of the bombardment will be intense.

        (b) A map shewing the lift of the barrage during the
assault is attached.

    5. (a) The position when gained will be at once consolidated.
A support trench will be dug south of the enemy's trench
behind the crest of the hill, starting from the western
corner of HIGH WOOD and running north h-westwards. To dig
this trench two companies 24th Bn. Manchester Regiment (Pioneers)
are placed at the disposal of 20th Infantry Brigade.

                                                    (b)

The 95th Company, Royal Engineers' War Diary entry for July 17, 1916,
detailing the secret plans for an attack to be mounted the following day.

From Mabs
The Bedford, Newport, IW.   Friday, March 24, 1916
My Own Dear Boy,
I am glad to hear that the leave has started again. Now, I don't believe you would ever guess what I am doing as I write this. Well, I am actually smoking a cigarette. Don't think I am getting into bad habits because it's only a sample one, but I must confess I don't dislike it when I'm on my own. By the way, Ashley and Maud are living just over the road, (41), just above Mrs Reynolds. They are not having any honeymoon, but we will, won't we, when we have our wedding? Did I ever tell you that we have some R.E.s at Parkhurst, I believe they are from Portsmouth. We get several of them here and they are very good chaps too (sure to be if they are REs). Of course, they know all about you – one can't wear RE badges without being found out. We also get an escaped prisoner of war here too, or rather we used to. I missed him this last week. He had been coming every night for three months before he ever said a word about his escape. It was a very interesting story when I did get it out of him (you needn't worry – he is married). I hope you see him when you come home. Harry arrived on board again all right and he finds that his name is next on the list to come down south so he will be happy now, if he does get down to Portsmouth. I hear that you have picked up some 'undesirable companions'. Have you been told of any way to get rid of them? I expect you have, but another way won't hurt you unless you have already heard of it. Mother says you want to look in all the seams of your clothes for the eggs, and get rid of them first; that will keep them down a lot. You will find them in little bunches of tiny white egg-like things. Kill any of those that you find and then they can't grow up. Another way to get rid of those that can walk is to smoke them out of the seams with tobacco smoke. Let me know if you try it, whether it is any good. It is very trying for you to have to put up with such things. Dad says it won't be much good trying to leave them in France when you come home because they might follow you here, even if they have to swim the Channel. I expect he is thinking of Jim's, that are as big as rats. Well goodbye my love and just wait till you come home. I shan't have to send love and kisses then.
From your ever loving, Mabs.

From Mabs
The Bedford, Newport, IW.   Wednesday, March 29, 1916
My Dearest Bobbie,
Yes, you are a dear boy– absolutely the best boy I know, and I hope it won't be much longer before I can see you to tell you so myself. You really must look after yourself, you know. I expect such narrow squeaks as that last one you had would soon make you feel a bit shaky but still, I can only hope you will always be as lucky because I'm waiting very patiently for when you come home for good. Fancy, it is 11 months since I saw you last; it scarcely seems possible and yet at times it seems like years rather than months. Well, there's one consolation. Each is a month nearer the end of the war so we must hope for the best, that is, an ending this year. Ern is in France now. The 2nd Hants have all

gone there from Egypt. We wondered whether you might be anywhere near each other; you might be lucky enough to meet sometime. We only heard this morning by the way.

If Ernest Gordon describes himself as a – any more, Mabel Isabel will bite his neck when she gets near him. The idea of such a thing! Talking about making me glad to get rid of you in seven days. What will you do when we are married? (Tut-tut! I am surprised). Dad is going on all right. He cheerfully announced the end of the war for June 21st. Of course, we asking which year. As to politics, if you want to raise a storm when you come home just mention Mr Asquith or Lloyd George or any of those and sure enough you'll get it. You would begin to wonder where you had landed. Do take my advice and don't as much as whisper politics within a mile of Dad. We still have the old club but there are not many of the old members left. Mr Seal, Arthur Stratton, Ashley Russell, Mr Warne, Mr Brimson and Roy and about six others are all the old ones. I'm very sorry if I don't give you more home news, but there always seems a letter full before I have begun and I usually write in a hurry as you know. I suppose you will say, "Well – don't write in a hurry". Mother told me about two months ago to tell you that you never send any answers to all her postcards that she has sent. With fondest love and kisses,

I remain ever your loving Mabs.

I sent some tobacco in your Mother's parcel from Morry.

From Arch

28, Barnard Road, Clapham Junction. SW.   Wednesday, March 29, 1916

Dear Bob,

As I got out of the train at Victoria this afternoon, I noticed a crowd of trenchites had just arrived. They were a grimy lot. Among them were a number of Belgian fellows who were met and carried off by an 'impossible' gendarme with "Independence Belge" round his arm, like a Derby Schemer's armlet. He was like one of those French gendarmes you see in comic papers about 10 years old. The Belgian contingent seemed to find him quite in order. They treated him like their prodigal father. He took them away and you could hear his excited shouts die away in the distance. I ran into the whole lot again later on. The gendarme was driving his flock into the "Independence Belge" Office. The other arrivals were Scots and English and colonials with here and there, a light Poilu* in a tin hat. I noticed that whereas the English and Belgians were covered with mud and looked as if they could do with a hair cut, the Poilus were all spick and span. I suppose they are familiar enough to you. We had a hurricane last night which was some gale. When I saw all them soldier boys just across from France and Flanders I wondered what sort of crossing they had and moreover, whether you by any chance had been picked for the journey. In London the gale quite casually tore up trees and blew off chimney pots and forced some windows in, and some out. On Lavender Hill a tailor shop had a big plate glass window blown clean out. Someone must have opened the door just as a big gust of wind ambled along; you will see in the papers what a rotten night it was. If George

---

* A French term of endearment for the infantry, meaning literally, hairy one, referring to the fact that many of them came from an agricultural background, often sporting beards and bushy moustaches.

was on Special Coppering I know he must have enjoyed himself. As a matter of fact, these Special Coppers have lots of little things to make up for their discomfort and one thing is that the Police canteen is open for their delectation. I have heard sundry tales of the good choice dispensed in the police canteen although wild horses should not drag any particular names from me. It is said, and vouched for on good authority, that the closing hours enforced in common low down and ordinary pubs are disregarded in the sacrosanct police canteen and the "Special" coming off duty at 2 am can drop into the canteen and call for such delicacies as time and the hour suggest. After all, there may be something in this Special Coppering.

I hear that Mrs Newman has sent you out a goodly bundle of titbits; the old duck now eagerly awaiting a line from you as acknowledgment. When you send this she will carry on like she got a love letter from a sweetheart and make up a special round of visits to tell her pals of the conduct of the war as specially detailed to her by her pet lonely Soldier in the Trenches. You must think up a few lies that will pass the censor for her especial benefit. After all our discourse on rats and lice it is quite appropriate to see in this week's Punch a picture with rats for the "motif". I wish I had known before that Punch would be acceptable out there. I would have been sending it before. You can't beat Punch any which way you look at it. By the way there's a Captain Bruce Bairnsfather who sends excruciatingly funny "Fragments from France" to the Bystander.* I think some of the funniest things that have been drawn of the British Soldier in the war. The drawings have been collected into a separate book after the style of Hazeldens "Reflections" and are published separately. I must get hold of a copy and send you. I think the gallant captain is a RE so, of course, he would be a genius. On Saturday next I'd take Beeb (DV & weather permitting) to the Island. I wish your leave would eventuate at the same time. I have reached my three mile limit here so will finish. Love from all of us and kisses where applicable.

Ever your loving brother, Arch.

From Mabs
The Bedford, Newport, IW.   Saturday, April 1, 1916
My Own Dear Boy,
It seems weeks since I wrote before. You'd never believe what a job I have sometimes to stop from writing every day. We are still patiently waiting for you to come. No doubt our patience will be rewarded in time. One of my RE cousins is here. He is from Bethune, or whatever its name is. Your mother told me to tell you to leave instructions that should a parcel arrive for you after you have left for home, you might tell the boys to have it but I guess that is what you would do without being told to. I showed the REs your postcard. They were delighted and said that they couldn't get them when they were there. Some of them were at Bethune. Two were there 14 months. It is a glorious day today; it makes me wish for the old times again, but hang it all – it's no use wishing and thinking it over. It only gives one the blues. The front room is always to let now. Kath told Gordon she would lend it to him for his girl, but he says he will leave it to us

---

* Bairnsfather's cartoons were a national favourite. They appeared in *The Bystander*, a popular weekly magazine. Mabs kept a collection of Bystanders which are now in the posession of Richard Brimson. The Bairnsfather cartoons which appear on various pages throughout this book are all taken from Mabs' original copies.

(cheeky young monkey). I haven't seen Ron since Boxing Day. He is a nice lad. They all seem to grow up so, now. It hardly seems possible that they can be the same little ones I first knew, but I suppose six years is a long time. Just fancy six years since I first knew you. What a lot has happened in that time. I only hope we can have those dear old times again soon but there – it's no use me trying to express my feelings on paper. I never could and I don't suppose I ever shall be able to. Archy and Bee arrived yesterday afternoon and Archy is going back tomorrow (Monday) morning. Poor little Bee does look ill, but I think a little Isle of Wight air will soon put her right again. Morry was here last night so we had a family gathering, or something of the sort, at your house. It wanted you, Ern, Harry and Wallace to make it right though. I shall have to cut this short, with fondest love,

I remain yours, Mabs.

War Diary : "Morlancourt, nr. Bray - Resting."

From Bob

BEF   Sunday, April 2, 1916

Dear Mother and Father,

We are having the most beautiful weather out here; the trees are beginning to look green. Sometimes when the guns stop firing you would hardly believe there was a war on; everything is so peaceful and quiet and the larks singing too, but if you had been round this way last night you would have thought all hell had been let loose – such an awful bombardment on both sides. Our billets are on top of a hill and we could see the shells bursting right along the line; it was a proper stream of fire. I was glad I wasn't in the trenches at the time. Of course it makes a lot of work for us chaps when they smash the trenches in. Thanks very much for the postcard but if you find things going hard you mustn't send any more, and also limit the parcels to one a month. We have been paid a little more often lately so it hasn't been so bad. How do you manage about coal? According to the papers the price is enormous. I hope you manage to get along all right. I am glad the summer is coming along so fires won't be needed so much. The French burn things the shape of an egg; they are black like a lump of coal too, and it gives a decent heat. I have heard from Archy. He tells me the kiddies are all right again now. Give my respects to Doctor Reardon and all the others at Whitecroft, and Mr. Holt and family. Well I must close now, with my best love to you and Kath.

Ever your loving son, Bob.

War Diary : "Morlancourt, nr. Bray - 1 section at work in No. 2 Redoubt, cleaning it and rendering it habitable for one section. Remainder of company on night work, cutting trench in continuation of Lucknow Avenue. S Lancs Pioneers deepening and cleaning trench between Suffolk Avenue and Wellington Road."

From Bob

Royal Engineers. BEF   Monday, April 3, 1916

Dear Arch,

I received your welcome letter yesterday and I am very pleased to hear the kiddies are all right again, and also that you will be likely to pay a visit to the Island. Time keeps rolling on so I expect my turn will come shortly for leave. Some of the fellows who came out in my draft have already been home and it is now getting on for my ninth month out here. We are having lovely weather this way; in fact it's jolly hot in the daytime. I expect you will be having similar weather shortly. We also had a gale out here somewhere about the same time as you had, I expect. The leave was stopped for a couple of days. We put it down to the Channel being too rough for crossing.

After all you can't blame Jim if he has a staff job. He will be better off in more ways than one. We had some of his regiment stationed close to us, a Pioneer Battalion. W. Beard is also in the same village as we are. Their company has a mascot in the way of a large monkey, between 3 and 4 feet high – an object of curiosity to the French people round here. Y.M.C.A's have gradually worked their way up the line. You find them a matter of four miles behind the trenches, which is a fine thing for us. They are well patronised, too. By the way, one of our fellows had "Fragments from France" sent him. We've had many a good laugh over the illustrations. I may say he doesn't exaggerate them too much either. According to what Mabel says he is at Parkhurst Barracks attached to the 3rd Battalion. Well Arch, I must close now.

Your affectionate Brother, Bob.

From Mabs
The Bedford, Newport, IW.   Thursday, April 6, 1916
My Dearest Bobbie,
I am afraid this letter will be a bit late – but better late than never. I received yours yesterday and I am glad to hear they have moved you out of that shell region. I hope they won't start shelling that village, too. Ern is in the 29th Division. They were out at the Dardanelles so I suppose the whole Division has moved to France. We haven't had another letter from him yet. Jack Bull and Ernie White are there too, in the same Division. You must look up those Warwicks. I should think you will be sure to find someone amongst them who knows this place. I hope you find Bert Hannam or Cherry Horton. Mickey Walsh is gone to France again but I don't know which battalion he was sent to. I didn't see him while he was at Parkhurst. He never came near the house to see any of us so I suppose he is another of them. The weather here is just glorious now. I hope you are getting it as good.

With best love and kisses, I remain yours sincerely, Mabs.

From Kath
49, Carisbrooke Rd, Newport.   Sunday, April 9, 1916
Dear Bob,
I'm writing this out in the garden. Dad is all right again now and has been able to get to work this last fortnight. We are having lovely weather now.
It's a good thing you are too and it is lucky you are so close to Walt Baird – he'll be company for you. We are still expecting to see you walk in any minute. They

do seem a mighty long time letting you off. I suppose next it will be some time in May. I shall believe it's what Arch says – you don't make enough fuss about it. We have got Bebe down here. Arch brought her last Saturday, April 1st. She has been here a week and has already begun to improve but she is as thin as a match; you can hardly see her when she's got her dress off.

Bee and I went over to Mabel's to tea last Wednesday. They have been very good to Bee. Mabel bought a cod's liver and made her some cod-liver oil and Mrs A gave us some port wine for her although Beeb doesn't think much of it. We are out in the yard. It's hot enough to bake us. You must have been having a dreadful time of it lately, by all accounts of your letter. You have never 'expressed' yourself like that before. You tell Mabel you've moved away from the firing. I expect you thought it was about time too. That was a lucky escape you had from the shell that exploded on the other side of the road. Good gracious! It seems hard to understand it here excepting when we hear there has been some more Zepp raids. Never know when they will take it into their heads to pay us a visit. We do get a good few A'planes about now, though. Mother will tell you what a surprise we have just had. We'll leave it for her.

With best love and kisses, ever your loving sister, Kath.

From Mother
49, Carisbrooke Rd, Newport.   Monday, April 10, 1916
Dear Bob,
I went to the door to answer a knock and there was C. Dyer as large as life and looking as well as ever. I was so glad to see him – I did wish it was you though. I hope you will be here soon now and he says you may come along any time while he is here. He only got here this morning. He says tell Bob to try and get an extra day for travelling, for he has got one. I got the card and was glad you got the parcel. Mab put in the tobacco and chocs so you must thank her. We are having beautiful weather. Now Bob, I will close as Kath has told you everything
Goodbye my dear son,
Ever your loving Mother, E. Brimson.

From Mabs
The Bedford, Newport, IW.   Monday, April 10, 1916
My Dearest Boy,
You ought to be here, but I suppose I might just as well say you ought to be in America. Well anyway, Charlie Dyer is here if that isn't a good enough reason. I saw Charlie strolling up the Mall, so of course I went out to catch him as he passed. He was surprised to hear that you were not home. I am quite sure he was looking forward to seeing you. Never mind. You still have yours to come, but it is hard work to wait and be patient but I suppose it is no use to growl about it after all. It is such a beautiful moonlight tonight, just like one of our old nights only you are not here. I have just been going over St George's Down with you again – but imagination isn't any good. It doesn't seem to bring you here. Still, perhaps we shall have a nice full moon when you do get here. I shan't have

any teeth left if they stop your leave again. They will be all mashed away with rage.

I had a letter from Ern today. He has cheered up again now and is looking forward to his leave. Percy Blow went away yesterday to join up under the group system. Morry isn't gone on board the Royal Sovereign yet, but he expects to go any day now. The best of it is he asked his girl (one of them) to come down for Easter. She is coming this week and he is in a fix now because he might not have a chance to see her. She may be in Portsmouth for a fortnight. Oh, the trials and troubles of this wicked war. Straff that Kaiser. Now what do you think the latest is? Well, the new Minister next door has a son who isn't very strong and as they haven't any garden of their own, he must want ours. So Dad has let him have the vegetable half and they began working on it today. He is a lieutenant, but only in the office, because he is too delicate to go in for much. It must be very hard for him because he is quite young. He wants the garden to amuse himself, but he can't dig it himself. He can only look on at that.

Goodbye my love for a little while and you can have all the kisses when you come home.

I remain your ever loving sweetheart, Mabs.

From Arch

28, Barnard Road, Clapham Junction. SW.   Tuesday, April 11, 1916
Dear Bob,

We are glad to think you are back from the firing line again. Kath tells us C. Dyer is home on leave. This is a dirty trick – him getting leave before you. However, she says C. Dyer came home by way of London and put in a night here in town because he couldn't get home that night. This may be the same for you and if so, don't forget that we shall be only too pleased to have you. Kath says C. Dyer looks as well as possible. He gives you a good character and says you look very fit.

I took Beeb down to Mother last Saturday week. Morry was over for the evening, and Dad and Roy and I went over as usual just to see that the Bedford didn't run away. Laurie came over home after to see Mabel back safe, and also to see that two bottles were properly unstoppered. Jim says the same thing happened when he was down there last, only Jim couldn't count the bottles. Every time he reached out for his glass he missed it. In the end it was Mabel who did the seeing home, I guess. Mabel is looking very well and is getting anxious for the time of your leave to arrive. There was some 'orrible singing going on in the Bedford when I was there on Saturday week. It seemed like to me that a soldier with a violent stomach ache was trying to sing the 'Rag Time Violin' through his nose. I didn't go into the room to put him out of his misery but he was chucked out at closing time like the rest of us. Mrs. Chiverton was there with her old man, sharing a pint, as of yore, and that old woman whose daughter always comes in with her and talks to soldiers; they was in. I don't know their name but you would know them right enough. The old 'un usually starts dancing after the 15th drop of gin.

I served a divorce petition on an old soldier today. He ain't in the Army no more now but I took his wife down to identify him. When she saw him coming she started trembling all over, like, and I had to prop her up against the wall. I asked her afterwards what was up and she said she thought of the last time she saw him. The last time she saw him to speak to, it appears he punched her hard on the end of the nose and done two months for it. That was eight years ago and she's been saving up for a divorce ever since. I saw the woman he lives with now and as she had two beautiful black eyes I guess he had been educating her. If you manage to get home now, you will get back at the best time of the year. Even our garden begins to look up and Dad's garden will be lovely in a week or two when those pear trees come into blossom. The white violets are all about. Do they have primroses and such in France and Flanders? I suppose that sort of information may reasonably be asked for and given. I tell you what, if you get the chance take Ma home a little root when you go. She would think no end of a little plant what she could think came from some plaguey battlefield.

We got a stationery wallet for you. It shall reach you as soon as possible. I haven't been able to find one such as I should have thought would be made. I shall have to design one I can see, and if I thought anyone would give me anything for the design I'm blamed if I wouldn't. The things they make and sell as folders or stationery wallets are putrid.

Well I'm at the end of my invention now and must finish. I wish the war would also finish. Sometimes I get almost tired of the repetition in the papers and still you seem bound to read it all. Even when you have read it all, you are not much wiser and everyone has heard something from a man who saw an aeroplane that had a flying man in it who once spoke to a relative of the Prime Minister's cook's young man, and so got certain information as to the conclusion of the war – and so it goes on.

However, I live in hopes that the war will end sometime or other. Captain Bairnsfather in his 'Fragments From France' seems to foreshadow that. Horny-headed and bearded Tommies within the distant years discuss the arrival of the War Babies Battalion. Did you see that picture? So long Bob, love and kisses and all that.

Ever your loving brother, Archy.

War Diary : "Morlancourt, nr. Bray – Work in trenches. Heavy rain at intervals."
From Bob
Royal Engineers. BEF   Thursday, April 13, 1916
Dear Mother and Father,
Sorry to have kept you waiting so long for a letter but I have been expecting one from you. I received the parcel all right. Thanks very much for it. The pineapple was a treat and so was the cake and the tarts. The tobacco was the right kind, a decent change from the light kind they give us out here. We are very busy now, working from seven in the morning till six at night. We have to drive six miles to the trenches in pontoon wagons. We have to take a circular route to avoid the shell fire; that is the reason the journey is so long. This morning we passed six horses lying all of a heap in the road, all killed by one shell – it was rather a nasty sight. I believe there was only one driver wounded out of the lot.

We had rather an exciting experience the other afternoon. We had been working under shell fire nearly all day and when we knocked off we had to cross some open ground to reach the wagon, when the Germans opened fire on us with three inch shells. Then we had to run the gauntlet. We can hear shells coming through the air and of course, we immediately lay down flat, which is the safest way. Luckily they all pitched a few yards on our right and no one was hurt. Since then, we have finished that job and are working in a quieter place.

Did you send a letter with the parcel? because if you did, I did not get it. Have just had some papers from Archy. Hope Dad and you and Kath are keeping quite well. I believe it is Kath's turn to write again. Am writing to Mabs tomorrow, all being well. Still get the County Press all right. Must close now, with fondest love to you all.

Ever your affectionate son, Bob.

From Mabs
The Bedford, Newport, IW.   Thursday, April 13, 1916
My Dearest Bobby,
We have just had Morry home again. He thinks this is the last time as they will probably go out on Monday. His head has been troubling him again lately, too. It must be beastly for him, always being plagued like that. He can't get any sleep at night through it. It is a good thing he is going on a bigger ship this time or I am sure he would never survive another trip on a little one. We can only hope the sea air will do him good on this one. Ern has been having exciting times lately. We haven't heard from him for about a fortnight, but one of the men on leave told me he said that Ern was one of the bombing party a week last Sunday, and one of the bombs exploded too close to him and blew him into the air, but fortunately he wasn't hurt. I don't suppose you ever hear from Wallace? We only hear about once in a blue moon. I suppose he thinks it is all right as long as he is alive. He must be coming home again shortly (for good) but I will tell you the reason when you come home. Very likely I shouldn't be able to explain properly here. I haven't said anything to Kath yet and I don't think I will unless he is really coming for good. Things go on much about the same here. I sometimes wonder if Newport ever will change. I expect it's impossible.

Well, I must close now, I remain your loving sweetheart Mabs.
I hope you are lucky enough for the end of the month.

From Charlie
87 Field Co. R.E. Battalion 12th Division, BEF.   Sunday, April 16, 1916
Dear Bob,
Just a few lines hoping it will find you fit. I have been home this week on my leave and going back tomorrow. Have to stop here tonight in London. Glad to say that I had a very nice time. Went in and saw your mother and father. Glad to find them well, anxiously waiting for you to come home on your leave. We are stationed at 'Sally Labouise' – been there for the last two months. All the boys wish to be remembered to you. We have sorted the Major, he has gone to

the 19th Division, made Colonel. Lieutenant Alderson, he was killed, also Lay Latham and Sapper Renaugh. I should be very pleased to have a line from you when you have the chance. Hoping to come across you again soon.
From your old chum Charlie.

From Mabs
The Bedford, Newport, IW.   Sunday, April 16, 1916
My Own Dear Boy,
Poor old Charlie went off again this afternoon. He is happy enough over it and tells your mother not to worry a bit about you, because you are all right. I expect you will wonder why my letter is late but it happened that I had to rush off in a hurry to Portsmouth because Morry wanted me to meet his girl for him. I came back yesterday afternoon. Portsmouth is still the same as ever, except that it is full of khaki and blue. Of course, there are always plenty of blues about but not as many khakis. Morry is still on the Amphitrite, the other ship isn't ready yet. He was over this afternoon with his girl. By the way he tells me I shall have to get his wedding present before he gets mine (tut-tut). He must be smitten. Bee has been into the country with me today; we thought it would do her good. We went in a car all round about Westover, Calbourne and Newbridge. It would have been much better if the showers had kept away but we didn't get wet and Bee enjoyed it. I can't get rid of the idea that you are coming. I even watched for you at 11 o'clock in case you came with that early morning train from Waterloo, but there was no sign of Bob. It is a glorious moonlight night again; a full moon this time (beastly, I call it). I wanted to be away over the hills in the moonlight but it's go to bed instead. There is a pretty little song out now called "Just take two and the moon". You must hear it when you come home. The REs are waiting for you to come home but I expect they want to talk about old times. Are you anywhere near the 92nd Company? Let me know if you are. Au Revoir for now,
I remain ever your loving sweetheart, Mabs.

From Kath
49, Carisbrooke Rd, Newport.   Wednesday, April 19, 1916
Dear Bob,
We were all ever so glad to get your letter today, you have been having some dreadfully exciting times and no mistake. It makes anyone quake to think about it. We do want you for Easter. Arch expected you last Sunday, Chris says in her letter. All the day he saved a cigar for you. They are coming down tomorrow (Thursday). I have had it in my head all along that you would be here as well. Easter, if you don't turn up, it will be a dreadful disappointment for us and you must be sick and tired of waiting.
Doris is here strumming on your guitar. She plays it very well; she'll be another Roy. She says she wrote to you in school today so she will put it in here. She has been up the Barracks with her school, entertaining the wounded soldiers, enjoying herself no end.
What do you think of poor little 'Stump' snuffing it. Dad says he wanted to go

Soldiers returning from the Front are given a welcome home at the
entrance to Ryde Esplanade railway station, 1916.

out and do some more painting just before he died, poor little chap.
Gordon came in again just now to show us his new khaki. It's just the same as
the I.W. Rifles. He looks fine; looks mighty proud of it too. Poor little Bebe is
picking up again now. Mother keeps feeding her up. Mabel took her out in the
Bakers' motor Monday, all round Calbourne way.
It was nice to see Charlie. I gave him Arch's address. He said he would like to
call if he had time. Well, I can't think of any more to tell you now.
    Heaps of love and kisses from us all, ever your loving sister Kath.

From Doris with Kath's
31, Melbourne Street. Newport.   Wednesday, April 19, 1916
Dear Bob,
It is about time I wrote again. Uncle Jack is coming over Easter Monday. We
went out Gatcombe House again yesterday, Tuesday. We had a fine time (that
blessed teacher has got her eyes on me).
Had a game of football with the soldiers after tea. We didn't half cheer up when
we came away. Daddy is working at Saunder's aeroplane shed*, doping
aeroplanes with some celluloid and chloroform mixture (I don't know whether
this is what they do it with or if this is what it smells like). He says there are the
most terrible smells all over the place down there. Each room has its own
peculiar 'perfume' or 'aroma' (or 'stink' is most like it). The men told him that
he has not had half of the scents yet. He says he reckons he's had enough.
I met Mabs and Bee going home from school on Monday. They were waiting for
Week's motor van (bread cart) to take them into the country. I was galloping
along with two other girls (dinner time, you know) and nearly rushed headlong
into them. Mabel had to yell out to me before I stopped (that bally teacher
again). That was a quarter to one. At quarter past I was going back and was just
in time to see them get in the car. I was off to hard work (I don't think! For we
had a rehearsal all the afternoon) and they were going to Calbourne in a motor.
We are going to give a concert to the wounded at Parkhurst this afternoon (tres
bien, n'est pas?).
Little Albert out the asylum is dead at last. The paint did not agree with him.
We are breaking up this dinner time, 12 o'clock (very nice too). I went in 49
Carisbrooke Road last night. Kath was writing a letter so this goes with it. I am
supposed to be doing history now. It was fine up Parkhurst. Only the wounded
were allowed to come in so all the rest stood round the YMCA hut and looked
in at the windows, joining in the chorus's. We had a free bath coming back – it
was pouring with rain.
The kids broke up yesterday. I have not anything else to say, so I shall not say
it.
                          With love, Doris.
PS. Daddy breaks up tonight at 4.30 and goes back Tuesday morning. Uncle
Archie will be here. I bet they will enjoy themselves. Bell has rung so I can't do
any more.

---

* Saunders of East Cowes, later, Saunders-Roe.

1916

From Mabs
The Bedford, Newport, IW.   Sunday, April 23, 1916
My Dearest Bobby,

I am sorry to hear that your leave has been stopped again, but there – I suppose we must make the best of it. It is all very well to come but I had already jumped a bit further and thought about the going away again. Well, never mind. We won't think about it at all, because I know I shan't want to let you go away again. Maud Reynolds was expecting her future husband home and they were to be married tomorrow (Monday) and he hasn't arrived, so I suppose there are some worse off. He is a Grenadier Guard. Now what do you think has happened? You know I wrote about a girl coming down to Portsmouth to see Morry? Well, it seems to be a case this time for he has bought her a ring, (not a plain one) and he says I shall have to buy his wedding present before he buys mine now, so I think it looks like business. There are two confounded cats out in the garden who ought to be shut up, with anything that howls, for the next ten years, (beasts), (howlers). Drat 'em. Morry is on the Royal Sovereign now; went aboard last Monday. I suppose those German blighters will be after her now as soon as she moves. I do hope they soon start your leave again. Why, if you are not home before May 10th it will make twelve months since I saw anything of you. Just fancy – twelve months. It seems like years sometimes. I saw Archy Strutt and Tom Barton today. I felt inclined to knock their heads together for a pair of microbes. Fancy such creatures thinking they are men. If they had any really good reason for still being here one could pity them, but they make me feel tired, but I suppose their time will come – and the sooner the better. We all spent Good Friday out beyond Betty Aunt, or whatever its name is, getting primroses and white violets. Countryside is just glorious now with primroses. We only wanted you to set things right, then Roy was there. We had sweet (?) music all the way home because the tyre came off of Kathie's chair and they couldn't make it stop on again.

I had another letter from Ern on Thursday. I haven't the least idea where he can be, yet he says he is still trying to find you. Well, I believe I have about exhausted my supply of nonsense so I must finish now. Goodnight my love and do please take care of yourself to come home safe.

Your ever loving sweetheart, Mabs.

From Mabs
The Bedford, Newport, IW.   Thursday, April 27, 1916
My Dearest Boy,

I have had to go to Osborne House today with Alice Barlow.* We went on bicycles and enjoyed it very much. It is glorious weather that we are having now. When will you be here to enjoy it? Morry is home again this afternoon until tomorrow morning. Lucky beggar. I hear that young Sharp is home again, too – Cheek! How dare he? Mrs Brimson and all of them are off to the pictures tonight but I'm not going. I don't like pictures this time of the year. According to the papers you must have been having hot times your way again. I hope the worst is over again now, for a time at least. What dreadful doings in Ireland

---

* Alice married Morry, Mabs' brother, later in the year and following his death in 1954 she became the landlord of the Bedford until its closure. See photograph page 17.

again. I think the people must all be going mad. Things are quite bad enough
without any of that sort of thing to make it worse.* I will finish off now. With
fondest love heaps and kisses,
          I remain ever your loving sweetheart, Mabs.

*War Diary : "Morlancourt, nr. Bray - Work commenced on Advance dressing station
Wellington Redoubt."*
From Bob
Royal Engineers. BEF   Friday, April 28, 1916
Dear Mother and Father,
I expect you are wondering when I am going to answer your letter. Glad to hear
C. Dyer has been home. I should like to have been home at the same time. I hope
you had a good time at Easter all together. Of course, we were working just the
same. Our Easter Sunday meal consisted of what they call 'iron rations,' that is
bully and biscuits for breakfast, dinner and tea. I think something must have
gone wrong with the transport. However, better luck next Easter.
I expect it will be some weeks yet before I shall be home as they keep stopping
and starting again. Have not had the County Press this week. Did you send it?
Sorry to hear about Albert Toogood's death but perhaps he will be better off
after all, poor chap. Remember me to Peter when you see him Dad, and also the
rest of the staff at Whitecroft. I hope you are still drawing the money all right
and that you are both keeping in good health; also Kath. We are having glorious
weather here now; quite hot in the daytime. In fact I slept out in the open last
night under the starry sky. Well Mother, I have no news to tell you this time.
Shall be glad to hear from you again soon.
                    Ever your loving son, Bob.
A parcel will be very acceptable – only don't put yourself to too much expense

From Mother
49, Carisbrooke Rd, Newport.   Thursday, May 4, 1916
My Dear Bob,
My mind was eased yesterday on receiving your letter. When I don't get one I
keep thinking you are coming home. We were so glad to see C. Dyer. I saw his
mother the other day. She tells me they have to address his letters as Corp.
Dyer. He seems to be getting on but he told me that he will be quite ready to
come out of it when the war is over. I hope you are in the same mind but I
expect you are for it seems awfully rough times for you poor fellows out there.
I lay in bed and think about you often. I hope you got the County Press. I send
you it every Saturday afternoon – what there is of it.** George is still in Egypt,
Jack Cornish is still at Winchester. Goes up to London with three more
sergeants every day to fetch the Derbys down. He says they do have some
trouble with some of them. They have to look sharp after them for they would
lose their stripes if they let them go. One got away once and they had to chase

---

* The Easter Uprising had been launched by Irish republicans who wanted an end to British rule
** Due to paper shortages the County Press had shrunk to eight pages, rather than its normal twelve.

him and found him in bed. They pulled him out and marched him off. We take the Daily Mail now. C. Dyer says he gets the best of food. I think it is a great shame for you to have such poor food. Is it always the same? I haven't sent lately, for everybody said you would be coming – that they were coming home in batches and C. said you would likely walk in while he was at home.

Easter passed nice and pleasant. We only wanted you. Everybody says, "We only want Bob." Yours was a poor affair. We must make it up next Easter. Now goodbye my son.

From your ever loving mother, E. Brimson.

From Mabs
The Bedford, Newport, IW.   Thursday, May 4, 1916
My Dearest Boy,
I received your letter yesterday morning and it was a treat, I can tell you. Of course, I don't get very anxious when you don't write because I am quite sure if anything happened to you we should hear at once from someone in the Company. I hope you take great care of yourself in that 'Happy Valley'. One of the RE's who came here has been there and he was also in a place with a long curious name beginning with M.*

Maud Reynolds has had her wedding after all. I went over to it and we had a very nice time, but I will tell you all about it when you come home, that is if you are interested. It was a very pretty wedding. May and Emma were bridesmaids. As to our wedding – well, I will leave that to you. It would be nice to make sure of it when you come home but I expect it would be nicer after all this trouble is ended. Still, if you are really serious, well, I will leave it to you to decide. I dearly hope you will soon come home. You can't tell how I am longing for a sight of you again. It will be twelve months next week since we last saw you here. It is quite time you had a leave. Some of them can get home often enough, especially the Officers. Ern hasn't said any more about coming home so I suppose their leave is all off too, for a time. We had a letter from Harry this morning. He is all right but busy as usual. Mother is sending a parcel off for you tomorrow. We wanted to send it today but we couldn't get any bread from the baker's whose bread keeps best so we must wait until the morning. We thought bread and eggs and things like that would be a change, as you told your mother you had been living on bully beef and biscuits. You would have had parcels for Easter, only we were so sure of you coming home that we didn't send in case you did come. I am glad you like the 'cigs.' It is impossible to know what to send. I hope I shall be able to send some more of Morry's tobacco soon. I usually give it to your Father. Well, I'm glad they have settled this compulsion affair at last, it is about time. It will come rather hard on some, but it will just be what a great many of them deserve. Well, must close again now my dear boy.

With love and kisses,
remain ever Mabs.
PS. Sid Upward is married now to a kid of about 16. Tut-tut.

---

* For much of April, the 95th were based at Morlancourt.

For reasons unknown, this next letter is the last one in the collection from Mabs in 1916. Her letters do not make a return until January 1917.

From Mabs
The Bedford, Newport, IW.   Monday, May 8, 1916
My Own Dear Boy,
I hope by this time you will have had your parcel. It is a nuisance when we want to send things to France. We can only send seven pounds and the boxes seem to weigh that before we get anything in them. Tell me whether you like that kind of parcel and then we shall know what to do. Your mother will send you one this week so you will have a little change. I believe they are starting on the daylight saving game here next week. If they do, we shall have to put the clock on an hour.* It is a very good plan, too, I should think. Florrie White had a son yesterday (Sunday) so I expect they are feeling mighty pleased about it. She wanted a boy. I wonder if there will be any chance of you seeing them when you come home. Now don't get alarmed – you are not obliged to go. Another kind friend gave me a nice present tonight. It is a silver cake knife. Now, don't you think I was born under a lucky star? First to get you, you dear old treasure (excuse me calling you names) and then all these various nice things that keep coming. I own I'm not content, but I suppose that isn't my fault. We must blame the Kaiser for that. How do you find it out in France? Better than this I hope. We had quite a party here on Sunday. All the Reynolds came over. They are a jolly family when they are together. Well, just wait till you come home for good. There will be celebrations then. Twelve months ago today, you were here for the last leave before you went to France. It is about time they let you come home again. They are giving leave already to that lot that left here about three months ago. I suppose some will be lucky enough to get it and the others will have to wait till their turn comes round, as you have had to wait for yours. Morry was home again Saturday. I hope they don't take him out just when you are coming or else he will get wild, after keeping him over there this time. Kath, Doris, Bee and myself have just been out for a little run to get some fresh air, as the sun came out for a few minutes after tea. With fondest love and kisses.
From your loving sweetheart, Mabs.

War Diary : "Morlancourt, nr. Bray - Work commenced on Advance dressing station Wellington Redoubt."
From Bob
Sapper E. G. Brimson 46870, Royal Engineers. BEF.   Wednesday, May 10, 1916
Dear Mabs,
I received your letter and also the parcel all right. Thanks very much. It was a treat to get such a lovely load, and fresh butter and the eggs – I can tell you I had some good feeds. We have been awfully short of food lately but it is getting a bit better now, and being in this camp it is impossible to buy anything. I started to write this but the pipe band of the Gordon Highlanders, who are in the same camp, are playing just outside our tent so I had to stop, so as they have

---

* British Summer Time was introduced on May 21, 1916, following its introduction in Germany on April 30th.

1916

now finished I can continue.

I think myself after all, it will be as well to leave our affair until the world is at peace again as it would be awful to have to leave you again so soon and besides, we can have a nice long holiday if everything turns out all right.

I can see Roy and Gordon both being called up together. I think they will have enough troops soon. Leave is still going on all right and I am patiently waiting for my turn to come. I shall soon have been out here ten months. I'm getting quite an old campaigner. No signs of any Hants knocking about yet, almost any other regiment but those, but I expect I shall run against them sometime.

I haven't any thrilling news for you this time. Things have been very quiet for this last few days. Archy has suddenly ceased sending the Sunday Pictorial. Has anything happened? I used to look forward to that.

There is one thing I should like to mention and that is that it is jolly hard lines on us fellows out here, considering what we have to go through, and then those cursed Irish people acting as they did. I am glad they are doing the right thing shooting them. Well Mabs, I must close now as the postman is waiting to take the letter.

Best love and kisses ever your sweetheart, Bob.

From Roy

31, Melbourne St. Newport.   Sunday, May 14, 1916

Dear Bob,

It is getting near time for one to be up 'somewhere.' It do make me mad. I don't want to be humbugged about. Gordon was 18 years of age last Thursday so he will have to go soon. Jacobs came home a fortnight ago. He said he should never come back to stop again in Carisbrooke. He was looking well, they said. When I go up Carisbrooke Sunday nights, there are only about six of the old boys left. It is miserable here now.

The Red Lion is shut up. 'Gill' has gone away and no one will take it. Of course, there is no business to be done now. The rent is only £10 a year. I am working down Cowes at Saunders Ltd., mostly on airships and planes. There are about ten girls working with me but it is very poisonous work. I had to stop home for a day or two. We all take turns with it. They have all been bad. Morrie Attrill was home Friday and Saturday – we had a Friday night together. He is off to sea again Monday, 15th of May so he didn't know whether he should come back again.

Did you know 'Farmer' Gaster, Perce Gaster's brother? They have had his letters returned lately. We were all together a few weeks ago. He has only just gone out. Starks is still down dock. He often asks for you.

We have been working very late – 6 am until 10 pm – but I catch the 8.30 pm up, get home at 9 pm, up in the morning at 4.30. It is a long day.

Your affectionate brother, Roy.

Things have got very expensive here.

War Diary : "Grovetown, nr. Bray – Work in trenches and on Grantown and Georgetowns camps as previous days. Work stopped in trenches by very wet weather."
From Bob
BEF   Monday, May 15, 1916
Dear Kath,
I think I will write to you this time as I owe you a letter. I got the parcel all right thanks very much. They are very acceptable, those kind, you can have a good feed after a day's work. I got Mab's parcel quite safely too. I have written and told her the Company Pay Corporal has asked for my home address, so you can expect me to be home any time now unless the leave is stopped again. I want Mother to have a clean change of underclothing for me and if you can find that pair of low shoes, to get them soled – or a pair of boots if there is any about, as mine are too big and heavy. Thank Mabs for the shaving stick.
I hope you are all keeping well at home. We are having very changeable weather out here; hot one day and torrents of rain the next. They have taken our blankets away from us today so in future we shall have to sleep in our clothes; we shan't have the trouble of dressing for the first parade. The other night we actually had an open-air concert got up by the Gordons before they went in the trenches and at intervals we had a selection on the pipes and drums. I'm almost sure the Germhunds could hear them but our big guns at the top of the hill were sending over souvenirs for them, just to keep them quiet. We had some very good singers among the Jocks and one fellow had a violin which had to take the place of a piano. It lasted up until about 10 o'clock. We had a very decent time. It's been raining today so they have issued us a tot of rum all round.
Well I must stop now. My best love to you Mother and Dad. Hoping to see you all soon. Remember me to all our friends,
                                        ever your loving brother, Bob.
Don't send any more parcels.

Bob was granted leave, from May 21st to June 1st, his first leave since arriving in France in the August of last year.

War Diary : "Grovetown, nr. Bray – Usual work in trenches and intermediate line etc."
From Bob
BEF   Sunday, June 4, 1916
My Sweet Little Pet,
It was a treat to get your cheery letter yesterday. I can tell you I did feel a bit downhearted coming back, and I was only one of thousands of others that felt the same. I spent about an hour or two in Southampton wandering round on my own, left all my things at the soldiers' rest. I wish you had come as far after all. The boat left about 7 pm. I am enclosing a photo of her, the Viper. She done it in six hours. They can get us back quicker than they get us here.
We had a tiring railway journey; everyone was fed up. I got to the railhead at 7pm and there was a driver waiting with a dogcart to drive me to the camp, which is a journey of about eight miles. He made the horse step it out, so it didn't take us long before I was once more within sound of the guns. There is a big one firing now, close by us; a 9.2 by the noise she makes.

County Press advertisements, 1916.

Well, when I arrived in the camp I thought I should have to tramp up to the trenches to join my section but as it happens, I found I was attached to headquarters for two or three weeks, so I found a wigwam for myself and here I am still. We had another concert last night given by the Manchester Regiment. They had a brass band as well and a stage rigged up with a piano. There are a lot of Indians in an adjoining camp and they flocked over and one of them got upon the stage to give us a song. He made it up of what English he knew something about, 'We came here and got some beer,' and then running off into 'Jack and Jill' and finished up with 'Pussycat, where have you been?' I don't believe he knew what it all meant, only it was a bit of English and that's all he cared about. Of course, he was loudly applauded and felt very proud before the rest of his comrades.

Well Mabs, there is one thing that has been worrying me and that is, I forgot to pay for the bottle I brought away. There is only one thing to do and that is to let Mother know and you can take it out of my money she draws from the Post Office. I didn't remember it until I reached Southampton.

And I did have a good time at home Mabs – the time of my life – only it went so quick I hadn't told you half I wanted to and I didn't have a quarter of the kisses I wanted, or it seems to me I didn't. It seems like a dream to me now, and the lovely drive we had on Sunday. It doesn't half make you homesick when you think of it, but we've got a lot of work to do out here yet.

Last night I think some of our lads caught Fritz napping. They made a bombing raid and brought it off very successful too. I dare say you will see it in the paper.* I watched them march off last evening. I was glad of the provisions that you and Mother put up for me. They have kept me going right up till now and still I've some left yet. Well Mabs, I must close now with my best and true love and heaps of kisses.

Ever your sweetheart, Bob.

Remember me to all at home and friends as well.

War Diary: "Grovetown, nr. Bray – Work in trenches. No infantry working parties arrived thereby disorganising and delaying the whole day's work."

From Bob
BEF   Tuesday, June 6, 1916
Dear Mother,
Have heard about the Queen Mary going down and I see by a paper I got today that only 14 were saved. Let me know as soon as you can if Harry is all right.** I've been anxiously waiting for a letter. Things looked very black according to the rumours we got at first out here, but they seem to be a lot better now. It seems as if the Germans got the worst of it after all. I am going on all right and getting settled down to it again. I hope you are all well at home and let me know as soon as you get news. Best love to Mabs and all of you.

Ever your loving son, Bob.

---

* There is no reference to the raid in the War Diary.
** Harry's ship, the battleship Queen Mary, was sunk by the German battlecruiser Derfflinger during the Battle of Jutland. Over 1200 men were lost, including Harry, aged 29. The wreck of the Queen Mary was discovered in 1991 and has been declared an official war grave.

War Diary: "Grovetown, nr. Bray - Work in trenches. Wet in morning. Cleared later."
From Bob
BEF   Wednesday, June 14, 1916
Dear Mother, Father and Kath,
This is to all of you as you all have birthdays this month. I wish you all many happy returns of the days and that the next you have, I will be home with you all for good. It's impossible for me to send you presents so you must take it out of the money in what way you like, and we will have a good time when I do come home. That week's leave went like greased lightning. I can hardly realise I've been, sometimes. I wrote you a letter some days ago asking about Harry. Did you happen to get it? Poor old chap. I can't think he's gone yet. I'd still some hope of him being alive. Poor little Mabs must feel it awfully, and her people. I've just had Kath's nice letter this evening with Arch and Chris's enclosed. I'm very glad that Bebe is getting so much better again give her a big kiss from her uncle Bob. I haven't heard from Arch and Chris for ages now, neither have I had a Sunday Pictorial. Do you think you could manage to send Lloyds as well as the County Press? Now, as the Russians are doing so well there is something to read. It looks as if business has started at last. It was jolly hard lines about Kitchener;* the troops were awfully downhearted about it for a while. I expect Robertson will take his place.
Well, I've no exciting news to tell you so I will wind up. Hoping to hear from you again soon,
       I remain yours affectionately, Bob.
They are only getting six days leave now, so I was lucky after all.
PS I often think of the drive we had, too. It's just like a dream.

War Diary: "Grovetown, nr. Bray - Work in trenches. Wet in morning. Cleared later."
From Bob
BEF   Wednesday, June 14, 1916
Dear Little Mabs,
I received your letter yesterday. I am awfully sorry you have heard nothing definite about poor old Harry. Like you, I am hoping for the best. We can only get a paper occasionally here, so we had to gather what we could from them. The victory was on our side, there is no doubt about that, but we had to pay an awful price for it. I only hope that Harry was amongst the survivors. It must be an anxious time for you and your people. I wish I could be with you, my pet, to share your trouble instead of being miles way out here. I do miss you awfully because I had such a grand time the few hours I was with you. It seems like a dream now. I like to think of the afternoon we walked over St George's Down. That did seem like old times again, just you and I together, and also the afternoon we all went up to the Castle and the drive we had. It's nice to think about it all out here. I think I am more fed up with the war since I came back than ever I was, but still, it can't be helped. We've got to finish it off and I've got a score to pay off on the Hun now – that is, if the worst has happened – but whether it has or not, they will have no mercy from me after this.

---

* Kitchener was was one of more than 600 drowned on 5 June, 1916, when HMS Hampshire sank west of the Orkney Islands, Scotland, after the ship struck a German mine.

Well Mabs, I was jolly pleased with the tobacco as I happened to be short and it came just right. It's Dad's birthday today as well. I should have liked him to have had a letter from me. I am writing tonight so better late than never. There are three birthdays this month, but I got mixed up in them. Was it Kath's on the ninth and is it Mother's on the 21st? I am sorry I forgot about those bottles. I can't remember paying for them now, but I was a bit worried about leaving you all again. I dare say you understand. Well Mab's, I must close now, with my deepest love for you and heaps of kisses.

Ever your true love Bob.

Write again soon Mabs and let me know if you hear.

From Kath
49, Carisbrooke Rd, Newport.   Thursday, June 22, 1916
Dear Bob,
We have got a young varmint here. I told you that Frank Gaiger's boy was coming for a week. Well, he has come. He is great pals with Gordon already. He is only 16, and a lot taller than Gordon, and looks about 20 and comes in as early as 12 o'clock at night. He goes up to Roy's after being out with Gordon till somewhere about eleven. He is a nice kid though. At present he is sitting opposite to me, writing home to his mother to tell her he is going to stay here and going to get work at White's* as a clerk and lodge with us. He has gone barmy over the Island.
Thanks ever so much for telling us to get something for our birthday with your money but I think it will be best to wait till you are home next birthday – that will be the best present. People keep saying it is going to be over this autumn. I wonder if it's true.
Arch is coming down for Beeb the first of July. I don't know what we shall do when she is gone, but I suppose they will be bringing her down again for the winter and it's only six months through Christmas. Someone was saying the other day, "they will be glad when it is over".
Mabel took Bebe and I out last night so I couldn't finish it. The boys came home later. Mabel had her scent spray ready filled with peppermint. We gave it to them; they couldn't think what the stuff was. It was sticky stuff mixed with Eau de Cologne – smelt rather queer.
Mabel has just come over to tell us she has had a letter from you and that it is true what we keep hearing about – we shan't get any more letters from the Front for a while. We will be writing to you a lot more yet.

Heaps of love and kisses from your loving Kath.

From Mother and Father
49, Carisbrooke Rd, Newport.   Thursday, June 22, 1916
My Dear Bob,
I hope you have got your parcel all right and that you will enjoy it. Will send another soon. Mrs Dyer tells me Charlie is very close to you and he hopes to see

* J.S.White, shipbuilder. White's yards at East and West Cowes were the biggest employer on the Island. The company ceased trading in the early 1970s.

you. I sent the County Press, also the Lloyds. Will do every week. It is bad for the Attrill's (*see below*). Mrs A feels it bitterly and I can't bear to see Mab in deep black again. It was so comforting to know you four boys was all right now. The break makes us feel nervous for we are always wondering what next will happen. I do hope you do all you can to keep out of danger. Of course, we all believe in doing our duty.

Dad is keeping up very well. The weather has not been very hot. Mab has just been in and tells me she has just had a letter from you, which sets me right, and that you have the parcel all right and you enjoyed the onions and cake.

I have been told that the orders have been given that no letters are to be sent from France. I didn't believe it till Mabs tells me it's all right and that you will send a letter if possible, won't you? Oh dear, what trouble it all is. I will send you some more ointment. Be sure you use it.

Believe me, ever your loving Mother and Father, E. Brimson.

County Press, June 10, 1916
NEWPORT - KILLED :

Leading Signalman Harry George Attrill, HMS Queen Mary. Leading Signalman Attrill was the second son of Mr and Mrs M. Attrill of the Bedford, and was 29 years of age. An old Carisbrooke and Newport National-school boy, he joined the Navy as a lad over 12 years ago, his splendid character and capabilities gaining him substantial promotion. He was a typical son of the sea and was in all three battles in the North Sea, serving on HMS Tiger in the Dogger Bank fight.

From Kath
49, Carisbrooke Rd, Newport.   Wednesday, June 28, 1916
Dear Bob,

We do miss your letters so; I think it is a beastly shame having them stopped.* You might let us have a postcard now and then just to let us know you are getting on all right. We hope you will like the parcel Mother has got together. The onions are a change I expect. Ma will send some more soon. She has just gone down to get you some baccy. Mabel took Bebe out to Atherfield yesterday; they stayed the night and came in by carrier today (Wednesday). Of course, that suited young Bebe just right. Roy hasn't heard anything about being called up yet. What do you think? Gordon's latest – talking about joining the London Scottish. He's as bad as you – thinking about the pretty uniform. Mind you take care of yourself,

ever your loving, Kath.

From Kath
49, Carisbrooke Rd, Newport.   Monday, July 3, 1916
Dear Bob,

We are all quite sure you must be immensely busy just about now and that's why we haven't had a card. We have been anxiously waiting for one but there

---

* Letters were not stopped from other parts of France. Possibly this was in preparation for the Somme battle, due to begin on July 1st.

June 5, 1916 THE DAILY MIRROR Page 3

"GERMAN LOSSES ARE HEAVIER THAN THE BRITISH"

New Admiralty Statement Shows Jutland Battle Was a British Victory.

GERMANS LOSE AT LEAST 18 SHIPS

2 Battleships, 2 Dreadnought Cruisers of the Most Powerful Type, and 4 Light Cruisers.

9 DESTROYERS AND U BOAT ALSO SUNK.

Brief Taste of Britain's Naval Might Sufficient For German High Seas Fleet.

PRESS BUREAU, Sunday, 9.50 p.m.

The Secretary of the Admiralty makes the following announcement:—

Until the Commander-in-Chief has had time to consult the officers engaged, and to write a full dispatch, any attempt to give a detailed history of the naval engagement which began on the afternoon of May 31 and ended in the morning hours of June 1 would evidently be premature.

But the results are quite plain.

The Grand Fleet came in touch with the German High Seas Fleet at 3.30 on the afternoon of May 31.

The leading ships of the two fleets carried on a vigorous fight, in which battle cruisers, fast battleships, and subsidiary craft all took an active part.

The losses were severe on both sides, but when the main body of the British Fleet came into contact with the German High Seas Fleet, a very brief period sufficed to compel the latter, who had been severely punished, to seek refuge in their protected waters.

This manœuvre was rendered possible by low visibility and mist, and although the Grand Fleet were now and then able to get into momentary contact with their opponents no continuous action was possible.

They continued the pursuit until the light had wholly failed, while the British destroyers were able to make a successful attack upon the enemy during the night.

Meanwhile, Sir John Jellicoe, having driven the enemy into port, returned to the main scene of action and scoured the sea in search of disabled vessels.

By noon the next day (June 1) it became evident that there was nothing more to be done.

He returned, therefore, to his bases four hundred miles away, refuelled his fleet, and in the evening of June 2, was again ready to put to sea.

The British losses have already been fully stated, and there is nothing to add to or subtract from the latest account published by the Admiralty.

The enemy losses are less easy to determine.

That the accounts they have given to the world are false, is certain—and we cannot yet be sure of the exact truth.

But from such evidence as has come to our knowledge, the Admiralty entertain no doubt that the German losses are heavier than the British—not merely relatively to the strength of the two fleets, but absolutely.

There seems to be the strongest ground for supposing that included in the German losses are:—

Two Battleships.

Two Dreadnought Battle Cruisers of the most powerful type.

Two of the latest Light Cruisers (Wiesbaden and Elbing)

A Light Cruiser of the Rostock type.

The Light Cruiser Frauenlob.

At least nine Destroyers and a Submarine.

TOLL OF SHIPS IN GREAT NORTH SEA BATTLE.

BRITISH LOSSES.		GERMAN LOSSES.	
BATTLESHIPS: Tons. None.	**DESTROYERS:** Tons. Tipperary ...... 1,850 Sparrowhawk .. 935	**BATTLESHIPS:** Tons. None.	**BATTLE CRUISERS:** † Lutzow or Tons Derflinger? 28,000 Pommern 13,700
BATTLE CRUISERS: Tons. Queen Mary .. 27,000 Indefatigable . 18,800 Invincible 17,250	Nestor .... 935 Nomad .... Shark 935	**DREADNOUGHT BATTLE CRUISERS:** Tons Kaiser Class.. 24,700	1 disabled, 1 damaged. **CRUISERS:** None.
CRUISERS: Defence ...... 14,600 Black Prince . 13,550 Warrior 13,550	Ardent .... Fortune .... Turbulent 71,850	Three others hit. **DESTROYERS:** At least nine	**LIGHT CRUISERS:** Wiesbaden .. 5,400 Rostock type.. 4,900
LIGHT CRUISERS: None.	**SUBMARINES:** None.	**SUBMARINE:** One sunk (Approx.) 800	Frauenlob ... 2,715 Elbing 5,600

THE KAISER AND 'OUR FINE SUCCESS.'

Saxon Decoration Conferred on Vice-Admiral Scheer.

AMSTERDAM, Sunday.—The Emperor William has sent the following reply to the congratulatory telegram sent him by the King of Saxony in reference to the battle in the North Sea:—

"Heartiest thanks for your telegram on the occasion of the fine success of our fleet in the North Sea.

"I know how you feel with me in view of this event, because you have always shown the warmest interest in the development of our naval power."

The King of Saxony has sent the following telegram to Vice-Admiral Scheer:—

"I express to your Excellency my heartiest and most sincere congratulations on the grand success over the mighty English Fleet.

"We all hail our proud fleet, which, like our army, has succeeded in conquering in an heroic battle a far superior enemy. In appreciation of your brilliant commandership I confer on you the Cross of Chevalier of my Military Order of St. Henry."—Reuter.

THE QUEEN MARY'S HEROIC SACRIFICE.

Bore for Five Minutes Fire of "the Whole German Navy."

A thrilling story of the sinking of the Queen Mary comes from an East Coast town. The mighty battle-cruiser was sunk by the gunfire which the German cannot always concentrate upon her.

She is said to have sacrificed herself for her sister ships. For a full five minutes she bore single-handed the fire of what officers describe as "the whole German Navy."

A magazine exploded with stupendous force in the forepart of the ship, which was blown away almost immediately. She sank within two minutes.

A ship's steward of the Princess Royal says the shell firing churned up the seas with countless columns of water 30ft. and 40ft. high.

Two men of the Princess Royal who returned from leave the day after the battle were bitterly disappointed to find that they had missed the historic fight.

Deep regret is felt at Jarrow at the loss of the Queen Mary, which was a Jarrow-built ship.

BELIEVES 34 GERMAN SHIPS WERE SUNK.

Officers who landed at an East Coast town during the week end were astounded to find that the public thought the British Navy had suffered defeat.

"Officers of the Fleet believe that they accounted for thirty-four enemy ships and that they may have some of the Germans further up in neutral waters," said one who saw a lot of the great fight.

"My ships discharged eleven and a half tons of high explosive, irrespective of weight of shell metal," he added.

"The deployment of British ships in entering and sustaining action was perfect.

"The ships went for the enemy at top speed, black smoke belching forth and the engines throbbing as we deployed right and left at a given signal, as our flagship manœuvres.

"Every minute the German got a sound thrashing and every man participating knows this."

An officer from one leave from the front who witnessed the return of part of the British Fleet which took part in the naval action on Wednesday, says:—

"The return was most impressive. Although the majority of the ships showed little or no signs of having been in action, one who saw a battle, if comparatively insignificant, scars.

"The ships' crews vehemently insisted upon the —to them—indisputable fact that the German Fleet had suffered a pounding far heavier than was received by our boats.

TRIED TO CUT ENEMY OFF FROM HIS BASE.

A survivor of H.M.S. Warrior, interviewed, stated that the British battle and light cruiser squadrons, with destroyer flotillas, bore away in an endeavour to cut the enemy off from his base.

"After some hours' steaming they succeeded in their object, and managed to get behind the High Seas Fleet.

Orders were given to engage the enemy till the arrival of the main fleet.

One—after another of the British battle cruisers and destroyers were put out of action in the heroic attempt to cut off the enemy from his base.

Late in the afternoon the first of the British Main Fleet units was sighted, and the Germans attempted to retire.

HOW BEATTY FOUGHT TILL HELP CAME.

Faced Overwhelming Odds in Order to Hold Foe.

WARSPITE'S VICTIMS.

How Admiral Beatty forced a fight and hung on grimly in order to detain the enemy in full strength until reinforcements came is told by an Edinburgh correspondent.

It was about 4 p.m. on Wednesday, when the British squadron was about 100 miles west of the coast of Denmark, our advanced guards sighted the enemy, and it was soon apparent that he was out in great force, there being in all about 100 ships, including at least twenty battleships and battle-cruisers.

Apart from the fact that the Germans were probably three times as strong as Admiral Beatty's squadron, they had the advantage of the light, in so far as they adopted a favourable trick of hugging the coast and at the same time assuring a safe retreat.

Then the atmospheric conditions took a change which still further helped the Germans.

Notwithstanding all these conditions Admiral Beatty, true to the traditions of the British Navy, never hesitated for a moment in throwing himself into this, a much greater battle.

Then came the Queen Mary, the battle-scarred Tiger, the Princess Royal and Indefatigable.

From fifteen miles the range of battle rapidly came down to ten miles, and then to five, and by this time a perfect inferno was raging.

At first the British gunners were plainly superior, and not long after the battle had started in earnest one of the big German cruisers was seen to receive a direct hit, and a moment later she was enveloped in flames and sank.

Up to this time the stout of the fighting had been done by the German battle cruisers, but the vessels of the enemy's Kaiser class of battleships had joined in the fray, and their smashing power gave the Germans an enormous superiority.

Having succeeded in at length drawing the whole German Fleet out of its safe quarters, Admiral Beatty, although greatly outnumbered and running heavy risks, evidently determined to hang on grimly in order to detain the enemy in full strength.

AFTER TWO HOURS.

The reinforcements came on the scene after the fight had lasted for about a couple of hours. Then there hove in sight the Invincible, the Indomitable and the Inflexible, Admiral the Hon. Horace Hood, the second in command of the battle-cruiser squadron, flying his flag on the Invincible.

Still, however, the odds were all in favour of the Germans.

The Invincible, after fighting with the greatest gallantry and doing considerable damage to the enemy, met her doom, and she sank quickly.

Further and much more formidable aid was now at hand, however, and Sir David Beatty was very soon relieved of anxiety when there appeared on the horizon the battleships of the Grand Fleet—the Valiant, the Barham, the Malaya and the Warspite—appeared on the horizon.

The Warspite bore the brunt of a terrific attack by no fewer than twelve German battleships or cruisers. She put up a glorious fight, and rather savagely or seriously damaged at least three of the German battleships. But it was hot fighting, credit is due to the Valiant for instance and sunk an enemy.

HAMBURG RUMOURS OF MORE GERMAN LOSSES.

COPENHAGEN, Sunday.—A person arriving here to-day from Germany says that rumours are current in Hamburg that two more German warships, the Westphalen and the Lutzow, were sunk in the recent naval battle.

1916

Harry, second from right, on board HMS Queen Mary, with half the ship's compliment of Signalmen.

Harry can be seen in this *Daily Mirror* photograph of sailors exercising on the deck of HMS Queen Mary; he is joint first, on the left. The photograph first appeared in the paper as a morale booster in the early weeks of the war and ironically, was used again, on June 5th, 1916, to accompany the news of the sinking in which Harry lost his life.

A commercial postcard of the tea garden at the rear of the Bedford. Standing at the table are Mabs and her father, Maurice.

seems to be such big things going off just now that you can't have time to think – let alone anything else.

Only for goodness sake take care of yourself as well as you can. Don't go running into danger just for the sake of picking up rotten old bits of shell, like you told us you did. So long as you come home safe and sound, that's all that matters. Arch came down Saturday for Beeb. Mabel took us down the station to meet him, he looks very well. They had to go back by the 4 o'clock train Sunday. As usual, Bebe was quite ready to go, although she said she would come back again soon. Arch says he doesn't think he will have much holiday this summer but he will send Chris and the little ones down same as usual. The poor old chap seems to think he might be called up in September. Says it is quite likely and if it did happen he would join the 'Hampshires' and be sent to Winchester, then he would shut the house up and pack Chris and the children down here. He doesn't suppose he would be sent abroad because the doctor didn't pass him. I believe he rather likes the idea. I think he feels a bit out of it now.

We had Mr and Mrs Attrill to tea Sunday. Arch had to be off before tea so Dad and Mr Attrill went down the station with them. We had tea in the front room and I think they had a nice comfortable little time. We wanted you, of course. It is the Asylum sports next Saturday. I don't know if we shall go. Roy has just come up from work and brought me an autograph book to put something in for half a crown. I don't mind that; he can bring as many as he likes like that. Well, dear old lad, I can't think of any scrappy bits more to tell you this time. With the very best love and kisses from us all,

ever your loving, Kath.

From Mother

49, Carisbrooke Rd, Newport.   Sunday, July 16, 1916

My Dear Bob,

Mabel let us read her letter, which was very kind of her, but what a dreadful time for you all. But things seems to be getting ever towards the end – that is if it keeps going on so well. I have been told that it is no good to send papers out to you, that they won't pass, but I have sent them all the same so will you let me know if you get them? I sent the County Press last night..

I suppose you are back in the trenches again by this time. Oh for the time when all you poor boys come home again. Arch expects to be called up in September. He says he will join the Hampshires and go to Winchester in an office.

They heard from Charlie yesterday. He is all right. George is still in Egypt and all right. They heard from Ern yesterday and Morrie today. Now goodbye my son.

Ever your loving Mother, Ellen Brimson.

From Kath

49, Carisbrooke Rd, Newport.   Monday, July 31, 1916

Dear Bob,

I have been thinking about you and keep saying, "I must write to Bob today," but something usually happens and puts it out, and I have been busy too, with those pictures I told you about that were ordered some weeks ago. I didn't begin them till last Monday but I have nearly finished one – the one like you and Mabel have of Sir Thomas Lawrence that I made into Wallie – I don't like doing the same ones over again – and the other one is the one I made up of the Swans.

Well, we were ever so glad to have your little letter. Anything is better than nothing and we always feel better when we get even the cards. You will be surprised to hear I am writing this up in the Castle trench. Doris and I have come up for the afternoon (it's her holidays) and, the silly fat-heads that we are, we have brought something to eat with us and no water – not a drop and we are that thirsty we could drink buckets. Doris began writing to you too, but she says you will be sick of her letters if she keeps on, (nice excuse). She feels lazy and she sent you six pages.

Now I must tell you about our holiday yesterday. Mabel and Doris and I went down to Cowes yesterday afternoon (Sunday), it was like an oven in Newport. It was just glorious down there with the sea breeze. We had a lovely time; had a nice tea and the aeroplanes – they were as thick as flies. Of course, there might have been only half a dozen of them but they seemed to do nothing but fly round and round. I just about got fed up with them for once. Then after tea we went across in the floating bridge to East Cowes. We heard Saturday night that there was a fire at one of Saunder's places where Mabel and Roy work.* They heard about it Saturday night and so Mabel wanted to go and see what damage was done. We found it was the one called Maresfield** so it didn't happen to be either of theirs, much to Roy's regret. He did hope it was his 'dope shop'. Anyway, the place was burnt right down to the ground, not a stick of anything left. It must have been a terrible blaze. Mabel took us to show us her workshop. She is proud of it, I think. I like to hear her when she is talking about aeroplanes to call it one of 'ours'. We do miss her trotting in and out at all times of the day, especially on Thursday afternoons, but she still manages to come over two or three times a week in the evenings, when she is not working overtime, and Sundays, so we haven't lost her quite; good thing too when she comes to talking about going to Rugby, or London, or munitions work. We are back home now and have both had our fill of water. On the way home the beastly tyre came off and just sort of spoilt our little outing.

I forgot to tell you, we went to Cowes by train. Ma was afraid you would think Mabel and Doris pushed me all the way. I went into the guard's van; it's all right in there; I'm quite used to it now. Rather like it.

Mother would like to know if you enjoyed the onions. She sent two lots so if you did like them she will send some more. Well I must finish this now. We hope you are still keeping all right every day. Good night now.

Ever your loving Kath.

---

* See photograph page 178.
** To cope with wartime aircraft construction, new buildings had been erected in Maresfield Road in 1915. They were completely destroyed by a fire on the 29th July 1916, together with all stock and work in progress. The buildings were replaced by early 1917.

Mabs (standing back row, first left) with colleagues at Saunder's Works, East Cowes.
"Mabel took us to show us her workshop. She is proud of it, I think. I like to hear her, when she is talking about aeroplanes, to call it one of 'ours'." Kath to Bob, July 31, 1916.

Two Cowes men, Ralph Lashmar, 29, and his brother Allan, 24, were killed during the test flight of a new J.S. White aeroplane, the 'Wight Landplane Bomber.' The plane suffered an unknown mechanical failure and crashed in farmland off Cockleton Lane, Gurnard.
" We saw an aeroplane come down, 'smash', and heard the crash too, on our way to Thorness. We heard afterwards the two poor men were killed." – Kath to Bob, September 27, 1916.

The next letter, written by Bob on August 4th, is a notable one. It is not what it mentions that makes it noteworthy, rather what it does not mention. The first item of note which Bob has chosen not to share is that since writing his last letter he has taken part in the Battle of the Somme.
The battle had begun at 7.30 on the morning of July 1st and for the British was to be the worst battle in the entire war – by the end of the first day alone nearly 20,000 British soldiers had been killed.
Secondly, at some point in the battle another important occurrence took place. Bob refers to this event obliquely in the letter, when he asks for menthol and eucalyptus lozenges to be sent to him, "as I've had rather a cough lately." What he does not, indeed cannot, reveal is that at some point he has been gassed. The 95th War Diary for July 20th contains the entry: '8.30pm - A forward RE dump had been formed close to Brigade HQ by use during the night of 19/20 and whilst drawing stores there we were subjected to a very heavy bombardment of High Explosive and gas shells. Two or three men were slightly gassed before they realised that gas shells were being used.' There seems little doubt that Bob was one of those 'two or three men' since this is the only reference to gassing in the entire diary. The fact that Bob had been gassed was eventually revealed to Bob's mother by an unknown third party (See Kath's letter of November 19th, page 190).

War Diary : "Tirancourt - 10 am. Inspection of 20th Infantry Brigade, HQ and 95 Field Co + 1/3 Durham Field Co. by the Army Commander. Court of Inquiry into Pioneer Marsh's death in afternoon*. 20th Infantry Brigade sports in afternoon."

From Bob
BEF   Friday, August 4, 1916
My Dear Kath,

Sorry to have left you so long without a letter. I received yours and Mother's all right and also one from Doris. I also got the parcel but sorry to say, as it had been such a long time on the road, the things had turned a bit. All the eggs were broke too, it would have been better to have packed them separate, but the cake was all right and some of the other things. A tin box is the best to send the things in after all. Well, we've had a decent fortnight's rest. I expect we shall be moving again shortly somewhere. We have been staying at a village by the river and it's just beautiful now. We've had fine weather all the time. I hope Mother and Dad are keeping all right. Dad must find that walk out there rather tiring this hot weather. Ask him to remember me to all at Whitecroft. Could Mother send me a few menthol and eucalyptus lozenges, as I've had rather a cough lately. Well, this is not a very newsy letter, but it's rather more than a field postcard. I'm sending Arch's letter back to you. I expect you miss Mabs a lot now, but it's all right of her to turn out on munitions. It all helps to get this rotten affair over and done with. Well Kath, I must close now as it is dinnertime. My best love to Mother and Dad and you,

ever your loving brother, Bob.

* The War Diary entry for the previous day includes the remark: 'It was reported to me that Pioneer Marsh had been drowned in the Somme. His body was recovered in the evening.'

From Kath
49, Carisbrooke Rd, Newport.   Thursday, August 10, 1916
Dear Bob,
We are sending you the cough sweets. Hope they will do it some good in the way of stopping it. We were so glad when your letter came yesterday. It's what we had been looking and looking for. It was grand for you to have a fortnight's rest and by a river too! Do you know there was a photo in the Daily Mail the other day of some of the soldiers at the front by a river bathing, and I was sure I saw you at the back with your cap on. The others were in the front behind towels. I showed the picture to Ma and Dad and Mabel and they all agreed with me that it was like you. I'll show it to you when you come home and you must tell us if it is. We always look for you in the pictures.
Here's young Doris galloping on like mad with her second sheet; she puts my writing in the shade with her neatness. I suppose Doris is telling you all about the Scouts. Just fancy! I've actually seen Baden Powell (from our window). He is a nice old chap, to ride by slowly to be looked at and the Scouts were fine. They called in Mrs Attrill's for some tea, (I don't say all of them), but she didn't happen to have enough bread in and no one to get any, or help, so she couldn't take them; nearly broke her heart but Mabel said she really was dreadfully put out because she had to refuse the poor little hot and tired nippers. They looked like angels.
They are going to give the girls down at Mabel's place a weeks holiday; that's more than she expected so she will be able to get off while Chris is here, and they have stopped overtime now.
Poor old Teddy Morris has lost his brother out there, he was telling her last night.
Dad hasn't come in yet. I expect he found it hot today. I'm sure you do when you are not in the river. We were awfully sorry the eggs were 'niffy' by the time they got to you; hope the next parcel turned out better. We will send another while Chris is here. With heaps of love and kisses from all,
                        ever your loving, Kath.

War Diary : "Buire - Company drill. Overhauling tool carts. CRE Lt Crewdson inspected site for Camp for Company."
From Bob
BEF   Tuesday, August 15, 1916
Dear Mother and Father,
Just a few lines to let you know I am still going on all right. I wrote to Kath the other day but don't know whether she received the letter. It seems such a long while before you receive them, and also before I get yours. I still have the newspapers all right, but the parcel you sent me last, took about eight days to come. It was smashed open a little and all the pastry and the small loaf was black with mildew. The other things were all right, except that the meat had turned a little. It's a rotten shame after you had taken all that trouble and we always look forward to our parcels too, and that's two that I've had like that. Well, better luck next time. I haven't heard from C. Dyer for some while but I

think he must be round our part of the line somewhere and I hear that Ern's division is too, so I might have the chance of meeting them yet. I often wondered whether H. Edge came over with the Anzacs. I keep my eyes open on the chance of meeting him.

I was very pleased to get dear old Kath's letter the other day. She still finds plenty of painting to do. I wish I was there to help her. I suppose there will be a time when this affair will come to an end. We get fed up at times, especially the sights we've seen lately. Well, I hope you are all keeping quite well at home, managing to get along all right. I must close now with my best love to you all,
Ever your loving son, Bob.

From Mother
49, Carisbrooke Rd, Newport, IW.   Friday, August 18, 1916
My Dear Bob,

I have been very busy lately, having Archie and Chrissie with the two little ones. Have sent off the papers to you. You will be sorry to see poor Dick Murphy's death. How sad it is and they tell me his wife has very bad health with five children so I hope they will find friends. It will upset poor Mrs Simes again, and Fannie, his sister. Her health isn't up to much.

I get Mrs Snow in to tea every time she comes in to see her mother, so I get any Ventnor news from them. I sent you some cough drops that you wanted, in a letter. Did you get them? I hope that cough is better but one can't expect much in the wet as you are. There seems very satisfactory news in the papers lately which makes one think the end can't be far off now. Won't it be glorious to think that all these dreadful hard times will be over for you poor fellows.

I am so thankful that you have been able to keep all right as yet. I lay in bed and wonder where and how you are sleeping but I know you are brave and keep up a good heart so we will keep looking for a good time to come, won't we?

Your father keeps pretty well. He is home today for it was so wet he would be wet through by the time he got over there. Now my dear Bob I will stop.
Your loving Mother, Ellen Brimson.

From Kath
49, Carisbrooke Rd, Newport.   Monday, August 21, 1916
Dear Bob,

We do talk about you a lot and wish you were here very often, especially when we are sitting down to dinner or tea. Mabel came to tea yesterday. Her Mother and Dad went out so she came over to us. Of course, you know, she has got a week's holiday. Mabel and Doris are going to ride to Shorwell about six in the morning on the mailcart and then walk to Ventnor. Nice to be them.

Mother, Chris and Doris and I went to the pictures one night last week to see 'The Rosary'* which was very good. I enjoyed it very much. They had some jolly nice music for once, piano and violin. It was all very nice until the 'Stage' then someone came on that was described as a charming young soprano in the County Press. Well, she warbled 'Come sing to me.' At the very first line Doris

---

*An American film telling the story of an Irishman who gives up the love of a woman to join the priesthood.

groaned out "Oh goo' Lord." In fact, we all groaned, only quietly. When she got to "Give me your hea-a-art," Chris said "It's like an East End music hall singer." Of course, there was various not complimentary remarks passed by us, especially by Doris you may be sure, but when it came to the last verse I couldn't put up with it any longer so I stuffed my fingers in my ears. There was a person sitting next to Doris who kept glaring at us. We thought it was because Doris wasn't quiet enough. We were in the round curtained seat at the back. It came to us as a great shock when, after the critter had stopped 'singing,' she went out. This woman got down off our seat and went out with her – it was her daughter! I remembered then, I had seen them come in together, also I understood why the woman glared at us so fiercely. When I told Chris and Doris they nearly had silent apoplectic fits. Poor woman! It's a wonder she hadn't eaten young Doris. What! She must have suffered to see we didn't appreciate her daughter. But what we appreciated most was some pictures of you boys at the Front coming and going to the trenches and things that happen through the day and finishing up with a queer sort of comic concert and a sudden interruption to rush off with the ambulance motor wagons. I suppose that's old stuff to you but it showed us a bit. I just about expect you are fed up with it all, poor old chap. Wish to goodness it would make haste and end. Well I must close now, Bob. With heaps of love from us all round.

Ever your loving Kath.

War Diary : "Fricourt Wood – Quiet day. Standing by all day waiting to consolidate Ginchy but not required."

From Bob
BEF   Tuesday, September 5, 1916
Dear Mother and Dad,
I was very pleased to get yours and Kath's letters the other day. I've got an hour or two to spare, so I am answering them now. I received all the papers quite safely and also a bundle of County Press's from Mabs. I'd only written a few hours before saying that I hadn't had any for a long while. They were very welcome as all the boys like to read them. Well Mother, you were asking me if I would like anything like tea and sugar and suchlike sending in the parcel. We can always get plenty of tea and sugar, so don't trouble to send any. As regards the fruit, the box Mrs Attrill sent, the majority of the pears were all right and also the other fruit. Don't go and spend your money, as I know how beastly dear things are now. One of your cakes is always welcome. It's what I like as much as anything, or the tarts that Kath makes for me – if they would only arrive here the same as they were sent. Even the little loaves of bread had turned bad that you sent me, but the weather is much cooler out here now and we have been having tidy drop of rain. A tin of pineapple and apricots just to make up, that is if they do not cost too much. I know they weigh pretty heavy but there is no chance of them going bad. In fact, anything you send me is always welcome. We haven't been so bad off for food out here for some while now. It has improved a lot lately.
I had letters from Roy and Doris today so I'll write a few lines to Doris. I can

never get a line out of Archy now, he can't be all that busy. Of course, I know Chris is always busy. She can send me along a few books to read if she likes. I hope Kath's been enjoying herself lately and Dad is keeping quite well. Remember me to all at Whitecroft. He must take it easy in the coming winter. They all say the end of the war is in sight, so I suppose it is. I hope so anyway. Well I must close now.

Ever your loving son, Bob.

Ginchy - War Diary pages from September 17th to October 26th are missing.

From Bob
BEF   Monday, September 25, 1916
Dear Mother and Father,
I received your letter of the 18th and was very sorry to hear of Dick Murphy being killed out here. He has such nice kiddies too. His oldest boy was the very image of old Dick.
We have moved again and are in another part of France altogether, the place where George Urry was killed. I'm going to have a look for his grave and see how it is kept up. It is awfully quiet round this way, after where we've been, and the people nearly all talk English to a certain extent, and we can buy almost anything here – only the money doesn't run far. But it is nice to be amongst civilisation once more, and about ten minutes walk – we are in Belgium.
I thought I told you that I got the menthol and eucalyptus drops that you sent in the letter, but the ones you sent with the pears – the moisture had melted them and you couldn't tell which was the paper or the sweets. All the papers came quite safely. I also had a letter from Chris and another from Arch.
We are having some lovely weather here again now. We've got decent huts to sleep in with beds made of canvas and a place to have our meals. It's almost like being in Barracks again.
I'm glad that you are all keeping so well and you've been having a nice time together by all accounts. Please remember me to Aunt and Uncle and also Harry when they write. Kath has still got little Bee with her. It will be something to pass the time off in having her to look after. We had a lovely bath this morning; large tanks almost big enough to swim in, of hot water and a clean change of clothing to put on when we came out. Well, I think I must close now, with my best love to you both and Kath and little Bee,

Ever your loving son, Bob.

From Bob
Sapper E. G. Brimson 46870, REs. BEF   Monday, September 25, 1916
Dear Chrissie and Arch,
I was jolly pleased to get your letters. I began to think you weren't going to write any more. I hope you have had a good time while you have been staying in the Island. I'm pleased to hear that Bee is keeping so well; it will do her no harm to stay behind for another month or two. I think the climate that way suits her a lot better (I know it does me) and according to what Archy says, there is

no place like it.
We are away in another part of France now, where it is not quite so noisy, almost within a stone's throw of Belge. It's all right up this way, so are the people. The towns are well built, just a little damage done with the shelling here and there. Mrs Urry's son, George, was killed up this way. I haven't seen Mick O'Brian since last November, and he wasn't well then, and I believe they were sending him down the line to hospital. He looked pretty bad, too. We have got very nice quarters where we are now, and quite comfortable. We have also been issued with a blanket I could put the winter in, in this place all right. Well, I must finish now as I can't tell you half the news I should like to. We hardly know what to say in our letters as the censorship is so strict. Well, goodbye for the present.

Ever your loving brother, Bob.

From Kath
49, Carisbrooke Rd, Newport.   Wednesday, September 27, 1916
Dear Bob,
I think it's about time I let you have another one; really I ought to write regularly every week, I know, but the weeks spin by so quickly – at least these have. We have got Beeb here again. They left her behind for the winter so she keeps us going. What do you think of the 'Tanks' she has drawn for you? The one in the square she remembered from those we sent you, the others she made up. We do want to know what you think of those monsters – I suppose you have seen them – the real ones, I mean. Mrs Attrill came over for your address; she is a dear old soul. She is sending you such a lovely parcel; chicken and grapes and things. Mother says she is sorry she put the potatoes in, she is afraid they won't keep fresh, but never mind, the other is grand stuff.
Mrs Attrill went up to the post and came back to tea with us. This is Mabel's last week at work. Chris is sending you a parcel. We had a card from Chris yesterday. They say they haven't been Zepped yet but they had had them pretty close, and that they had sent you a parcel, so you will get theirs and then Mrs A's, and Mother will send you one next week.
We were supposed to have had a visit from a Zepp on Monday over Portsmouth but nobody seems to know the exact truth about it – all sorts of thrilling tales were told. One of the night nurses saw it over the Asylum; somebody else said they saw it over Pan Down. You feel most mightily thrilled when you are in bed and the light's out, I found out, waiting for 'em. They don't seem worse than moths in the daytime. Best way is to go to sleep quick and then it doesn't matter.
But that's not a quarter as bad as the aeroplane we saw come down smash and heard the crash too, when Chris and Arch were here, on our way to Thorness.* We heard afterwards the two poor men were killed but I suppose that is old news to you – you have had plenty of letters from people since then. But it was dreadful. It looked like a bit of war, it was so close to us. Isn't it a beastly shame about poor old Dick Murphy? I haven't told Chris yet. Gordon has been to

* Two Cowes men, Ralph Lashmar, 29, and Allan, his brother, 24, were killed during a trial flight of a new aeroplane manufactured by J.S. White for whom they were test pilots. See photo page 178.

London a fortnight. Enjoyed himself just about, says he would like to live up there now. We have been having such a lot of rain this last day or two but it generally keeps off for Dad to go to work but it will be very wet for him to come home tonight. Well, do you know what we keep hoping now? That you will be able to come home for Xmas. Don't you think you will ? It would be grand. It would be something worth looking forward to – but we wouldn't want you to go back again, that's worst of all. I must finish now, so good night dear old boy, heaps and heaps of love and kisses from all of us,

ever your loving, Kath.

From Chris
28, Barnard Road, Clapham Junction. SW   Sunday, October 8, 1916
Dear Old Bob,
Our last letter to you was rather unfortunate. Archy wrote last Sunday but didn't put sufficient address on the envelope so back it came. I expect it got to France before they found out. I'm so glad you got your parcel. You must tell us what you liked best. It's such a job to know what is best to send. Do you know about those vests the men are getting from home? Soaked in some sort of disinfectant to keep vermin away. If you know about it, can tell me what to do and I will see to it for you. I expect Kath has told you all about our Beeb's birthday and how they went for a motor ride. I expect Beeb fancies herself now she is seven. Bab goes to school regularly now, she was saying tonight she wished Uncle Bob would come home at weekends, it would be all right, wouldn't it? We saw the remains of the last Zep that was brought down yesterday, in the pictures.* What an enormous thing. I hope you found that pencil I put in your parcel. Writing with the other was getting so faint that we thought you must be in need of one. Kath and Mabel went to see the war pictures the other day. They did some good because Kath said she would have to write to you more than ever. I suppose Mabel will too, so you ought to get plenty of correspondence now. I will say goodnight now Bob.

Your loving sister Chris.

     War Diary : "Pont de Nieppe – Trench work. Batt HQ at Surrey Farm strengthened. Repairs to screen at Motor Car Corner begun."
From Bob
BEF   Thursday, October 12, 1916
Dear Mother and Father,
Just a few lines to let you know that I am still in the pink. The weather is getting cold and we get plenty of wind and rain. The country round this way is awfully flat and they have big dikes to drain the land or else I think it would all be submerged. It's impossible to dig a trench more than three feet deep because it is so sodden. Please tell Mrs. Urry that I will do what I can as soon as I get the chance. I got Chrissie's parcel quite safely. I've also had letters from her and

---

* On October 1st, 1916, eleven Zeppelins were launched at targets in the Midlands and London. Chris had seen a newsreel on October 7th of the only one to have reached London. It was shot down, crashing near Potters Bar. All 19 crew were killed.

Royal Engineers repairing a bridge on the Somme.

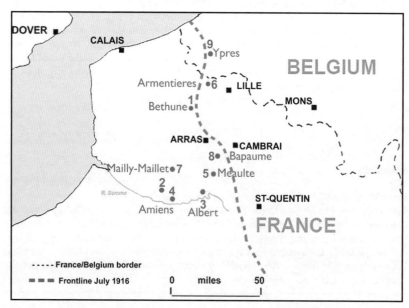

The numbered points on the map indicate the sequence of approximate locations of the 95th Field Company from September 1915 till October 1917.

Archy, also Mrs Attrill's arrived quite all right. I should like to know if you could send me a couple of writing pencils, Dad. I would take great care of them. I've got a lot of writing to do. I should like a small one and a large or those that you can really spare. The ones they supply here are only common camel-hair ones so I've had to borrow a sable off of another chap. I hope you are getting along all right at Whitecroft. I shouldn't risk it in wet weather. I only hope you are managing all right at home and never want for anything as I know what an awful price stuff is, so don't deprive yourself for my sake unless you can really spare it. I see by the County Press that Francis Hess has died in the Persian Gulf. He was a gunner in the Howitzers.

So you didn't care about the Somme battle picture?* I didn't expect you would. Mabs didn't mention it in her letter so I don't know what she thought of it and Kath, perhaps she could tell me next time she writes. Leave has started again. I only wish I was having another seven days but there are some fellows who have been out here over a year and haven't been home at all yet so I mustn't look for another just yet. Well, must close down with best love to you all at home and kisses. Hoping you are in the best of health.

Ever your loving son, Bob.

War Diary pages from September 17 to October 26 are missing but the entry for the 27th shows that the 95th was at Pont de Nieppe.

From Bob

BEF   Thursday, October 26, 1916

My Dear Kath,

Just a few lines in answer to your letter that I received yesterday with the postcard and the pencils. Thanks very much for them; they were just the thing. Also, thank Mother and Dad very much for the postcard. I'm glad that you have got plenty of work to do for Xmas, it will help to pass the time along better, especially if you can make a little out of it. I should very much like to be home for Xmas, but I very much doubt it as there are a lot of lads that haven't been home at all yet. I had letters from about all Roy's household. Clem's, Ivy's and Kathleen's were very laughable, I'm sending them on later if you haven't already seen them. The other afternoon a Hun aeroplane had the cheek to come right over and attack an observation balloon which is close to our camp. It was flying our colours as well, that is, the rings instead of the black crosses. It flew round the balloon firing with his machine gun and when he thought he had made enough holes, he set it on fire and the man in the basket began to drop rapidly but luckily, before he had gone too far, he managed to get out of the basket and descend with the aid of his parachute, and I'm sorry to say the Hun escaped to his own lines again. Well, Kath, I must finish now.

Ever your loving brother Bob.

I was very pleased to get the parcel with the lovely cake, it arrived quite safe and I had a good feed of the salmon at teatime. Thanks also for the sweets and tobacco.

---

* In 1916 the Government commissioned the making of a documentary film, 'The Battle of the Somme,' showing the early days of the battle. The film toured British cinemas and was a huge success, seen by about 20 million people.

From Mother
49, Carisbrooke Rd, Newport.   Thursday, November 2, 1916
My Dear Bob,
We had Mrs Attrill in for tea this afternoon. Quite cheered us up. They expect
Morry this Saturday. Mabel is still away. They expect her next Wednesday. She
is at Chester now but I expect you know. We miss her very much. We have got
so used to her coming in and out all times of the day.
I suppose you haven't had time to see H. Urry's grave yet and perhaps it is a
good way from where you are billeted. I am sorry you think that you won't be
home this Xmas. I will try and send you a good parcel. Let me know if there is
anything special you would like. I will do my very best to get it for you. Glad
you liked the last one also. It wasn't so good as I would have liked but I know
you won't mind for you are sensible enough to know how dear everything is
now. The prices are really dreadful. We get 12/- worth for the pound so you may
guess what things are like now.
Can't you get the cards now Bob? For if you can send one every few days, I feel
so cheered. When it runs to two weeks, you might be dead and buried for all I
might know. You will try and be as careful as you can won't you, for we all want
our Bob back again.
You are seldom out of our thoughts for long. Now, goodbye my son. Every one
says "give my love to Bob when you write."
        And your ever loving mother sends her best love, E. Brimson.

War Diary : "Le Roukloshille - Cleaning up billets and clothing and settling in."
From Bob
BEF   Friday, November 3, 1916
My Dear Mother and Father,
Just a few lines hoping you are all keeping well at home. I am still going all right
although we get a lot of rain and it has turned very cold.
We have got two blankets though, so we sleep warm enough at nights. Thanks,
Dad, for the pencils that you sent; I've had a leather case made for them so I can
keep them in good condition. I should have liked one about midway between
these two as the majority of the size of letters I write is about two inch. Of
course, the small pencil comes in just right for writing the names on crosses –
I've had a good many of them to do.
I've had a nice parcel from Chris and Archy and I also heard from Archy
yesterday, telling me about Flo's wedding. I think I shall get married next time
I come home so you can all get ready for it. Kath will always have Mabs with
her then. I've had a bundle of books sent to me by a Mrs Wilcox who lives
somewhere in Berkshire. Can you tell me who she is, and her address, as I
should like to thank her.
Well, Mother, I must close now and I want Dad to remember me to them at
Whitecroft. My best love to you all at home.
                    Ever your loving son, Bob.

From Mother
49, Carisbrooke Rd, Newport.   Monday, November 6, 1916
My Dear Bob,
I am afraid you are having an awfully rough time of it by the papers and your letters. I hope the time won't be long before you will get your holiday. I don't think I've ever known the weather so cold and such frost as we have had lately. I'm glad you mentioned the allotment money but it has done no good. I went to Mr Alderslade, he said as it's been in my name from the first they can do nothing, but Archie will see about it I expect, when he comes.
I am sending you a parcel this week, the best I could do. I hope you will be able to make the pudding warm. I wish I could send you some rum or whisky but they won't allow anything of that sort. I am so glad you have fire in your billet. There don't seem any chance of an end to this dreadful war. I expect you get downhearted sometimes, poor boy. Try and keep up your heart, it may stop sooner than we think.
I saw Mrs Dyer. She says Charlie has not heard from you for some time. He is quite well.
I wonder what sort of Xmas dinner you will have. Every soldier is to have a lump of plum pudding, the paper says. I think there will be a shortage of luxuries everywhere as things are so scarce and dear now.
Now my dear Bob, I will conclude his letter. Have sent the lozenges and Vaseline.
                    Ever your loving mother, E. Brimson.

From Mother
49, Carisbrooke Rd, Newport.   Sunday, November 19, 1916
My Dear Bob,
You seemed sorry to leave the little village. What sort of a place are you in now? I hope it is nice for you.
The people at Whitecroft are all well and they often ask after you and wishes to be remembered to you. Minnie is gone to the Asylum at Dorset somewhere for a change. Mr Holt asked Dad if you had a stripe yet, and they have taken on another painter. He had been a patient from Ryde, a young man about Roy's age. The brush Dad sends you. He thinks you will be glad of it.
Now, he was talking the other night about my not getting the old-age pension. I said it was because I received 7/6 from you. Mab was here, so she says "Why, that should not make any difference as that is Kathie's money, for Bob told me he was leaving it for her." I wish I had understood that at the first for I am sure I could get the pension, so I think if you will put it in your letter to me in some way that they will know it was a mistake all round, I think it would be all right, so if I get it and Dad is stopped from work it won't make things so bad.
And now Bob I will stop and look anxiously for a new letter. We all send our very best love to you.
                    Believe me, ever your loving mother, E. Brimson.

From Kath
49, Carisbrooke Rd, Newport.   Sunday, November 19, 1916
Dear Bob,
You will be thinking it is about time you heard from me again. I think it is too
so I'm writing while I've got the chance tonight. I shan't have much chance
tomorrow – there is generally so many visitors on Sundays; Mabel and the
children. And I'm dizzy doing my cards.
I think I told you I had finished the miniature and big picture of Harry.* I charge
ten shillings for the picture and four shillings each for the little ones. They were
very pleased with them. Mrs Attrill wanted them to send to Rugby, to Mrs
Collins and Nelly and Kitty.
Mother didn't like to hear about your being gassed, second-hand. She thinks
you ought to have told her before. Have you really got over it? Doesn't it leave
any after-effects? She wants to know. I suppose that had something to do with
the 'cough' and that was why you wanted the lozenges. I begin to see daylight
now. Don't you ever keep us in the dark again about things like that – we
would rather know. You will have to tell us all about it when you come home.
I do wish you could come for Christmas, another measly one, of course. It won't
be quite so bad as it was last, because Chris and Arch will be here but it won't
be a real one till we have it all together again. But Gordon will have to go after
Xmas; he has made up his mind to it, poor old chap.
Here is Dad and Roy just come in. Dad is putting up a little greenhouse outside
of this window. We have got an extra lot of flowers this year. Dad went down
and got some wood and a large window for three shillings. Mr Woodbine has
offered to help him. They were just setting to work this afternoon when it
started raining.
Mabel has talked to us about what you want to do when you come home, but it
is only for Mabel to decide. Of course, it is right enough what you want, but
Mabel will be more concerned in it than anybody else so it's only for her to do
as she thinks best. There's one thing – there wouldn't be a great big fussy
wedding.
You know Minnie has left, I suppose, and poor old Peter – Dad says he is dying.
There won't be much sense to 'Fete' days with Minnie and Peter and Stump
gone. Mother and Bee are busy packing your parcel. We hope you will enjoy
what we have sent you. It's not half as good as we would like. We all wish you
the very best of luck and hope to goodness next year will be better.
        The best love from Mother and Bebe and your loving Kath.

From Ernest Attrill
6330 Hants Rgt., B. E. F.   Tuesday, November 28, 1916
Dear Mother and Father,
I am in a convalescence camp again now, not far from the hospital, but I don't
know how long I shall be here as I am booked for another place at any time. I
was for Blighty but the chap in the next bed had the scarlet fever and me and
the chap of the Royal Naval Division were kept in quarantine for ten days and
as I was a bit better at the end of the ten days I was marked convalescent, so I

* See photo page 140.

don't know what they will do now. They may send me straight on leave from the base, as it is due. I have not heard any more of Jack Bull. I could tell you more if I saw a chap of his Company. I heard from Morrie. Hoping this finds you all quite well as it leaves me, still safe, but they are leaving the pieces of shrapnel in me so I shall soon be a walking Krupps advertisement. I shall have to pack up now.

With love from your affectionate son, Ernest xxxxx.

War Diary : "Mailly-Maillet – Work continued on 6th Avenue + communication trench W. of Wagon Road. 2 coys Manchester Pioneers continued new front line trench during night of 30/11/16 - 1/12/16. Lt Dutton laid out continuation of communication trench W. of Wagon Road to this new front line. Enemy very active with sniping, especially in vicinity of Duckboard Walk + Left Battn HQ."

From Bob

Thursday, November 30, 1916

Dear Chris,
I got your two letters last evening and very pleased I was to get them. Speaking about the weather and the mud, don't mention it. In some of the trenches the mud and water is nearly up to your waist. You should see the kilties, their mud caked kilts flapping against their legs. In fact, they and everyone else who are in the trenches are the same. I've never seen mud in England like we get out here; it is so strong and sticky that when you once sink in it takes four men to pull you out or else they all come in as well. Let's hope this will be the last winter out here. We completed a thirteen day march last week, arriving back on the battlefields. I expect we shall be here for Xmas. We have pretty comfortable billets, that's one good thing.
I hope you will be able to get down home for Xmas, it will be better for all of you to be together. It's impossible for me to be at home, anyhow; perhaps better luck next year. I suppose you heard about poor old Dick Murphy* being killed? Hard lines for his wife and kiddies. The lads are getting their leave now. They are going one a day so perhaps I might stand a chance of another next spring sometime, all being well. Thanks very much for the Sunday Pictorials you send. The Germans are dropping a few shells outside our billet, so I think I will pack up for the present because I might have to move, so goodbye for the present. Love to you all and a big kiss for Babs.

Ever your loving brother, Bob.

From Charlie
87 Field Co. R.E. Battalion 12th Division, BEF.   Saturday, December 2, 1916
Dear Bob,
Just a few lines in answer to your most welcome letter which I received quite safe last night. So glad to know that you are still keeping quite fit. As for myself, well, I am in the pink at present. Yes, I was wondering what had become of you. I heard about two months ago that we were near you but we are a long way off

---

* Corporal Richard Murphy, born Godshill, of the Hampshire Regiment Battalion, killed in action, Flanders Sept 9th, 1916' : *War Graves Commission Entry.*

now. Fancy you seeing Sapper Wilkinson's grave; it must be 15 months since we buried him. How the time flies. What you wrote after that in your letter was torn off. What names was it on the wall? I think I know the Convent you mean. As you say, we are having some weather. It has been very wet, up to our knees in it, but it is much better just lately. Ern Attrill wounded again. He seems very unlucky. It is in a nice place – the leg. Good old Blighty for him. I heard Jack Bull is missing; hope they will hear some news from him. All the boys wish to be remembered to you. I suppose you are sweating on your next leave. My number is 90, not too bad. Shall go home by next Xmas. Not too Bad. I hear from Jack he wished to be remembered to you. Plenty of work for them out there now. Well, I think that is all for this time.

From your old chum Charlie.

From Kath
49, Carisbrooke Rd, Newport.   Wednesday, December 6, 1916
Dear Bob,
We were so glad to get your letter Sunday, after such a long time of waiting. We had begun to wonder what was wrong. I expect you are getting it cold; it's bad enough here. Dad was glad that the pencils suited you but it's not a very cheerful job you wanted them for – a nasty cold job, I should think. Dad has had to do some fancy dress work for the nurses out there sticking gold paper letters on calico. One was 'England' and the other 'France' and there is another one 'Tipperary', that's for Sallie. I suppose she is going to be an Irish Colleen.
Dad and Mr A were coming home along the Nunnery Road one night from work – poor old Mr A was knocked down in the hedge with a bicycle. It did shake him up. Dad says the poor old chap was in a rage; he never heard him swear so much before. The man came back to see the damage and directly he saw who it was he said, "If only I'd known it had been you, I'd have run right over you." They happened to know each other it seems, but it made Dad laugh to hear Mr. Arum swear so. It's a good job they come home together. They are proper pals.
Did you ever get the Oxo that Kit and Ron sent you some time ago? Ron bought it from his shop – two bottles – they pack it down there. It will be a pity if you lose it. I will write again before Christmas. Arch says he keeps telling you you have got to get home for then. I wish to goodness you could.

With heaps of love and kisses from us all, your loving Kath.

From Chris
28, Barnard Road, Clapham Junction. SW   Sunday, December 10, 1916
Dear Bob,
The last Xmas we hope that you will be out there. Your parcel is packed and will be sent off tomorrow; hope you will get everything safely. The cigars Archy bought, he packed up so carefully so that you should have them whole. He says if they get broken you can smoke them in your pipe. The card, Bab worked herself and thought you would like, and the Father Xmas she bought for your

mascot. We are trying to get down to the Island for Xmas but they don't seem to want to run any passenger trains, but we shall certainly try to go. The cake we all had a hand in, for luck. We are not sending you any pudding because you will get one from Mother, also from the newspapers. We were pleased with your letter. It was good of you to find time to write to us. I sent mine on to Mother and she sent hers onto us.

We feel very worried about you poor boys having to be in that mud all the time. I suppose you wear high, watertight boots – even then I don't see how you can keep dry. I'm very glad you have got decent billets. Perhaps you can get nice hot water for your feet. I expect you have to thaw them occasionally. I see you asked Mother for vaseline. Was that to rub them with? Have a good time and keep cheerful. You are all good boys. Wish your pals a happy Xmas and good luck from me.

Ever your loving sister Chris.

War Diary entries for December 15th to December 20th are missing but prior and subsequent entries show the 95th located at Mailly-Maillet.

From Bob

Friday, December 15, 1916

My Dear Mother, Father and Kath,

I'm writing this letter and putting it in with Mab's, in the green envelope. I had a letter from Chris this evening and also an amusing letter from Doris. By the way, I should like to send all Roy's kiddies a card from France but we are in a deserted village – no civilians and no shops so I can't buy anything to send but I've sent a Divisional Xmas card* to each of you. I think they are very nice this year, don't you? I want you to keep them and I'll have them framed when I get home.

Chris says they are trying to get down for Xmas. It will make it a lot better for you all. I shall probably be dropping a line to aunt Eliza in a day or two. She has been very good in sending me books. Thank you very much for the nice cake you sent me in Mab's parcel. I'm very sorry about the allotment money. I hope Archy will be able to arrange it all right. I will let you know what sort of Xmas we have. We have got a canteen in the billet. We get stout at 7d a litre and it's very good too. Dad and Mr Arum, I think, had better have someone to look after them. Wait till I get home next time I'll take them both out on the spree and I'll see they don't get knocked in a ditch with bikes.

Tell Roy and Kit that I never received the Oxo they sent. I expect it got lost on the road. Our fellows often lose their parcels but I have been pretty lucky up till now. I get the papers all right. Oh, by the way, you needn't bother to send 'Lloyds' any more for a bit as the postman brings us a paper nearly every day. I'm glad to hear that Bee has improved in health. Tell her uncle Bob sends love and kisses.

Ever your loving brother, Bob.

* See photograph page 196.

From Doris
31, Melbourne Street.   Saturday, December 16, 1916
Dear Bob,
We are setting the kiddies to write to you to keep them quiet. Nice game isn't it?
Last week it was an awful examination week, (by the way, this is some of the paper I brought back). When we had finished, every one of us prigged all the blotting paper, pens and nibs we could lay our hands on and when dear Munkus came into the room she says to me, "Get me a piece of blot, please." I went on and pretended I hadn't heard. I pity the other poor jigger that had to fetch the blot that wasn't there, for the room was absolutely bare of everything except desks and chairs so I had (the week before) to pull the violin strings undone and the mandolin as well, so as I should do a little bit of work.
I expect I had better write on both sides hadn't I? I yand arf god a coud id be dose.
Newport isn't half a beastly place with no lights, and a thick mist laying over all day. Gordon doesn't seem to mind. He goes up to Carisbrooke every night now. There wasn't half a nice concert at the Drill Hall but of course, I couldn't go because of the exam. Gordon went with a girl or two. They took off the FY&N Railway line a treat. The man says, "I was on the 11.69 to Freshwater. Suddenly the train stopped, then there was an awful crash (the man at the piano touches the top note so as you could just hear). Carriages were piled on top of each other. The guard got off to investigate and found – A fly on the line! He went to pull the passengers out. He helped out one fainting person. She looked at him and said, "Guard, is my hat on straight?" Gordon didn't half get some digs from his pals, I think.
His Lordship, Gordon, has just come in and I shall have to stop. He has been to work today at Ningwood and wants his dinner.
                              With love from Doris.
PS. Weep no more for Lycidas,* Old Peter now is dead.

From Roy
31, Melbourne Street.   Saturday, December 16, 1916
Dear Bob,
One more year round. Well, I had a great surprise last night, Saturday. I went into Bartons and who should I meet but George Berch. He was wounded on the Somme in the Hampshire's through the back of the head and five shrapnels in the thigh. He says he left old Bill Scott out there.
Gordon has not had his papers yet; it is a fortnight over time. His manager says it is impossible to let him go, so we don't know what will happen.
I am still on machines. Getting them out as fast as we can. You know Peter Jeffreys is dead? There won't be many old chums left there when you come back. Food is still getting dearer here. Doris finished her schooling this week so she will be doing something very soon, which will be making things better. There is only Dad, Percy Gaster and myself down at the Bedford now, bar

---

* Doris is mis-quoting 'Lycidas," a poem written in 1637 by John Milton : "For Lycidas your sorrow is not dead, Sunk though he be beneath the watry floar."

married women and soldiers. It is getting rotten at home.
Well, I am just going to Carisbrooke now as usual. So I must wish you as happy
a Xmas as possible,
                from your affectionate brother, Roy Brimson.

From Ivie
31, Melbourne Street.   Saturday, December 16, 1916
Dear uncle Bob,
I am so sorry you are not coming home for Christmas but have you got Aunt
Chrissie's parcel and Grandma's? I hope you have got them, but we have all sent
you a letter. On new year we will send you another parcel – at least daddy said
he would. The bird has moulted and on the top of his head is a red group of
little feathers. Its colour is yellow black brown white red it's chest is brown. Last
Xmas Gordon shone a flashlight on our faces and woke us up so we got up at
once and began looking in at them because we were so anxious to look at them.
                From your dearest cousin, Ivie.

From Clement
C. Brimson   Saturday, December 16, 1916
I hope you will be all right for Christmas we had a nice tune up to night. Ronald
works down Kitbread. I have a sailor hat and Ernest has a new jersey.

From Charlie
46869, 87 Field Co. R.E. Battalion 12th Div, BEF.   Monday, December 18, 1916
Dear Mrs. Brimson,
I had a letter from Bob the other day. So glad to know he's keeping fit. He is in
one of our old billets. Telling me they are getting plenty of rain. Well, we are all
alike, but glad to say it has been better just lately. We are a bit lucky. This Xmas
Eve we are out on rest, so we are looking for a good time. I don't expect it looks
much like Xmas at home. Hoping to see you all again soon. Well I'll now close.
  Wishing you all a very happy Christmas and bright New Year, from Charlie.

From Kath
49, Carisbrooke Rd, Newport.   Thursday, December 21, 1916
Dear Bob,
We had your lovely long letter yesterday. It cheered Mother up, and all of us.
And we do hope you will have as decent a Christmas as anyone can expect out
there. I suppose it's no use wishing you a happy one. I expect you will have
some kind of fun though, with all the boys. And I don't believe they are coming
down from London; it seems to be such a bother with the trains. We do hope
you will get your parcels safely, only we wondered how you would manage to
keep the pudding and cake till Christmas.

County Press advertisement.

7th Division Christmas card, 1916. See page 193.
"We are in a deserted village – no civilians and no shops so I can't buy anything to send, but I've sent a Divisional Xmas card to each of you." Bob to Mother, Father and Kath, December 15. 1916.

I must tell you what everybody is doing for me. Instead of buying me separate little presents they are putting all the money together (all Roy's family, Mabel, Arch and us) and getting me a box of 'miniature materials', ivory and all; then I'll be able to charge the proper price, (when I get 'em to do). I couldn't when I only did them on little bits of paper. Young Da' and John Arum had some more adventures last night. Dad's umbrella blew inside out, coming up the lane in the copse. John shouted, "Turn round quick." Dad turned and it blew right way out again. Then, coming home, Dad must needs slip down a grating. He had just put out his lantern and being quite dark out nowadays didn't know where he was going; he had a hard bump. Your letter was waiting here telling them they would have to mind out, as you would have to come home and take care of them. Dad says, "I wish he would."

I don't know if anyone has told you – poor old Peter is dead. I must finish now.

Hoping to goodness you will be home next Xmas for good, Kath xxx.

From Ernest Attrill
X Company. 6330 Hants Rgt. BEF   Sunday, December 24, 1916
Dear Mother and Father

Just to let you know I have got an attack of rheumatism so I am having a short rest again. Rather hard luck but I shan't be here long so if you get any letters back from the Regiment you need not be worried. I will let you know as soon as I shift again. Hoping this finds you all quite well as I am improving.

The above address will find me as they can forward to unit if I have gone back.

I will now close, from your affectionate son Ernest. Au Revoir xxxxx.

From Ernest Attrill
2nd 6330 Hants Rgt., I Coy. No 5, Con Camp, A.P.O. S23
Friday, December 29, 1916
Dear Mabel,

Just to let you know I got your letter and fags and was very pleased with them. The cards were very pretty, also the verses in them. Well, it is as you say, these camps are very good as they save sending us to Blighty. Of course, I don't know exactly when I shall be home as I shall no doubt get a quick order myself and find myself walking in the bar door – but not just yet.

We had a splendid Xmas here. Plenty of everything; also concerts, but they always remind you of home. You wish to know how I have been going on all this time. Well, we have got some good doctors here so I am nearly well again. I can walk about now but I have not quite reached running pitch yet. I can't tell you how long I shall be here; it may be days or weeks. I have a little walking exercise each day till I am up to the mark, so I cannot grumble at this life.

Hoping this finds Mother and Dad and yourself in the best of health.

From your affectionate Brother Ernest xxxxxx Au Revoir.

1916

From Doris
31, Melbourne Street,   Sunday, December 31, 1916
Dear Bob,

It is raining, absolutely pouring. We have just finished Christmas. It wasn't much but we've been so busy this week that we have only just started to get your parcel together. Mabel sent us a pretty Christmas card. We only had about four altogether. People seem on the saving system in that direction. Chrissie, Kath, and the two kiddies with Gordon, and I went over to Mabel's to tea on Thursday and got home about 11 o'clock. It was raining when we went and so dark that we couldn't see where we were. None of us had a light and you ought to have seen, or else heard, Gordon and I groping for the steps – we sounded like burglars. I said, "I have got them." Gordon said, "Where, where? Hurry up!" I slid down them somehow and Gordon comes on top of me, jumping on my toes and I don't know what.

Uncle Archie went back Wednesday at 1 o'clock and he says from 25 miles out of London the train absolutely crawled along and he got home at 7 o'clock instead of 5. Electric trains got lost, so the papers say, for one ran onto the wrong line and they cut the electric current and the passengers were stuck for two hours and nobody knew where they were.

We received your card. I do think it is a nice one this year; better than last year's almost. Kathie showed me some Christmas cards she had from Mr C. Dyer – two worked ones and one divisional. I don't think his divisional card is half so pretty as yours.* It is not printed the same.

Gordon has gone to work today but this will be the last time he will have to go on Sundays because the trains are going to be altered after tomorrow. There are going to be two trains in and one out from Freshwater on Sundays. Cheerful, isn't it? So if you want to go out to Freshwater and back from Newport, you will – you have just got to go on wanting now. I expect Gordon will have to go in about a fortnight's time.

Sir Sam Fay is going to try to get him into the Railway Operating Corps. I think it's attached to the R.E's. I have never heard of it until last week but that is a minor detail. Sir Samuel is the head of their line. I have applied for Gordon's place when he goes because I am not going back to school again.

Did you know George Brown at the Asylum, because he has been and hit his head up against the lamp post in the dark and he's got three eyes now. It's teatime now and I'm getting hungry.

With love from all, Doris.

PS. A drier new year.

---

* See photo, page 196.

Calendar of Events of 1917
(Bob's activities shown in italics)

January 31 – Germany announce unrestricted submarine attacks on all shipping including hospital ships.

March 15 – Tsar of Russia Nicholas II abdicates.

March 23 – Move to Ervillers billets.Work on water supply and road repairs.

April 6 – America declares war on Germany.

April 9 – Battles of Arras and Vimy Ridge.

May 2 – Battles of Bullecourt and third Battle of the Scarpe begins.

May 25 – First great aeroplane raid on Kent and Folkestone, 290 casualties.

June 17 – Battle Messines.

July 7 – Severe aeroplane raid on London, 250 casualties.

July 17 – Proclamation changing name of British Royal House to Windsor.

September 6 – After 15 months Bob has second leave while in France, for 12 days.

September 20 – Battle of the Menin Road Ridge (Ypres) begins.

October 12 – First battle of Passchendaele (Ypres).

November 1 – Division inspected by HM King of Belgium.

November 3 – British troops begin arriving in Italy.

November 12 – 95th begin to move through France for Italy.

Nov 21 – Bob arrives with 95th and the 7th Division in Italy.

November 30 – 95th moved to Campo S. Martino.

December 1 – 7th Division at Montello.

December 2 – Russian and German Armies suspend hostilities.

December 17 – Armistice signed between Russian and Central Powers.

From Arch

28, Barnard Road, Clapham Junction. SW   Monday, January 1, 1917

Dear Bob,

This letter must, in the first place, record our good wishes for 1917. All sorts of things we want to happen in 1917. I suppose all being well we ought to see you and Mabel tied up this coming year – that's one of the things. Another thing we want to see is the Huns whacked and peace proclaimed on our terms and an end to all this fearful war and waste of life, destruction of property and bankruptcy of wealth. I note that your CO did not take any notice of my oft repeated commands for you to come home for Christmas. We went down to the Island, and in fear and trembling on account of statements in the newspapers. However, a good many people were frightened off it and the journey passed off without incident.

I had a sort of hope at the time that you might turn up at any moment, as there were any number of chaps home on Xmas leave. Amongst others I saw Woolly, the motor car driver. Of course, he was grumbling like anything but looked in first class condition. Curious how the conversation in the pubs has altered in the Island. Everywhere the talk is munition talk. Most everyone is on munitions. Even "Peace" Gaster – I believe that's his name. He used to be a kind of fishing bloke what never done no proper work but gets conversational in the Bedford after the first pint. Well, they all talk of machinery and shells and "dope" and aeroplanes and such. Roy says he may have to join up in the New Year.

However, I reckon they won't take him off his munitions. Gordon will be in the Army soon, in the Railway Corps. I believe that this is a branch of the R.E.s and he do say that after about a month of training he will be shipped off to France. I myself can scarcely see why a chap in the Railway Corps needs any 'train'ing. Joke. The children had a good time. Thank goodness they don't understand anything much of the misery and frightfulness going on all over the Continent. Your divisional card is very nice. We were glad to have it. Ma has since had one from Chas Dyer. His is not quite so nice as yours. Mabel is looking very well. The latest is that Mr Attrill thinks all the pubs are going to be shut up and he will go down to Rugby. Mabel says if he does she will come to London and get a job on munitions or something. I don't think they will close the pubs but I think they will put them under state control and dish out drink cards. I wonder how old Mother Denham and her precious daughter would go on if this happened.

On Boxing Day, Roy and I followed the hounds. They put up a fox the other side of Bowcombe Down but the fox was too clever and ran right through a herd of sheep and got clean away while the hounds were attending to the sheep. Being about halfway to Shorwell we went on and had some bread and cheese and pickle in the Crown. The Five Bells was deserted but in the Crown we found old 'Cherry Blossom'. Do you remember he was in the Five Bells that time we all walked out there? Morry and Harry were with us. That was three years ago. This time we came back on the mail van and lucky we did, as it started to rain just as we got into Carisbrooke.

I came back on Wednesday, and Chris and Bab on Saturday. Bee is quite contented but was very pleased to see us. She has been very busy on various little things and has, also under Mabel's tuition, been learning the piano and some dancing. Kath and Mabel had, on the quiet, been making some fairy frocks for Beeb, Bab and Ivy, and of course, there was a party where dancing etc took place to show off these said frocks. Poor Kathleen hadn't got no fairy frock and was inclined to be a bit down in the mouth about it, saying that Ivy was looking so diaphanous, but she got over it. Wally was down for Xmas and went back same day as me. We went together as far as Clapham Junction. He and Gordon lounged about together, considerable. Gordon is full of ragtime songs of the latest breed and he sings very deep bass. He is the greatest authority on footer in the Island. I noticed you have utilised every word possible in your Field Service postcard. I had not noticed before that you could wangle part of sentence number two into sentence number one. Mabel tells us that you were gassed some time since. I hope you are feeling no ill effects now. To be gassed here, and to be gassed somewhere in France, are two quite different things. Chris will be writing next Sunday, but as for me, I must finish. It will take you a week to read all this. Many were the enquiries for you this Xmas, so you can see that you were in many people's thoughts. But in one household you were constantly remembered, and in that household we count Mabel. Keep smiling and let's all hope that the New Year will see you back well and hearty. Best love from us all and kisses where needful.

Ever your loving brother Arch.

1917

From Kath
49, Carisbrooke Rd, Newport.   Tuesday, January 2, 1917
Dear Bob,
It's about time we let you know what sort of Christmas we had. We had a letter
and some cards from Charlie Dyer; he happens to be having a rest for Xmas.
Well, Chris and Arch did manage to come down after all. It was a good job. I
had begun to look forward to a nasty lonely Xmas. They managed to come on
Saturday all right. Arch stayed till Wednesday and Chris till Saturday. Chris
would have stayed longer, only they are putting the fares up double for the
New Year.
The holiday went off all right. The children had the best of it; they were just
pleased with themselves because I made them some fairy dresses. Ivy, Bebe and
Bab, they got what they have always wanted at last.
I think I told you that Dad took two golliwogs out to Mr Holt's little girl and
Peggy Green, last Saturday. Who should come to the door but Mrs Green to say
how pleased she was. She thought it was so kind of us and all that. She seemed
very nice and friendly. She finished up by saying she would be sending a dozen
eggs in for me and I wasn't to think of it as a payment (I told her we didn't want
to be paid for it) but as a present from her. She asked after you ever so kindly
then she bought another golliwog to send to the Doctor's (one before this one)
little baby. She is a decent old sort.
I have got my miniature box; it's a beauty. They all clubbed together. It came to
one pound eleven. They expect to see something done now. Well I must finish
now,
                              ever your loving Kath.
Harry Harvie is on his way home to join up. He has passed the doctor after all.

War Diary: "Mailly-Maillet, Bertrancourt – No's 1 and 2 Sections at work in Camps No's
3 and 4. Proceeded to billets in Mailly-Maillet. Paraded at billets and marched to Station
TR reaching there at 1.08 am."
From Bob
                                        Tuesday, January 9, 1917
My Dear Mother and Father,
Just a few lines to let you know that I am still going on all right. Kath got her
letter all right but since I wrote that we have moved back from the line a bit. I
had a fine parcel from Roy and Kit and family. It arrived quite all right. Shall
drop them a line soon. I'm also very pleased to hear that Gordon is trying to get
in the Railway Corps. I wouldn't advise him to go in the London Scottish or any
line regiment.
Things are looking very much brighter out here and we are expecting great
things when the weather is properly settled. I hope the leave will carry on. If
Mabel has had her letter she will have told you of the extra 4d a day I am
getting. It's a nice little rise for me. Did Archy see about the allotment when he
was down at Christmas? I hope you are managing to keep going. Sugar must be
a big luxury now at home. We always get it all right out here, in fact living with
us has been a lot better lately. I wrote to C. Dyer the other day and I have heard

once or twice since they have been back resting for some while. We are expecting to go back for about six weeks later on.

Sorry to hear of old Peter's death. Mr Holt will miss him, I expect. Kath had a very nice present I hear. I hope to see some of the work she has done with it when I come home. Well, I must finish now. With my fondest love,

Ever your loving son, Bob.

From Chris

28, Barnard Road, Clapham Junction. SW.   Friday, January 12, 1917

Dear Old Bob,

We have had a most exciting week. Archy has had a cousin come all the way from Australia, a soldier, and stationed on Salisbury Plain. Most of them have been in London on four days leave, so of course this boy came to see his relations, bringing a friend with him. Last night they put in with us. They are very nice fellows. It would be nice for you to meet them and tell them a few things. You must be getting quite a Frenchman by now. We got your service postcard today. You can't think how glad we are to get them, Bob. I haven't seen a line from you since long before Xmas. I want to know what sort of Xmas you had, and what you had to eat, and how you spent it, and all that. I expect they told you of Dad's accident. We hope he is getting all right again now. I've only had a postcard from Kath since we came back. I suppose she is busy with miniatures. She ought to make her fortune now. What you'll have to do, Bob, is to come home on leave and come London way. We want to see you. We haven't seen you since you went out there nearly 18 months ago, so just see about it. Archy will tell you in his next letter all about the jaunt round London with the cousin.

Ever your loving sister, Chris.

.

From Arch

28, Barnard Road, Clapham Junction. SW.   Sunday, January 14, 1917

Dear Bob,

We were glad to get your card. Since my last letter we have had, as Chris mentioned, a great time. A cousin of ours, (one of my mother's sister's sons) has joined up in an Australian Regiment and came up to Town from Salisbury for four days leave. Back in the dim and distant past he came to the Isle of Wight with his Pa and Ma after a journey from Jamaica and was unquestionably an unmitigated nuisance. Now he has turned out a real nice chap, a regular colonial with curious phrases and an unlimited stock of conversation. With him came a silent youth – a broth of a boy from the Back Blocks. If ever there was a contrast, it was in those two chaps. The cousin (Percy James Millmore) was all life and talk – especially talk – while his friend, George Glasscock, was all repose and silence. They had the time of their little lives. They arrived with a train full of other Australians thirsting for London and women and wine etc etc and made their way down to Magdalene Road ("Magdallan," Pearce called it). They put up the first night there. Next night they stayed over at Sam's place, and the third night with us, returning on the fourth to Salisbury. We took them to the Grand, to the Pictures and to the Victoria Palace, and also for a short run round the historic parts of London such as Westminster Abbey, the Law Courts, St Pauls, the Temple Church, The Bank, Mansion House, the tubes, the rolling staircase, and Alf Squire's Colonial Bar. Also, to lunch in the London Restaurant where friend Percy got confidential with the waitresses in next to no time, and friend George said nothing but looked about with considerable admiration. I had a little business to do in between whiles, at Somerset House and the Law Courts, and I had to leave them in the waiting room at the former place while I went to see a man. When I returned, I found the indefatigable Percy bewildering an ancient Somerset House attendant with considerable conversation, questions and anecdotes. He was detailing the position and rights of Trades Unions in regard to the registration of births, deaths, and marriages in Australia when I came and rescued the old attendant. He, Percy, was very particular that his young protégé should in all respects behave as a Soldier and a man, and kept a vigilant eye for the approach of Officers. Every now and then he would nudge the dreamy George and point out the advent of some "Brass Stars." I believe the Colonials have a name for slackness in respect of the salute. It won't be Percy's fault if this is not remedied. He is one of them blokes what mocks reforms, I should say. By talking. If ever in your travels somewhere in France you come upon a crowd of men silent, but one who is telling everyone how everything is done, and why, and when, and where – that will be Percy. Some of the words he uses are strange but he understands them and he don't mind much if you don't talk back. He goes right on. I begin to see why he was with his pal George. George never says nothing and Percy talks for himself and George, and all the honour of the Regiment. Mind you, he ain't bragging or anything – only just talking. He has been sent over to stop the war. He is going to talk the Germans stiff. He can do it. He hits it off with children all right. And wants to spend his money, (both of them did) right and left.

They have gone back to camp with a fixed determination to get some more leave and spend it in London. If Percy starts talking to his Commanding Officer about it he'll get his leave all right, at about the end of the third day.

Music Halls, they call the "Vaudeville." The Vaudeville they saw knocked spots off any previous experience of theirs. Some village, London. There was a big Australian on Waterloo station when we went to see them off – one of Percy's 'crowd' – he said "some village, London, but we struck it at Hell's Damnation time for blasted weather," and he was quite a mild man to look at. He was quite right about the weather. It snowed and froze, and rained and hailed. When they went back Waterloo station was a sight, covered with Australians and girls seeing them off. One who was considerably drunk tried to get his Officer to shake hands with him several times. Whenever in the course of his rolling perambulations he came anywhere near the Lieutenant, he looked sloppy at him and held out his hand. The Ossifer took no notice beyond recommending him to find the Sergeant. One sergeant I saw, and he was obviously capable of taking in hand any situation. He was a man. All the crowd took the time from him when he said anything. And when he did say anything it was an Order. What he said, went.

I am afraid I have been talking as much as Percy. I shall therefore stop. Hope your leave comes along soon. So long old chap. Love from us all and kisses from Chris and Babs.

Ever your loving Brother, Arch.

If I don't get a chance to write before the 23rd, let me here and now wish you many happy returns of that auspicious date.

From Mabs
The Bedford, Newport.   Thursday, January 18, 1917
My Own Dear Boy,
Just a line to wish you the best of luck for your birthday, and I hope that the next one will be spent under better conditions than the present. I feel sure it will be all right by then.

I was glad when your postcard turned up for your Mother was getting nearly frantic because the letter you promised me had not arrived. It was no earthly use to tell her you were busy – she wouldn't have it. Unfortunately, the cards took 10 days to come this time which is the longest time of any we have had from France. I hope you have your parcel in time, I posted it on Tuesday and made the cake and pudding all myself, so I hope it won't kill you.

There have been several chaps we know on leave from France, so we are looking forward to seeing you soon. We had a letter from Ern again today but he doesn't say much about himself.

Painters and paper hangers have arrived today to do the house right through so you can guess there is a lively time in store. I am up to my neck in needlework so you will know what I am at.

From your ever loving sweetheart, Mabs.

From Mother
49, Carisbrooke Road, Newport.   Thursday, January 18, 1917
My Dear Bob,
This is to wish you a happy birthday from me and all of us. We hope you will be spared to come home to us quite safe and live to spend many more. Mabel is with us this afternoon to tea. She says she has written to you today. I would like to send you a postal order for a few shillings but things have not been very bright lately. All the same, I do hope you get enough money. Let me know else. I hope you have plenty of warm clothes.

You haven't written much lately. By that I expect you have been hard at it. We got your Field Cards which you wrote on the sixth. We got it on the 16th. It seemed a long time coming. I got it in my head, Bob, that you have not been all right. I hope I have been mistaken. Have you heard from C. Dyer lately? I hope he is all right. We haven't heard much about the getting married lately Bob. You must let us all know your mind on the matter when you write. Kath and Mab is full of it; plenty of talk between them. Gordon don't know how soon before he will have to join. Hope you get the County Press all right. I hope you will get

Mab's parcel for your birthday safe. This will make three birthdays you will have in the Army. We didn't think that once, did we?
Well, it seems by the way things are going, people says it won't be much longer; that is our comfort and I hope it will prove true. Now my dear Bob, I will say we all send you all kind wishes,
ever your loving mother, E Brimson.

From Chris
28, Barnard Road, Clapham Junction. SW   Sunday, January 21, 1917
Dear Old Bob,
To begin with, I must wish you happy returns of your birthday and may you spend the future ones in quieter times. I will get a parcel off to you sometime in the week. We were glad to have your card the other day. I suppose you can only have so many. We went to see the film pictures of the 'Battle of the Ancre' the other day. My goodness, you don't know what war is till you have seen what the boys are doing on the pictures. We also saw some 'Tanks'. Some tanks is a good expression, they are marvellous. I'd like to see one in reality. I suppose you are quite used to them now, I expect. You have heard a rumour by now of the terrible explosion we have had close to London*. I expect you can guess where. It must have been terrible. It shook our houses and made the windows rattle. Everyone thought it was Zeppelins. I had a note from Mother the other day. She says Dad is still at home, although he is better from the accident. I don't suppose he will go out to the Asylum again this winter. I wish they would get their pensions – I should feel more comfortable about them. We do what we can but times are hard for the best of us.
Mother tells us you might be getting married when you come home, Bob. Of course we can't blame you. All we can do is wish you good luck and let us know when you can. In one of your letters you were telling us about the mud. We saw some of it in the pictures and they were taken in September. What it must be like now, I can't think. Never mind, it can't last forever – I think you are all splendid. We also saw how the letters were dealt out. I expect you know heaps of chaps that never get any letters at all. I'd write to them myself if I knew. We will give you your birthday present when you come home. Save me a badge Bob. I haven't got one at all. Love from us all. Best wishes and luck for your birthday.
Ever your loving sister, Chris.

---

* On 19 January, 1917, a TNT factory in Silvertown, East London was destroyed when a fire detonated 50 tons of high explosives. The factory was destroyed and over 70,000 properties were damaged in the biggest explosion ever seen in London. 73 people were killed in the blast. An inquiry found the owners were negligent in the running of their works and judged that Silvertown was a totally unsuitable place for a TNT plant. The report remained secret until the 1950s.

" There Was a Young Man of Cologne "

(I've forgotten the rest of the poem, but it's something about "a bomb" and "If only he'd known ")

Bairnsfather cartoon from *The Bystander* magazine.

From Mabs
The Bedford, Newport.   Tuesday, January 23, 1917
My Dearest Sweetheart,
Today is your birthday, the third war birthday. Fancy, three gone by since you
left here; it scarcely seems possible. Certainly seems impossible that a year has
gone since the last, although so much has happened, and there are times when
time seems long. However, we have great hopes for your next birthday, when
the war is over and you are home again. I'll see you don't go away again unless
I go too, but I don't think you would want to. You will be only too glad to rest.
I have received your letter dated the 14th and I am pleased to hear that you are
doing so well. You may as well carry on and do all you can while you have the
chance. Fancy a conduct stripe! I didn't think they gave them to the New Army.
I suppose they make it different for you because the old soldiers had to wait
three years for one, I believe. I am glad you are a good boy and I hope you
always will be, but I know you will be – for you can be trusted, my love. I would
trust you anywhere. Even if there are French girls.
We have had nasty weather here the last week, bitter cold, and inclined to snow,
but I believe it is too cold to snow.
Gordon has been to Winchester today and has passed fit for General Service. He
thinks he will get into that Railway Corps all right, but it isn't settled yet. You
might meet poor old Uncle Will Collins out there soon. It is too bad. He didn't
join up till about November 9th and he is on leave for a draft. I'll let you know
if he is sent to the 2nd R.W.Rs then you may have a chance to cheer him up a
bit. He ought not to go really because he has some very bad varicose veins, but
they don't seem a bit particular now.
My old friends the chilblains are back again but I have only got two broken so
I am lucky so far. I have been plagued with neuralgia since about three weeks
before Christmas.
Ern hasn't arrived here yet but he is still coming. He is much better now. Morry
says he hasn't had a letter from you yet. He thinks you must be busy, but he
seems doubtful what sort of business. Oh! I am glad you changed your mind
about the wedding and now please don't change again until after the war – then
we will have a wedding.
     Au Revoir and best love from your ever loving sweetheart, Mabs.

From Kath
49, Carisbrooke Rd, Newport.   Thursday, February 1, 1917
My Dear Bob,
We had a letter from Arch this morning and they sent down your letter, (to
them) last one. They say they have sent you another parcel last week. Mother
will be sending one next week, as you have been having other people's lately.
They had your letter up at Roy's on Monday. I expect you have had some awful
weather since Xmas – we have. The water in my hand basin and flowerpot have
been freezing over and they are only a yard from my nose in bed. It's taken me
all my time to keep that from freezing too.
Dad hasn't felt up to going to work since Christmas so he and Mother have sent

in their pension papers and are waiting to hear the result only they, the pension people, are never in much hurry. I've been busy just lately, painting another 'Viking' picture. There is to be a sale of work at the Drill Hall this afternoon in aid of the wounded soldiers; the War Supply Depot have got it up. Anyone can send anything they like to sell to help, so I have sent my picture and Doris has painted two little seascapes.

You will see in the County Press that she has passed her last exam. She is very proud of it. She said she wondered if Bob would see it.

Poor old Gordon had to go to Winchester last Tuesday to be examined again. He is waiting now to be called, same as you had to. I think he is sick of waiting. Of course, he doesn't know when he will have to go.

(My hands are beastly cold now, I can hardly hold this pencil). Mabel and Doris and Beeb and I have just come back from the Drill Hall. They have done ever so well so far, too crowded to move. Won't it be grand if you can get home next month. Arch says he heard there was going to be another big push on the 16th February, bigger than has ever been before and that everything will be rolled up and all opposition done in and all will be well. Is that true?

Arch says, too, that we ought to go and see the Picture of the 'Tanks' if they come here. I should like to. You don't tell us if you see much of them. Are they so common that you don't take any notice of them now?

We hope you will like this parcel all right Bob, and cake. It's the best Mother could manage this time; says she will try and send a better one later.

Heaps of love from us all, Kath.

War Diary : "Beauquesne - Church parades for all denominations."
From Bob

Sunday, February, 4, 1917

My Dear Mother and Father,

I have kept you rather a long time without a letter but I have written to Roy, Chris and Mabel so you will know that I am still all right. We are still having awfully cold weather. The frost is the most severe I have ever known. Everything is frozen. Even our daily ration of bread is like a lump of wood. It's as much as we can do to cut it – and then we have to thaw it on the fire. I think I would rather have the swarms of flies that we are pestered with in the summer. How are you managing at home? Can you manage to get enough coal? You must be having hard times of it. I hope you are getting all right again now, Dad.

I don't think the time is far off now when it will all be over and finished. Germany seems like a rat in a corner. She knows that she cannot win and so she is having her revenge on everybody and everything that comes in the way. We have all great hopes of being home before next winter so try and keep going until then and tell Kath to begin getting ready for the wedding.

Leave has started again. They are going one a day from here but I don't fancy my chance just yet; it might be the end of March. I had the County Press all right up till now. I was very pleased to see Gordon's success as footballer – five goals out of the seven is jolly smart work – I can see him becoming a professional yet.

I am surprised to hear of H. Harvie being on his way out so soon; another one I must keep a lookout for. I heard from C. Dyer the other day. He is still going on all right. I don't know what part of the line he is in now. Chris tells me she went to see the new war film the other night. Fancy her mentioning that place. We had the band of the R.E's from Chatham here the other day. They are on tour in France. It was quite nice to hear them once more. Well, I must close now.

Ever your loving son, Bob.

You might send the khaki muffler out sometime please. No hurry.

From Arch

28, Barnard Road, Clapham Junction. SW.   Sunday, February 4, 1917

Dear Bob,

Many thanks for your letter. We have had yours to Dad and Mother forwarded and have sent ours down to them. This happens to all your letters. What a good thing to be back of the line again and having a rest. From what I have read, a rest back of the line is sometimes harder work than being in the front lines. Well, the Huns seem to have gone too far with the Yanks this time. Even old Wilson seems to have got the blight with them at last. They always blunder somewhere, despite being the race of Supermen out to teach Kulture to the world. This will be a sad day for Old Moore – he did not foretell America coming in. I confidently expect that the Daily Mail, after having cursed America all along for standing neutral, will now tell them they'd better leave the war alone.

We sent you a parcel about ten days ago – I wonder whether it reached you. We saw just after we sent it that no parcels were being sent from Southampton for 15 days, or words to that effect, but we sent it and so far as the tinned stuff it contained, it ought to be all right. We hear these Australian cousins, what were here the other day, are now laid up with influenza. Both in hospital. I guess the talkative one has talked the nurses blind, deaf, dumb and paralytic. We had a letter from him on Friday. He's a rotten writer. Got plenty to write about but difficult to make it out. Writes like an inky spider crawling over the paper.

It has been snowing and freezing, and snowing and freezing all along and tonight it has snowed proper. All the streets white and gangs of girls out snowballing. I got one on the back of my neck. I didn't stop to return the compliment in consequence of George being with me, and I didn't want to shock his morals. Besides, he was in a hurry to get into the pub. What I say is that there are getting to be too many girls about. It ain't safe for a poor confidin' young man to go out. As George says, all the girls what comes into the pubs seems to have got wedding rings on, and they orders their gin like they knew exactly what to do and don't want no male person to tell them what's good for the constitution. And then you notice that it's mainly females as are concerned in the conspiracy to murder Lloyd George. Shockin' I call it. 'Taint as if we was in the times of suffragette raids and similar excitements. No – the fact is they is a lot of females what ain't got no shells to make and no husbands to make a fuss of and no work on the land where they can put on trousers. So they gets morbid and wants to be talked about and consequently has a go for Lloyd George. That's where they slipped up. They ought to have tried someone less artful like

Balfour. They won't half cop it now, I reckon.

Lots of rumours flying around just now. I 'spose the latest Hun frightfulness is the cause thereof. From the state of things at present it may be even yet necessary for me to be mobilised in one form or another. I can see me working on the land, or minding pigs, or urging reluctant hens to lay. All the young blokes goes automatic into the Army or Navy now, and in course of time, everything would work out like a mathematical problem and we should always have millions of soldiers, and millions of sailors, and millions of ships, and millions of girls to work to keep them fed and clothed and supplied with munitions, so I warn Germany here and now what is in store for them. Supper is now ready so this is where I finish for now. So long Bob, lots of love and kisses where proper.

Ever your loving brother, Arch.

War Diary : "Mailly-Maillet – February 7th, "Work on 6th Avenue. Ground like iron." February 12th, "Work as usual. Weather considerably warmer."

From Bob

Unknown date in February 1917, but before the 14th

My Own Dear Sweetheart,

I don't know what has gone wrong with the mail. We have only had one in about eight days, and that day I had yours of the 8th, which must have taken some while to come. We have been back in the line 17 days now. Ours wasn't a very long rest. We never do seem to get much in our poor old Division. I think it's a case of wearing the old ones out first, but you will read all about it when the war's over. The frost and the cold has gone and we have got the old sloppy mud back again, but it is much warmer – that's one good thing.

As your birthday is close handy, I will wish you very many happy returns of the day next birthday. All being well, I shall be able to wish you the same personally. This village that we are living in has no civilians left as it is not very far from our trenches, therefore there are no shops. I am sorry I cannot send you any little souvenir this time. We don't care where we go now much, so long as it helps to finish this kind of life out here. I'm jolly glad we are doing so well with the new War Loan. I should have liked to have invested a few fivers myself in it. Leave has been stopped for some while now, and I don't know when it will start again. If it does start, I shan't be home in March.

Three of our fellows had got actually to the station and were recalled. Sorry to hear that Ern hasn't got home yet. Rouen is a funny place to get to; they don't consider the ordinary Tommy there, in fact most of the fellows I know have been glad to get out of it. I'm awfully sorry to hear that your Mother has been so unwell lately. I do hope it is nothing serious. Harry Leal, he is in the Dorset Regiment. I was going up through the street and I heard someone shouting Bob! Bob! I turned round and there, I couldn't recognise him for a minute or two until he told me. He couldn't stop long as he was going into the trenches that evening. I haven't seen him since.

Well Mabs, my pet, I must close now. Fondest love and heaps of kisses.

Ever your own true love, Bob.

From Chris
28, Barnard Road, Clapham Junction. SW.   Sunday, February 11, 1917
Dear Old Bob,
Archy told you last week how pleased we were to get your letter and to know you are resting a little while. We always feel relieved somehow when we hear you are slacking it a bit. We did get your service card and very pleased we were with it too. We have been thinking a lot about you boys out there lately in this severe weather, but it has broken now, I think. It is bitterly cold and coal scarce, that's the worst part. I hope Mother has got plenty. We had a long letter from Kath the other day and she didn't say a word about them being short. I suppose they have told you all about the bazaar they went to, and how one of Kath's Gogs was raffled for £2.16s. 0d – What a price for the old chap. I wish she could make a few to sell at that price.
We are hoping every day to hear of you getting some more leave. I want a souvenir. We went to someone's house the other night and they had several relics to show us. One was a ring made from a German bullet or something, and another, a little cross made from a piece of bell. She also had a lovely scarf bought out there but that was an expensive thing. I don't expect anything like that but I should like a relic of some sort to show off (not a helmet).
Hope you get the Pictorial all right every week we send regularly. Fancy it being Mabel's birthday on Wednesday. I have forgotten how old she is – don't suppose you have. I will write to her for the occasion and perhaps send her something for that bottom drawer of hers. I should think it is about full by now. Kath tells us that Mother and Dad are likely to get their pensions soon now. I hope so. I am sure, of course, when the weather gets warmer Dad would be able to do odd jobs. I don't know if he will go to the Asylum again. I expect he'd like to. I'll say goodnight now, Bob.
                          Your loving sister Chris.

From Doris
31, Melbourne St, Newport.   Sunday, February 18, 1917
Dear Bob,
I had your card a long time ago but I have not had time to answer. I am going down Gordon's office now to see what it's like because I am going to take his place when he is gone. I don't know when it will be, as the two men he went up with have had their reply and are going next Friday, but nothing was said about Gordon. He doesn't think he'll get into the ROC because he is too young.
It's quite decent down the office. There is a fire to roast chestnuts on. One of the other clerks brings bull's-eyes and I provide the chestnuts. Then the fun begins. We're going to get a teapot and kettle etc, to make tea, then when you come home we shall invite you to a cup of dishwater (perhaps). This all happens between 1 o'clock and quarter past two as the manager goes home to dinner at 12 and doesn't turn up till a quarter or half past two. We go at 12, get back at 1 (perhaps) and then the other clerk goes and doesn't come back till 3 o'clock. So Miss Scamill, Gordon and I are left on our lonesome. Don't we work too! Gordon has a yarn over the telephone with his pal on the Central Company, and uses the manager's phone and forgets to pay. Miss Scamill and I read and eat.

Fine, isn't it? I go home at four.

The weather here is lovely and warm at present. I don't know how long it will last. Is it any warmer out there? I forgot to tell you about our new creature. It's a black dog this time; you know the kind, one of those skinny kind, always hungry. I think it's called a greyhound – though how they ever make it grey, I don't know – it's as black as soot with a white band round its neck. I've taken it out twice as yet but never no more. The first time it pulled me down over the embankment to the road at the Castle and nearly broke my toe (how sad!!!) Then some wounded stopped me and asked if it was a bulldog, of all creatures. I had enough first time but I thought it had better have one more chance so I put the strap on it and took it up the Castle again. Then I took the strap off so it wouldn't pull me down over and the blessed thing turned tail and bolted home as fast as it could go and left poor me standing there, looking; and then it had the sauce to turn round and look at me. There were some boys up on the Keep and they all started to sing "Love me, love my poodle." That just about finished me so I turned round and followed the poodle, or bulldog or black greyhound – whatever the little beast is.

I went down to Mabel's to tea on Wednesday with Bee and Kath and Bee was coming up here today, only Ernest has got a cold and is not very well. Daddy keeps on saying he's going to write to you, but he finds he has not got time. He has gone back to Cowes to work now. He does not like it so much as at the Medina Hangar. Too much to do!

I will write a readable letter next time, but I'm trying the fountain pen Gordon gave me. It's more like a poker.

With love from Doris.

PS I don't know if you saw it in the County Press, but I've passed my examination.

From Kath

49, Carisbrooke Rd, Newport.   Thursday, February 22, 1917

Dear Bob,

Mother is out and Dad is reading. Beeb is busy looking at Dad's history books says she would like to stay up all night and look at them. Poor old Gordon has had his papers to say he has to go March 8th and he won't be in the Railway Corps after all. They said on account of his being under 25 he has got to be in some line regiment. It is too bad – we thought he would be all right. He doesn't mind, seems pretty joyful to think he is wanted same as the rest. He was in here just now in the cadet uniform; says he went down this morning and had his photo taken. Makes a smart soldier.

That old pension affair isn't finished yet. Mother will tell you all about it when it is settled. They haven't had anything from it yet.

Seems a mighty long time waiting for you to come home. We do hope it won't be long now. Mother wasn't very pleased with the way that cake turned out; she will do better next time. I expect you will like it better than hard biscuits, anyway. I must finish now Bob,

with heaps of love and kisses, ever your loving Kath.

How are you getting on with that mouth organ?
Mother writes on edge of letter : I hope things are all right with you Bob. We have been waiting for news. Even a card is very welcome. Poor Mab looked hard for her birthday card, Mother

War Diary : "Mailly-Maillet – Work on Wagon Road with whole coy."
From Bob

Tuesday, February 27, 1917

Dear Mother and Father,
Received your welcome parcel this afternoon. I was jolly glad to get it and also to hear that you are all keeping well. We go seven or eight days without mail therefore, you mustn't worry if you don't hear every week. The parcel was a big luxury to me as the food we have been getting lately hasn't been up to much, although we can't grumble as things are at present. I expect you find it very hard to rub along now. Let me know exactly about the pension and if you find it impossible to draw it I will try and arrange to have the allotment transferred to Kathie. It seems the only way to settle it. I wrote to Mabs some while ago but she did not say whether she received it. I hope she will get it. I heard from Doris today. She tells me she is in the office. Tres bon.
Have been getting the County Press all right; the last one you sent came yesterday. The weather out here is a lot warmer now; almost like spring. I hope you are having it the same in the old Island. Tell little Bee that Uncle Bob sends love and kisses and will bring her a big present when I come home.
Well I must close now, with my best love to you all. Hoping to see you soon.
Ever your loving son, Bob.
Will drop Kath a line soon, I was ever so pleased to hear of the great success she had with her picture. She's getting on fine.

From Mother
49, Carisbrooke Rd, Newport.   Sunday, March 11, 1917
I am sorry I could not send you a parcel this week. Things have not been going so well. The weather has been so bitter cold and wet, or snow. It knocked your father up last Friday. He hasn't been outside the door and has been in bed three days but I am pleased to tell you he is getting all right now. The doctors saw him before he came home and gave him a large bottle of medicine. It's very nice – I believe it's half wine. I am sending you a 1s 8d postal order; it isn't much but I thought it would come in useful.
It was Doctor Reardon who gave him the medicine and he enquired for you. Dad says he always do. The nurses and patients do also; they will be so glad to see you when you come home.
Roy is still up at the prison at work. Kath keeps all right. I need not tell anything about them over the way, of course – Mabel does that. Charlie is expecting to be sent off. He is anxious to go. They heard from Harry. He tells them the

Doctor wouldn't pass or I suppose he would have been home. I hope you will see Dyer again soon. Wish you could come home together. Dad says most of them have joined up over at the Asylum, in the group. Now goodbye my dear boy,

ever your loving Mother, Ellen Brimson.

From Mother and Kath
49, Carisbrooke Road.   Sunday, March 11, 1917
Mother : After reading of such dreadful times you are having in the paper it is so nice to know that you are all right. I am sorry to keep you so long but I've waited to know the result of the pension affair, but as they are still silent I can't wait any longer, but directly things are settled I will write again and let you know. What a shame to keep people waiting. I don't know whatever we should have done if I had not the help of your money, but it has hurt me very much to use it. Gordon has joined in the 3rd Hants and is over at Gosport at present. They are all well up there, also down the Lane.
Kath : Beeb was very excited about your message and wondered what your big present can be. So do I. I told her perhaps it would be a German helmet; she turned up her little nose at that.
Roy and family went down to have their photo taken 'family group' because of Gordon going away. Clem came in today, says they have the proof "and Ma says I'm the best looking one in the family." Kathleen comes next with the remark that ,"Daddy looks soft." We haven't seen it yet; I expect you will get one... Doris has just come in with it and they look fine, every one of them.
You're a mighty long time coming home for your rest. I dreamt you were here the other night it did seem so real. I must finish now.

With best love from your loving Mother and Kath.

From Bob
                                                    Monday, March 12, 1917
Mailly-Maillet : War Diary entries for March 1st to March 16th are missing.
My Dear Kath,
It's about time I wrote to you a few lines, so as I am writing to Mabs I'll slip this in with hers. I hope Mother has got over her bad cold. The weather has been bad enough lately but we have got the best to look forward to – that's one good thing. How are you getting on with the painting now? I expect to see a lot when I come home, and the next time I come home I don't expect to come back here again. I seem to think that the war will finish this year all right.
I forgot to tell you of a bit of sport we had out here in the village we were resting in, a few weeks ago. An old barn caught fire about 9 o'clock at night and after it had been burning some while the ancient village fire brigade arrived on the scene – old men with long beards. They all came up to look at it first with the captain. It was the time when the very cold weather was on so they all stood there and had a warm first and then the captain suddenly shouted "Allez!" And they all hobbled off down the road and presently returned with big helmets on

and dragging a very ancient fire extinguisher on wheels. Then they all stopped to light their pipes, after which they fixed a hose on it, then they had to draw it close to the fire to thaw it before they could pump. When they eventually got it going the roof and walls fell in, so it saved them the trouble of trying to stop it. There were crowds of Tommies round watching it and having a warm so you can guess the chafing that was going on. It was a scene worthy of Fred Karno's.* It is impossible to describe it as we saw it.

I hope you are getting the pension business settled up at home. I'd write them a letter myself if I knew where to send it. Tell Mother the cake was tres bon. I wish I had another like it now. The mouth organ has refused to give any sound at all now but there is a chap with a mandolin in the billet so we get a bit of music sometimes.

Well Kath old girl, I must close now, with best of love to you, Mother and Dad not forgetting little Bee.

Ever your loving brother, Bob.

From Doris
31, Melbourne Street, Newport.   Friday, March 16, 1917
Dear Bob,

As I have not anything particular to do this afternoon, I thought I would write to you once more. The manager is in the next room. I expect he will come in here when a little bird tells him I am not working but I have got to risk that. Gordon's at Gosport in the 3rd Hants. I am glad he never got in the ROC for one thing, namely that the ROC badges are like the REs and I have got one of them, so now I shall have two. There is plenty of work to do down here if you like to do it, but that's it – you see, at present I've got a tired feeling for such stuff. Don't I get some fun on the telephone? Especially dinner hours when I am here alone, except for Miss Scamill, the other clerk.

Sir Sam Fay, our boss, is coming down here tomorrow (Saturday). Isn't it a nuisance? I shan't have my half-day off now. I'm going to Portsmouth next week to see Gordon. He says his clothes is baggy and the food is awful. Mr Batten, the manager, told me to tell him that God sent the food and the Devil sent the cook. Very good isn't it? Mabel went over to see him on Tuesday. He told her that the chaps in his room are very good, except for the fact that they had five murderers in with them for a week or so. One of them was had up for boxing with a man. He hit him too hard and killed him and it was turned into manslaughter. The same man is teaching him boxing. Yesterday I nearly knocked Miss Scamill's glasses off with a great bundle of tickets I threw at her (but first she nearly knocked my nose off). Today she bumped into me and now she has nearly got a black eye and I've got a blank brain – she has knocked my memory out.

Daddy is down at Cowes again, but he doesn't mind now because it is warm again. Up the other place he used to sit over the fire all day long, I believe. Silly old Ron is still on the buy. We've got another rabbit now; keeps on saying he's going to get rid of them but still they all hang on. It is nearly as good as a farmyard, what with the fowls, the dog, the rabbits and the field mouse we've

---

* Fred Karno's Circus was a famous entertainment troupe. Any chaotic organisation became known as 'Fred Karno's Army'.

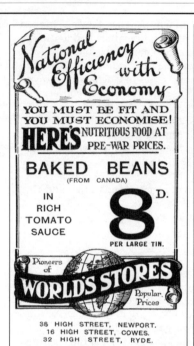

County Press advertisements, 1917.

tamed. I nearly committed suicide this dinner time. I was walking down the line and forgot the train was coming but I turned round – (manager keeps on wandering in and out. Here he comes, I wonder why people always come when you don't want them). It's nearly teatime. I hope you've had your tea or dinner whatever you call it when you read this, else you will feel hungry, make your mouth water, you know. Well, 5 o'clock; time is up, so I'll write again.

With love from Doris.

From Chris
28, Barnard Road, Clapham Junction. SW.   Sunday, March 18, 1917
Dear Bob,
We are thinking about you all the time, and talking about you every day, and wondering about where you are. We are having good news lately as regards the fighting out there and Archy has bought a map; he spends a long time studying it. I suppose it is better for you while the weather is fine – for advancing, I mean. We are always anxious, you know. It is about time you had some more leave. It will be very nice about Easter; that is the time you ought to manage to come. It would cheer Mother up no end. She seems to have been very queer lately but Kath said in her last letter she was improving. Of course, it is money troubles that has been worrying her. It does seem too bad that they should be treated like that at their ages, too. I believe Mabel is doing all she can. We do too, although it is hard for us all. If the weather keeps on like this we shall be having Beeb home again, then Mother won't have her on her mind all the time. I noticed in your letter home you promised her a big present. It's kind of you to think about her but bring yourself safely Bob – that's the chief thing. I want to know what you meant in one of your last letters, when you spoke about me going to the pictures. You said "fancy Chris mentioning such a place." What did you mean? It was when I had told you about seeing the tanks. They tell us Gordon has gone now and having a rough time of it by all accounts, poor chap, scrubbing floors etc, – never did one before in his life, I don't suppose. Oh, I do wish it was all over and the boys were home again.

Ever your loving sister Chris.

War Diary : "Ervillers – Billets, water supply + road repairs in neighbourhood of Ervillers. Construction of dugout for 20th Brigade (Inf) HQ began."
From Bob
Monday, March 26, 1917

Dear Chris and Arch,
I received your letter of the 18th. Very glad to hear that you are all keeping well. I've only these two sheets of writing paper left so it won't be a long letter. We have been having a decent time lately, scotching old Fritz up. We are a good 20 kilometres from our old front line and as I suppose you have seen in the papers he has burnt down or blown up every house in every village, and mighty big craters on every crossroads, and blown up or cut down every tree – fruit trees

as well, big and small. You would think there had been a terrific earthquake that had destroyed everything.* We have one consolation – he has left us plenty of firewood and plenty of stones so we are not short of fire. We had to trek across country as we could not use the roads after a certain point. It's a poor way of showing his hate in destroying the private property of the French peasants. It appears as if he has driven them out of their homes and would not let them take any of their furniture, as it is laying about all over the place, smashed up. Well, he'll have to pay for all this in the long run.

Well Chris, it's rather awkward for me to let you know what to send in parcels as there are lots of things it is difficult for you to obtain, so I will still leave it to you. We are right away in the wilds now so it's impossible to buy anything so I've got to depend on you folks at home now, although I know it's hard for you too. Last week we were sleeping in a tent pitched among the shell holes and it was jolly cold too but now we are in a wooden hut with three stoves in so we are pretty comfortable.

I hope Mother and Dad will soon get the pension business settled. They don't tell me much about it and I don't like to think of them wanting anything and poor old Kath and you might as well ask for your ticket as ask for leave now. I think it's a case of waiting until the war is over.

Well I must close now as it is near bedtime and I'm sleeping in one of old Fritz's beds (I think he took all the souvenirs with him on his shirt), they are a different kind than ours anyway. Well, so long for the present. Heaps of kisses for Babs.
                              Ever your loving brother, Bob.

From Kath and Mother
49, Carisbrooke Rd, Newport.   Monday, April 2, 1917
Dear Bob,

Arch came down on Saturday to take Beeb back. They couldn't do without her any longer although it isn't quite the right time to take her up there.

Poor old Arch couldn't manage for them all to come down this Easter, or for me to go back with them, as they had intended to. Arch thinks he might be called up but he is going to try to get on as a 'Special Constable' – he thinks that way he might get out of it. I hope it will be all right. I can't imagine Arch being in the Army can you, Bob? I've finished my first real miniature on ivory, not an order but just to keep for show. Arch is going to try to get an order from his boss to have his little girl done. Everybody says it's all right, especially for a first attempt. I'm not blowing my own trumpet, only telling you. I believe it was you made me manage it because you keep telling me you expect to see something done when you come home. Roy has had the sack down at Saunders but he didn't waste much time; he was on at Whites the next week. We never knew Roy so eager to work before? He sticks to it like anything; fairly loves it. All the same, it didn't prevent him having his joining up papers sent in again last Saturday but he seemed quite proud of it. Arch and Morry consoled him with the thought that beer would be much cheaper in the Army, after rubbing it in with all the worst things what he would have to go through. Poor old Roy; he doesn't care a hang about anything, he says, except the drilling, marching and

---

* See photograph page 246.

writing letters. If poor old Kit thinks she is going to get a letter every week, she is mistaken and that's how the silly beggar keeps on every time he moves. He shouts "left, right," just to get himself used to it. I don't know how he will get on about his 'papers'. Perhaps Whites will get him off.
Gordon is 'putting up' with it at Gosport pretty well. He doesn't think much of it. Good night now old boy.
With heaps of love, Kath.

War Diary : "Puisieux - 1 section wiring Ervillers defences. 1 section making good diversion round crater in Ervillers. 1 section water supply in village."
From Bob
Tuesday, April 3, 1917
My Dear Mother and Father,
I believe the last letter I had from you was the 13th of last month. I've already written to Kath. I hope she has got it all right; anyway I'm answering yours tonight. I'm very sorry to hear that you have been so unwell lately and I hope this letter will find you all right again. You must try not to worry. I'm glad to hear that Aunt Eliza is helping you a little; it's very kind of her. It's quite time that business of the pension was finished. If I only knew those people's address I would write to them myself and let them know what I think. They are a lot of rotters. As for my money, don't be afraid of using it; I'm only too pleased to know that I can do something for you. Remember me to J. Cornish if you see him again.
We had a bit of excitement about an hour ago. A German aeroplane flew over here and attacked two of our observation balloons. He swooped down from a big height and fired his machine gun into the envelope and then threw a fireball which set the escaping gas light and it soon burnt up. The two observers escaped with their parachutes. After he finished that one off, he swooped on the other one and served that the same, but meanwhile they had seen what had happened to the other and they were already on their way to 'terra firma'. Fritz then made off for his own lines. All the time, our guns were firing at him and infantry were shooting at him with machine guns but I think the cheeky beggar got back all right. I think he done this in revenge for us fetching down one of his planes this afternoon. I expect he will get the Iron Cross for his smartness.
So, poor old Gordon is going through it. I'd give a lot to be in Barracks in Blighty scrubbing floors – any job for a change at home.
I should be pleased to have a family group portrait. I'm anxious to see what it's like, so tell them to send one along please. Has Dad managed to get any seed potatoes for the garden yet? I hear they are worth their weight in gold now. We see them about once a month out here and then we might get half a one. I can't make out what you people are living on now. I suppose you drink your tea without sugar too. I've noticed the French people, when they are drinking coffee, put a sweet in their mouth first; they are just as bad off for sugar.
If you can keep the garden going it will help you a lot; you have got the best of the season coming on. It will be just right for Dad; look after it. I've broken that

little comb you sent out to me, but I've picked up a half of one since.
Well, I must finish as it is nearly bedtime. I shall be glad to hear from you as
soon as possible.
Give my love to little Bee and also best love to you all at home,
                                        Ever your loving son, Bob.

From Mother
49, Carisbrooke Rd, Newport.   Wednesday, April 11, 1917
My Dear Bob,
We got your letter this morning. We were interested about the aeroplane. We
expect to have a lot of good stories when you come home. We read in the papers
today about the 11,000 German prisoners and how the English soldiers cheered
them. Was you one of them? I could kill some easily, the brutes. Yes, Bob, the
food and anything else you buy is double and treble – so dear – but don't you
worry. If I am a good manager we get enough, such as it is. We mustn't
grumble. They say it will be worse yet but I must tell you we have the pension.
It came last Friday. 5/- for Dad and 5/- for me. What do you think of that? And
besides, they paid us the back money from February which was two pounds
each. Wasn't that grand? I had two pounds to pay for back rent and paid other
things so now I have plain sailing and will be able to get along.
I know you will be glad to know all this, so whenever I can manage I shall put
in the bank for you again. I wish I could get up to £50 for you by the time you
come home. I'll do the best I can. Dad is getting on with the garden all right, but
we have had so much wet and frost and snow that it throws it all back.
I am surprised that potatoes are so scarce in France, that being such a country
for vegetables. We can only see seed potatoes in the shops and not many of
them. I cook rice or beans with the stew.
 I am sending you a parcel tomorrow. I would put in a loaf if there is room. I
will see. I hope the comb is all right.
I will close now, hoping you will get the parcel alright and that you get the
County Press. Mab has just come in. She sends the cigarettes with her love.
Good night my dear boy.
                Take care of yourself for my sake and all of us, Mother.

From Mabs
The Bedford, Newport.   Saturday, April 21, 1917
My Dearest Love,
I do wonder what is going on out there all this time. What excitement there
must be and work, but what a terrible cost. Although, I suppose taking all into
consideration our losses are very slight and yet they seem tremendous. Just
think of it – 31,700 prisoners alone in 10 days and 14,000 taken by our lads. What
on earth can their total casualties be? With killed and wounded they must be
something awful. They deserve to be wiped off the earth, the horrible fiends.
They make me feel sick at the thought of them and their latest games and so I'm
sure I shall see German written all over all the pigs in future. Away with the

Germans. We will have something nice for a change.

The weather is behaving splendidly; it couldn't be better than at present. It is such a treat to have the warm sun again; we hardly know where we are. Your mother is talking about sending Kathie and I off by the sea all by ourselves for the week. Don't I wish you could be there?

It is Gordon's birthday soon so I thought we could get him a cigarette case for a present. I have got my eye on a nice plain leather one so that he can have his initials on it. I thought they wouldn't be so likely to steal the plain one. I expect he will like a present from 'us'.

Dad gets off working on the lane now; he has one of those plots up at Whitepit, about 7 rods, so that will keep him busy. I've got my garden in a box in the backyard. I'm growing green peas in it. The Minister is still keeping our other piece. We didn't think he would after the boy died.

Take care of yourself my love, but don't forget to give Fritz beans, because we owe him a good many grudges. At least, I suppose Fritz can't help it; his superiors are to blame. With every good wish for your safety,

I remain always your loving sweetheart, Mabs.

> War Diary : 'Puisieux - Company resting. Two church services (C of E + Non Conformist)"

From Bob

Sunday, April 22, 1917

Dear Mother and Dad,

I was jolly glad of the cake and the loaves; it's a change to get anything like that now. Thanks also for the comb. The end of the war seems to be in sight at last. The French troops are doing splendid work away on our right. I saw on a message posted outside a wireless station today that we and the French had taken 33,000 prisoners and 330 guns, from the 9th till the 20th, and we know that a lot more has been taken since. We are gradually pushing them off the map that Mabel sent me; I shall soon want a new one. I am very glad that the pension business is settled at last. You will feel more settled now, also the best time of the year is coming on. Archy sent me the tickets in the Sunday Pictorial, I suppose they were the ones they had for the boat across from Ryde to Portsmouth. Got the County Press today. I see that H. Jolliffe of Shanklin is in hospital with interns at Cheltenham. I wonder if it is Harry.

Don't bother to send soap – we get plenty issued. I managed to have a washing day today as we had a few hours off. I'm getting quite smart at it now (only don't tell Mabs). Glad to hear that Kath has been able to get out lately. The weather here has improved a lot.

I had the job of painting the badge on the steel helmet of an Officer in the 2nd Dragoon Guards, and also wrote a cross for his servant that was killed in action up here. I decorated the cross a bit – he was very pleased with it. Our Major and other officers came to see it. He gave me a tip of 10 francs. I get crosses to write for lots of other Regiments. I designed a fancy letter for them and combined it with a little decoration. They don't look bad – everyone admires them, anyway. I also get a good bit of signwriting to do – mostly the names of the villages and towns; also direction boards, as the Germans destroyed the originals.

I had rather a narrow escape the other morning. Part of the gable end fell on the place I used as a workshop but I happened to be on parade at the time. Fritz had blown the lower part away and there happened to be a strong wind on, which fetched it down. Anyway, a miss was as good as a mile, after all.

Well I must close now with love to you, Dad and Kath.

Ever your loving son, Bob.

From Mab

The Bedford, Newport.   Wednesday, April 25, 1917

My Dearest Love,

Just a line to tell you that your parcel has started at last. I posted it this evening and I do hope everything will be all right this time. I am rather doubtful about the fruit tarts; I am afraid they will get crushed.

We are getting impatient for news of you again. I do wish you would think of us at least once a week and drop a postcard. You worry your mother to death when you leave it so long. It isn't any use to say anything to her for she is always convinced that something has happened to you. Don't think I am grumbling, lad, because I know you must be having an awful time now and you know I wouldn't want to make it any worse for you. No, Bobbie, it will be the happiest day of my life when Peace is declared and I know you are out of danger. Oh, let it be soon.

Morry was over on Sunday, he is coming again on Saturday for a weekend. I expect he will often be over here now until he gets another ship. We have had a letter from Ern. We sent him some bread and fish and various other eatables and he says they did enjoy it and he could have got quids for the bread and fish alone. Would you like some fish?

Of course, it would have to be haddock or bloaters as nothing else would keep long enough. We would have sent some today but there was none in the town this afternoon and that was too late, because we had made the other things. I haven't any extra special news after all except that the IW Rifles are in action again and some have been killed. One of the killed is a boy of 19 who lives quite close here.

Spring seems to have come to stay at last; it has been beautiful lately. Well, if I don't stop soon the parcel will be forgotten about before you get the letter. With best wishes for your good luck and tons of love and kisses,

I remain your ever loving sweetheart, Mabs.

From Charlie

46869, 87 Field Co. R.E. Battalion 12th Division, BEF.   Sunday, April 29, 1917

Dear Bob,

Just a few lines in answer to your most welcome letter which I received quite safe. Glad to hear that you are keeping all right. If I can find out where you are I will come and see you as I should like to have a chat with you. Glad you saw H. Leal. You want my opinion of the war? Well, I don't think it can go on much

longer at this rate.
We are getting warm – nice weather now. Hope it will continue. We have had
several of the old boys to see us lately. It is nice to see them; and leave is out of
it altogether. Hope we shall soon be going for good. Glad to say that I am quite
well at present. Cannot say much, as you know. I think that is all for the time.
Hope to meet you soon. Wishing you the best of luck.

From your old chum, Charlie.

From Doris
31, Melbourne Street, Newport.   Monday, April 30, 1917
Dear Bob,
I had a postcard from you. I don't know when but I did have one so I am
answering it now. Of course, I am not writing this at the office (you know, that
great big place at the bottom of Hunnyhill) – never do such things as that!
Especially as the manager is at Southampton and there is only me here!
Gordon came over yesterday. Doesn't he like the Army? (I don't think). His
food, like yours, is most delicate – stewed mice and onions for lunch; I think half
a slice of bread minus dripping for tea. I won't mention dinner for you may not
be able to eat yours after it.
What do you think of the weather? In Newport everyone is being sort of
parboiled (like you do the sausages before you make the sausage rolls).
Telephone bell just went. Makes you say things sometimes, but I don't mind
when I know who it is at the other end, like I did this one. There was no one to
overhear me, so it was all right. (Hope your letter never heard).
Do you remember me telling you about a certain black skinny dog? Well, the
same was sold for 3d, as it was always hungry, poor creature could not help
itself. After many days it returned skinnier than ever. We fed it again and also
again and for many agains, but this was no gain. So when he returned the third
again, we sent him empty away (by the way that is a bit of the Bible – I am not
quite heathen – for one thing, I am going to be confirmed soon). After many
days we hear of poor Gyp no more, for he went back and coveted, stole and
demolished 9.65476843 (don't forget the recurring) of a suet dumpling, which
was not legally his. There is a commandment which says "Thou shalt not covet
thy neighbour's house nor his ox, nor his ass nor anything that is his." Well the
dumpling was his (his neighbour's I mean). Also there is one which says, "Thou
shalt not murder." Well, the dog did murder. He murdered the dumpling, so the
poor creature had to go to the better land where they have got suet dumplings
to covet. I suppose they live on the wind up there. This is the end of Dog Gyp.
Never mind, we have another rabbit now. It's very ill at present but
nevertheless it's a rabbit up till now. It has eaten too much I think. Poor dog
could never have done that.
The writing is getting worse and worse. Soon you won't be able to read it at all
so I will stop now and write again when I can write better.

Love from all, Doris.

From Mabs
The Bedford, Newport.   Tuesday, May 1, 1917
My Dearest Boy,
I am glad you have learnt how to do washing for if you don't write once a week
in future to me, you see if I don't make you do all the washing. I will, see. I'll
pay you out. Sorry the beginning is a bit wobbly but I tried to write by
moonlight and it was no great success. You see, I had only one match left in the
box and I managed to let it slip and of course, it could not be found, so I tried
to do without the candle but had to give up and hunt the match again. After ten
minutes frantic search I unearthed it and here we are. I am very sorry to say that
we have had very bad news of poor old Ern again. One of the nurses wrote, and
tells us that he is wounded and dangerously ill. That is all we know at present
but he is evidently very badly hit this time. Well, I think he has had his share of
trouble and I hope this will be his last. It is about time he had a rest and perhaps
it will be more settled by the time he is fit again. Your letter came with that news
this afternoon.
Yours was delayed as you had forgotten to sign your name outside so it was
specially censored at the Base. It was passed alright and not a word scratched
out. Please remember always to sign in future. Fancy talking about all you will
have to make up when you come home, as if all we can do for you pays you for
all you are doing for us.
I went out to Newbridge today, Monday, and the country is just glorious with
the primroses and everything just bursting into life again. I am going to
Atherfield tomorrow so I shall find some more beautiful country there I expect.
I have got the cigarette case for Gordon. It is only a plain leather one with a
silver edge. I thought they wouldn't be so likely to steal it if it was plain,
although it is a very good one. His initials are on it and it looks alright. I hope
he won't lose it, for it cost about 7/- altogether. I hope you won't think me too
extravagant.
I often have dreams about you coming home but it doesn't get you home any
faster. Dreams are stupid things after all – aggravating nasty beasts. I meant to
tell you that Gordon has a thief in his room because I sent him a letter with a big
packet of BDU's in and some wretch stole it, for Gordon said he hadn't had it
when Kath asked about it. I wish there had been a man trap inside.
I didn't finish again yesterday so I can tell you about my trip to Atherfield. All
went well (except my back brake) until I wanted to come back. Then I had to
find a lot of tape in the form of a patch on the front wheel to prevent the sudden
inclination of the inner tube to come out through a big split in the outer cover,
so I couldn't use that brake then. Result, walking down all hills and a new tyre
into the bargain. Just my luck in these hard times.
Morry is never tired of talking about the old joyride, but I hope when you start
joyriding again it won't be that sort or I shall get fierce, but you must remember
Morry is a poor old married man now with someone to keep him out of
mischief. Morry was here on Saturday and Fred Ballard happened to be on
leave too, so they were able to have an evening together.
To finish up Morry took him over to your home to finish off the evening with
Roy, but Roy's wife had taken him home so they had to manage without him.

I couldn't get Morry to move till about 11.40 pm and then he was quite disappointed because he had to go before 12 o'clock. An airship came over us yesterday afternoon when we were going to Newbridge. 'We' means Molly and I. Well, it is time I went to dreamland to dream some more beastly old nightmares I suppose. The only thing you need worry about is getting yourself home and I shall be quite satisfied and that will make up for everything. May your good luck be always with you is the loving wish and only thought of your little sweetheart, Mabs.

I hope the parcel has arrived. I am afraid you are a very naughty boy to want V.C's novels,* but I will try to get it. You make me blush at the thought – dreadful.

Having left Saunders, Mabs applied for employment at Parkhurst Barracks.

Parkhurst. I.W. Organising Officer   Saturday, May 5, 1917
Women's Work. Section I P.G.
Bring this letter with you as a permit to enter the Barracks.
With reference to your answer to my advertisement in the I.W. County Press, if you will attend at 'The Library,' Parkhurst Barracks at 2.30 p.m. on Tuesday, May 8th, 1917, the Officer Commanding will see you with reference to your application for War Work. The wages are from 19/- to 23/- per week and 2/- War Bonus according to the employment, and the hours – 48 hours per week.

From Bob

Saturday, May 5, 1917
Bullecourt : The War Diary entries for May 1st to May 9th are missing.
My Dear Kath,
It's a long while since I heard from you so I'm going to write you a letter to ask you what I've done wrong – or perhaps you've been too busy. There is a thunderstorm raging at present after a good spell of hot weather. It'll lay the dust, so it doesn't matter. I am longing to see some of your paintings especially the miniatures; I know they must be A1. I want somebody to send me out a nice little sketchbook, one that I can put in my pocket. What's put me up to it is a R.H.A. boy who was in a bivouac close to me. He's a bit of an artist and carries a sketchbook and he has made some natty little pictures of places he has been in, up and down the line. A bon souvenir. I can't imagine Arch being in the Army – only as an officer – and I think he would make a jolly good one. I've met some rotten ones out here and Arch could knock spots off them. Got Doris's letter today. She's some wench and no kid about it – I don't know whether you're ever read one of her letters. Well, Gordon must be getting broken in by now. Let's hope Roy won't have to follow. If he does, I'll put him up to a good job, that is R.E. Water Transport. All he has to do is to help manoeuvre the

---

* There seems little doubt that this is a reference to the works of novelist Victoria Cross, 1868-1952. Her 'racy' books dealt with themes of female sexuality, extra-marital sex and, on occasion, inter-racial love affairs. A prolific writer, her 1912 novel 'Night of Temptation' sold over 6 million copies.

barges up and down the rivers and canals of France and Belgium, and not too close to the firing line, not too much work. Grub, money and clothes found and a cheap tour through the Continent. Well, Kath, must close now with my love to you, Mother and Dad, also Kitt and the kiddies.

Ever your loving brother, Bob.

Write soon

From Mother
49, Carisbrooke Rd, Newport.   Monday, May 7, 1917
My Dear Bob,
I so often think of you painting the crosses. Are there many that you know? The papers say the French are keeping the graves beautiful with flowers and give them great attention. It shows how grateful they are to the poor fellows and that the ground is given to them for ever.
Sad news came to Mrs Attrill's today, officially, to say poor Ernest is wounded and dangerously ill. They had heard before from the nurse – I expect Mabel has told you. Isn't he unfortunate, poor chap? He is a rough one, Bob, but I liked him very much; he was so homely with us. I hope he will get over it. It has been sad times out there lately, by the papers. I long every day to hear it will all soon be over. Of course, as things are, leave is stopped for everyone.
We posted the County Press yesterday. We are having lovely weather now and things are coming on well in the garden but my word, the goods is dear and not a single potato can be got. Kath don't like that, for you know how much she is for potatoes, and the bread is like eating sawdust almost. I will make a wholemeal loaf for you when I send. Mab says she sent you some pastry, how was it when you got it?
I left off writing yesterday to get ready and take Kath to meet Mabel. She went to Atherfield in the morning. Dad went with us and we got so far as Buckum (*sic*) village. It is a nice walk but very dusty. We didn't go any further, so turned back. Mab caught us up at Clatterford.
They haven't heard anything of Harry for three weeks. He was alright then, and Charlie is. Now goodbye my dear boy.

Ever your loving mother, E. Brimson.

From Mabs
The Bedford, Newport.   Wednesday, May 9, 1917
My Dearest Boy,
More trouble since the last letter. Ern is in Manchester again, but I am very much afraid that he will never be quite fit again. He has managed to write himself, but as usual he says very little about himself except to say that it will be a long time before he is well again. The official report says he is seriously ill with a gunshot wound in his face and fractured vertebrae so you can guess things are serious. Now I will tell you something to make you smile. The ASC* advertised for women workers. They wanted clerks, librarians, tailors, orderlies, postmen and storekeepers. Of course, I thought that a librarian would

---

* The ASC, or Army Service Corps, provided the food, equipment and ammunition for front-line troops.

suit me down to the ground, so I applied for that, or tailor. They told me I was far too young for a librarian as the work would be too much, so there was only the tailoring part left. They only wanted two of them at Parkhurst and there were three of us there, so we had to trek off to the tailors' shop and the men had to hunt up some coats for us to patch. Then we had to set to work right away. One of the girls had had 10 years experience so they took her, but they wouldn't have me. I didn't mind because I don't think I should survive a weeks patching of seven hours a day. Fancy me sitting still, sewing all that time. Of course, I used to at Cowes, but we had a change round to some other work every few days.

Gordon is coming home this week for his six days draft leave, so I suppose the poor kid will soon be out there. He was pleased with the cigarette case. Kathie is still up to her neck in Gollywogs; she has just finished two monsters. Now she has two more to do and one must be finished tomorrow. What a rush, but I suppose he will get done all right, we must all help.

Morry and Wallace are going on all right and I will let you have any news of Ern as we get it. With fondest love and kisses to my dear old boy.

Remain always your devoted Mabs.

War Diary : "Mory – Three sections working on Vraucourt - Homme Mort defence line."

From Bob

Sunday, May 13, 1917

My Darling Mabs,

I'm so awfully sorry to hear about poor old Ern being wounded again. If ever a man has had his share, he has. I do hope he will recover all right and never have to see the fighting line again. We have moved further forward since our last little push and we are bivouacked. Old Fritz strafed us unmercifully this morning although none of our fellows were hurt, as it happened. Others suffered.

You must excuse my writing as it is awkward writing a letter on your knees. We are having glorious weather now and I would much rather be camping out. Your splendid parcel came all right and everything was in first class condition. The pastry was very welcome, also the ship's tobacco. I enjoyed the best smoke I've had for months as the baccy they issue to us is rotten stuff. I must also thank you for the cigarettes and cheroots you sent me. I see it is going up in price again in the next budget; the poor working man again has to pay.

I hope you are still keeping on with the piano. We had charming music about half an hour ago – a Scotch piper blowing his inside out on the pipes. They can't seem to play unless they walk up and down all the time. The bombardment has just started again. I expect we shall get a few more souvenirs from Fritz tonight. It was very kind of you to give Gordon such a nice present. He'll be awfully pleased with it. Take care of yourself my pet. Heaps of love and kisses

From your ever loving sweetheart, Bob.

War Diary : "Ablainzeville – Two sections training. Two sections on billet repairs."
From Bob

Monday, May 21,1917

My Dear Mother and Father,
Just a few lines to let you know that I'm still going on all right. This is the anniversary of my going home on leave last year. I might have mentioned that leave is still going at the rate of one in five days, and as there is nearly a score to go before me I've got some while to wait yet.

We are back a few miles behind the line for a rest at present in one of the wrecked villages. We are bivouacked in an orchard in one of the few villages that possess a few trees. For all the destruction of the Huns the country is lovely roundabout. I usually go for a stroll of an evening round the old German trenches and down the dugouts. There's no doubt about it – they made themselves comfortable and never meant to leave it.

I'm surprised to hear of Gordon being ready for active service so soon. It doesn't seem long since he was called up. Let me know where he goes to. Glad to hear that Kath has got plenty of work with gollywogs; that's what I like to hear.

Got Kath's letter all right also the County Press. There's one little thing I'd like you to send me some time and that's a shaving brush, one that the hair doesn't come out of.

Well, must close now, with fondest love to all at home. Shall probably be home for a few days before the summer's over yet. Love and kisses,

ever your loving son Bob

Since writing this have received parcel. Everything in splendid condition. Enjoying it very much. Thank Kath for sketchbook.*

From Mabs
The Bedford, Newport.   Tuesday, May 22, 1917
My Dearest Boy,
I am expecting you home. I keep on looking for you. I suppose you will be lucky enough to get a leave one of these times. Ernie White arrived today. He is from the 29th Division. Suppose you are still having an awful time out there, but the news is always good, except for the casualties, although I suppose taking into consideration what is being done they are not so very heavy. We can't afford to lose men like that though, we haven't enough. Don't you think the Huns are about finished. They ought to be – the brutes.

I have been in charge here since Sunday. Dad and Mother have actually gone away and left me. They went up to Manchester to see Ern. I don't know when they will be back. He is very much better and the Doctor gives great hopes of him getting all right again. He hasn't been under the x-rays yet so they can't be certain yet how he will be.

I am glad your parcel was in good condition. I have heard that food is a bit scarce in those parts at present. Twelve months tomorrow since you arrived home last. I wish it was tomorrow you would arrive again, but perhaps it will be better later, as Mother is away. Things go on in the same old sleepy way, we

---

* Bob used this Rowney Sketchbook to document scenes on the Front. See sketches on pages 260-262 and front cover.

never get anything fresh. As to business – well it's just about as brisk as one could expect with beer at 6d a pint and tobacco 2d an ounce more. I must write again in a day or two when mother gets back with news. Au revoir, my love and take care of yourself from those 'straffing Huns.'

    With fondest love, I remain ever your loving, Mabs.

From Arch
28, Barnard Road, Clapham Junction. SW   Sunday, May 27, 1917
Dear Bob,
We were very pleased to get your letter to learn the parcel arrived after long travels. It seems to me as if sometimes the things are lucky and get through quickly, while at other times they lie about in sidings and places for weeks. We were afraid this parcel had been torpedoed. The war still goes on, don't it? That seems to be the one thing that does go on. The general public goes about trying to get another half a pound of sugar, and treats the war more or less as a fixture. We shouldn't know what to do if we hadn't got it. We are all sick of it but if we hadn't got it as an excuse, the Lord alone knows what would happen. Now and again some unpatriotic schemer manages to work people up into a strike but strikes can't last long nowadays; the union strike pay haven't got no war bonus in it. That's the fatal reason why. Blokes what are getting higher wages than ever before, and a 10 shilling a week war bonus, soon find out that it is unpatriotic to strike. And there's a sequel to that, now I see. Blighters what come out on strike had some home truths told them about striking, when they were paid about £5 a week, while Tommy and Jack at a halfpenny a day were fighting for them. Well, the strike blighters have gone back to work, and so that people may think well of them they are agitating for more money for Tommy and Jack. All very well, but will they help provide it by knocking five shillings a week each off their war bonus? Not on your life they won't. That's a test to their patriotism what would very soon find out where they lived. There would be very few remarks made for Brother Tommy and Brother Jack. The people what makes strikes haven't got the faintest idea of the science of political economy. They couldn't, for the life of them, tell you the mysteries of revenue and taxation or all the vast organisation necessary to be kept going in order to provide the general public with highways, powers, sanitation, lighting, railroads, food, ships, home defence, foreign service, naval defence, and all the thousand and one things necessary for the preservation of national life. And yet – they goes and strikes. As I said, they don't strike long in wartime, but when the war is over they will. For while they are living on the war and getting fat on it, what do they care if things are twice as dear as they used to be? Sugar is three times the price it was. Never mind, there is the money for it, and let the old woman go and stand in a queue for it if it can't be got otherwise. People in one town suddenly realises there's a war because aeroplanes drop a few tons of bombs on their heads. But the people in the next town goes on just the same. They ain't hurt. People says to each other, "How awful," and goes on into the next shop for half a pound of sugar quite calm. It's just like in peace time – someone dies, we say, "Ah, well, poor old so and so's gone?" "Yes, he's gone,"

Freshwater, Yarmouth and Newport Railway office, Hunny Hill, Newport.
"It's quite decent down the office. There is a fire to roast chestnuts on. Miss Scamill, Gordon and I are left on our lonesome. Don't we work too! Gordon has a yarn over the telephone with his pal on the Central Company, and uses the manager's phone and forgets to pay. Miss Scamill and I read and eat. Fine, isn't it? I go home at four." - Doris to Bob, February 18, 1918.

Mabs, Beeb and 'Tiny'.
"Now, what do you think I had for a present today? It is a dear little dog. A biscuit coloured Pom. It is a real beauty and I am sure you will like it."
Mabs to Bob, May 28, 1917.

says No. 2. "Not a bad post," says No.1. "No," says No. 2, "and what's yours? another half a pint?" and the incident closes. You don't realise things till you're in them. It's the same with this war. We know we're in it because everything is three times the price and we hear every now and then of a poor one we knew being either killed or wounded, and we read everlasting accounts of fights and battles in the papers but we don't know nothing about it really. It will be about five years after the war before we really know anything about it and by that time we shall have forgotten it. What I would like to see happen would be a great migration of people back to the land. When you come home, Bob, and gets married, never you go into a big town. You watch out and find a place near a town where you can have a garden big enough, and live as much in the garden as you can. That's my advice to all and sundry. If everybody tries to produce their own food after the war, the prices are bound to come down, and beyond that we shall revive the race with a healthier crowd than we had before. It has needed this war to find out how many unhealthy ones there are. Put people back in the country and they will get all right or die off. The war has trained lots of blokes fit and then outed them. Why not in future train them fit and make them useful in food production? Well, anyway, blow the war – them's my sentiments first, last, and all the time. So far as other things are concerned, we learn that Gordon, who was booked for a draft has not been sent yet and perhaps he may have another six days leave. Who knows? The ways of the Army are strange. Jim still sticks at Windsor, wangles leave as often as poss and rails at the army, maintaining all the time, however, that the Coldstream Guards are the only people alive. We hear that Ern is recovering from plenty more wounds, and that his father and mother have gone to Manchester to visit him. Probably you have later news of him than we have through Mabel. We here, have been having very nice weather punctuated with a thunderstorm or two, and have been devoting ourselves to living as much in the 'back to the land' style as we can. The children are pretty well and are very rapidly growing tall, and send Uncle Bob any amount of hugs and kisses. I am looking every post for re-examination papers, and I can tell you, me boy, that I should be quite as much at home as a Private as if I held the King's Commission.

Having wrote all this blamed stuff and reached the last page, I must put on the closure. We are going to see if we can't have a little outing tomorrow down into the country where the smoke of the town and the buses of the suburbs cease from troubling.

What I should like to do would be to have a week right away from any railway somewhere, where there was a wood, and a body could sit in the shade of a steamy hot evening and smell wood smoke, and sweet briar, and damp earth and ferns, and see little bits of blue sky through green leaves, and know that when I had to light my pipe I could wander off to the village pub and call for a pint. Gott straff the Kaiser. Amen. So long, Bob, old man. Take care of yourself and make haste home and let us foregather and talk. Oh, let it be soon. Lots of love and kisses from Chris and the children,

Ever your loving brother, Arch.

From Chris

28, Barnard Road, Clapham Junction. SW   Sunday, May 27, 1917

Dear Old Bob,

I'm afraid it is a long time since we wrote to you but you must forgive us – it's your parcel we have been getting together. We sent it off yesterday with the pipes. Archy has to go to bed early on Sunday evening to get up again at 1 o'clock to go on duty at two. He has had to be re-examined and they have classed him C1. That means garrison duty at home, so we don't know what's going to happen next. Bab tried to tell you in her letter that we were at Victoria station and saw crowds of boys home from the Front. You seem to have been having it wet out in France just the same as we have here. It was miserable. We thought of you boys out there. I suppose you are a long way from Gordon or Archy's cousin, the Australian. I will put in his name and number. You might come across him. He will keep you alive with his chatter – nineteen to the dozen – you'll know him by that. Then I suppose Har Harvie is out there now. Have you seen Percy Dyer yet? When is this war going to end? We are sick to death of it, everything is so dear, but we are getting plenty of vegetables and potatoes etc especially beans. We can't seem to eat them quick enough. We would like to send you some. Let me know if the cakes were all right. I made them all this time. I hope you get them quickly and that you find the pipes are nice, and the chocolate. I suppose I must go to bed now. Archy has been gone hours. He goes on duty twice a week and gets called out for raid scares, there was one tonight. Come home soon Bob. Best love from us all.

                                    Your loving sister, Chris.

From Mabs

The Bedford, Newport.   Monday, May 28, 1917

My Dearest Boy,

I was so pleased to get your letter yesterday. You are a dear boy and you know I always trust you anywhere, so I am not alarmed at the nurses a bit. I feel sure you would never abuse that trust, Bobbie, my love. You ought to know that if I wasn't quite confident of you I could never love you as I do. No doubt you have had a great many temptations out there, but I expect you always remember me as I always do you in such cases. I have met no end of real good chaps since you went away, but there are none like my boy.

I feel fed up tonight, when I think of 12 months ago. More still when I go back to times before war but there, it is no use getting down, that won't win the war and we will be able to make up for it afterwards. I am afraid this nonsense will give you the hump so now I will switch off.

Now, what do you think I had for a present today? It is a dear little dog.* A biscuit coloured Pom. It is a real beauty and I am sure you will like it. The only thing that disappoints me is the cat. I am afraid she will never make friends, but I do hope she will because I wouldn't like to part with her for the dog, as she is such a dear old puss.

I am pleased to say that Ern will be all right again after a few months. He happens to have the cleverest doctor in England for these cases and he is very

---
* See photograph, page 230.

interested in his case. He said Ern is doing splendidly, all his wounds have healed.

Charlie Godfrey and that Mr Tring were in tonight, enquiring for you, and they wish to be remembered etc.

I am still waiting for you to come. I shan't be surprised to see you any day. I have sent all your books off at last and I am very sorry I kept you waiting especially for E.W's as I know you wanted it so badly.* You will find you are quite right about it's being another 5 n's. It is. (shocking).

Our Kath read it, and she calmly told me she couldn't see anything in that book – she had read worse ones than that – but I will take care not to let anyone know that you want any more of them.

Well this is the 29th. I wonder if you remember what happened five years ago today? I am nearly asleep so I had better stop. With the best wishes from us all,

    I remain ever your loving and devoted sweetheart, Mabs.

From Mother
The Bedford, Newport.   Thursday, May 31, 1917
My Dear Bob,
I sent off your shaving brush this morning. They said at the shop that it was a good one and Mr Attrill says it is. Do you want shaving soap?

Gordon is over at the base. Have sent his address; am glad you keep up with C. Dyer. When I saw his mother she tells me Chas had a letter from Bob and he is all right, so that makes another one for us to know about you. I think I told you Charlie Harvie is in the ship 'Bristol' and was in the last battle. They haven't heard lately from him or Harry.

I do hope you will soon have your holiday for we are all anxious to see you,
                    from your loving mother, E. Brimson.

From Doris
31, Melbourne St, Newport.   Saturday, June 2 and Thursday, 14, 1917
Dear Bob,
I am writing this at the office as usual. Mr Butten has been and went and gone to Southampton and jolly good job too. He wasn't half in a temper yesterday – threw all our letters all over the place, yelled at everybody who went near him. He started telling me off and just because I smiled he says, "Oh! This is no laughing matter." So next time I am going to start howling, see if I don't. Perhaps he will like that better.

I had a fine time Whit Monday. Went down the river all the afternoon with —— (don't know him, do you?) It started to thunder about four o'clock so we had to turn back. Shame, wasn't in it? Never mind, we made up for it in the evening. Pan Down is a nice place, isn't it? Gordon likes Ventnor best. Don't blame him, do you?

---

* This is almost certainly a reference to Edgar Wallace, at one time the most widely read author in the world and a prolific writer of mysteries and thrillers offering readers, in his own words, "crime and blood and three murders to the chapter." Mabs is gently chiding Bob for his liking of what were known as 'pot boilers.' Wallace also wrote 'King Kong.'

Must tell you of the new additions to our family now. Item 1, six small rabbits (all hungry, worst luck). Item 2, one silver grey rabbit (hungrier). Item 3, one Belgian hare, ditto, (hungriest monster that I ever came across). You bet this is Ron's doings again. (Ain't somebody swearing next to me. It's old Jimmy Thomas, commonly known as "James dear," in our office)

But he is 'no go' because he is – well, to tell you the truth, I believe he is 53, or anything between that and a hundred. So you can understand.

Isn't the telephone bell ringing? Well let it ring on – so long as I can't hear what the man at the other end is saying. Don't expect it is very complimentary, do you?

14th June – Look at the date. I started this on the second and I have just come across it half finished so I thought I would finish it and let you have my work of art. Swish!

Now I will tell you about the discovery I have made. It's this : – You are my godfather. Hope you are doing your duty by me and seeing that I behave myself and all that. But I don't need much looking after. I am a good sort of 'critter'.

I am going to have one (not six as last year) week's holiday this year and I am going to visit Londing Town. I expect I am what they call a country bumpkin or pumpkin or something.

Tell you all about it when I come back – that is if I don't get Zepped, and if I don't get submarined on the way over, and if I don't get smashed up in the railway going up, and if I don't get knocked down up there, and if I don't stop there when I get there. So with love from all, I remain, yours to a cinder. Your giddy god-granddaughter. PS is there such a word as this?

Cinders. Talking about cinders reminds me of a nice little rhyme I learned at Sunday School It's a hymn I think : Ashes to ashes, dust to dust, If God doesn't take you the —— must, and so on.

     I don't know what the Kaiser will do – he won't go anywhere.

From Mabs

North End, Portsmouth.   Sunday, June 3, 1917

My Dearest Sweetheart,

I was hoping the war would finish all at once but sometimes I think it never will end; but there, it can't go very much longer. Have your books arrived alright? I hope they have. I went to see 'The Bohemian Girl'* last night with Morry, Alice and May. I like operas. I wish you had been there too; it would have been a lot better.

We went over to Stokes Bay in the afternoon but our afternoon was spoilt over there by the discovery of a body in the sea. It was some poor seaman who had evidently been in the water for at least two months.

Morry had to help drag it up out of the reach of the waves. I didn't envy him his job. There was only a soldier and him who would do anything to it. Have you heard anything about leave yet? I am still expecting you. I haven't had any more news of Ern so I can't tell you anything different.

     With fondest love and heaps of kisses, I remain, ever your loving, Mabs.

---

* An opera ballad; a story of love between the classes. Written in 1843, it remained in production until 1932.

1917

War Diary : "Ablainzeville - Two sections water supply Logeast Wood. 1 section training."

From Bob

Tuesday, June 5, 1917

My Dear Mother and Father,

This is the month of the three birthdays, so I am writing this to wish you two and Kath very many happy returns of the days, although there will probably be another letter before the 14th, all being well. The shaving brush arrived this afternoon quite safely for which I thank you very much. I have also had the County Press. I expect the garden is looking A1 now. I wish I was home for a leave as this is the best part of the year, I think. We are having glorious weather out here. I hope you are all keeping all right at home and taking things comfortable. There will be an end to all this some day, I expect, and then we shall settle down once more. Well, I've got nothing interesting to tell you this time so will write again later on. Love and kisses to all at home.

Ever your loving son, Bob.

From Mabs

The Bedford, Newport.   Sunday, June 10, 1917

My Dearest Boy,

I received your Field Postcard this morning. Glad to hear everything is all well. It makes one a bit anxious now with all these fierce attacks and 'pushes' going on. Reports are still good but it does seem it's a little bit won for such heavy lists of casualties. As you say though, there will be an end to it somewhen but I wish it would hurry up. The worst of it is that now those —— no they can't win, they are out to do all the worst things they can. (The blank supplies all the evil things I can think of). One lad I know was telling me how a few weeks ago he was on a decoy ship and a submarine came along demanding their provisions. Of course, they gave them provisions all right, in the shape of a shot that sunk them, but while they were doing that another beastly submarine came up and torpedoed them. He happened to be one of the lucky survivors. He was picked up by one of our ships, but the sub had bolted. It is a pity they couldn't catch her too, now I suppose she will go off and tell tales to the bastards.

The little dog is alright; she hangs on to me like a limpet. She is afraid to let me out of her sight for a minute and she makes a proper guardian, for she won't allow any stranger near me until I tell her it's alright. You have got a rival now, she is dreadfully jealous and won't allow me to talk to the bird, she gets that mad if I do. One good thing, no one dare interfere with me when she is about. How much longer before you get leave? Lots have been coming from different parts lately. The last one is that Harry Seal that you met out there. He told me how he came across you, but he says he hasn't had another chance because they are in another part of France now. He is still here.

Ern is getting on all right again. He is allowed out any afternoon that he feels fit enough to go and he is in another hospital in Stretford, Manchester.

It is just the part of the day that we used to enjoy at Ventnor. Don't I wish we were there now, but there is no use wishing these days. We must be patient and wait for the end – if there ever is an end.

Perhaps this summer will see the worst of it through and then it won't be long. I hope there won't be another winter for you under the same conditions as the last one.

I saw Charlie Stent and Ernie Milhuish last night. They both wish to be remembered to you. Ernie is in the Army now. It was the first time I had seen him in khaki. Well, I suppose I must close again my love, with fondest love and heaps of kisses to my brave soldier boy.

I remain ever your loving sweetheart, Mabs.

From Kath
49, Carisbrooke Rd, Newport, IW.   Sunday, June 10, 1917
Dear Bob,
Your letter came exactly on Dad's birthday and the card on Mother's. It seemed just right.

Gordon surprised us very much. He has changed from the Hants to the Royal Inniskillings Fusiliers. He says he has been turned Irish and that it's a pretty good Regiment. He has joined his battalion which is resting at present, and in billets. He says he wrote to you before he came up and expects any letters that were addressed to the Hants will follow him up. Mind you write to him, Bob. He will look for it. He wants me to write sometimes to let him know how we are getting on at home. They seem to have been having some terrible times in London lately, don't they? Chris is getting quite nervous.

Jim is moved up to the orderly room at the Wellington Barracks near Buckingham Palace, Arch tells us.

Harry Harvie came home last week for three days leave before he goes to France. He looks better than he did when he came the last time. I do wish you had one of those hats; you would look fine.

I suppose I'm getting short of news now but I must tell you we, that is Mabel, Doris and I, went on one of your favourite walks last night over St George's Down. We took the spyglass. We did wish you were there too. Only then, two of us wouldn't have been wanted. We got back about 10 o'clock. I really must finish now. For goodness sake make haste and get your holiday, only you mustn't go back again.

Love from Kath.

From Mabs
The Bedford, Newport   Monday, June 11, 1917
My Own Dear Boy,
Many thanks for that nice letter which arrived this morning. It took such a mighty load off my mind. I was afraid you were mixed up in this new 'push' but I was glad to find you are not, after all.

Bobbie, my love, I expect you can just guess how much I miss you now and unfortunately, the longer you are away the worse it gets, although no doubt you will be pleased to hear that it is so. Sometimes I wonder if the old happy days were only a dream after all. It is nice when I dream of you though, especially a very vivid dream for it hangs around for days and makes me feel that you have really been home although it is a rotten disappointment when the waking up time comes.

Here I am again scribbling all sorts of nonsense – when shall I mend my ways? Not till war is over I suppose. Well, I don't think I have altered in 12 months, at least not very much, only to grow 12 months older (and thinner p'raps). No, I don't believe I am thinner though, as I don't think my weight has altered. Some old owl told me tonight (now keep your hair on) that I get prettier every week (shh) but I wasn't to tell anyone. I nearly told him that I was sorry I couldn't say the same of him.

Oh! By the way, why that reference to the 'nice boys'? My word, if you were here or I was there, (it doesn't matter which) I would bite your neck, see. Wretch, what meanest thou? Didn't I tell you to beware certain damselles who you mentioned in your letter? I am surprised.

It was rather nice of that Lieutenant to hunt you up. I should think he must be a very nice chap or he wouldn't have troubled. I will let you know if I hear anything of him, but at present all I know is the little bit I read in the County Press a week last Saturday. I expect you saw that, too.

I'm sorry about the Picture Posts but as long as you got them it's all right. I might have been 'loony' enough to put 75th on them instead of 95th, else I had better take lessons on how to write legibly. They showed that picture in Cowes about Christmas time, but I suppose Newport is too religious for it. Rather hard on Gordon to have to do Ern's share of the business. Poor kid. I think it was too bad to send him out so soon, although at present he is only at the base. Quite far enough for a start. It is to be hoped they keep him there. Uncle Will is still at the base; I believe he is in Rouen. Gordon makes a splendid little soldier and provided he pulls through all right, soldiering won't do him any harm. He looked better than ever he did before. Morry was quite struck with him and told me he makes a better man now then his father ever will. Roy does get abused one way and another but there, it serves him right. I don't pity him.

Well, this won't do or this will grow into a proper dispatch, as Ern always calls my letters. He can only answer my letters in bits because he never has patience to read right through them straight away.

Good night, my loved one, and be a good boy and take care of yourself to come home safely to your everloving and devoted sweetheart, Mabs.

The new potatoes were put in the parcel because Mother was determined to have them put in, so if you can manage to cook such things please let us know and you shall have enough to eat next time. We posted a parcel this morning. I hope you get it alright.

From Gordon
   Private G.R.Brimson, 35303, 14th Hants Regt., 3rd I.B.L, Church Army Recreation Hut. B.E.F. France   Saturday, June 16, 1917
Dear Bob,
I expect you have heard from home that I have arrived here at last. I have had a good few letters from home this week but until then I had heard from no-one. As you will see by my address I am still at the base, but as I have now finished

my training I expect to be moving farther up very shortly. I may go into any of our battalions so I expect to look across a pal of mine, Ike Cave from Carisbrooke, who has been promoted since he has been out here.

The pack and rifle makes one sweat this weather, does it not? My leave home was very enjoyable and everyone was quite alright. Of course, it was not half long enough to have a good look round but I saw most of the home folk I knew. I went out along the railway and saw all the staff, also a girlfriend of mine (a pal of Dolly's who I hear is home again). The railway is still pegging along in the same old way. Passed quite close to Daddy's place on the way out. I am sure he would not like this work.

My training in Blighty was very short. Still, I got two week-ends home. How is Charlie Dyer? Well, I must now close. I have a few more letters to write home.

From your loving nephew Gordon.

From Mabs

The Bedford, Newport   Tuesday, June 19, 1917

My Own Dear Boy,

How do you like the summer? It is so hot but we mustn't growl I suppose, for it is certainly glorious weather, although we want some rain. I expect you have heard by now of the dreadful storm in London and the Thames valley. Poor London people what an awful life it must be what with air raids etc. They must be worried to death. Oh, those horrible Huns. I hope you 'straff' them well when you get the chance. Fancy, 153 poor little innocent babies killed and injured by the vile beasts.* Each thing they do seems to be the worst possible thing that can be done, and yet they can still find something worse. It must make any decent feeling Hun hate his country. I know I should, if Englishmen did such things as they are continually doing. Away with Germans and to — with the Kaiser. No, I think the best thing for the Kaiser is to be crippled in an air raid and then imprisoned in a real prison cell for the rest of his life and he ought to live for ever to enjoy his thoughts.

Has your parcel arrived yet? I hope it has. I haven't been able to get any more books yet but I am living in hopes. Naughty boys – I am surprised at you all. The little dog gets on alright, but the question now is whether I belong to the dog or the dog belongs to me. It is quite amusing in the evening when I am serving in the different parts; she trots to and fro all the time after me. It is a very sensible little thing and seems to understand every word we say to it, but I don't admire her name which is Tina or Tiny; she comes to both but we thought about changing it to Tony. I wish you were here (not to see the dog) but there, it is no use wishing – that wish must be nearly worn out. I have wished it every day that you have been away. I was going out to initiate Doris into the mystery of keeping her balance on a bicycle but I think I shall have to put it off till tomorrow. She is crazy to ride; she nearly went mad when I told her I would teach her how to do it. It is your mother's birthday tomorrow. How the time

---

* On June 13, 1917, twenty German bombers attacked London. 162 people were killed, including schoolchildren. Zeppelin airships, described in propaganda as 'baby killers', made about 51 bombing raids on England during the war, dropping over 5,000 bombs and killing over 500 in total. By 1917 aeroplanes had replaced Zeppelins and carried out 27 raids, killing over 800.

does fly. Why, we shall have summer gone before we can look round. The garden is beautiful now and you should see the roses. They are a picture. Well this won't do. I suppose I shall have to pack up once more. With fondest love and best wishes,

I remain ever your loving sweetheart, Mabs.

From Chris
28, Barnard Rd. Clapham Jnc., London S.W.11.   Thursday, June 21, 1917
Dear Mother and Kath,
I must wish you both happy returns. The book is for Kath and the enclosed for you, Mother, to buy something you want. Now mind you do. Wish it could have been more. We have been nearly worried to death with air raids; last Wednesday we could see and hear explosions. It was just before twelve in the morning; I rushed to the school to get Bab, left Beeb with Mrs Newnham. Next day Archie was called out, and the next three times. Can you wonder we are worried? This week has been rather calm (touch wood). Exciting times now. Love and good wishes.

Best love to all, Chris.

From Mabs
The Bedford, Newport.   Monday, June 25, 1917
My Dearest Bobbie,
So you are up to the line again or rather, I suppose you are there again now. Hard luck isn't it? But there, it must be done. It is better than shirking after all. It fairly makes my blood boil when I think of Conscientious Objectors (grrrrr). I wish they would let me do as I like with them – although there is a worse type of creature than those and they are the ones who are dropping into the munitions jobs left vacant by one who has joined up. They earn (?) all the money and then have the impudence to strike for more. Of course, we don't class them all alike, but there are some of that sort and they will eventually do as much harm to England as ever the Germans will. Hang them! Let's have something pleasant – if there is anything pleasant now.
Ern is still getting on all right; he wrote a day or two ago. He wished to be remembered and hoped you were still in the pink. Morry was home from Saturday until Sunday morning. He is supposed to be going to join the 'Furious' today. She is another new man o' war, the biggest and fastest in the world. I hope she will smash some Germans when she gets hold of them. Why wasn't I a boy? I would be a sailor then and have a chance of paying out. I do want to be a sailor. We have been travelling over some of our old haunts lately – over St George's Down. I went up to look at the place where the tall foxgloves grow. I always do when I go that way. If only you had been there. I guess it would have taken much longer to admire the foxgloves. On Sunday evening we went on that walk along Alvington and through those fields and out on to the road at Betty Aunt, whatever its name is. I believe it should be 'Ant'. It wasn't like old times though, because you were not there, Bobby my love.

If I were the only girl in the world And you were the only boy etc.
Well it would be all right but it is a shame to set you longing again to be here.
By the way, I have got a VC book for you, but I am afraid you will be
disappointed in it. I expect you will like it, only it shows VC in a new light, quite
goody-goody.
And now, while I think of it, if I was there I would bite you, see. How dare you,
wretch, miscreant, and everything else I can think of. How dare you, I say, write
such things about fascinating young men! Young man – beware of jealousy. I
don't possess such a feeling for you, or at least with regard to you, and I don't
expect you to, either. I don't believe you love me a bit or you wouldn't say such
things; you would trust me a little better than that. I hope he stays here now. It
will just serve you right and give you a bad time for a week, if you go on being
jealous. I am surprised at you if that is the sort of insults you mean to give me
for behaving myself and never so much as looking at another man. I have had
three letters from him now. He does write regularly. That's more than some
people I know do! You can read them all when you come home, or I will send
them out if you like. They have all been censored.
Grandpa hasn't been very well lately. His eyesight has got very bad, and he fell
down some steps that he didn't see. It shook him up a bit and he hasn't been
much since. He had a bad heart attack on Saturday but he is much better today.
He will be 87 on July 1st so I suppose we can't really expect anything else
although he can't understand why he should be like it.
Charlie Dyer hasn't come home yet. I dreamed he did one night last week. I
suppose you think that if you say you will be home before the end of the
summer you might hit nearer the mark. While we must have patience, it is
something to know that you are safe and well after all your experiences. Au
Revoir, with fondest love and best wishes,
                    from your ever loving and devoted, Mabs.

From Mother
49, Carisbrooke Rd, Newport.   Tuesday, June 26, 1917
My Dear Bob,
I have been so glad to get this parcel together for you and I do hope you will get
the things alright. I hope the onions will not spoil the leeks; I know you like
them. Father got them from the garden. I should like to send a lot more things.
Mabs gave dad some cigars on his birthday, so he said, "I shan't smoke them,
put them in Bob's parcel." The salmon I hope you will like. I will buy all I can
and get up another very soon.
I often wonder which part you are in and if you will fall in with Gordon. Then
there's Harry Harvie – you might just chance to meet him. He is a good sort. I
hope you will be home for the pears Bob; they are coming on alright. I hope
Archie has remembered your papers and written to you. You get the County
Press all right don't you? – so that you can see the list of war news and who are
lost that belongs to the Island. I expect you know some. It's all very sad; one
never thought it would last all this time. Arch will have told of their troubles of
air raids. It's making Chris nervous. They have been lucky as yet.

Now goodbye my dear boy. Hoping it won't be long before we shall see you. Ever your loving mother, Ellen Brimson.
PS. You might tell us if you was pleased with the bit of butter – if it was a treat – for I like to send anything that is.

From Gordon

Sunday, July 1, 1917

Dear Bob,

Thank you very much for your letter dated the 17th which has been forwarded on to me from the Base. My address is now as follows, Pt. GRB 41356,15th Platoon, D, Coy. 1st Enniskillen Fusiliers, BEF. I am writing this – *placename scribbled out* – and it is a little lively. Hope you will be lucky enough to get your second leave. The Island must be looking grand about now.

I had the County Press this morning from my mam. Yesterday had a letter from Daddie who writes every Sunday evening before leaving for his usual walk. He says my garden is going fine. I should think so with the work I put in last summer.

When I joined my new battalion we were back resting in billets and on one Saturday we had Divisional Sports, but I never came across my pal Cave from Carisbrooke, although his battalion was there. The French lady at our billet used to cook us eggs for 2 ½ centimes each and her cider was tres bon. She treated me one day to the taste of cherries and strawberries. We have a good few Irish fellows in this battalion but I would have preferred going to my Regiment. I had an Island chap with me, but he is in another Company.

By the way, at the base I saw about four Newport chaps, three from I.W.Rifles and one who had just come down from the Line. Well, I will now close this letter.

From your loving nephew, Gordon.

From Mabs

The Bedford, Newport   Monday, July 2, 1917

My Own Dear Boy,

I hope you are still going on in the same old way – that is to say no worse than it has been. I know it won't be any better for some time yet. Still, I suppose there is a better time coming. You may get a leave soon. There have been several R.E's home lately, but there are so many companies of R.E.s it is a puzzle to find out much about them and where they come from. Nelly Barlow (Morry's sister-in-law) was married last week. Her boy is an R.E and he was expecting leave last January when you were and he has just got it; 12 days too; just think of it. My word, what if you get 12 days! I hope you do. Won't we make the best of it. I am still expecting you any time. I wonder each day if you will come wandering up the Mall loaded, just as you were before. I hope you won't have another dreadful time as you had then.

Morry has gone to the 'Furious'. We had a card this morning. He says he is settling down but there is one serious drawback. The beer is always sold out about an hour after it arrives. Terrible. We have had no trouble yet with ours, but many of the houses have had to close till they can get a fresh supply. In Cowes most of them close all day except for an hour in the evening from 8 to 9 pm because the supplies won't hold out.

What with sugar, potatoes and beer I wonder there are any sane shopkeepers left. I am sure that potatoes and sugar especially, will hold their heads a few inches higher than everything else. To think that they have been so much sought after. We don't trouble about sugar at all now. We never have any on the table so we shan't miss it that way, when we can't get any at all. Fancy Dad doing without sugar. S'marvellous. The dog goes on all right; it is just like my shadow, I can't move without the little villain.

Ern is still going on all right, but he doesn't say anything about coming home yet, but he is well looked after there, so he is better off. Wallace is still alive and that is all I know of him. He is coming here for his summer holiday soon but I don't know how long it will be. I wish you could get home then, to see him; I don't believe you would know him. I am trying to pare a corn off my toe as I am writing this. Fancy me with a corn. It is only a little one but I don't want it to grow any bigger.

I am going out with Doris and the bicycle after. She will soon be able to ride now, although I have only been out with her twice. Well, my love, I must close now, but I will write again in a day or two. Bon soir. (soyoz gentil). I believe I have spelt that bit wrong.

Heaps of love and kisses from your ever loving Mabs.

War Diary : "Mory – Sundry back area work, eg., Div. Bathhouse. 'What-Nots' Theatre. Div HQ Camp. Gas school."

From Bob

Monday, July 2, 1917

Dear Mother and Dad,

I received the parcel this afternoon. It was tres bon; everything was quite all right except the s- in the little tin which unfortunately spilled itself onto the cake, but that is only a detail. The cake is very nice. I might mention also the produce from the garden. It was good of Dad to send me the cigars and tobacco. I hope he doesn't deprive himself, all the same.

Will you try and let me know what Division Gordon is in, and then I can look out for him. The idea of putting him into an Irish regiment – it's hardly right in my opinion anyway. Glad to hear that Kath is getting plenty of outings. Wish I could be there too. Heard from C. Dyer today. He is going on all right and was lucky enough to drop across the Island R.E's. Was pleased to hear of H. Harvie coming to see you. Well, must close now.

With fondest love to you all at home, ever your loving son, Bob

From Mabs

The Bedford, Newport   Monday, July 9, 1917

My Own Dear Boy,

Do you know that it is 17 days since I received a letter from you? But there, it may come tomorrow. That is what I keep on thinking, and keep on hoping that you will come tomorrow too. I suppose there will be a tomorrow when you will land in Newport again, but I do wish it could be for good. You mentioned the contents of the little tin which spilled itself in the cake. Did you mean the one with the roses? I am sorry if it was, because I put them in. What were they like when they arrived? I didn't think any water could get out. I only made the rag damp and damped the flowers a little.

We had our annual trip to Whitecroft on Saturday but times have changed even out there. I expect we missed the old faces. The patients enjoyed it just as much as ever. It is a treat to see them. They all seemed so happy that day. The wounded soldiers who were there enjoyed it. It was quite a novelty for them.

I went to Ventnor on Friday, on the bicycle, but it isn't Ventnor without Bob. I went with Mrs Reynolds and her sister. Will Reynolds is in Egypt now. Your letter has arrived at last. It came this morning, you bad lad. It's well for you, you didn't mean what you said in that letter. I'll let you off now – such remarks as those make me grow fierce (Fieeeeerce, see).

I hope the orchestra will get on alright; it must be a nice treat for you. I hope they will be able to keep it up. It will pass away a good many hours which would be very miserable. We never have any of our jolly old concerts here now. We have lost all our boys; they are nearly all in France. I do wish you could drop across some of them. That would cheer you up.

Ern hasn't arrived home yet but I suppose he is still improving as we haven't heard any different. Doris can ride the bicycle so she is happy now. She managed it quite easily, except for the jumping off part; she had a curious way of her own for that, but she does it right now.

I thought Gordon liked his new Regiment. He said that he liked it in his letters home but perhaps he told you what he wouldn't let them know. In any case, as you say, it was too bad to put him there when he would have been more at home in the Hants. One thing, if he pulls through all right, as it is to be hoped he will, he will make just such another as you, my love. It has made a tremendous difference already. It seems to be just what he wanted to set him going.

Well, I can't go on forever, it is bedtime. Goodnight and be good till you get that leave.

With best love and kisses, I remain your everlasting, Mabs.

From Charlie Dyer
46869, 87 Field Co. R.E. Battalion 12th Division, BEF.   Sunday, July 15, 1917
Dear Bob,

Just a few lines in answer to your welcome letter which I received quite safe. So glad to hear that you are still keeping fit. Sorry to hear about Harry Williams. He was wounded rather badly when he was with us. Suppose it is the old wound troubling him again. Fancy young Gordon in the Irish Battalion. I will drop him a line. I had a line from Harry Leal. He got to Blighty sick; had 10 days leave. He is at Weymouth now. He wrote and told me where he saw you. I know you were at that part but was not able to get to see you. Yes, I saw it in the County Press that poor George Birch was killed. All the boys wish to be

remembered to you. How is everyone at home please? Remember me to them. I had a line from Bern Jolliffe the other day. John says it is time we were all back again. Everyone all right out there, plenty of changes in the staff. Glad to say that I am quite well at present. Pleased to have a line from you any time.
Wishing you the best of luck, from your old pal, Charlie.

From Kath
49, Carisbrooke Rd, Newport, IW.   Tuesday, July 17, 1917
Dear Bob,
Mother is beginning to worry again. She says she is sure you are looking for a letter every day. She has just gone out. I'm up in the summerhouse writing this and Dad is doing little bits to the garden. Ma told me I must tell you that she has bottled lots of gooseberries, black and redcurrants so that you can have some pies when you come home. We do wish you would make haste and we have been wondering if you are anywhere near where the King and Queen have been – Messines, isn't it? And I am to tell you that Archie Brett is out in France. Nr. 38083 Cpr. A.J.C.Brett, 355 Siege Battery, R.G.A. BEF. France.
I suppose you have heard from Mabel that we went to the Asylum sports, Saturday before last. That is, Mother, Dad, Mabel, Doris and I. And of course, Dolly and Bert must needs come in while we were gone. He is home on leave. She has had enough of London and wants Roy to see if they will take her on down at 'White's', then she will lodge up at Elm Grove. Charlotte tells Mother that Charlie's boat touched "somewhere" where George is, so they were able to see one another. They went and had their photos taken together. The photographer is sending them on home. In Charlie's letter he says "What price the whiskers," so they are expecting to see him with a beard. Won't he look awful?
Doesn't it seem dreadful the way they keep raiding poor old London.* Arch said in his last letter that a whole army of 'planes' looked just as if they were making straight for Clapham Junction and when he got in, all the neighbours were crowded into their passage drinking brandy. What a time they must have had. Arch said it was putrid stuff too (the brandy, I mean). (There is an aeroplane going over now). I expect poor old Chris wishes she was down here.
Ever your loving Kath.

War Diary : "Mory – Tower Trench revetment and wiring - Two sections. No Infantry owing to Brigade reliefs."
From Bob
Wednesday, July 18, 1917
My Dear Kath,
Just a few lines to let you know that I am still going on all right and I hope this letter will find you in the pink. The correspondence seems to get very slack from

---

* On 7 July, London and the East End were attacked by German bombers – 57 people were killed. The raid caused great anger about the lack of warning and the lack of effective defences. From September, street lights in central London were turned off.

home now and it seems ages since I heard from Archie or Chris. I think the air raids must be knocking them sick up there. I wrote to them some time ago but have had no answer. Hope you find plenty to do at home. Shall expect to see heaps of new pictures and different things. I've done a bit myself, in the book of yours.
Well I must close now as I want to catch the post tonight, Goodbye for the present, ever your loving brother, Bob.
Love to all at home.

From Mabs
The Bedford, Newport, IW   Sunday, July 22, 1917
My Own Dear Boy,
I received your letter of the 15th this morning. So you would 'choke' me off, would you? You ought to, considering the time I usually have to wait to get so much as a scrape of a pencil out of you, but you see it wasn't my fault after all. There now – you will be getting wild but you needn't get alarmed. I know you well enough.
I am glad you are being so well looked after as regards food. It is the proper thing to see to our men first, not that we are short at all, but I mean if things did get as bad as that. However, I don't think we need worry about that for we shall always get something. Hun U-boats don't get it all their own way. All that worries me is the end of it, or rather how long it will be until the end. It can't be very much longer. The Russians will be able to keep them busy on their side again so that there will be a better chance on this front.
Ern is leaving the hospital tomorrow (Monday) so he will be home, I expect, before this reaches you. We shall have plenty of company for the next month. I will get those books for you and send them at intervals. I have one more to send you now, but that is another tame one but it will be something to read.
I went to Ventnor Thursday afternoon with Doris, so we thought we would walk along the cliffs by the hospital towards Woody Bay but after climbing the cliff at Steephill Cove we found that the path had quite gone. It doesn't seem possible that it could alter so much since we walked along there. There isn't even a piece of the cliff left to walk on by the hospital. It is a shame that our lovely walk has vanished.
I had a letter from Chris on Wednesday. A letter of three pages – just think of it! I believe it is about the second one this year. They are all well, recovering from the raid by degrees. That last one must have been terrible for them, but Archie said he didn't believe the damage was as serious as rumours led us to believe, which is a very good thing, though no doubt he has let you know all about it by this time. Marjorie seems to have been most upset by the raid. Poor little maid. Chris said she kept waking up frightened several nights after.
I can't collect my brains a bit to write today so I shall have to give in for the present. I still look for you every day. One day, I hope patience will be rewarded. Au revoir my dearest and best love and heaps of kisses.
From your loving and devoted, Mabs.
I am sorry I never mentioned G. Birch to you, for I quite intended to. He is another good lad lost.

Ervillers, France.
We have been having a decent time lately, scotching old Fritz up... I suppose you have seen in the papers he has burnt down or blown up every house in every village, and mighty big craters on every crossroads, and blown up or cut down every tree. You would think there had been a terrific earthquake that had destroyed everything." Bob to Mabs, March 26, 1917.

"Try and get hold of the Daily Mirror of 30 July. In there you will see a photo of a signboard I wrote out here, a very large one. Cut the photo out of it, it will be worth keeping; there is a Tommy kneeling down beside it." Bob to Mabs, July 31, 1917. The original caption read, "Captured villages, being unrecognisable, are now indicated by means of a signboard."

From Gordon

Monday, July 23, 1917

Dear Bob,

Thank you for your letter received some time ago. I have been away from the Battalion on a pigeon flying course and of course, I was delighted to be amongst pigeons again. But the course did not last very long and I rejoined my battalion. I cannot state by divisional number as we are not allowed. I am in the same as Ern Attrill was, by the way. I passed close to their battalion, but did not have the chance of seeing any.

I was in luck's way this week, a parcel and a registered letter, so I have been visiting some of the local shops. Aren't they bare places? I wonder how so many live in one small house.

They have been hunting some of my pals out at Newport who have just come of age. We are back resting for a short while, having had a rather warm time. One of my pals was killed; he joined the same time as I did at Gosport. We are getting together a concert tomorrow night and I got my pal to give a song. He has just gone out to give a rehearsal.

When shall you be getting home again? The time is creeping on. I had a letter from my boss who said he thought I was lost as I had not written for such a long time. Charlie Dyer is on another Coy. to you, is he not?

Well I must now close, getting near bedtime.

From your loving nephew Gordon.

(This letter contained some small dried flowers.)

From Mother

49, Carisbrooke Rd, Newport   Wednesday, July 25, 1917

My Dear Bob,

 I have just seen Mrs Dyer. She tells me Charlie says he has heard from you. I suppose you haven't heard anything about leave yet. He told them he thought it wouldn't be long before he would be home.

We are to have the 7/6 Pension proper next month, in fact everyone is who is entitled to it, without any reserve. It will be acceptable, for everything is still very dear. They talk about altering a lot in the paper but they are so long doing anything.

I have bottled a nice lot of fruit from the garden. I could do that without sugar. That luxury is not to be got, only a very small quantity sometimes – and 7d per lb instead of 2d. I am getting ready to take Kath out so I will stop. Everybody sends kind love, same from me.

Ever your loving Mother E B.

They are expecting Ern today.

From Mabs

The Bedford, Newport   Thursday, July 26, 1917

My Dearest Bobbie,

This is just to let you know that Ern is home at last. He arrived last night but I don't think he should have come home yet. He looks fairly well but his limbs are a bit useless – he hasn't much control over them. He has only eight day's leave so he won't have much time to pull up now before he joins the regiment again. He thinks that he will get his discharge – he ought to for he will never be fit for France again.

Mother has gone to Ryde today so I am in charge of the cooking. Don't I wish you were coming to dinner? I know you would enjoy it even if there was no dinner, just to be in Newport. Gordon's regiment is in the 29th Division with Ern's regiment. They are, I believe, at Poperinghe, west of Ypres. It would be fine if you could see him, poor boy. I'll bet he would be pleased to see you.

We, that is to say Kathie, Doris and I, went to see a sketch called 'Come Inside' at the Rink. Those dear boys / sailors did enjoy themselves and at the end of the show they had a mad five minutes dancing to the tune of 'Are You From Dixie'. You will read all about it in the County Press. They did it once at Freshwater; the sailors took most of the female parts themselves; there were only two real girls in the show.

Au revoir, adieu, and all the rest of it.

I remain always your loving sweetheart, Mabs.

War Diary : "Mory – Work on London to two sections and 40 Inf. deepening and revetting with U frames. Digging out bad part from just East of China Lane by night .1 Coy Inf. Wiring material trammed up to Tower Trench and carried to site of work. 1 and 1½ Coy, Inf. 2 sections."

From Bob

Tuesday, July 31, 1917

Dear Mother and Dad,

Got your letter all right. Very pleased to hear the news about the increase in pension. It will be a great help to you. An account has been received from Chatham saying that I am about £13 in debt. I can't see how that has happened as I've never overdrawn my money, and I think the allotment money seems to have been paid all right. You couldn't have drawn any more than I have allowed. They've made a mistake some where and I shall see about it. There are other chaps in the company worse than me.

I shall probably be home in a few weeks now if leave still keeps going. Fancy Archy Brett being out here and a full Corporal too; that's another one to look out for.

Try and get hold of the Daily Mirror of 30 July. In there you will see a photo of a signboard I wrote out here, a very large one. Cut the photo out of it, it will be worth keeping; there is a Tommy kneeling down beside it.* I've already told Mabs about it. So that's what they do in London, is it? Drink brandy when there's an air raid on? I shall have to see if we can't have tots of rum when the Huns start blowing our camp to bits – a very good idea. Heard from Gordon a few days ago. He's a pigeon flyer now. Most important work is done with pigeons, so he will be just the chap for it. Haven't heard from Arch or Charlie yet; goodness knows what's happened to them. It must be a couple of months since I heard. The food we get has improved a lot of late. We actually get frozen

* See photograph page 246 .

rabbits and bread puddings two or three times a week, and also boiled rice. We also have a dry canteen now, where we can buy all sorts of tinned stuff, in fact anything we need, sauce and pickles etc.

I forgot to tell you – we have three regimental pets, a goat, and a magpie that's just learning to steal, and a nice old black dog. I've made a bit of a sketch of him in the book.* Jolly fine ratter and can almost talk with his eyes. Many walks we've been on together. The goat is rather a nuisance as it will eat anything but what is good for him. I had a few pounds of red lead amongst the paint I look after and it had a good feed from it, but seemed none the worse after. It has also fed off of 'claroude de lime'** and still lived; it has an inside made of cast iron. The magpie we brought up from a youngster and clipped one wing so it can't fly, but it hops about the camp and watches the boys go out and then pops in to see what it can pinch – anything bright attracts him. But I must finish now, with love to you all at home,

ever your loving son Bob.

From Mabs
The Bedford, Newport   Sunday, August 5, 1917
My Dearest Boy,
I am glad to hear the news of the leave and let it be soon. I also hope that you will have good weather and what is better still, I hope you will come in with the lucky people who get 14 days.

I haven't time to write much more, but as I don't know when I shall get another chance I thought I must do it now.

There is a wedding coming off here tomorrow so I shall be very busy all day.

About that money affair – I hope you will fight it out. It may take some time but they can't make you pay it without proof that you owe it to them. Have you got your paybook alright? It will be quite alright if you have. One thing, those fat headed clerks are always making mistakes so perhaps that has happened in your case.

We have all been out today, Kathie and Marjorie too, for a drive. We went through Arreton to Shanklin and back through Godshill. The only thing that upset it a bit was the horse and he managed to fall at Lake, but he did it so quietly that we hardly noticed it except that we all had to turn out of the wagonette. The poor thing cut himself in two or three places but he went on quite all right again after. No one was the least bit alarmed and we have all arrived home quite safe. Well this won't do as it is now 10.45pm and I must be up again at 6 am, so I will write a respectable letter next time. With every good wish and fondest love and kisses,

I remain ever your loving sweetheart Mabs.

Morry's address, Maurice W J Attrill, Ships Cook, HMS Furious, c/o GPO London. We have found the signboard (Daily Mail).

---

* See sketch, page 259.

** A reference to chloride of lime, a chemical used to purify drinking supplies in the trenches. The process left an unpleasant taste in the water, a source of much complaint.

From Kath
49, Carisbrooke Rd, Newport   Sunday, August 12, 1917
Dear Bob,
I have just woke up to the fact that it's time you heard from me again. Your card came this morning and the nice long letter last Sunday. We don't know what to make of it about that money they are trying to make out you owe. Mother has heard of lots since who have had the same bother and they all say you mustn't let it drop – you must try all you can to have it put right. The beasts will make you pay if they can.
Mother met Mrs Dyer. She has heard from Charlie. He says he is coming home and has sent for a timetable. Shall we send you one? Wouldn't it be grand if you could come while Chris and Arch is here? I suppose you know we have got Bebe again? Jim came down for a weekend and brought her. We didn't get the telegram to say they were coming till the same day. Something went wrong with the train; the one they were to have come by was too full so they couldn't get a seat so had to get a later one. We had given them up for the night and had gone to bed. They got here about 11 o'clock. We soon came down again though. Beeb was just as lively as if it had been in the afternoon. She doesn't look as well as when she went away. Jim has something the matter with his neck and is under medical treatment. He doesn't look well at all.
You heard from Mabel, I daresay, that they have had a crowd of youngsters from Rugby. Wallie, of course, and Kitty and her brother and then Albert from France. They have heard from Gordon. He tells them he is moving into the trenches, doesn't say much.
Beeb has put a letter in for you with her love. She was delighted to hear about your pets. I wish you could bring that dear old dog home with you; he will miss you when you come away.
Well I can't think of any more to say. We are taking in the Daily Mail so we found the picture you spoke about but it was only a small one, just the signboard alone. It does look fine. Mrs Williams is getting the Mirror; we think it will be bigger and better. We are very proud of it. I have sort of been wondering if the Tommy kneeling down is you; that's why we want to see the larger picture. I hope it is. I must finish now with heaps of love and kisses from us all.
                    Every your loving Kath.

From Mabs
The Bedford, Newport.   Monday, August 13, 1917
My Own Dear Boy,
Another week gone. It is marvellous how the time slips along. One thing – thank heaven each week is a bit nearer the end of this wretched war. The soldiers keep on saying that the worst part will be through before Christmas, if it isn't finished. If only it is, it will be grand.
How are the pets getting on? I hope the goat hasn't died of indigestion yet but I don't believe there is any limit to a goat's digestive powers. We went to Southampton yesterday to see the crowd off. They all went off to London together. Charlie Dyer expects to be home this month; I wonder if you will have

the luck to meet here.
Archie has been passed for home service; I hope they will leave it at that and not
put him on active service. I think they had better put him in Jim's place and give
Jim a change. Ern is at Sutton Coldfield (Birmingham) now. He says it is a very
nice place and beautiful countryside. They are carrying on the massage for his
back. News is very scarce again and I am not good at writing letters out of
nothing so I suppose I must give in. With fondest love and kisses,
                    I remain ever your loving sweetheart, Mabs.

From Mabs
                                                    Wednesday, August 15, 1917
Dear B.
Do you recognise this place?* It is the first time I knew the name. Thanks for the
F.P.C's. Three arrived this morning: What's the joke? Love from Mab.

From Mabs
The Bedford, Newport.   Saturday, August 18, 1917
My Own Dear Boy,
This is Saturday night and bedtime but I thought I would start a letter even if I
didn't get it finished; I am expecting yours in the morning.
My cousin Fred arrived from France this morning. He is in the Army Veterinary
Corps but he is a wheelwright. I think he came from the Arras district; that's
where Albert is too. I hope you don't arrive early in the morning with the mails
or I shall be fast asleep and shan't be there to see you. If you are where I think
you are, they seem to have been busy just lately; again, I hope it won't make any
difference to your leave. I suppose St. Quentin will soon be won now. It is
usually the last straw when they start setting fire to things. It has been a tough
fight for it but I expect it will only be a heap of ruins when it is captured. It is
awful the way everything is being smashed up out there. We have got a lot to
be thankful for. I believe that there are plenty of people in England who don't
realise that we are at war, or at least they don't know the serious side of it.
Your cousin has been to your home for the weekend. She is a very nice girl I
should think, but I only saw her for a few minutes.
I do hope they will let you come soon or all the summer will be gone but I don't
suppose you will care a hang about the weather once you get here. It is better,
to have nice fine weather at home for I guess you get enough rain. Toffee said
it was raining like the 'man below' when he wrote.** I believe our men will
always think of France at the sight of rain and mud.
Ernest is still going on all right and enjoying himself. Morry, I believe, just puts
up with it because there is nothing else for it. I'll bet he would like to get home
with you. Well, this won't do; it is time to stop again.
        Adieu mon ami or mon amant (it's both the same). Heaps of love and kisses
            from your ever loving and devoted sweetheart, Mabs.

---

*This was written on a picture postcard of 'Dropping Rock Cottage,' St. Georges Down, Newport,
a remote cottage long since disappeared.
** Toffee, Albert Everton, went on to receive an honourable discharge due to sickness and was
awarded the Silver War Badge, January 24, 1918. He died at Hampstead in 1921.

1917

From Charlie Dyer

46869, 87 Field Co. R.E. Battalion 12th Division, BEF. Sunday, August 19, 1917

Dear Bob,

Just a few lines hoping that you are still fit and well. Well, I am glad to say that I am expecting to go on my leave this week. No such luck as seeing you home as well, I suppose? Never mind, you will have yours soon now, I should think. It is 17 months since I went. How the time goes by. Our three years is nearly up. I suppose we shall then start on the Duration. All the boys wish to be remembered to you, W Chappell and Len Thornton – not many of the old boys with us now. Glad to say that I am quite well. Will call in home when I go.

Best of luck from your old pal, Charlie .

Write me a line if possible please.

The next letter is the only one from Bob's father in the entire collection.

From Father

49, Carisbrooke Rd, Newport.   Friday, August 24, 1917

Dear Bob,

We have just received your welcome letter this morning, 21st of August. We are sending a one pound note. Hope it will arrive in time. We are all well. I must finish to get the post. hoping to see you soon and in good health.

Your affectionate Father, C. S. Brimson.

From Mabs

The Bedford, Newport.   Sunday, August 26, 1917

My Dearest Bobbie,

I hear you will soon be home – about time too. Dyer was to arrive today but I don't know whether he has yet. Morry has great hopes of getting home when you do. I hope he does. It will be fine. It is three weeks today since I had a letter from you, young man. I shall get some more young men to write me letters if you don't buck up. See, you are a bad lad.

Doris and I went off to Ryde on Thursday to see a play, 'Ghosts'. It was a horrible thing although it was good and played splendidly. I will tell you about it when you come home. There will be a lot to talk about when that time comes. I hope it won't be long now.

I can't collect my brains to write. I've nothing to write about and Nelly is kicking up a row on the piano which won't allow me to think a bit. Another thing – if you don't write letters more than once a month I can't answer the same one five or six times.

The children were pleased with their cards, especially with what you had written on them because I had told them you would come out with me all the time and of course, they thought I really meant it, so Bab said that shows you won't. You will have quite a lot of calls to pay when you come home so you will keep busy. I can guess what you are saying now, but you wait. Well, adieu au revoir, mon amant.

I remain, ever your loving sweetheart, Mabs.

In September Bob had two weeks home leave, his first in fourteen months.

War Diary : "Scottish Wood – All four sections working on trench board track from Xroads at J.7.d 90.15 to Polygonne VXXX (J.10.a.7.8). Very heavy shelling. Sappers Frost, Ramsey, Armitage, Jones, Nash and Blayney wounded."

From Bob

Thursday, September 30, 1917

My Dear Mother,

Just a few lines to let you know that I am going on all right and about settled down to it again. We are having lovely weather just now and as you can see by the papers, making the most of it. I have written to Mabs and she knows where I am, near enough. I was certain that was where we should land at the finish and it turned out right. It's worse than the Somme ever was, but we don't mind as long as it will get the job finished.

I was jolly glad of the food you gave me to bring back, in fact I don't know what I should have done without it as I was delayed for a while. I found out that you can never take too much in a case like that. I also want to thank you for your kindness to me while I was at home. I had a jolly good time and it is something to look back on, only it passed all too soon. I haven't heard from Gordon lately and I left his address at home, so please will you forward it on, and tell Kath not to forget the photos I left with her. Dad can send me a few tomatoes if he thinks he can manage it but don't bother if you find it inconvenient. They would need to be sent in a strong box. I got last week's County Press all right. Tell Mabs she needn't bother writing me letters in ink if it is a bother to her, anything will do as long as I get them; I didn't think she would have taken it seriously. I am writing this letter but it is a job to think as the guns are kicking up a terrible row since yesterday evening, without stopping. How Fritz can put up with the continual rain of shells on him, I can't understand. Well Mother, I must finish now.

Ever your loving son, Bob.

War Diary : "Scottish Wood H35.d.28. – 1 Section maintaining 20" Inf Bde track. Sandbags and picks taken to forward dump by pack mules. 2nd Cpl Hall and Sapper Calder killed and Cpl Darville wounded (hospital)."

From Bob

Thursday, October 25, 1917

Dear Kath,

Jolly pleased to get your letter. It seems a long time to me, as well, since I was home and I might mention, we have had some exciting times since I've been back. Given you had a fine time at the birthday tea with them, many happy returns from me – better late than never. Can't send any postcards as there are no shops where we are.

 I'm trying to get this written before it gets dark as we have Fritz over here nearly every night, dropping his bombs (don't think it's only in Blighty that he drops them). It's a new experience for us, all the same. Of all the different Fronts we've been on, we've never been pestered with those things before. We much

Unappetising

Moments when the Savoy, the Alhambra, and the Piccadilly Grill seem very
far away (the offensive starts in half an hour)

Bruce Bairnsfather cartoon published in *The Bystander* magazine.

rather prefer the shells and bullets. You can pretty well guess where they are coming. Had to stop this letter again but tonight it is raining and very cloudy, so I think I shall be able to finish it.

I got the parcel today. Thank you all very much for it. You made a decent job of the photo case and I'm very pleased with it, xxxxx. Those are kisses from me. The tomatoes were as fresh as if they had only just been picked and the cake was fine, also the radishes – I had a jolly good tea. Thank Dad very much for the tobacco – my old favourite – also little Bee for sending me the nuts. Also, thanks for the cigarettes and the lovely fruit. I noticed you didn't put the picture of Mabs that you painted for me in the case. Are you touching it up again? Did I tell you we were only about 10 miles from Gordon? There's no chance of getting to see him until we are out of the line and its 10 to 1 chance, then.

Well, I must chuck it now, will write again soon. Best love to Mother Dad and Bee, not forgetting yourself,

ever your loving brother, Bob.

War Diary : "Racquinghem – Drill by sections and company. Inter-section football match. xx v. No.4."

From Bob

Tuesday, November 6, 1917

My Dearest Sweetheart,

We moved back from the line last Tuesday to a small village close to the Belgian frontier, stopped a few days there and then went on trek to another village well behind the lines in France. We are likely to be out some while to reinforce. We are also being inoculated again and it's not 'bon' as we get the all dose at once, not two editions as we did in Blighty. I've got my turn to come. The King of the Belgians inspected our Division yesterday; probably you will see the photographs in one of the papers.

Had a letter from Chris and she told me about you staying with her for a bit; hope you had a good time; you just missed the air raid by all accounts. I suppose you are at home now and settled down once more. I shall look forward to a long letter from you, kiddie. I was glad to hear about Ern getting along again all right. I hope he will never have to come out here again. Had the 'Weekly Telegraph' and was very pleased to get them too, as I had run a bit short of reading material.

Still patiently waiting for the photo of you and Tiny, or has the old lady claimed her again? I expect she was sorry she gave her to you after all; rather a cheek to want it back though. I've run up against the 14th Hants just lately, but could see no one I knew. I was hoping it was the 2nd when I first saw them.

Well, my pet, I must close now, with best love and kisses.

Ever your loving sweetheart, Bob.

1917

War Diary : "Bergeneuse – Making up equipment etc of company."
From Bob

Friday, November 16, 1917

My Dear Kath,

At last I've got the chance of answering your letter. I wrote one to Mabs on the 6th but we have not been allowed to send any until today as we have been on the move again, so I hope you will get this all right. Yesterday we were marching through an out-of-the-way village, where there were a lot of Australians billeted, and who should I see standing outside the doorway but Harry Harvie. I managed to have a few minutes talk with him and then we went on again for about another 3 kilometres to another village where we are putting up for a day or two. Of course, as soon as I had my tea I set off back to find Harry again. I found him out and so we spent the evening together talking over old times and I'm going to see him again tonight, all being well. The worst of it is I hadn't a ha'penny on me. I don't think I've been so bad off for money since I've been out here, and there is nothing so bad as being on the march with nothing in your pocket – and goodness knows when we shall get paid again.

I was jolly pleased to meet old Har and so he was me. He has been up on the same front as we have just come from and been through some stiff fighting too. I had a letter from Mabs today. I wonder what's up with her. I hope she isn't getting tired of writing. I've done my best to keep up correspondence and of course, if they won't let us send them it isn't our fault. Never mind, better one now and again then none at all.

Well, Kath, I must finish now. With heaps of love and kisses for you, also Mother and Dad.

Ever your loving brother, Bob.

Will write again soon, I forgot to tell you that all the fellows took Har to be my brother – a compliment to one of us!

Italy had begun the war as an ally of Austria and Germany but in 1915 transferred their allegiance to Britain, France and Russia. In late 1917 Italy was overwhelmed by invading Austrian and German forces and over 300,000 Italian soldiers were lost. The Italian government requested help and British and French troops were moved from the Western Front to halt the advance. In just a matter of days Bob found himself transported from the wintry trenches of the French battlefields to the blue skies and sunshine of Northern Italy, "a splendid place," as he tells Mother.

War Diary : "Enroute to Italy – Moved to Noventa Vicentina. (About 18 miles)."
From Bob

Sunday, November 25, 1917

My Dear Mother,

This is a short letter I'm putting in with Mab's to tell you that I'm quite all right but have gone a little further from Blighty. We are now in Italy. We were four days and four nights travelling here through some of the most famous French and Italian resorts. It was a lovely ride and lovely weather too. We are now on the march. We crossed the frontier through the Alps at night. I happened to be on guard so I was awake all night and I saw the sunrise – the most glorious sight I've ever seen – and the most beautiful colours. The Alps were covered with snow and it was awfully cold but we didn't mind that. We were taken up the mountains with electric cars, one on each end of the train; very powerful they were, too. You could look out of the window far down in the valleys and look up at the snow-capped peaks far above your head. This is a splendid place, far better than France or Flanders.

Must close now as I want to catch the post.

ever your loving son, Bob.

Could you please send some money as I don't know when we shall get any.

War Diary : "Enroute to Italy."

From Bob

Sunday, November 25, 1917

My Dearest Sweetheart,

This is just a short note to tell you that we have left the Western Front and are now in Italy. In future you must address the letters 'BEF Italy,' but don't put the number of Division as you used to. This is the most beautiful country I've ever seen and such lovely buildings. Every house has its vines and of course, they are all over. We came through Paris and all through the Champagne and the Chamoise, and through the Alps (Sunplan tunnel). Will describe it more next time. It's like being transferred back to summer again, lovely blue skies and quite hot in the daytime.

Hope you are all quite well at home, please write soon as you can.

ever your loving sweetheart, Bob.

The first part of the War Diary of the 95th Field Company ends with the entry for 30 November 1917. Bob's subsequent locations are referenced from known movements of the 7th Division.

From Bob, St. Martino Dilupari, Italy.

Wednesday, December 12, 1917

My Dear Kath,

It has seemed months since we had any mail from home; of course, it takes a few days longer now. I've never felt better in my life. We are close to the mountains and the air seems to suit me somehow. I don't believe I've ever possessed such an appetite. We get very severe frosts during the night and the early hours of the morning but when the sun gets up it is quite warm. The people seem to be very decent in this country but I suppose that is only because we are rather a novelty to them.

Don't bother to send that muffler out as I've already got one. I got Mab's parcel yesterday and it arrived in splendid condition, considering the long journey.

Well, I must close now, with best love to you, Mother and Dad.

Ever your loving brother, Bob.

When sending parcels please do not put Italy on the address but simply 'BEF.' I do not think that this also applies to the letters. Could you send me an English-Italian dictionary?

From Bob, St. Martino Dilupari, Italy.

Wednesday, December 12, 1917

My Dear Mother,

I received the parcel of 1st December yesterday and everything was in excellent condition considering the time it has been on the road. Thank you very much for your kindness. This is really a letter to you all as this is the last day for us sending Xmas letters, so I wish you all a joyful Christmas and I hope you will all be as happy as you can under the circumstances. We must look forward to better ones in the future. I'm sorry I'm not in the position to send you anything. We are all rather badly off in that way. I wrote to Mabs and I thought I should have time to send her another in time for Xmas but find I shall not be able to, so please give her and her people the compliments of the season for me.

We had a fall of snow during the night and the mountains look lovely this morning with the sun shining on them.

I'm glad to hear that Gordon has got home all right, also that he is so near home, poor old chap. He had a narrow squeak and I'm convinced that Kath was the means of saving his life, as we have known cases like that before. Gordon is safe enough now for the rest of the winter in Blighty. Had a letter from Arch yesterday, two County Press and two Sunday Pictorial, and also a parcel of books from Aunt E. The mails are coming all at once now. I hope you are getting mine all right. I told you in one of the previous letters that I got the postal order all right and it was very welcome. The tobacco and cigarettes came just right as I'd run right out of both. Hope Dad is keeping fit. Should be glad of a map of this country if possible to get one. Must close now, again wishing you all a good time,

ever your loving son, Bob.

From Geo. C. Parcell

49312 RE Italy   Sunday, December 30, 1917

To Spr Bob Brimson,

I expect you will be surprised to receive this letter from me but my folks at home keep worrying me to write to you and make enquiries as far as possible as regards the death of Syd King who as you know was killed on October 1. By what I am given to understand he had mentioned that you were the only one he knew in the Company, and when I was at home on leave his folks were asking if I knew who you were and asked me to write to you. Of course, his people were very much upset about it and what made matters worse was that he had only been out a very short time. As I daresay you know, I saw him once or twice before he went into the line and he was killed just about a week after. I would be very pleased if you would kindly drop me a few lines and inform me, as far as possible under the conditions, of the details of his death and how it came about.

My address is Spr. G.C.Parcell, 4th Pontoon Park, RE (Motor Transport), BEF Italy.

I still get a letter now and again from Bert Cubitt and he is still as well as ever. I saw the 87th once, that was just as they were going into the Somme and as you may guess there were not many left. Bob Briggs has been wounded three times and Sealy has gone home on munitions and had married the girl used to walk out with down at Seaford. Lieutenant Brims was Captain in charge of transport. I must close now, hoping this will find you in the best of health.

I remain, Yours Sincerely, Geo. C. Parcell.

This watercolour of 'Nita' is the first painting to come from one of Bob's sketchbooks (see introduction).

"We have three regimental pets, a goat, and a magpie that's just learning to steal, and a nice old black dog. I've made a bit of a sketch of him in the book. Jolly fine ratter and can almost talk with his eyes. Many walks we've been on together." Bob, July 31st, 1917.

"Ablainzeville, May 29, 1917."

Ablainzeville was one of the many small villages in the area to the south of Arras which had the misfortune to become fought over by both sides, who wished to establish their respective Front lines. The village was almost totally destroyed in the battles.

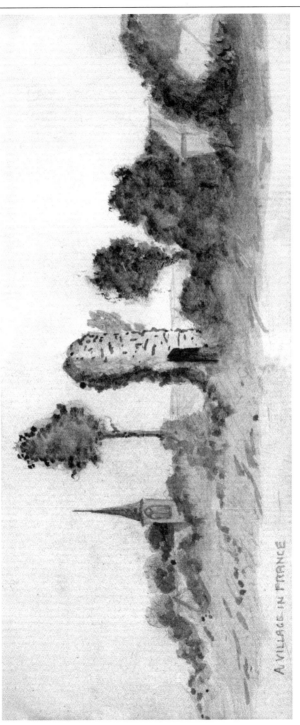

"A Village in France."

"Bullecourt under shellfire," August 8, 1917.

The German and British armies had both established a frontline outside Bullecourt. The area was lost and won several times and by the time Bob made this sketch, the village had been totally destroyed.

Calendar of Events of 1918.
(Bob's activities shown in italics)

January 14 – German destroyers bombard Yarmouth, Norfolk.
January 15 – 7th Division at Montello.
March 28 First Battle of Arras, Corp. Charles Dyer killed in action on the Western Front.
July 15 – Second battle of the Marne begins.
July 20 – German forces retreat across the Marne.
September 28 – The Allied Flanders Advance begins, Messines retaken.
October 3 – Armentieres retaken by British forces.
October 24 – Italy Battle of Vittorio Veneto begins.
October 27 – Austrian Government ask Italy for an armistice.
November 9 – Kaiser Wilhelm abdicates.
November 11 – Armistice signed. End of war.
December 1 – British and United States troops cross the German frontier.
December 4 – Demobilisation of the British Army begins.

From Kitty Walcroft *
Expeditionary Force Canteen HQ. A S C.   Sunday, January 6, 1918
My Dearest Mabel,
Thanks most awfully for writing to me, and also for the sweet card. It was real good of you. As I have no doubt you know by this time, I had a troubled time getting back here; got hung up at various places and arrived here three days late. I missed all the dances too, perfectly rotten! It seemed good to get back to the camp after being nobody's child for some time, although I really hated going back when I was at Newport.
Yes, I wish you were out here too, Mabel; I'm sure you'd have a quite good time. One advantage about being hung up at Boulogne is that I met a very charming boy, whom I love ten hundred, but then of course, I love lots of very charming boys ten hundred.
And now for a very important thing. The best of everything to you in the New Year and may your shadow never grow less. I don't want mine to grow more; I really have got fat, haven't I? But 'ca ne fait rien'! Excuse the bit of French but it's such a byword here, otherwise I wouldn't spring it on you. Two of the girls from my hut have gone on leave today and my pal has not returned yet. Wish she would, I miss her horribly.
Our hut really looks charming. It's decorated up with holly and mistletoe and the girls have made shades for the lights. We've an awful shortage of water again; have to get it from the stream. It is a nuisance but I managed to scrounge a bath whilst I was at Folkestone and we have an 'up as far and down as far' behind the screen in the hut – only the girls are such beggars and pretend to peep and to knock the screen over etc. There's a girl bothering me to show her

---

* Little is known of Kitty, who was clearly a close friend of Mabs. She was a telephone operator in Berkshire before going to France with the Army Service Corps. She died in 1919, aged 25, in unknown circumstances, still attached to the ASC.

the Highland Fling and will you excuse this letter 'cos it's being written under difficulties. Au Revoir Mabel, a happy New Year to you all, kindest regards to your Mother and Dad,

love to yourself from Kitty.

*From Bob, Montello, Italy.**

Saturday, January 19, 1918

My Dear Mother,

I was jolly pleased to get your welcome letter of 31st December, also the enclosed order – thank you very much for it. I hope you are not depriving yourself by sending them. We are in the line again now, not in the mountains, but on more level country and there are very few civilians about here. Still, we have got good billets and are very comfortable. I was so glad to know that you all spent such a nice Xmas, and such a big party of you, too. I should like to have been there but still, it can't be helped; better luck next time I hope. I was surprised to hear that C. Dyer had such a narrow escape from capture; he must have been in that reverse on the Western Front. I haven't heard from him for some while. I think I told you in one of my other letters that I got the book Kath sent all right and also the cards, and today I got the County Press of January 3rd, and the Sunday Pictorial, so you can see how long the mail takes to get here. I hope Kath is still keeping busy with her painting I think she might get one or two ready for me. Tell Dad to remember me to all at the Bedford.

Well, I must finish this off now. Best love to you, Dad and Kath,

ever your loving son Bob.

From Charlie
BEF.

Wednesday, January 30, 1918

Dear Bob,

I was very pleased to have a letter from you as I know that you were gone to another Front, so was expecting it any time. Very glad to hear that you are still keeping fit and well, also that you like it out that way. They say a change is as good as a rest and the people being able to talk English makes it better for you chaps. Expect you will have plenty of hillclimbing now. So you heard about our do? Yes, it was very close but some of them were taken. They have heard from them and they are all quite well when they wrote. Will let you know more when we meet. Hope it won't be long. Fancy you meeting some of the old boys out there. I know the chap you mean very well. Remember me to Parcell when you write to him again. Glad to hear that Gordon is all right again. I was not very far from him when he was wounded, by what I saw in the County Press. I had a card from Kathy and also Mabel. Glad to say they are quite well, also, Mother and Dad and my mother often meet yours so I hear how you are getting on. I heard from Jack he is quite well. Plenty of changes at Whitecroft. We are having some grand weather here, like spring. What sort of a time are you getting? Len Thornton and Bill Chappell wished you the best of luck; shall be pleased to have a line soon, if possible. Not much news. Glad to say that I am A1 at present. Yes, a good job we could not see the future, as you say. Hope it will soon be over,

Best of luck from your old pal, Charlie.

---

* See sketch, page 278.

From Bob, Montello, Italy.

Unknown Day, February, 1918

My Dear Mother,

I have been unable to write just lately for reasons of which I am unable to explain here. We are out of the line for a bit and the weather has been scorching hot but now it is just the opposite again, and very cold. I have got the extra money, that is 9d a day, but we are not allowed to draw it. We get the same as we always did before but of course, it will go into my credit. I don't want you to send me any more parcels as we are getting very good rations out here. If I want anything particular I will let you know. Fruit is very cheap out here and we also see the lemons growing on the trees in some parts. Eggs are very cheap too, we buy them for 2d or 3d each new laid. I'm getting the County Press all right and the Sunday Pictorial from Archie. That supplies us with the news of the Western Front and at home. Are you on the food rations yet? By all accounts it is a success. It's a thing that should have been done a long time ago, to my idea, as everyone will get the same amount. Well, I must close now

Ever your loving son, Bob.

From Bob, Signoressa, Italy.

Saturday, March 16, 1918

My Dear Kath,

Got your letter of the 9th alright, but if you or any of the others wrote letters about the 23rd to the 24th, they are at the bottom of the sea, so it was read out on our Parade the other morning – the Huns done it on us for once. Let me know if anything was sent off about that time. I sent three more pieces of edelweiss, I hope you got it all right. I like this little writing pad, just a nice size. I have made a couple of sketches in the book. We were in a little village, near the line, deserted by the Italian people so we occupied their houses. They left beds, tables and chairs behind so we had furnished apartments just like being in lodgings. We had a lovely view across the country of the snow-covered mountains held by the Austrians. It was quite evident that he could see more than we could, for one day he shelled our billets and kept us in a dugout for an hour and a half. It got so hot that we had to desert that village and move further back. Now I'm better off than ever – I've got a room to myself with a spring mattress. I rigged up a table and scrounged a chair, and also rigged up a stove. Don't think it's only the R.E's that are living cushy like this – even the infantry up in the line are just as well off. The Italians build good substantial houses of solid stone and they take some knocking down. We are not very far from the sea and not far from the place where you drive about the streets in boats. We are getting very decent food now and I've been reading in the Sunday Pictorial about the awful trouble to buy food even when you've got the money, so I don't think you had better send any more parcels. You must have an awful trouble to live. I think we must be really better off than you, after all. Had a letter from C. Dyer today. He's going on all right now. Well, I must dry up now. My best love to you, Mother and Dad, ever your loving brother, Bob.

PS. We are having glorious weather, sunshine day after day, proper blue Italian skies. How is it at home?

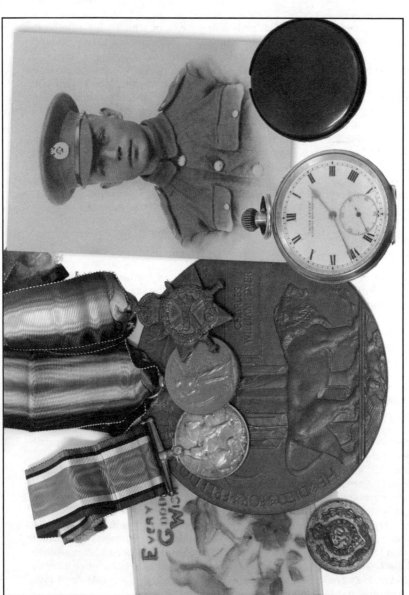

Charlie Dyer's medals and posessions in a 2015 auction catalogue.

"I got the County Press with the account of C. Dyer's death. I can't get over it yet... I had great hopes of his getting through all right, especially as he had escaped nearly three years without a scratch. He was always a plucky chap, was old Charlie. He's a chum I shall never forget." Bob to Mother, April 28, 1918. (Charlie was likely to have been a victim of the 'German Spring Offensive' which began on 21st March.)

The "letter from C. Dyer" that Bob referred to may well have been the last letter that Charlie ever wrote. The 'Killed In Action' column of the County Press for April 20th carried the following announcement :

DYER – March 28, killed in action, Corporal C.W. Dyer, R.E., son of Mr. and Mrs. W. Dyer, 7, Clarendon Street, Newport, aged 26.

From Archie
28, Barnard Road, Clapham Junction, SW11   Friday, April 19th 1918
Dear Kath,
When I started this I was going to have a little letter for each of you. However, for some reason or other which escapes me at the moment, I didn't finish it. Well, next night, young Nip turned up.* He had had a long and uninteresting day at the Central Recruiting Office and was, in the first place, told he could go home for seven days, I believe. We were very pleased to have him. We played 'nap' all that evening and he went up again next day. He was there all day again and was then told that the Air Service was full up but if he came up today he might have a chance for the R.E.s, so he went up and have not come back.

We were rejoiced, Wench, to get your letter and Nip read it before he went off. By the next post came a parcel from Mabel containing primroses and butter. Nip went off before he had any chance at the butter. We are sorry he has gone. He slept all right and was quite at home. He seems quite able to take care of himself although he does seem so very much of a boy to have to join up – It seems a shame to take them so young. We were very glad to have Bob's letter, and more than glad to note that he is still in Italy. Had he been in France he might have shared the fate of poor Charlie Dyer. This is very sad to think of, and both Chris and Bab, who met him when he was home on leave, are very, very sorry. Mrs Newnham ain't very well. Got a pain in her tum. She gets this every so often and kids herself its appendicitis. It may be. Chris has to go up every now and then and see to her and 'course, Bab goes too; took the old duck some primroses etc. This letter must now stop. The next one I write will probably be to Beeb so you can tell her to look out for one. Give her lots of kisses from us. Also love and kisses to you. Good night Wench.
                    Ever your loving Brother, Archie.

From Bob, Carriola on Mont Pau, Italy.
                                                    Sunday, April 28, 1918
My Dear Mother,
Mail seems so very scarce now. I've only had one letter from Mabs since the 30th of last month, also one from Kath, and this one from you. I don't know what becomes of the mail. Letters are very welcome now that we are cut off from civilisation. I was very upset to hear of poor old Charlie's death.** I had

* 'Nip' is Wallace's nickname.
** In June 2015, Charlie's medals, watch, death plaque and photograph appeared in the catalogue of a forthcoming auction to be held by Warren & Wignall Ltd. of Lancashire (*see opposite)* but for reasons unknown they were subsequently removed from auction. Their current whereabouts are unknown.

great hopes of his getting through all right, especially as he had escaped nearly three years without a scratch, but if he happened to be one of Carey's lot he must have been in some stiff fighting and he was always a plucky chap, was old Charlie. He's a chum I shall never forget. Please tell Mrs Dyer I send her my deepest sympathy. All the lads must be having a terrible time on the Western Front now and that is the reason we don't mind the hardships we have to suffer up here. Had a letter from Arch and Chris yesterday so I must try and answer it soon. Sorry to hear about poor Collyer, too. I knew him quite well. It's sad for his poor wife and kiddies. Remember me to H. Harvie. It's a good thing he is out of it for a while. I got the County Press with the account of C. Dyer's death. I can't get over it yet. Well, I must finish now with my best love.

Ever your loving son, Bob.

From Bob, Carriola on Mont Pau, Italy.

Sunday, May 26, 1918

Dear Mother,

I got your letter of the 12th a few days ago. I was away down on the plains when it arrived, for a couple of days. It's awfully hot down there but everything looks lovely, especially now the vine leaves are out. Fruit is plentiful; that is one good thing. Don't send any more cards as I've got a couple of packs. Mabel seems to be getting on pretty well at Portsmouth. It seems rather funny work for a girl – her hands will get terribly rough. Still, it's better than the other thing she was going into. I expect you do miss her. Well I must close now.

Ever your loving son, Bob.

From Bob, Crossing The Piave, Italy.

Saturday, June 22, 1918

My Dear Mother,

It's a long time since I wrote to you but I hope you are not anxious about me, as everything is going all right up to now. We have had it pretty quiet since we've been out here and the others have been having it rough in France. Now we are having our turn and as you can see by the papers we are holding them up in most places, especially on our portion of the line. By what I've seen of the prisoners they look as if they could do with a good meal. They are Austrians, Slavs and Czechs. The Italians have taken 15,000 and we 3,500 and the French 2,700. They are wild with excitement over....*The rest of this letter is missing.*

From Doris
31, Melbourne Street, Newport.

Friday, July 5, 1918

Dear Bob,

Don't feel like doing any work today so I am writing to you (yes! actually writing to you!). You see, it's like this – I went to Sandown yesterday (Thursday) and we took the kids out in a boat, about a dozen of 'em. Bloomin' 'eavy they were, an' all! Well, Daddy sat in the stern (trust him for a soft job – he's a

Brimson, so am I!) Ron and I rowed against the tide with all that bloomin' lot right to Shanklin and back. I am as stiff as blazes! And hot wasn't the name for it. I've got blisters all over my hands today.

Ron and I went in a shop for some tea, but we bought a cake as well. The girl said, "Don't eat that cake in the shop will you?" "OK, no," said Ron. For tea we were allowed 1½ ozs bread, and the butter! Don't mench! It was about this size O, in a little ball to go over two slices. Well, after we got rid of the bread Ron says, "I'm still hungry," so we cut the cake under the table and started that. When the girl came in she said, "I thought I asked you to eat the cake outside?" "Oh," says Ron, "We have been eating it outside." We hung our heads outside the window, so that was alright. But didn't the girl row on?

What do you think! I have had a letter from my French girl. She says, "In Paris there was much raids and there are many deads." Some girl she is, I can tell you. S'true int it! Last Sunday, about 9.30 in the morning, I was in bed singing away like a lark (even though I says it, as shouldn't, and even though Daddy said it sounded like 50 cats let loose) because it was Sunday and I didn't have to go to work. (Don't like too much work, do you? 'T'isn't good for my health) Ron was having a bath in his room. (I suppose he was, at any rate I heard a few growls). Presently he sings out to Ernest, "For heaven's sake, tell Doris to shut up that darn row. The shirt won't go on." That's his compliment.

Well I am up to my neck in work so I suppose I shall have to push on with it. I had a siphon of soda water tipped down my neck last week. Golly, it was wet and cold, but I had my revenge of course.

Well Kath's alright, Grandma's alright, Grandpa's alright, Daddy's all right (Oh, I can't go through our little mob, but they are alright, so that's all right). Yours truly is all right and tennis is better than all right – I nearly live on the tennis courts – have a fine time up there. I am playing in a tournament next week. Swish! Wonder if I shall win. Well, must close now and I will write again soon.
With love from you know who, otherwise me, Doris.

From Bob, Magnoboschi, Italy.

Monday, July 22, 1918

My Dear Mother,

I received Lloyds all right and also the letter containing handkerchiefs, for which I thank you very much. Have been out sketching this morning – one or two nice little mountain views. They are very nice paints that you got. I could do with a tube of madder brown if you could manage to afford it. Will try and make it right with you as soon as possible.

We have been having awful thunderstorms up here lately, and cold, too. We have got a stove in our hut and we have it going at nights. Plenty of pinewood to burn round about. They are very nice handkerchiefs you sent me. Thank you once more. It will be a few more weeks yet before we return into the plains again. Fellows who come up from down below say it is 130° in the shade, and up here we have got to have a fire, so it will give you some idea what it is like. Well, I must close now,
ever your loving son Bob.

INFORMATION DESIRED.

REPORTED missing on Sept. 27th, in France, 2nd-Lieut. C. J. Tolman, 22 Squadron R.A.F.—Any information gratefully received by his mother, Mrs. W. H. Grace, Alverstone, Whippingham, I.W.

COWES.

Mrs. Gladdis, 4 Castle-road, has received official news that her son, Pte. Gladdis, was not killed in action on March 23rd, as reported, but died from gunshot wounds in the lung on April 6th as a prisoner of war in hospital at Le Cateau.

We regret to announce that Gunner Herbert Thomas Carter, R.G.A. (Siege Battery), son of the late Capt. Ivo Stodhard Carter and of Mrs. Beere, of Pandora, Arctic-road, was admitted to hospital, seriously wounded in the chest, on September 25, and died shortly afterwards, aged 24. Although so young, he had had eight years' service, six and a half of that time in India, but had only been 11 weeks in France.

Another promising young townsman has made the supreme sacrifice on the Western front, namely, Corpl. Archie John Froud, third and youngest son of Councillor J. Froud, of St. Giles, Park-road, who, on the 26th ult., died in hospital at Rouen from wounds received in the chest and right leg during the heavy fighting on the 21st ult. He was going on well when, unfortunately, the effects of gas poisoning developed, and he suddenly succumbed.

NEWPORT.

Lance-Corpl. George H. Woodford, D.C.L.I., aged 26, the eldest of four fine soldier sons of Mr. H. Woodford, 31 Royal Exchange, who had been missing in France since October 4th, 1917, is officially presumed to have been killed.

Pte. C. H. Hutchings, Wiltshire Regiment, the 19-year-old son of Mrs. E. B. Hutchings, of 98 Hunnyhill, has been severely wounded in legs, side, and right arm by shell fire on the Western front, where he was temporarily buried in a dug-out by shell explosion. Both legs have been amputated above the knee.

Mrs. Ricks, St. Aubyns, Staplers, has received the sad news that her husband, Pte. Alfred Ricks, Royal West Kents, aged 41, was killed in France on August 27th. He was formerly proprietor of the well-known restaurant in Lower High-street.

Mr. Alfred Peck, T.C., of the Britannia, Hunnyhill, has received the sad news that his third son, Pte. William George Peck, London Regiment, aged 22, died on the 24th September as the result of wounds received in Palestine. He joined up 3½ years ago, and, after serving on the Western front, went to Salonica, where he saw considerable service, and was afterwards transferred to Palestine. It was in the dash on Nazareth that he was fatally wounded. His officer spoke highly of this promising young soldier.

Mr. J. W. Raeburn, of Ingle Neuk, Avondale-road, has received the distressing news that his second son, James Wyllie Raeburn, Canadian Forces, was killed in France on August 12th. A native of Newport, deceased was well known in this town, where he was formerly employed in the solicitor's office of Messrs. Buckell and Drew. Eight years ago he emigrated to Canada, where he continued his legal training with such marked success that he qualified as a barrister before patriotically joining up last year.

County Press advertisements, 1918.

From Bob, Magnoboschi, Italy.

Sunday, July 28, 1918

My Own Sweetheart,

I'm awfully sorry to hear of your illness and I hope by the time you receive this you will be quite all right again. Was it Spanish Flu you had? I fancy that was what I had, only the doctors could not make out what it was, or how we got it, and they could not give it a name then. Over 80 of our company was down with it at once and some of them are not back yet. It leaves one awfully weak but I think the open air life soon put me all right again. What is this talk of our people leaving the Island and going to live with Chris? I just had a hint of it in Mother's last letter; have not got full particulars yet. I don't dislike the idea myself; that is, if they go to a decent town or somewhere near one, not too near to London. In reference to myself, I can see there would be more scope for me after the war is finished. I know you would not mind, would you kiddie? There would be the Island to go for our holidays every year. You see, I'm building castles in the air. Let me know what you think about it, pet, in a nice long letter. Must close now,

ever your own true love, Bob.

Enclosed you will find a curious kind of flower that grows on the mountain slopes.

From Bob, Magnoboschi, Italy.

Sunday, August 11, 1918

Dear Mother,

Pleased to hear you are all going on all right. Might send the palette, as it is easily carried about and very handy for me. I have met a chap from Newport in a hut a stone's throw from our billet through reading a little bit about him in the County Press. His name is Fred Williams. He lives in Chapel Street and he happens to know Ern Attrill quite well, He is in the Army Cycle Corps and so he comes over to our hut every night. It is nice to meet someone from our way. We are still on the mountain and it's a bit hot today. I expect you will read of our little success up here, what came off on the 8th. I bet they never heard a bombardment like it before in these mountains. I hear very little from Mabel now. I don't know whether she is too busy or too tired when she comes home – and then she only writes short letters. By the way, a new order has come out that "Italian Expeditionary Force," must be put in full on all letters and papers. Must close now,

ever your loving son, Bob.

Have done a few nice little sketches.

From Bob, Tezze D'Arzignano, Italy.

Thursday, September 5, 1918

My Dear Mother,

I haven't received the colours yet. Did you send them before the pad, or after? If I don't get it, don't bother to buy any more. Yesterday was the anniversary of

"Monastery," 1918.

Bob painted this watercolour of the partly damaged Sant' Eustacchio Abbey while it was being used as a lookout position by the Italian forces. It was later destroyed by Austrian artillery fire during the Battle of Piave River, June 15th

my enlisting so I get another penny a day more pay; it all mounts up. How is Archy going to manage about his business if Chris is going to live at Whitstable (where is it by the way)? Doris is in for a good time anyway.

Glad you went round to see Mrs. Williams. Have not seen Fred lately, since we have been out of the line. We left him up there. We had our Divisional Sports on the 3rd. Quite a gay time, thousands of British troops in topees and French in their light blue, Italians in grey, the signorinas in their flash colours and bands from all the different regiments. Our Division seems to run these things a treat. We shall soon be moving again shortly. Have taken some sketches of the two castles.* It took me about an hour to climb up to them, mostly through vineyards, a splendid view from the top, too. I was properly fagged when I got back. My hand is quite all right again now, except for a scar. Send my best wishes to Jack Cornish too; hope he will soon be better. Well, I must close now, with best love to you and Dad, and Kath, also Rory, Kit, and family.

Ever your loving son, Bob.

From Bob, Tezze D'Arzignano, Italy.

Wednesday, September 18, 1918

My Dear Mother,

I received the letter with the palette enclosed but it arrived in four pieces, worst luck, and the tube colours I haven't had, so I don't suppose I shall get them now. Don't write any more or send anything until I let you know. I will try and send field postcards whenever I get the chance and I will try and get another letter off in a few days. Of course, I can't let you know anything but you have nothing to worry about. I hope you don't mind me putting my letters in Mab's, but we only get one green envelope a fortnight and I can talk to you better in them. Tell Dad to keep the garden going alright as I expect to be home again in about six weeks, all being well, and I expect Kath to have a lot to show me.

Ever your loving son, Bob.

From Kitty Walcroft
E.F.C. HQ, A.S.C., BEF

Tuesday, October 1, 1918

My Dearest Mabel,

I've been going to write to you dozens of times but somehow I've never quite managed it. How are you getting on? I wish you had passed for overseas and were out here with me. It's not really a bad life. Our working times are from 9.00 until 6.30 with an hour and a half for lunch. Being a telephonist, times are different. Every other evening I have to work until 8.30 then we get a half day a week and every other Sunday. We are stuck right out in the heart of the country so we have to manufacture our own amusements and for a great relaxation we sometimes walk into the nearest village – of any consequence – five miles away. So you can guess we're reduced to pretty desperate straits sometimes. The boys who are stationed around here are getting up concerts for us and recently they installed a cinema – gee! It is crowded too. We have the pictures once a week – on Saturdays. We have real up to the minute films.

---

* See sketch, page 274.

"Tresino, 1918."

This is one of two pictures of Tresino sketched by Bob, probably during September or October 1918 when the area was used by allied troops for open battle training.

The weather is getting fearfully cold and although I sleep in my woolly coms and pyjamas and thick dressing gown and my stockings, I lay awake shivering and aching with the cold. Heaven alone knows how we shall get on when the really cold weather comes. Of course, we shall have stoves in our huts then. By the way, those huts Mabel! Do you know what Nissen huts are?

Love to yourself, from Kitty.

From Chris
28, Barnard Road, Clapham Junction. SW.   Monday, October 28, 1918
Dear Old Bob,
I have just had a letter from Kath and she enclosed your last letter. What luck for you to design the Xmas cards. You are coming out. I hope they will put your name on them. You will have made your fortune. Don't forget to send me one.*
I should like to have a letter from you sometime, Bob. I don't understand what you mean about me hinting at money troubles concerning Mother and Dad. You know there are always money troubles, especially in war time, with us all – even us. But what's the good of talking about it? We must do the best we can, and I think we are, considering everything is so expensive, but all that is nothing compared with bad health. If we can only get our little Beeb stronger, we can face anything. Now Archy has got a bad attack of flu and Mr Hanne has had to close the office.** Hope you soldiers are keeping fit out there, this wretched flu seems to be raging everywhere. Kath tells me you have been up the mountain and seen Romeo and Juliet's castles – just fancy. You will have a lot to tell us about your travels when you do come home. I'm so glad you think the end is so near. Shan't I be thankful? Hope you are keeping well; you have had one or two nasty attacks of illness, haven't you? It's a good thing you have got over them all right, that fever weakens and so you looked a lot thinner in your photo. We shall be very glad to see you home again. It's just what I thought. They would go and stop all leave. That keeps you out there until after Xmas, I suppose. You must come home for good then and get married and settle down, but I hope you haven't developed a roving spirit – you have travelled a bit in this last four years. Goodnight now Bob. Keep fit, love from us all.

Your loving sister Chris.

The war came to an end at 11 o'clock on the morning of November 11, 1918. Sadly, no letter survives from Mabs or Bob, nor any other member of the family, to mark the occasion. Instead, it is left to Kitty Walcroft, in a letter to Mabs, to celebrate the historic moment.

From Kitty Walcroft
E.F.C. HQ, Gwynfa Camp A.S.C., A.P.O. S1   Monday, November 11, 1918
My Dearest Mabel,
What about the war now, Mabel? We are frantically excited. We are going to celebrate tonight, have a dance and one thing and another. All the rest of the

---

* See photographs, page 280.
** In 2016, Archie's employer, solicitors Hanne & Co were still trading in Clapham Junction.

1918

Castles of Montecchio, "November 30, 1918.

"Have taken some sketches of the two castles. It took me about an hour to climb up to them, mostly through vineyards, a splendid view from the top, too. I was properly fagged when I got back." Bob to Mother, September 5th, 1918.

staff had the afternoon off. We poor blighters in the phone office have to work. However, I'll make up for it this evening or I'm a Dutchman. Oh Mabel, I feel so excited! I just hate having to stop in this office answering stupid old calls. I want to jump, dance, sing, shout and generally go mad. Still, when I think of my great age I sober down some. Your letter smells awful good; such a treat to smell scent. One of the boys I know is going to get me some scent for my birthday so I'll be able to have nice smelly writing paper too. It's simply pouring with rain. I shall get wet through going home but – now for some swank - Ce na fait rien!

Yours, Kitty.

From Bob, Montecchio Maggiore, Italy.*

Wednesday, November 30, 1918

My Dear Mother,

I have been travelling a lot lately and that is the reason I have not written letters. We thought we were going right into Austria at one time but of course, they surrendered and there was no need to chase them any further. We got nearly as far as the River Tagliamento and then turned back. I shall never forget the sights I saw on that march, and the attitude of the poor civilians, and the relief after so many months of tyranny under the rule of the enemy. In one village where we stopped the night, all the senoritas sang patriotic songs, the first time they had been able to sing them for over a year, of course. We gave them some songs too and we had quite a jolly night. The majority of the people had their cattle stolen, and everything they had in the place, and they were practically starving. Of course, food was rushed over for them in motors.

I can say this much, that the engineers working hard, night and day, under shellfire and bombs from enemy planes, persevered and bridged the Piave, a river running at ten miles an hour. A few were drowned, some wounded, and one fellow from Winchester died of wounds. Our company got great praise for their work, as without the bridges the attack could never have been made. Within a week Austria was finished, as you all know, then it wasn't long before Germany packed up and it's all over at last.

It's just a matter of waiting now until we get demobilised. I suppose it will take a bit of time; don't expect me home for Xmas anyway. I'd give anything to be able to be with you all but I don't think there is much hope. We will have a good time when I do arrive. We are allowed to put in a pass for any place in Italy but of course, you have to have plenty of money to go with it. I'm going to have a day in Venice** if I can get enough money. It's rather an expensive place by all accounts. Do you think you could send me out a couple of flannel shirts and a couple of pairs of pants, the kind I used to wear in civvy life? We can't get them now, only old second-hand ones from the baths and they are not always clean. Don't send socks as I've plenty of them. Make a strong parcel of it and address it plainly and then I'll get them all right.

Very glad to hear that Dad has recovered from the flu. A lot of the regiments out here are still suffering from it, but we are all right so far.

Well, I must close now with love to you, Dad and Kath.

Ever your affectionate son Bob.

---

* See sketch page 276.
** See sketch page 284.

"The Montello."

"I've been doing a bit of watercolour sketches lately, as I've been wandering over the hills." Bob to Kath, January 26, 1919
The Montello plateaux was the site of fierce fighting during June 1918 but the Austrians failed to capture its summit and were pushed back to their original lines by the end of June.

From Mother

49, Carisbrooke Road, Newport   Monday, December 9, 1918

My Dear Bob,

I've enclosed a ten shilling postal order for you. I do wish it could be more but I really couldn't manage it. Kath, me and Dad has been making dolls. Dad does the stuffing and I and Kathie the rest. We have had a good many orders for Xmas and have nearly done now, so that has enabled me to do for you, but not so much as we wish but I know you will take the will for the deed.

I hope you will manage to get to Venice and will enjoy yourself; Kath is full of it.

We have just had Harry Harvie to see us. He goes back to France and expects to come again before he goes back to Australia so perhaps you will see him. Hoping you will have a very happy Xmas. We shall be quiet but will hope for better times later. Goodnight my son. Kind love from us all,

ever your loving Mother, E. Brimson.

From Bob, Orgiana, Provincia de Vicenza, Venetia, Italy.

Tuesday, December 17, 1918

My Dear Mother, Father and Kath,

This is to wish you all a very happy Christmas – at least as happy as you can be under the circumstances. I suppose it will be rather quiet for you with not having Chris down this time, but it is only a matter of weeks now until I shall be home for good. They are supposed to be demobilising 671 men a day from this country when they do start, so it won't take long. I hope you got the Divisional Xmas cards all right. Those I done have come now, so I will try and send you one. They are selling them in our canteen at 5d and they are going well.

You may have noticed that I have written the place where I am. We are allowed to do that now. I don't expect you will find the name of the village on the map as it is too small. It is a place between Verona and Vicenza. They are buying fowls for Xmas and a variety of vegetables and other stuff so I don't expect we shall have such a bad time.

I'm going to try and get £2 forwarded on to you from Chatham as I am now about £17 in credit. I hope you will get it in time. The shirts and pants haven't arrived yet but I expect they will any day now.

 I didn't hear about F. Ball, only that they hadn't heard anything of him for a long time. Has he turned up yet? I expect he has had a rough time. You might have a look at my suits of clothes just to see that they are all in good condition. I expect they will fit me. If they won't, Dad will have to have them. Kath, I expect, will have plenty to keep her busy; she generally does. Well, must close now.

Ever your loving son, Bob.

While in Italy, Bob was asked to design the Company Christmas card for 1918.
"I hope you got the Divisional Xmas cards all right. Those I done have come now, so I will try and send you one. They are selling them in our canteen at 5d and they are going well." Bob to Mother, Father & Kath, December 17, 1918.
Top, Bob's original draft design. Bottom, the printed version.

From Chris

Tankerton, Whitstable, Kent   Wednesday, December 18, 1918

Dear Bob,

I was in hopes you were going to be at home this Xmas. I expect you were, too. It seems unfortunate because we can't go, so they will be rather lonely. I suppose you will get leave pretty soon, then you must all make up for it, only we shan't be there.

It is a long time I heard from you, just a field card about two months ago, and nothing long before that, but I am expecting a letter soon with one of your cards. I have not heard from Mabel lately. I expect she has been rather busy. I don't know whether she is still going to Cowes. She will write in a day or two; sure to.

I should like to hear all about the place where you are, Bob. It must be beautiful up on the hills. Write and tell us about it – no censor now is there? Make haste and come home. It seems such a long time since we saw you and we should like a nice long talk. You must have such a lot to tell us. The children often talk about you. Bab has grown such a great big girl. She is taller than Beeb now. Well Bob, we must wish you Happy Christmas, but come as soon as you can after.

Love from us all, your loving sister Chris.

*From Bob, Campolongo, Italy**

Monday, December 30, 1918

Dear Mother,

Just a few lines to tell you that I received the parcel of underclothing quite safely, and the other things, for which I thank you very much. I remitted Kath £3 about ten days ago. I hope you have heard something about it by now and will draw it from the Post Office.

We have moved since I wrote to you last and the scenery is very pretty where we are now, some decent walks when the weather is fine. We had one of the finest Christmases I've had since I've been in the Army. Everything went off a treat – plenty to eat and also good sport. Did you have anyone for Xmas or did you go over the road? Mabs tells me they would probably have it quiet. Fred Ball seems to have had it pretty rough, He won't want to hear Germany mentioned for a good while to come, I bet.

Mabs sent me a fine parcel of tobacco and cigarettes, also a card from Mr and Mrs A. I heard from Chris two days ago – seems to have quite settled down in Whitstable. I was glad to hear that Bee was getting better again.

Well I must finish now as I want to catch the post tonight. Will write a longer one next time.

Ever your loving son, Bob.

* See sketch page 282.

"Campolongo, my last Billet in Italy."
"We have moved since I wrote to you last and the scenery is very pretty where we are
now, some decent walks when the weather is fine." Bob to Mother, 30 December, 1918.

From Bob, Ju Campolongo, Villa del Ferra, Venitia, Italy.

Sunday, January 12, 1919

Dear Mother, Dear Kath,

Received the PO for ten shillings for which I thank you all very much. It must have travelled a few hundred miles, especially if it has been to the 75th Field Company, which I believe is in Germany. However, I've got it safe at last and very welcome it was too. I also want to thank you very much for the tobacco pouch; very nicely made. Of course, I know what it is made of. I have it in use and the tobacco keeps very moist in the rubber lining. I hope by this time you have heard something about the £3 I sent you. I hope you understand that you have to go to the Post Office to draw it, as that is where they send it from Chatham. I wanted you to have a £1 each and buy whatever you fancied. It's not much in these times, but better than nothing. They have stopped censoring letters out here now so that is the reason I have to put my name on the corner of the envelope.

Well Kath, will write you a longer letter next time. I hope I shall have more news to tell you all,

ever your loving brother, Bob.

From Kath

49, Carisbrooke Rd, Newport

Saturday, January 18, 1919

My Dear Bob,

I do hope you will get this on your birthday. We wish you could have been home for it – you will be next time, I hope – and we also wish you the same old wish, only heaps of happier returns. There! That sounds a little bit different to the usual doesn't it? I'm getting a bit fed up with writing the same old thing year after year. I wish you would look sharp home and then I wouldn't have to write so many letters. I can't think how you manage them – bad enough writing 'em on the table. Mother wishes she could have sent you a nice cake but she will be sure to have a big one when you come home. She'll scrape some currants up from somewhere, if we have to grow them ourselves.

We were very glad you got the money safe at last and that you were pleased with it. Hope it helps you to have a jolly time. Are you still going to try and get to Venice? I shall be glad if you can – almost as glad as if I went myself. Do you still get the County Press every week? Mother thinks because you never mention it, that you don't. Nothing in the silly thing, only P.S.A. meetings.

Mother, Dad and I went to the pictures on Thursday; it was one called 'Thelma', one of Marie Corelli's books. We read it some time ago and I tried to paint a picture from it so I wanted to see if it was anything like mine. Have you read it, Bob? It's about all Norway. Very beautiful pictures of the midnight sun they showed.

Ivie came running down with a letter she had written to you. It had been in her pocket a week. She hopes you will be able to read it.

Do you know what the Italians call you soldiers? "bright stubby-nosed Englishmen!" That was in the paper yesterday (aren't you glad you haven't got a stubby nose?). I think they have a jolly good cheek. Only to make up for it, they also said they were the best soldiers in the world and the most cheerful.

"My last view of Venice,"

Bob had wanted to visit Venice since the war ended and on the 1st February 1919, he got the chance.

They were comparing them with their own "noble aquiline-featured" Italians. Well, that seems to be all there is left to talk about so I had better finish up. Hope you won't get too gay on the 23rd.

> With heaps of love from Mother, Dad and Kath.

A letter from Ivie was included in the envelope.

Dear Uncle Bob,

I have not written to you for years but I am now. We have had a lovely Xmas; we had five parties. Xmas day, Boxing Day we went down Grandma's. The Monday following, we had our little friends in. On the Tuesday Kathleen and I went to a birthday party; they had a Xmas tree and I had a box of doll's furniture, a hanky and books and six pencils.

Gordon is coming home soon and I hope you will too. I wonder what Italy is like. I expect it is hot, isn't it? I expect the soldiers had some fun on Armistice Day. I am in Standard IV now and in May I shall try for a scholarship at the Technical School. Well, tonight I have written to Gordon, Beeb, Bab and you. I hope you are well, so goodbye until another time. Hope you had a happy Xmas.

> Good night, with love from Ivie.

From Arch

5, Henley Villas, Tenterton, Whitstable, Kent   Sunday, January 19, 1919

Dear Bob,

This is just to wish you many happy returns of the 23rd and one happy return to Blighty in the near future. Oh! Let it be soon. When you get back you must try and look us up here. We like this place. I suppose the first thing you will be thinking of will be matrimony when you get back – there are many worse things. Jim will shortly be out of khaki now, I expect, and has a job already to go to. There appear to be signs in the land of reawakening of the builder so that should be a good thing for you in your line of business. All the best of good wishes. Your design for the Xmas card was top hole.

> So long old bean, ever thine, Arch.

This is the last letter from Bob while posted abroad.

From Bob, Ju Campolungo, Villa del Ferra, Venitia, Italy.

Same old address, Italy (*sic*)   Sunday, January 26, 1919

My Dear Kath,

I've got some good news to tell you. I'm going to Venice.* On Thursday 1st, that is, all being well and nothing happens. Will tell you all about it next time I write. I've remitted the £15 so I hope it will come through safely. I still get the County Press every week – it's about the only thing that does come regular. The leave train that left Italy last Sunday came to grief on its arrival in Northern France and as far as we can make out, there were 41 killed and over 100 injured. Our captain and three sappers were on the train but we haven't heard anything about them yet. I've been doing a bit of watercolour sketches lately, as I've been wandering over the hills. I've discovered lots of pretty little places, deep ravines

---

* See sketch opposite.

with water mills at the bottom and snowy mountains for a background. Was it in the County Press that you saw that letter about us having stubby noses? Because if it was, it was from a letter written by one of the H.A.C. Their Batallion is in our Division, only they are in the Austrian Tyrol representing the British Army of Occupation, and he said it's what the Austrians said about them. They seem to get on very well with them. I wrote to Doctor Erskine last night to see if he would put in a letter of application for me. I hope he will do his best to get it through quickly as I'm fed up with the Army now, especially as a lot of the old boys that have been through the lot from 1915 with me are going home to their jobs again.

Well Kath, must close now. With best love to you, Mother and Dad. Shall be able to write a longer letter next week; all about Venice.

Ever your loving brother, Bob.

From Mabs

The Bedford, Newport   Thursday, February 13, 1919

My Dearest Boy,

I am glad to hear that you have been to Venice after all. Won't you have something to talk about when you come home? You will never know when to stop. Perhaps I had better come for a honeymoon – wouldn't that be fine? I think I should just love Italy. Wallace has had a few days leave before going to Germany; I wish you could have seen him. He went back again today.

Ern isn't out yet, but expects to be soon. Morry is taking trips round about Ireland and Scotland at present but will be back at Rosyth on the 18th. There was a rumour that they would go to America later – can't say when that will be. We don't get much in the way of news to report; nothing much ever happens here. Arthur Bull is on leave again for a fortnight, he is in the Fishguard and George Almer (who used to be a groom at those stables just above your house) is home pending discharge. Phil Snow has been to Newport. He sends his kind regards etc. I forget whether I told you last week. He is stationed near Dublin at present. Well, I am afraid must cut this short as it is getting late.

Fondest love and kisses from your ever loving, Mabs.

From Mother

49, Carisbrooke Road, Newport   Sunday, February 16, 1919

My Dear Bob,

I wonder how many more letters we shall send to Italy. Not many more, I hope. We all thought we should have had you home before this especially when we keep hearing of men being home from Italy but I suppose a little more patience is wanted over the matter. The only comfort about it is you will not have to leave us again. We were delighted with your last letter. It seems you did enjoy your visit to Venice, you described it all so well. Kath was glad.

I got £14. They said that you was entitled to it so I put it in the bank the same day. I have been anxious for you to know, that is why I am writing tonight. There don't seem to be very much news this time so will finish,

your loving Mother, Ellen Brimson.

Fovant is a small village in Wiltshire, located between Salisbury and Shaftesbury at the southerly edge of Salisbury Plain. During the war it was home to Fovant Military Camp which housed over 20,000 soldiers on their way to France. When the war finished, the camp was used as a demobilisation centre for returning troops.

On February 20, 1919, just four days after Mother wrote the last letter of the book, Bob was demobilised at Fovant Military Camp.

The last piece of documentation referring to Bob's military career is an 'Identity Certificate' issued to him by the Dispersal Unit at Fovant. Dated February the 20th, it marks Bob's last day in the Army after serving for over four and a half years.

On the 15th of January, 1920, Bob and Mabs were married in St Mary's Church, Carisbrooke. Standing left to right are Ivie, Gordon and Doris Brimson.

My Grandparents by Richard Brimson.

I was fond of my grandparents. My grandfather was a quiet man who didn't say a great deal but my Gran enjoyed conversation on a broad range of topics. I knew my grandfather had been in the war when I was little – not that he talked about it much. I remember when I was quite young I asked him if he'd killed any Germans but he didn't answer. I remember him showing me some rifle bullets in a clip which he'd brought back from the Front; the cartridges had been emptied and the bullets refitted. He also had two or three pieces of shrapnel that he'd kept as souvenirs – probably because they'd just missed him. He treasured a small box with a piece of 'hard tack' like a piece of ship's biscuit, labelled 'Part of my rations on the Somme, 1916'. I remember him showing me a postcard he'd kept – a cartoon of Tommie's in France marching along a road of pointed stones – and he said, "When you marched along the cobbled roads in France for miles your feet got so sore you'd feel like you were walking on needles." He talked about being in Italy which he liked a lot but said,"We'd march for miles to the top of a hill only to see the next one to march up in front of you."

My Gran would talk about the Bedford. I remember her saying that before the war they opened at six in the morning. The men would come in on their way to work to get their pints and some of them just carried on and didn't get to work. Even though it hit their trade, Gran thought that restricting the pub hours was a necessity in the war. I met Kath when I was young. She died in 1959 so I couldn't have been more than eight; I remember seeing her in her wheelchair. Her parents died in the early thirties and because she couldn't look after herself she moved to London and lived with Chris and Archie, and later with Babs. Grandfather spent the rest of his working life as a painter, decorator and signwriter for Westmore's until he was asked to retire at 71.

Bob and Mabs with Richard Brimson in 1964.

After the war Bob and Mabs set up home in Trafalgar Road, Newport where they brought up their four children; Joan, Norman, Robert and Ralph. They remained there till they died, Bob in 1970, aged 85, and Mabs in 1982, aged 88.